High-Class Moving Pictures

✳✳ HIGH-CLASS ✳✳
MOVING
PICTURES

✳ ✳ ✳

Lyman H. Howe and the
Forgotten Era of
Traveling Exhibition,
1880-1920

✳ ✳ ✳

CHARLES MUSSER

IN COLLABORATION WITH

CAROL NELSON

PRINCETON UNIVERSITY PRESS

PRINCETON, NEW JERSEY

Published by Princeton University Press, 41 William Street,
Princeton, New Jersey 08540
In the United Kingdom: Princeton University Press, Oxford

LIBRARY OF CONGRESS CATALOGING-IN-PUBLICATION DATA
Musser, Charles
High-class moving pictures : Lyman H. Howe and the forgotten
era of traveling exhibition, 1880–1920 / Charles Musser in collaboration
with Carol Nelson.
p. cm.
Includes index.
ISBN 0-691-04781-2 (cloth : acid-free paper)
1. Howe, Lyman H., 1856–1923. 2. Motion picture producers and
directors—United States—Biography. 3. Motion pictures—United States—
Marketing—History. 4. Silent films—United States—History.
5. Motion picture industry—United States—History.
6. United States—Popular culture. I. Nelson, Carol, 1944–
II. Title.
PN1998.3.H69M87 1991
791.43'0232'092—dc20
[B]   90-39536

Publication of this book has been aided by the
Pennsylvania Humanities Council

This book has been composed in Linotron Goudy

Princeton University Press books are printed on acid-free paper,
and meet the guidelines for permanence and durability
of the Committee on Production Guidelines for Book Longevity of
the Council on Library Resources

Printed in the United States of America by Princeton University Press,
Princeton, New Jersey

2   4   6   8   10   9   7   5   3   1

Frontispiece: Lyman Hakes Howe (1856–1923)

* * *

For my grandmother,
GRACE WINTER GREENE MUSSER
who lived through this period and
still talks to me about it

In memory of my grandfather,
JOHN MUSSER
professor of American history,
who died before I was born

* * *

For my mother,
MILDRED G. SILBERMAN
who first told me about the
moving picture exhibitor from
Wilkes-Barre,
and my children,
MICHAEL AND DANIEL NELSON
who have grown up with
Lyman H. Howe

In memory of my grandfather,
LOUIS M. GIBELMAN
who operated a nickelodeon in
Minooka, Pennsylvania, and introduced me
to the movies with stories about
his teenage years as a projectionist
for the man he called Willy Fox

Contents

* * *

Acknowledgments

* * *

THIS BOOK has been a collaborative undertaking, delightful and deeply satisfying. If I have performed the task of writing these pages, Carol Nelson has been intimately—sometimes principally—involved at every stage. The result can only be seen as a work of joint authorship. Almost a dozen years ago Carol rediscovered Lyman H. Howe and then single-handedly sparked renewed interest in his activities as a traveling showman. Soon she was producing, and codirecting with Ben Levin, a half-hour documentary film, *Lyman H. Howe's High Class Moving Pictures.* Since I also had an interest in early cinema and was, in fact, working on a somewhat similar film project (a documentary about Edwin S. Porter, the maker of *The Great Train Robbery*), it was not long before we met at the Museum of Modern Art in New York and exchanged information. Her steadfast interest and enthusiasm for Howe quickly captured my attention, and we remained in periodic communication as her film progressed. Once it was completed in 1983, she raised grants from the Academy of Motion Picture Arts and Sciences and the Pennsylvania Humanities Council to finance a modest study guide to the film. I pleaded, and she finally agreed to let me write the text.

Carol had assembled such an impressive array of documentation that writing a study guide seemed simple at first glance. However, we soon realized that a film and a book required two quite different bodies of research. From our new perspective, available information often raised more questions than it answered. A new round of investigation was thus launched, building on what had been acquired for the documentary film. Lyman H. Howe was a master promoter who had left paper trails in many newspapers and other periodicals. These traces usually proved easy to locate, but the actual extraction of new information was time-consuming, if ultimately rewarding. Gradually, an undertaking intended to be about one hundred manuscript pages turned into something over four hundred.

Since this book was co-authored, it can be situated in two different contexts. Although it stands on its own as a portrait of an exhibitor and of a widespread cultural practice, it still functions as a study guide to the film. Simultaneously, it serves as a companion to two other books I have written about pre-Hollywood American cinema, *Before the Nickelodeon: Edwin S. Porter and the Edison Manufacturing Company*, recently published by University of California Press, and *The Emergence of Cinema: The American Screen to 1907*, published by Scribner's/Macmillan. We are con-

vinced that whatever we have accomplished can be largely attributed to
the overall scope and conjunction of these related projects.

Many people generously provided time and materials for this book. In
the process of making her documentary film, Carol contacted Dr. and
Mrs. Lyman H. Howe III, who graciously gave us access to the showman's
scrapbooks. Carol tirelessly located and interviewed people who had
worked for Howe or the Howe company. Many had documentation as well
as their memories to give. Maxwell Walkinshaw Hallet and Paul Felton,
Jr., relatives of key employees, also made scrapbooks available. Marlene
Chirinko undertook many trying research tasks on our behalf.

Studies such as ours cannot be written without the resources provided
by libraries, museums, archives, and historical societies. We are particularly grateful for the assistance provided by Burt Logan and the staff of the
Wyoming Historical and Geological Society in Wilkes-Barre; Mimi Bowling and Ed Pershey at the Edison National Historic Site in West Orange,
New Jersey; Brigitte Keuppers and Brooks McNamara at the Shubert Archives in New York; Eileen Bowser, Charles Silver, and Ron Magliozzi at
the Museum of Modern Art; Barbara Collins at the Tioga County Historical Society in Owego, New York; Jean Blanco at the Curtis Theater Collection at University of Pittsburgh; Mark Peterson at the Winona Historical Society in Winona, Minnesota; and Donald Crafton and Maxime
Flecker at the Wisconsin Historical Society in Madison, Wisconsin. Extensive research was also performed at the Troy Public Library; the Billy
Rose Theater Collection, the Annex and the Main Branch of the New
York Public Library; and the Osterhout Library in Wilkes-Barre. This
study could not have been made without the large newspaper collections
on microfilm at the Library of Congress and the state libraries in Hartford,
Harrisburg, Albany, Columbus, and Madison. Additional microfilm was
provided by many other institutions by interlibrary loan, through the assistance of Paula Jescavge at New York University's Bobst Library. Both
the Motion Pictures, Broadcasting, and Recorded Sound Division at the
Library of Congress and John E. Allen, Inc., enabled us to see a number
of Howe's original productions.

We were blessed with a patient, caring, and astute editor in Joanna
Hitchcock of Princeton University Press. Her steady guidance brought
this project to successful completion. We are also extremely grateful for
the comments of individuals who read drafts of this manuscript, including
Robert Sklar, Neil Harris, Donald Crafton, Kristin Thompson, Calvin
Pryluck, Lynne Zeavin, and the late Jay Leyda. Andrew McKay provided
us with much valuable information. Pat Loughney, Joyce Jesionowski, Su-
sanne Williamson, and Drew Willis assisted us with illustrations. Thanks
also go to Roberta Pearson, Russell Merritt, Susan Kempler, Harry Wade,

Timothy Mennel, Julie Marvin, William Simon, David Bordwell, and
Richard Koszarski.

Charles Musser
March 1989

WILKES-BARRE, Pennsylvania, has always taken great pride in its early
years as "the city of black diamonds" and the heart of the anthracite coal
industry, but by the 1960s the city's connection with early moving pictures had almost been forgotten, and the name of Lyman H. Howe had
slipped into oblivion. Little more than his palatial home remained to re-
call him. It was his residence that sparked my initial curiosity and led to
what some have quite properly called my obsession with Howe. At this
time, acknowledgment must be made of those individuals who helped turn
my obsessive curiosity into this manuscript.

For nearly ten years, the public television station WVIA has been constant in its support. It funded the initial research, sponsored all grant ap-
plications, and gave generously of its facilities and personnel. The cooperation of George Strimel, former general manager; Dr. John Walsh,
general manger; Ron Stravinsky, business manager; Jim Frushon, former
sound director; and Mindy Klaproth, public information director, must be
recognized.

The Pennsylvania Humanities Council provided most of the funding
for production of the film *Lyman H. Howe's High Class Moving Pictures* and
for the preparation of this book. Special thanks to Dr. Craig Eisendrath,
PHC executive director, who patiently administered the Howe funding,
which he describes as the longest continuous grant in the Council's history. Additional funds for this book have been provided by the Sordoni
Foundation, the Academy of Motion Picture Arts and Sciences, and a
generous friend who wishes to foster recognition of Wilkes-Barre's important heritage.

Personal documents and oral history have helped to make this project
unique. Many of the missing pieces were found through a group of gentle-
men whose lives somehow interconnected with Howe and his exhibitions:
Lyman Howe III, Maxwell Walkinshaw Hallet, James McDonald, Lloyd
Davey, Edward Plottle, Archie Winters, Bernard Burgunder, Frank Shaf-
fer, Dick DeFrenes, Ben Edwards, Ralph Hazeletine, Sam Hamill, Ervin
Marvel, Donald Malkames, and Ken Woodward. Sadly, several have
passed away since the research was begun ten years ago, but their role has
not been forgotten.

Whenever I have needed his advice or assistance, Ben Levin has always
been there, as has David Shepard. In addition, the financial expertise of
Joseph Silberman and Donald Dembert has helped greatly in the planning
and management of these projects.

The two people who have been part of this project for ten years have been my main support for more than a decade. Without them, I would not have had the courage to continue beyond the initial research. To Adadot Hayes, who served as photographer, sound recordist and sounding board, and Charles Musser, whose outstanding knowledge of early motion picture history, enthusiasm, and friendship, have made this publication possible, my sincere thanks.

Carol Nelson
April 1989

THE following individuals and institutions kindly provided photographs and permission to use them:

Paul Felton, Jr.: 9-1, 9-2, 9-5, 9-6, 10-4, 10-8

Maxwell Walkinshaw Hallet: 6-1, 6-8, 6-9, 6-10, 6-11, 6-12, 7-1, 7-2, 7-7, 7-11, 8-4

Dr. and Mrs. Lyman H. Howe III: 2-1, 2-2, 2-3, 2-4, 3-3, 3-5, 6-4

Charles Musser: 5-2; photographer Suzanne Williamson: 6-7, 7-9, 8-6, 8-7

Carol Nelson: 4-1, 9-4, 11-3, 11-4

George Eastman House: 8-9; photographer Paolo Cherchi-Usai: 5–1a; photographer Joyce Jesionowski: 4-2e, 4-2f, 4-2g, 4-2h, 5-1b, 5-5

John E. Allen, Inc.: 9-11a, 9-11b, 9-11c

Library of Congress: 4-2a, 4-2d, 6-6e, 6-6f, 8-2a, 8-2b, 9-7a, 9-7b, 9-8, 9-9; photographer Joyce Jesionowski: 10-7a, 10-7b, 10-7c, 11-2; photographer Patrick Loughney: 6-5a, 6-5b, 6-5c, 6-6a, 6-6b, 6-6c

Museum of Modern Art / Film Stills Archive: 4-2c, 7-6; photographer Joyce Jesionowski: 4-2b, 4-4, 6-6d, 7-4a, 7-4b, 7-5a, 7-5b

State Historical Society of Wisconsin, photographer Matthew Watt: 10-1

U.S. Department of the Interior, National Park Service, Edison National Historic Site: 3-2

Winona Historical Society, Winona, Wisconsin: 7-8a, 7-8b

Wisconsin Center for Film and Theater Research: 11-5

Wyoming Historical and Geological Society, Wilkes-Barre, Pennsylvania: 3-1, 3-4, 4-3, 4-5, 5-3, 5-4a, 5-4b, 5-6, 5-7, 6-2, 6-3, 6-13, 7-3, 7-10, 7-12, 8-1, 8-3, 8-5, 8-8, 9-3, 9-10, 10-2, 10-3, 10-5, 10-6, 11-1, A-1a, A-1b, A-2

Abbreviations

* * *

High-Class Moving Pictures

1

* *

Introduction

* * *

As THE nineteenth century neared its close, a phonograph exhibitor and motion picture entrepreneur toured northeastern Pennsylvania and New England boasting that he was "the Barnum of them all." Although he had enjoyed only a tentative, regional success over the previous fifteen years, wrapping himself in the mantle of Phineas T. Barnum's greatness would soon prove unnecessary, even inappropriate. In the aftermath of the Spanish-American War, Lyman H. Howe would marshall his own talents, create his own legend, and become America's foremost traveling motion picture exhibitor—a title he could credibly claim for the next twenty years. For Americans from Massachusetts to Kansas, he would bridge the gap between humbugger Barnum and movie mogul Adolph Zukor.

Howe belonged to the legions of traveling showmen who brought urban-based entertainments to the American heartland.[1] He was part of a way of life soon undermined by mass entertainment—first the storefront motion picture houses or nickelodeons, and then the movie palaces with their balanced programs. Touring a miniature coal breaker, he entered the world of show business in 1883, exactly fifty years after Barnum and thirty years before Zukor. He gave phonograph concerts during the 1890s and added motion pictures to his programs in 1896. His last road shows ended in 1919, shortly after the end of World War I. In his heyday he toured new, technologically based entertainments with important prerecorded elements. Howe flourished in one era, when performers journeyed from town to town almost exclusively by railroad; he grew old in another, when an evening's fun could be shipped in a film can.

Howe remains one of many shadowy figures from the era of "silent" American film. His presence is briefly acknowledged by Terry Ramsaye and Robert Grau, two early chroniclers of motion picture history.[2] Among more recent historians, Harry Geduld has discussed Howe's use of sound effects.[3] Yet the nature, scope, and duration of his activities have never been addressed. One concrete goal of this investigation, then, is to provide a professional biography of an exhibitor who was involved in motion pictures from the outset. It is not, and cannot be, a study of the man's inner life. No personal correspondence survives. Interviews and accounts focus on his public persona, providing only the barest glimpse of his private life and thought. A wide assortment of scrapbooks, some professional correspondence, and a few films produced by Howe are available. These, in conjunction with extensive research in newspapers and trade periodicals, have made it possible to create a portrait of his business activities and to illuminate the practice of traveling exhibition throughout the silent era.[4]

Howe's activities resonate with the concerns of recent scholarship. Social and cultural historians have increasingly explored the ways in which popular culture and leisure time activities shaped the lives of ordinary Americans as the United States emerged as an industrial nation and a world power.[5] How did commercial amusement—particularly the movies—become integrated into these people's lives? How did these early films reflect and influence their system of values and beliefs?[6] As Robert Sklar has pointed out, historians active in cinema studies explore similar questions.[7] Although Roy Rosenzweig, for example, emphasizes the social organization of leisure and ideology and Douglas Gomery economic and business history, both have been concerned with the site of exhibition and the conditions of reception.[8] In fact, a focus on exhibition lends itself to industrial history precisely because it must address the economic basis of the motion picture industry—the showman's ability to bring patrons through the front door. When historians have looked at the first fifteen years of motion picture exhibition, however, they have usually focused on vaudeville and the early nickelodeons.[9] We are looking instead at the almost forgotten practice of traveling exhibition. How did enterprises such as Howe's come to flourish and what caused their decline?

Exhibition history can also investigate the relationship between the films that were shown—and often still exist—and the people who originally saw them. What meanings did audiences find in them? This question is normally asked of films only within the framework of a textual reading, but this need not be the case. At least with Howe, enough evidence survives to analyze the ways in which exhibition helped to structure the reception of these films. Since exhibitors such as Howe mediated between motion picture producers and Americans of diverse environments, their study enables us to better understand the transformation of American culture in the new industrial age. In this respect, Howe's musical counterpart may well have been composer and bandleader John Philip Sousa. Both helped to construct what Neil Harris has called a "culture of reassurance."[10]

Early motion picture exhibition, however, was eclectic. Carnivals often carried a motion picture blacktop or electric theater, and dramatic repertory companies frequently showed films between acts of their plays. As Calvin Pryluck has remarked, wherever commercial entertainment existed, there were likely to be moving pictures.[11] Even among specialized exhibitors who used films as their principal or exclusive drawing card, it would be naive to suggest that Howe or any other individual was "typical."[12] Some traveling exhibitors had several companies touring the United States at one time, others only one. Some appealed to religious groups, others to lovers of urban, commercial amusement. If Howe is not and cannot be "typical," he proves useful for understanding not only traveling exhibition but larger issues involving turn-of-the-century entertainment. His uniqueness had definite limits. Wrestling with the problem of another unusual individual's typicality, Carlo Ginzburg remarks that "culture offers to the individual a horizon of latent possibilities—a flexible and invisible cage in which he can exercise his own conditional liberty."[13] Certainly this was true for Howe, who pushed against some limits even as he happily conformed to others.

Film practice in turn-of-the-century America occurred within parameters that allowed for significant though limited variation. To better explore the parameters of traveling exhibition, we will examine exhibitors other than Howe. Some were Howe's associates—people like Stewart Maxwell Walkinshaw, who became Howe's partner, and Edwin Hadley, who eventually went into business for himself. Others were direct competitors like John P. Dibble, prominent between 1897 and 1904; Archie Shepard, a successful traveling showman who became an owner of storefront motion picture theaters; and the Kinemacolor Company of America, which presented nonfiction subjects with its system of color cinematography from 1910 to 1915. Still others appealed to different audiences with different subject matter and formats. Among the illustrated lecturers using moving pictures were E. Burton Holmes, who was active from 1891 into the 1950s, the photographer and filmmaker Edward Curtis, and even President Theodore Roosevelt. Establishing similarities and differences among Howe and his fellow exhibitors, as well as tracing their interaction, defines the horizon of possibilities within the practice of traveling exhibition.

As even a brief glimpse at Howe's contemporaries makes clear, an exhibitor's prosperity was far from assured. He had to keep a repertoire of films that were novel and good enough to please patrons. He had to know how to present these pictures in the best possible light. This meant not only having up-to-date projection technology but also knowing how to solve a wide range of technical problems continually encountered on the road. An exhibitor's ability to promote his show was also crucial. Howe's achievement of these goals at any particular moment was not as unusual as his ability to sustain a high level of success over several decades.

Although traveling exhibition was a widespread phenomenon—more widespread than generally acknowledged—it might not merit such extensive study if these showmen did not often play a crucial creative role.

Particularly in the early years, exhibitors were responsible for what is called "postproduction" in modern filmmaking. They routinely assumed an editorial function, often by structuring their short films into longer narratives. They were also responsible for the sound accompaniment, not simply music but sound effects, synchronous dialogue, and live narration. In all of these areas, Howe generally represented the state of the art.

Approaching Howe as a subject for biographical inquiry highlights contemporary concerns about both authorship and an author's "biographical legend." In the first years of cinema and in earlier years of screen practice involving magic lantern shows, the predecessor of today's slide shows, the exhibitor was viewed as the author of the work, of the exhibition. The film director, whom we now usually consider the author, either did not exist as such or went unacknowledged. A history of this era of film practice thus requires us, as Michel Foucault has urged, "to study not only the expressive value and formal transformations of discourse, but its mode of existence: the modifications and variations, within any culture of modes of circulation, valorization, attribution, and appropriation."[14] Howe is particularly interesting in this regard because he continued to appropriate the role of author long after most exhibitors had deferred, first to the claims of production companies, and later to those of leading actors, directors, and writers.

"Lyman H. Howe," moreover, was often a construct, a commercial fiction. After 1899, the man no longer traveled with his show. After 1907, most decisions for the Howe enterprise were made by Howe's partner and general manager, Max Walkinshaw. *Lyman H. Howe's Hodge Podge*, a series of short subjects made in the 1920s and early 1930s, was initiated by a Howe associate when Howe was already seriously ill. It continued for ten years after his death. The relationship between the man and the authorial construct is an important one that is clarified over the course of our narrative. Inevitably, and purposefully on Howe's part, the man and the commercial construct merged; where one ended and the other began is difficult and sometimes impossible for us to tell. Although Howe's name is used in both senses in this study, we have sought to provide contexts in which the referent is clear.

Here, then, the question of authorship is tied to the concept of biographical legend offered by the Russian Formalist Boris Tomashevsky, and more recently applied to film by neo-Formalist David Bordwell. Tomashevsky claims that "the biography that is useful to the literary historian is not the author's curriculum vitae or the investigator's account of his life. What the literary historian really needs is the biographical legend created by the author himself. Only such a legend is a literary fact."[15] Bordwell argues that "we can situate a filmmaker's work in film history by studying the persona created by the artist in his public pronouncements, in his writings, and in his dealings with the film industry."[16] In the case of author Howe, public statements and newspaper puff were plentiful, colorful, often fictional, and sometimes contradictory. Some people accepted these pronouncements at face value. A few even elaborated on the myth he had initiated. Undoubtedly others who attended his shows were uninterested or even unaware of the Howe legend. But many retained a healthy skepticism towards the master showman's promotional schemes and myth building. As Neil Harris makes clear, such skepticism had been cultivated by Barnum in his prewar audiences and was never entirely absent in response to the showman's ballyhoo.[17] As with the meaning of a film, when we consider the notion of a biographical legend, we must take into account the audience's reception.

Although reconstruction of the author's biographical legend, too often ignored by historians interested simply in the film, can be progressive, it is not possible to recreate the moment of the legend. History changes our experience of a film; to deny that is to retreat into nostalgia. We do not sit in a period theater watching a period print on a period projector. Even if we could, we could not duplicate the period spectator's knowledge. What we know and how we know it are different. One of the historian's strengths is the ability to establish a biography of the author beyond the legend. Tomashevsky may be unhappy with biographers who "have been determined to learn at any cost the identity of the woman whom Pushkin so hopelessly loved (or pretended to love),"[18] but the biographer who establishes that Pushkin's lover was a respectable society woman does not destroy the legend; he provides the reader with a new and valuable perspective. We would argue that the historian must establish not only the legend (or its absence) but also an accurate account of the author's life and its conditions. The dialectical examination of one in light of the other will yield a new, richer understanding of the work.

Certainly the legend should not be dismissed and Bordwell has laudably drawn attention to some of its functions within an industrial system. Yet a biography of any public figure must be concerned with the individual's legend precisely because it often strategically obscures uncomfortable truths. Awareness of both legend and historical reality often leads to insight into a particular individual or a larger historical issue. For instance, in 1904 and 1905 Howe claimed to have produced certain films that we now know were made by the Edison and Biograph companies. What can be supposed from such assertions? It would not be enough simply to accept them as part of the Howe legend without concern for their factual basis, but it seems unproductive simply to treat them as embarrassing falsehoods, either to gloss over them or to condemn their perpetuator as a huckster. They should be situated within the framework of contemporary motion picture practice and analyzed. First, similar claims to authorship were made by many rival exhibitors and reflected the increased competition of this period. Second, as the creative role of the exhibitor was being reduced and the production companies asserted stronger control over the narrative, exhibitors tried to maintain their traditional claims of authorship by insisting that they had produced films that they had actually purchased. Contradictory claims must have made many film patrons skeptical and led to a new era in which the production company was acknowledged as the author.

Bordwell correctly asserts that "our task is . . . to analyze the legend's historical and aesthetic functions." But to produce more accurate, less self-serving biography, the historian must also "puncture the legend," replacing it not with some "easy truth" but with a more acute perception of the historical moment.[19] No understanding should be considered final; this text will inevitably be revised—by us as well as others—in the future. But to say that we have not attained or exhausted Truth, that new evidence will require refinement of our arguments, and that there will always be gaps in our knowledge does not make the undertaking any less fruitful or worthwhile. To distinguish between historical fact and fiction is a crucial labor, often difficult and frustrating, and therefore humbling.

In its examination of one figure and one aspect of the motion picture industry, this study usually does not bring its theoretical model to the fore. In terms that are materialist and dialectical we have sought to situate the cinema within social and cultural practice, and where appropriate, we have explored the ideological implications of Howe's programs and his relations with his contemporaries. We understand changing motion picture practices to involve the dynamic interaction between cinema's production methods (including not only film production but exhibition and audience reception) and its methods of representation. We have here inevitably concentrated on exhibition methods and their impact on representation and are also concerned with the commercial strategies of various showmen. Rapidly changing methods of production and representation not only open up new commercial opportunities but eliminate others and alter the rest. Correspondingly, commercial innovations transform these methods. The business side of cinema is likewise an integral part of motion picture practice.

HISTORIANS' discussions of film audiences often revolve around the opposition between the predominantly native-born middle class and the heavily immigrant working class, a distinction of limited value for Howe's entertainments since the immigrant working class rarely attended his shows. The American notion of the middle class is so broad that it includes almost everyone from salesclerks to corporate managers, from lawyers and doctors to small businesspeople. Greater specificity is needed.[20]

Howe became known for his ability to attract what were often called "the better classes" and "the leisure classes." Robert Grau later called them the "automobile clientele." These terms for the economic elite are not so narrow, nor so pejorative, as the term "ruling class"—a term that is usually absent from most studies as well. Harry Braverman has distinguished between those who worked within a traditional framework of small capital and the growing numbers of people who were employed by large-scale enterprises, the old middle class increasingly giving way to "the new middle class."[21] Likewise, "the new folk," according to Albert McLean, Jr., were members of the working and middle classes—either previously rural Americans or European immigrants—who had moved to large cities and found employment within an expanding industrially based economy. They were, he convincingly argues, the principal patrons of American vaudeville.[22] At least until the end of the nineteenth century, Howe relied heavily on patronage from smaller cities and towns still often dominated by "the old folk." In the communities that he frequented, the economic transformation was more gradual and occurred later than in the large urban centers, and his patrons' mobility—geographic, economic, and social—was notably less.[23] Nonetheless, he learned to bridge differences between "the old folk" and the new.

Historians commonly juxtapose two types of culture closely related to the overly simplified opposition between middle and working classes. On the one hand is the semi-official, elevated, Protestant culture with its stamp of social responsibility and respectability; on the other is popular commercial amusement with its promises of immediate pleasures and its challenges to traditional values. John Kasson, for example, contrasts Coney Island to Central Park and Chicago's Columbian Exposition of 1893 with their aspirations for more traditional cultural standards.[24] Daniel Czitrom illuminates the cultural threat that motion pictures seemed to pose by quoting a period sociologist who saw this confrontation as a battle between "warring sides of human nature—appetite and will, impulse and reason, inclination and ideal."[25] Although this simple opposition dominated discourse at many points in the late nineteenth and early twentieth centuries, a close investigation of Howe and his fellow exhibitors encourages finer discriminations. His activities make it impossible to equate motion pictures with popular commercial amusement per se, for Howe did not embrace popular entertainment in the same way as Coney Island and vaudeville. His activities make it clear that motion pictures operated within three distinct cultural clusters.

Associated with the better classes was the refined culture of the *Atlantic Monthly* and polite literature.[26] Its members, proponents of a enlightened, humanistic sensibility, operating freely within centers of power, had their own newspapers, theaters, and cultural institutions. They also had their own venues and genres for motion pictures. Thus, the Brooklyn Institute of Arts and Sciences presented the travelogues of E. Burton Holmes and Dwight Elmendorf, who also gave programs at Carnegie Hall in Manhattan. A morally conservative, church-oriented culture, tied to the old middle class, played a prominent role in many small towns. The extent to which the goals of these two cultures differed has been underappreciated, at least in relation to commercial amusement.[27] Although they did generate an uneasy alliance of reformers anxious to regulate motion pictures employed for mere amusement, their differences were often manipulated by the film industry and astute showmen.

It is little realized that the conservative religious community had a positive program embracing motion pictures. Groups routinely converted YMCA auditoriums and churches into temporary motion picture theaters. Religious subjects such as *The Passion Play of Oberammergau* may have been their favorite pictures, but in order to retain members or bring them back, the Methodist Episcopal Church and other denominations were prepared to adopt many of the amusement world's methods—and many of its films.

Around this question, there was, of course, serious internal debate. The struggle to define a cultural policy in the wake of industrialization in some ways paralleled the churches' attempts to develop a commensurate social and economic theory.[28] But action did not wait for consensus. A group of adept exhibitors built on a tradition of presenting lantern shows and phonograph concerts as part of a church's cultural activities. Mediating between the urban, amusement-oriented motion picture producers and the church groups themselves, showmen were often able to package films that epitomized urban pleasures in ways that gained these conservatives' endorsement. Indeed, although Methodists categorically banned amusements in any shape or form for its members, they became one of cinema's strongest proponents. Their film programs entertained rather than amused. If the distinction seems rather fine, for them it was nonetheless real.

Finally, there was America's vibrant, commercial, urban, popular culture, which attracted middle-class patrons, both "old" and "new," as well as those from the working class.[29] Its own distinctive genres included fight films and short, risqué comedies. Although both consistently received the clergy's strong condemnation, we shall see that filmed boxing matches, at least, enjoyed a brief vogue in elite circles. Vaudeville theaters, opera houses, and amusement parks were some of the outlets for this type of motion picture entertainment. The rise of the story film and the subsequent nickelodeon boom irreversibly associated motion pictures with commercial amusement and finally obliterated other associations from historical memory.

Howe was unusual precisely in his ability to appeal to all three groups. Building on his earlier experiences as an exhibitor, he commenced by establishing a strong rapport with religious groups. In 1898 and 1899, after solidifying these ties, he gradually moved his exhibitions into local opera houses and found additional patrons among frequenters of popular amusement. Finally, on the eve of the nickelodeon boom, he began to show pictures in prestigious urban theaters, where he attracted members of the leisure class who would not have felt comfortable in cheap nickel motion picture theaters. As Woodrow Wilson had written well before becoming president of the United States, "Someday we shall be of one mind, our ideals fixed, our purposes harmonized, our nationality complete and consentaneous."[30] Howe seemed to achieve this goal by finding a common ground among these often antagonistic cultural clusters. It was a heady but brief moment of triumph. As feature-length "photoplays" became widely accepted as art and travelogues were incorporated into the balanced program, the transcendence of these cultural divisions was achieved on a new level, and Howe's fortunes rapidly faded. It was the kind of cinema promoted by Adolph Zukor that achieved a new hegemony.

Howe had neutralized the tensions that pervaded American culture by finding a common denominator. This was one of the principal reasons why his programs collapsed in the wake of World War I. Religious opposition to popular culture has existed in America since at least the first part of the nineteenth century. Barnum had faced it and coopted it with his modifications of the museum, keeping its educational shell and filling it with forbidden pleasures. The nickelodeon era inflamed opposition from allied genteel and religious groups, but the creation of the National Board of Censorship soon dampened it. The three cultural groupings continue today, finding their way onto televison, where commercial networks dominate the airways but coexist with public television, dependent upon a cultivated elite for donations, and evangelical Christian programming which has experienced a recent setback with the scandals surrounding Jimmy Swaggart and Jim Bakker. Although these three distinct cultural orientations preceded and succeeded the period when Howe was active, this study investigates a time when they confronted a new era of mass entertainment.

2 ✳

Traveling Exhibits:
Howe's Early Years,
1856-1890

✳ ✳ ✳

> Those who have never been in or seen a coal mine or breaker, or even
> those familiar with the scenes in the Anthracite Coal Regions of
> Pennsylvania, will be pleased to learn that an opportunity is presented
> to them of witnessing a perfect Miniature Coal Mine, showing the
> entire operation of mining and preparing anthracite coal, the whole
> being such a faithful and exact representation as to make it a sight
> well worth seeing.
>
> Lyman H. Howe and Robert M. Colborn,
> "A Marvel of Mechanism"

THE TOURING OF informative, educational exhibits has a long history in
the United States, dating back at least until the early nineteenth century.
By the 1830s, many managers were traveling the country with a variety of
curiosities. In 1835, Barnum purchased and exhibited Joice Heth—an ancient, partially paralyzed slave said to be George Washington's nurse.
Touring New York and New England, Barnum enjoyed substantial profits
as she astounded patrons with details of the first president's early life. The
distinction between gossip and history may have been questionable, but
Heth was also a biological wonder, believed to be 161 years old. By the
1840s, Barnum had opened the American Museum in New York City,
even as he continued to send out such exhibits as the stuffed "Fejee Mer-
maid" (part monkey and part fish) and the midget Tom Thumb. Both
were promoted, at least nominally, as scientific curiosities of an educational nature.[1]

Demonstrations of new scientific and technological knowledge were
popular cultural events. A "Grand Exhibition of Nature and Art," given
by Prof. J. B. Brown and Dr. A. T. Johnson in the 1840s, toured parts of
the country promising to explain "the whole principle of telegraphing."[2]
Additional technological innovations on their program included the Boston Fire Alarm Bell and Colt's Submarine Battery. This fascination with

process and mechanical invention, often expressed through extensive, detailed analysis, is one aspect of what Neil Harris has called "the operational aesthetic."[3] Certainly this orientation was evident in Howe's exhibitions, particularly the miniature coal mine and breaker that began his career.

During the 1870s and 1880s small-time showmen continued to travel the United States presenting exhibits in halls or rented storefronts. While still claiming to educate their patrons, they offered subjects primarily sensationalistic in nature. Among these showmen were the New Englander Benjamin Franklin Keith (1846–1914), Italian-born Sylvester Z. Poli (1859–1937) and Lyman Hakes Howe (1856–1923) of Wilkes-Barre, Pennsylvania. Although each began by modeling himself on Barnum, their lasting achievements as showmen would come only after they found new ways to entertain an industrializing America.

Keith, after leaving a New England farm at seventeen, worked at Bunnell's Museum in New York and then with Barnum himself. Over a period of years, he took three different exhibits on the road and each time returned destitute. In 1882 he opened a museum in Boston and began to prosper, expanding his operations and forming a partnership the following year. Staying in one place, he needed a constant supply of new entertainment. "My only attraction was Baby Alice, a midget that at the age of three months weighed but one and one-half pounds," Keith later recalled. "But I installed a small stage in the rear of our room and secured several acts from the variety theaters."[4] After changing business partners, Keith introduced "continuous vaudeville." The off-color jokes and songs of the male-oriented variety show were eliminated and the program refined to be suitable for ladies and children. Moreover, the bill was repeated without interruption from late morning until the theater closed late at night; a patron could thus arrive at any time and see the entire program.[5]

Poli worked as a wax modeler at New York's Eden Musee, which opened on 23d Street in March 1884 with waxwork exhibits in its foyers and orchestral selections in its Winter Garden.[6] In 1887 the Musee sent Poli to Chicago, where he sculpted lifelike figures of seven anarchists condemned to hang for their role in the Haymarket Riot. Several statues were done from life, others from photographs. Poli then made duplicates of "The Seven Chicago Anarchists" and "The Story of A Crime," a narrative series from the Musee's Chamber of Horrors, and went into business for himself, renting a small Chicago storefront and opening a makeshift dime museum. When it proved successful, he took his exhibits on the road. Gradually Poli accumulated enough capital and experience to begin his own permanent museum. Briefly based in Troy, New York, he moved to New Haven, Connecticut, leased a hall, and opened Poli's Eden Musee in 1892. A theater with variety acts was added, and Poli soon followed Keith into vaudeville.[7]

LYMAN HAKES HOWE

Lyman Hakes Howe was born on June 6, 1856—the year that Sigmund Freud was born and the Bessemer steel process developed. He grew up in Wilkes-Barre, then the principal town in northeastern Pennsylvania. The surrounding Wyoming Valley was a mining center for anthracite, or hard coal. By the 1850s, anthracite's qualities as an efficient, low-pollutant fuel were widely recognized, and it was gradually adopted for railroad locomotives. This ensured general prosperity for the region throughout the second half of the nineteenth century.[8]

Nathan Howe, Lyman's father, depended on the area's growth for his livelihood, moving to the Wilkes-Barre area from Massachusetts in 1835 and soon establishing a brickyard. He expanded into contracting and constructed many of the town's public works as well as several early, small railway lines designed to transport coal from mines to the canals. In 1840 he married Margaret Robins. Lyman, the youngest of eight children, was born when she was forty-one and her husband thirty-five. Three of the children died in childhood, the two youngest girls when Lyman was two and four; the others had married and left home by the time he was fourteen. Like many of his contemporaries, Lyman began to work early in life. After two years of secondary school at Wyoming Seminary, a private college preparatory and business school, he and a friend started a small business as house and sign painters.

Howe soon gave up painting to become a traveling salesman or, as it was then called, a "drummer." The future traveling showman learned promotional tactics and became familiar with neighboring towns and cities, which he would someday visit as an exhibitor. This promising job might have led to a respectable position in a commercial house but for the severe economic depression of 1873. It was only the start of the young man's misfortunes. In October of that year, his father dropped dead on the street while conversing with a friend.[9] Nathan Howe's estate was near bankruptcy, and the family house on 233 South Franklin Street was sold: widow and son remained there only as boarders.[10] This son of an affluent contractor suddenly found himself in the working class.

With business conditions in disarray, Lyman abandoned his responsibilities as a salesman and found employment with the Central Railroad of New Jersey as a brakeman, a physically demanding and dangerous job. He chose, however, to list his occupation as painter and probably took odd painting jobs to supplement his meager income. Although Howe worked his way up to extra baggage master, it was not an easy time to work for the railroads. Owners repeatedly cut employees' wages. To save more money, they dismissed men and increased workloads for those who remained. Such management practices eventually goaded railroad workers into a strike that spread across the United States and into other industries.[11] In northeastern Pennsylvania, the strike was so powerful and effective that it had to be suppressed by the state militia. The fact that Howe stopped working for the railroads around this time suggests his active participation in the strike. As Oscar Jewell Harvey remarks in his history of Wilkes-Barre, "Some of the strikers sought and were granted employment in their old places, but hundreds of others, many of whom were to become prominent in other walks of life in later years, found that the strike of 1877 had finished their careers as railroaders."[12] Howe resumed his trade as a full-time house and sign painter, cultivating his taste and sense of design in the process. Slowly he accumulated capital, and in 1883, the twenty-seven-year-old made his first move into showmanship. He and Robert M. Colborn purchased, refurbished, and finally exhibited a miniature coal breaker.

A MINIATURE COAL MINE AND BREAKER

Howe and Colborn promoted their miniature coal breaker with themes that reverberated throughout Howe's later career. They described this "marvel of mechanism" as

> A perfect Miniature Coal Mine, showing the entire operation of mining and preparing anthracite coal, the whole being such a faithful and exact representation as to make it a sight worth seeing.
> The coal is separated from the slate by little boys known as slate-pickers, whose grimy faces and monotonous avocation must be seen to be appreciated. And is spoken of by the press as being the greatest mechanical wonder of the age.
> The huge lumps of coal as it comes from the mines in its natural state is hoisted up the slope to the top of the breaker, from whence it is run through the steel rollers and then through the screens, and so on till it has gone through the process of being reduced to its proper sizes ready for shipment.
> This Coal Mine and Breaker, which is operated by the most complete miniature steam engines of modern construction for that purpose, is of such size and capacity as to reflect accurately all of the interesting features of the real object, built at a cost of over $4,000.00 and weighs over 5,000 pounds. Showing the geological formation of the different strata where anthracite coal exists, and it also shows the miners actually working in the separate chambers drilling and blasting the coal.[13]

The exhibit revealed two processes: first, the operation of a coal mine; and secondly, that of an intricate, mechanically propelled model. Here

2-1. Howe & Colburn's Miniature Coal Mine and Breaker was a commercial failure in Baltimore (1884).

and in subsequent publicity materials, the model's faithful duplication of reality was emphasized. The workings of the mine were said to be shown in "a vivid and lifelike manner." Miniature miners were depicted with lights on their hats that illuminated their surroundings. It was all "set forth with realistic faithfulness." The illusion of reality was sought, even as the methods of achieving this illusion were exposed as part of the exhibit.

Realistic faithfulness provided a framework for additional elements in Howe's showmanship. Great emphasis was placed on its educational value. The miniature coal breaker was declared "interesting and instructive."[14] People unfamiliar with the process of extracting coal were urged to educate themselves. The miniature was meant to provide "an object lesson for students and scholars that they will long remember."[15] Crucial elements of the operational aesthetic—process, analysis, and education— were evoked. The gain in scientific knowledge, in the field of geology, was also promoted. Furthermore, Howe and Colborn contended that watching the miniature simulacrum was superior to entering the mines. Able to see the whole process at once, spectators gained a clearer idea of mining and breaking coal. It was also safer: "The danger and great unpleasantness, the dust of the breaker, the deafening roar and clatter of the machinery, also the drip and dirt of the mine and the anxiety lest blast or fall of rock may startle or perhaps injure you, are all happily avoided by a visit to this miniature."[16] The spectator's ability to experience a dangerous activity in complete safety would later reemerge as an important element in Howe's motion picture programs.[17]

In promoting his Automatic Coal Miner and Breaker, Howe emphasized its technological component. He declared that the working model was "built strictly on scientific principles" and was "the greatest work of mechanical art ever attempted."[18] (The showman's need to declare his entertainment superior to all others was already apparent.) He called the model a "mechanism"—the same term he later used for the phonograph and the motion picture projector. Using technology to represent a technological feat of a different order, the actual mines and breakers, the miniature mine served as a double testimony to human ingenuity, persistence, and daring. First, there was Howe and Colborn's ingenuity in making the meticulous model, their efforts in transporting such a heavy thing so many miles, and their willingness to risk so much money. Second, there was the courage of miners who worked day after day at their dangerous jobs. The miniature coal breaker testified to "the many lives lost and the dangers that surround those whose occupation it is to go down in the bowels of the earth to delve for that which gives us warmth and comfort."[19] The partners may have celebrated technological achievement, but they also were aware of its cost.

The showmen's choice of subject matter was noteworthy for its presentation of a typical yet striking aspect of Wilkes-Barre life. The region's coal was often called "Black Diamonds," and Wilkes-Barre, center of the anthracite industry, was known as the Black Diamond City. Howe was using his showmanship not only to promote his miniature coal mine but to boost his hometown. Remnants of what Francis Couvares and E. P. Thompson call "plebeian culture," evident in this celebration of localism as well as in showmen's idealization of the common man, peek through a heavy overlay of middle-class respectability.[20]

Howe's career as a showman did not begin on an auspicious note. Buying and carefully refurbishing the miniature coal breaker was a major investment for Howe and Colborn. Although the reported cost of $4,000 was almost certainly exaggerated, the miniature took their life savings and some borrowed money as well.[21] To recoup their investment, the partners exhibited the working miniature in Pennsylvania towns during the fall of 1883. On January 9, 1884, they opened at the Masonic Temple in Baltimore, Maryland (1880 population: 332,313).[22] Spectators paid ten cents to see "the mechanical wonder of the age" from 10 A.M. to 4 P.M. during the day and from 7 P.M. to 10 P.M. in the evening. Advertisements were placed in all the leading papers: the *Baltimore Sun*, the *Baltimore American*, the *Baltimore News*, and so on. Leaflets and brochures were printed and distributed.[23]

Howe and Colborn remained at the Masonic Temple for a month, competing with such amusement enterprises as the Dime Museum, which offered the "Mammoth Hog," shadowgraphs, a stage show, and diverse curiosities. Variety at Kernan's Monumental Theater included Prof. Kennedy's "Scientific Art of Mesmerism" and Neil Smith's Wonderful Dog Circus. Theatergoers saw such plays as *The Stranglers of Paris* at Ford's Grand Opera House and *Our Bachelors* at Albaugh's Holiday Theater. Those interested in cruder amusements might have witnessed a "Sparring and Rat Killing Contest" in which a dog killed five rats in 1 minute and 55 seconds—only to be defeated by a rival canine that did so in less than a minute.[24] Howe and Colborn did not find a ready audience for their high-class entertainment. Their exhibit lacked sensational appeal. Unlike Barnum's successful coups, the miniature coal breaker failed to rouse people's prurient interests or test their credibility. Although Howe and Colborn claimed that "thousands are witnessing its wonderful workings everyday,"[25] their venture, like Keith's tours before it, was a financial disaster. The model was stored in a barn, and the partners rode freight trains back to Wilkes-Barre. As showmen they had proved to be miserable failures.

Although Colborn abandoned the amusement field and eventually became a physician in Newark, New Jersey, Howe did not give up so easily. He bought out Colborn's share of the enterprise and made arrangements with officials of the Lehigh Valley Railroad to exhibit the miniature coal breaker as a summer attraction at Glen Onoko, a popular resort in Mauch Chunk, Pennsylvania. Now renamed Jim Thorpe, Mauch Chunk then called itself "the Switzerland of America."[26] The region's leading tourist attraction was a switchback railroad that zigzagged its way up the mountain to Glen Onoko. Near the mountaintop station Howe pitched a tent and set up his exhibit.

Glen Onoko proved a conducive setting for the presentation of Howe's mechanical wonder. The tent reduced or eliminated the costly rental of exhibition space. Instead of moving from town to town, he relied on the resort's constantly changing population of summer tourists. Because Mauch Chunk was renowned for its coal mining, and few other amuse-

2-2. Howe's exhibit at Glen Onoko (ca. 1885).

ments were available, tourists were favorably disposed to visit Howe's model. Howe's clientele was drawn from the "better classes"—people who could afford the luxury of a summer vacation. With disposable income, they could readily indulge their curiosity. Howe sharpened his appeal to this group by revamping his promotional materials and eliminating the last vestiges of plebeian culture. Materials distributed during his Glen Onoko exhibitions, for example, dropped earlier sympathetic references to the miners and breaker boys. Howe's emphasis was now entirely on process, ignoring the workers who did the processing. The valorization of process and technology went hand in hand. As a result of these changes, Howe prospered at his second attempt and remained at the resort for the next nine summers. Taking a failure and turning it into a modest success, he demonstrated the abilities of a true showman.

Poli, Keith, and Howe faced similar dilemmas before their careers took divergent paths. Should they travel from town to town with their cumbersome exhibits, or stay in one place? Their displays were expensive and time-consuming to make. Since they could not readily be replaced by new exhibits, the showmen were forced to move. Yet while they all took their attractions on the road, they found expenses high and patronage uncertain. Their commercial activities were thus more successful when less peripatetic. Faced with the difficult problem of attracting return customers, Keith and Poli moved into vaudeville. Howe settled for something less:

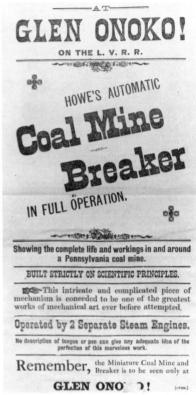

2-3. Howe at Glen Onoko (ca. 1885).

2-4. Handbill (ca. 1885).

part-time showmanship. Exhibiting his model during the summer, he returned to his old occupation as a painter during the other three seasons.

Poli and Howe (less is known about Keith's exhibits) offered lifelike images to patrons for a dime. Their interest in presenting a perfect model of some real person or event had wide application in the amusement field at this time. The Eden Musee, with its waxworks of famous people, executions and tortures, was considered an educational experience. With its pricey admission charge, twenty-five and fifty cents, and orchestral selections, the Musee catered to a somewhat refined and moralistic middle-class audience. Its opening, for example, was attended by the mayor, an ex-senator and prominent businessmen with their wives.[27] Shorn of these high-toned trappings, Poli's "The Seven Chicago Anarchists" and "The Story of A Crime" were perceived as closer to the heart of commercial, urban, popular amusement. In keeping with his own background, Poli appealed more readily to the immigrant and working classes, yet his museum still attracted certain middle-class patrons who enjoyed this sort of amusement. Howe's miniature, less ambiguous in its educational aspirations, catered to people with a more fastidious temperament. Not only class differences but divergent cultural outlooks within classes helped to determine these showmen's different audiences.

Although Howe's success remained modest, it provided him with new confidence and new possibilities. For example, he could afford to marry. Mauch Chunk was between Wilkes-Barre and Allentown, and it seems likely that he met Alice Koehler, the daughter of an Allentown farmer and miller, at the mountain resort. The two were married on September 26, 1888, shortly after he concluded his fifth summer season. During the following four seasons, they ran the exhibit together. Lyman acted as barker: meeting the train, selling the show to tourists, and leading them to the nearby tent. Alice acted as ticket taker while he lectured on the exhibit.[28] For the remainder of the year the couple lived with Howe's mother in Wilkes-Barre.

With free time to fill (painting was itself a seasonal business) and some money to invest, Howe looked for additional ways to enhance his income. He found one opportunity in the emerging telephone industry. By the late 1880s Wilkes-Barre and its vicinity had a rudimentary telephone network, and Howe became briefly involved in the merchandising of telephone equipment.[29] Much later an admiring reporter retold Howe's account of this adventure as a moral, educational tale of triumph over adversity:

> He met a man that had for sale several gross of telephone attachments which were to be placed on the transmitter and which enabled the user to whisper and still be heard at the other end of the line. . . .
> The man who owned them was discouraged and readily sold out and Mr. Howe bought them cheaply. He was warned against taking a hand in the game, but continued on his merry way. In Scranton, which he decided upon as the first field of his labor, he sold the transmitters right and left, ending by disposing of them all at a good price and in some cases selling them to people who had no phones but who might be expected to own them in the future.[30]

This short-lived enterprise reflected Howe's continuing interest in promoting and explaining technology. In the meantime, he waited for the right opportunity to apply his skills as a showman. Then the phonograph abruptly experienced a new wave of popularity. With it Howe returned to the life of an itinerant showman. He had found a technological novelty that could not only entertain and educate but make traveling as an exhibitor more practical.

3

$$* *$$

Photographers of Sound:
Howe and the Phonograph,
1890-1896

$$* * *$$

"Bottled Music," Such it seems to be; as though you drew the cork and set the voices of past and present free.

Bethlehem Daily Times, April 23, 1890

THE DEMONSTRATION of technological inventions found new scope with the phonograph concert. Unlike the telegraph and the telephone, which enjoyed brief vogues on the lecture circuit, the phonograph proved a more lasting vehicle for amusement.[1] Although these concerts, like many kinds of nineteenth-century entertainment, are now forgotten, hundreds of phonograph exhibitors entertained Americans in the 1890s. Daniel Czitrom has traced the development of media in American culture by focusing on the telegraph, moving pictures, and television. The disjunctions among these technological forms of communication are so severe as virtually to defy any sense of continuity.[2] However, the phonograph played a key transitional role as it bridged the gap between the telegraph (and telephone), media whose principal function was to facilitate practical communication, and moving pictures, which serve primarily an entertainment or artistic function.

The phonograph was invented by Thomas Edison in 1877, just a few months after the disturbing Great Railway Strike. After a period of depression and mounting class conflict, the invention's unexpected appearance contributed to a renewed optimism about America's future. Edison, the newly named "Wizard of Menlo Park," was soon showing his invention to an enthusiastic president in the White House. This original phonograph was a primitive instrument that used tinfoil as a recording surface. Its impression only survived for two playbacks. Despite such limitations, the following year saw its exhibition as a technological novelty through bookings made by James Redpath. In May, eighty showmen-lecturers were trained in the operation of the machine, assigned territories, and then dispatched across the country. Charging twenty-five cents, these eager demonstrators remitted 25 percent of their gross receipts to the Edison Speaking Phonograph Company, which was set up to exploit the invention.[3] Although the exhibitions were initially well attended and extensively reviewed, the novelty soon faded. By 1879, microphone, phonograph, and telephone demonstrations were being given as church fund-raising entertainments. One such program included

1st. Use of the speaking Telephones while the audience are assembling (rendering speech, music, imitations &c., over a long wire.)

2d. The Scientific Lecture (about a half hour.)

3d. The Singing Telephone (heard throughout the largest room by all present at once.)

4th. The Phonograph (heard distinctly throughout the largest Churches or Opera Houses.)

5th. The Microphone.

6th. Examination and trial by audience of Phonograph and apparatus, (when opportunity is given to all to ask questions.)[4]

Even these more modest demonstrations of the phonograph had virtually ended by 1880.

The phonograph lay dormant for almost five years, until a rival group of inventors produced the graphophone, a similar machine with a superior recording system. A wax compound used as a recording surface enabled sounds to be recorded with greater clarity and played back many times. Although forced to adopt his rivals' wax cylinders and a recording method of incision rather than indentation, Edison responded by making improvements on his original invention, unveiling them in May 1888. This "perfected phonograph" stimulated public curiosity and created a renewed demand for public exhibitions of the instrument.[5] That year, the North American Phonograph Company was formed to market both Edison's phonograph and the graphophone.[6] The company leased rather than sold the machines through approximately twenty regional subcompanies, usually started by local entrepreneurs, which acquired exclusive marketing rights to specific territories and were usually responsible for giving exhibitions. When John P. Haines, president of the New York Phonograph Company, gave a demonstration in Utica (1890 population: 44,007), in January 1889, vocal contributions from the audience were recorded and then played back. These were followed by "reproductions of speeches, Levy's cornet playing, letters, whistling, the howling of a dog and other sounds to demonstrate that whatever it heard was repeated verbatim."[7] The purpose of these demonstrations was to convince businessmen that they should rent the phonograph for office use at a uniform rate of $40 per year.

Edison and the subcompanies at first promoted the instrument along lines imagined eleven years before, as a business machine that could replace expensive stenographers. Less skilled and thus less costly people could transcribe an executive's dictation from the cylinder. Businessmen could send their correspondence via a "phonogram" or record, thereby saving the time and expense of typing letters on still primitive typewriters. Like Edison's quadroplex, the telephone, and the typewriter, the phonograph was meant to increase communication efficiency and ultimately decrease the costs of running an office.[8]

But people with no interest in renting a machine joyously attended the phonograph demonstrations. As one showman later remarked, "all that was necessary to fill a hall or church was the simple announcement that the phonograph would be on exhibition."[9] This demand encouraged individuals to rent machines and give concerts within the territory of the renting subcompany. According to the *Phonogram*, the phonograph industry's trade journal, M. C. Sullivan and his brother, M. J. Sullivan, were the most successful of these exhibitors. Based in New York City, they had worked for the Edison General Electric Company and had the necessary technical expertise to run a still-temperamental machine. Between 1889 and 1891 they were booked by seven of the largest concert bureaus and gave more than three hundred exhibitions in theaters and churches, at concerts, banquets, and dances.

> The exhibition was always preceded by a lecture on the discovery and development of the miracle of the nineteenth century in which its commercial features were strongly outlined. Then followed a programme consisting of the best obtainable cylinders.
>
> In many cases the selections were so perfect that a repetition was demanded by the audience; and a glance through their large programme scrapbook shows that in several instances the Edison Improved Phonograph, exhibited by Messers. Sullivan, was the only attraction.[10]

Unfortunately the Sullivan scrapbook, like most potential documentation of this phenomenon, does not survive.[11] Howe's phonograph scrapbook preserves a rare selection of reviews, the only available coherent selection on a single showman. In combination with other materials, they provide a unique overview of a phonograph exhibitor's career and a new understanding of this short-lived practice.[12]

HOWE AND HADDOCK, PHONOGRAPH EXHIBITORS

Early in 1890, Howe acquired a partner, a Mr. Haddock, and moved conservatively into this new field. Becoming year-round showmen, they rented their machine from the Eastern Pennsylvania Phonograph Company, which controlled Wilkes-Barre and the eastern half of the state.[13] Their concerts were modeled after demonstrations given by the North American Phonograph Company and its subcompanies in late 1888 and 1889. Though presenting a wide range of prerecorded material, some by well-known artists, these exhibitors rightfully claimed credit as the authors of their programs. Not only responsible for making many of their own recordings, they also organized them into coherent form, with appropriate introductions and juxtapositions.

Howe's attraction to the phonograph is easily understood. It not only piqued his interests in technology and mechanics but provided new challenges for him to master. Like many people entering the phonograph industry at this time, he had prior, if limited, experience with the telephone. But unlike most of these people, he came to this venture as a showman rather than a salesman or technical expert. The goal of creating a simulacrum of the real, which he had so lovingly and imperfectly tried to achieve with the miniature coal breaker, could now be easily accomplished. One critic expressed a common view: "Think of it! A song or instrumental selection is rendered by an artist in New York, is boxed up, carried to this place and then is reproduced by the phonograph as though the player, speaker, or singer, as the case may be, were standing on the platform in the presence of the audience which listens to its reproduction."[14] Howe's publicity had called his miniature coal breaker "one of the mechanical wonders of the age," but this was the familiar hyperbole of showmanship. Now it was newspapers that called Edison's newly improved invention "the greatest wonder of the age" and "the greatest achievement in science that this or any other age has ever seen."[15]

The phonograph offered other advantages over the the coal breaker. Since it was light and comparatively simple to break down and set up, Howe could easily move from town to town. The financial risks were also much smaller. He only rented the machine and could return it without further expense if the novelty's popularity faded. Although Howe had to purchase expensive records (as much as $5 apiece), from the beginning he was able to "phonograph" many of them himself. Howe's background, moreover, enabled him to make good recordings and coax quality sounds from a machine both complicated to work and likely to malfunction. Not only did the wax records warp or crack, but they were sensitive to seasonal changes in temperature and varied in quality. Users had to rely for power on bulky, undependable batteries, which were also in their early stages of development. Over the years, Howe had learned how to keep his coal breaker functioning. Now this experience could be applied to the phonograph.

Howe and Haddock gave their first phonograph concerts at Frothingham's Arcade Hall in Scranton, Pennsylvania (1890 population: 75,215), twenty-five miles from Wilkes-Barre. Open from 9 A.M. to noon, 1:30 to 6 P.M. and 7 to 10 P.M. every day, the partners gave over twenty daily concerts presenting a dozen selections and lasting about half an hour. Admission was ten cents.[16] Opening night, March 10, 1890, was attended by a small group of interested listeners including lawyers, doctors, and the press. From the start, the partners sensed how to entertain their audiences. Patrons heard songs like "The Old Oaken Bucket" sung by the Manhattan Quartette, banjo solos, a parody of Whittier's poem "Barbara Frietchie" and some miscellaneous conversations. Howe and Haddock received a warm response. After their exhibition, the *Scranton Truth* concluded that "an audience can be very agreeably entertained with songs and speech and brass bands thrown upon the sensorium of the instrument months ago."[17] A few days later, the *Scranton Daily Times* reported,

> The Phonograph, at the Arcade, continues to attract immense crowds. People sit in amazement and listen to the music, vocal and instrumental, recitations, speeches, stories, &c., produced by a machine. It is really the wonder of this wonderful age, and seems almost incredible for a piece of simple machinery to reproduce, perfectly, every sound uttered, of whatever nature. We would say to all: Don't miss seeing, hearing and being astonished at this marvel.[18]

Their ten-day run was extended to more than two weeks.

The operational aesthetic continued to play an important role in these exhibits. The novelty of the late 1870s was largely forgotten. Although people had heard about the phonograph, they found its mechanics difficult to comprehend.[19] Their confusion was relieved as Howe and Haddock explained the principles behind the machine, illustrating them with a diversity of recordings. To maintain interest, the partners recorded the city's well-known Bauer's Band (four selections) on March 19, the Germania Band on March 20, and the Banjo Club on the 21st.[20] When the Germania Band's recording of "Our Naval Officers" was played, it "was reproduced so naturally that it seemed as though the original band was playing in the room."[21] While the large crowds suggest that even people of modest means attended at least one concert, the *Scranton Free Press* reported that "it has been visited by many of our prominent people dozens of times, and each entertainment seems more interesting than the preceding one."[22]

By April 1, the partners had moved their exhibition to Allentown (1890 population: 25,228), Alice Koehler Howe's hometown. They occupied a storefront on the town's main thoroughfare and equipped it with chairs. The first concert was "visited by people from every walk in life . . . and excited the wonder and curiosity of all who heard it."[23] By the end of the week the room was filled throughout the day. The *City Item* reported that their entertainments were "holding the interest and attention of our best people."[24] Again the partners decided to stay an extra week. The *Allentown Critic* reported

A GREAT SINGER IN TOWN

We have a great singer in town among us at present who, owing to his extreme modesty, would be unknown to the public if we did not call attention to his presence. He is a most gifted musician, also, and a finished elocutionist. He was such a wonderful child that his parents found it a difficult task to find a suitable name for him.

He is now staying at 616 Hamilton street and may be seen any afternoon and evening for the next few days at the place named. But like most great characters he is very eccentric; never going without an attendant, very reserved in his manners and yet, when he is beguiled into a conversation becomes exceedingly interesting. What he says is, however, shrouded in mystery and can be seen by only a favored few.

This versatile chap will entertain those who call during the next few days at 616 Hamilton street from 1:30 until 6 o'clock in the afternoon and 7 to 10 in the evening, giving special attention to the ladies and children in the afternoon, and rendering a most delightful program consisting of songs, instrumental selections, readings, etc. He is a perfect mimic and can reproduce anything he hears as those who heard him give a perfect reproduction of the oboe solo played before him by Mr. Fred Bechtel, of the Allentown Band, evening before last can testify.

It costs but 10 cents to attend his wonderful concerts and—oh, we forgot to state it before—his name is Phonograph.[25]

Howe and Haddock experimented with their exhibition methods and varied their programs so that returning patrons would not be bored. To add to the conceit that the phonograph was a person in mechanical form, the showmen recorded a cylinder that served to introduce the concert and the phonograph as the show began. Only after "Mr. Phonograph's" opening remarks did one of the partners assume the role of lecturer. Selections included many of their Scranton recordings as well as cylinders purchased from the different subcompanies. As before, they infused these concerts with personal interest by phonographing well-known local personalities: the Allentown Band, Congressman Sowden of Allentown giving an anecdote in Pennsylvania Dutch, and an organ grinder who had been playing out on the streets in the afternoons.[26] The recording of the hand organ briefly transformed the organ grinder into a local celebrity.

The showmen applied many of the practices that Howe had developed earlier with the coal mine. The exhibitions were brief. Patrons came and went. Even the admission charge, ten cents, remained the same. Although the leisure classes, like those that Howe had entertained at Glen Onoko, found the presentation attractive, the informal atmosphere and the affordable admission fee encouraged attendance by working people of modest means. The novelty appealed across class and cultural groupings. Their advertisements boasted "a dollar concert for 10 cents." Certainly recitals and musical concerts with out-of-town performers could cost one dollar. For this reason, Howe and Haddock argued that they were presenting the same kind of high-class entertainment, but in a democratic form accessible to a larger portion of the population. This policy continued in South Bethlehem (1890 population: 10,302), where Howe and Haddock again occupied a storefront, Laufer's storeroom, near the post office. Performances were limited to the afternoon and evenings. They drew on a collection of recordings large enough to entertain interested persons for several shows.[27]

When the duo completed their week-long stay in South Bethlehem and moved to Bethlehem (1890 population: 6,762), they changed the format of their shows, lengthening them to two hours. Some of the logic behind this decision was explained by the *Bethlehem Times*:

> Those who visited the entertainments given by the phonograph in South Bethlehem last week were more than pleased with the work of this wonderful instrument, but those entertainments lasted for only half an hour, and as one had become nicely interested in the phonograph the programme came to an end. These entertainments at the armory will be relieved of that disagreeable feature and all who attend these concerts will be entertained for two hours or more by a programme that will include whatever it is possible for the phonograph to do, from the act of drilling the Rifles to the more difficult task of rendering the most artistic music. Everything can be distinctly heard anywhere in the room.[28]

These new exhibition methods allowed for smoother operations and larger financial returns over a shorter time span. Four concerts were given over a three-day period with evening concerts every day and a single matinee. The concerts were longer, the performance space larger, and the admission fee higher. Evening admission charges were thirty-five cents for adults and twenty-five cents for children, with slightly reduced prices for the matinee. The exhibition was held at the armory, in a spacious hall that accommodated many more people. Different commercial methods were also employed. The exhibition was presented under the auspices of the Bethlehem Rifles, a militia group that provided the hall and relieved the partners of many promotional and organizational responsibilities in exchange for a percentage of the receipts.

Howe and Haddock held the principal creative responsibility for their shows. They were not exhibitors in the modern sense: they did not simply present the works of creative artists. Rather, they functioned as directors, performers, and technicians. Their concerts can be more appropriately viewed as live performances with prerecorded components. These live

theatrical presentations were built around mechanically reproducible elements but were not dominated by them. One of the high points of their
Bethlehem concerts was coordinated with the sponsoring company of
state militiamen. The exhibitors recorded drill instructions delivered by
the commanding officer and then played the cylinder with a squad of the
Bethlehem Rifles following the commands. Mr. Phonograph thus assumed
"the duties of commanding officer as well, putting the boys through [their
paces] as though its days and nights had been spent on the battle field."[29]

TRAVELING ALONE

Howe interrupted his new career to show the miniature coal breaker at
Glen Onoko for the summer. When he returned to the phonograph in the
fall of 1890, he operated without a partner. One of his first independent

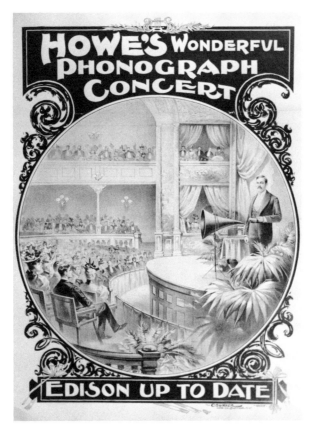

3-1. Poster (ca. 1893).

efforts was in Carbondale, Pennsylvania (1890 population: 10,833). Howe played for three evenings: on December 15 and 17 at the chapel of the Presbyterian Church, under the auspices of its Ladies' Aid Society, and on December 16 under the auspices of the YMCA at its hall. Admission on all occasions was twenty-five cents.[30] At about this time Howe began to use a standard contract that formalized his relation with these sponsoring groups:

TERMS AND CONDITIONS FOR
PHONOGRAPH EXHIBITION-CONCERT
BY THE PHONOGRAPH EXPERT, PROF. LYMAN H. HOWE

On condition that you and your society will agree to vigorously work it up—take every means of letting your citizens know of the quality and merit of this rare entertainment by placing the advertising matter where it will do the most good, have the work done, the bills distributed, etc. by reliable persons and also see that local notices appear in the local daily and weekly papers at your own expense, if any, I will agree to exhibit for you on the following terms, viz: You and your society to furnish place (hall or opera house preferred) to hold entertainment in, sell the tickets and receive for your share 40 per cent. of the gross receipts, on a basis of not less than a sixty dollar house. If the total receipts amount to less than sixty dollars you to receive thirty per cent of gross receipts.

I, Lyman H. Howe, agree to furnish the advertising matter consisting of large window bills, dates, handbills, tickets, pay all express and traveling expenses, etc., and receive for my share the balance of the gross receipts.[31]

His phonograph concerts became a way for churches, local YMCAs, and veterans organizations to raise money. Services were often donated by the local newspaper, and occasionally even the local opera house.

By 1891, Howe was touring from town to town in a manner that would continue—with significant modifications—for the next twenty-nine years. He usually played for only one or two nights at each location. If a concert was successful, he then usually arranged another engagement for some future date. At fifty cents admission, an exhibition at the YMCA in Milton (1890 population: 5,317) on New Year's night, 1891, was so well attended that a return was booked for Thursday, January 15.[32] When Howe played at the YMCA in nearby Danville (1890 population: 7,998) on January 12, the concert proved so successful that he returned two days later.[33]

For almost three years, until February 1893, Howe's phonograph concerts were confined to the territory controlled by the Eastern Pennsylvania Phonograph Company. He exhibited at Memorial Church and St. Aloysius Hall in Wilkes-Barre (1890 population: 37,718), at the Sons of America Hall in Lebanon (1890 population: 14,614), at Martin's Hall under the auspices of the Young People's Society of St. John's Lutheran Church in Lancaster (1890 population: 32,011), at the YMCA and later at the Christ Church lecture room in York (1890 population: 20,793), at the Academy under the auspices of the Young People's Society of Christian Endeavor in Waynesboro (1890 population: 3,811), and at the Memorial Lutheran Chapel in Shippensburg (1890 population: 2,188). Returning to Scranton and Allentown, he performed in local churches.[34] Howe gave exhibitions in almost every town and city in eastern Pennsylvania outside the immediate Philadelphia area, with Protestant religious groups providing a framework of support.

During this period, all phonograph exhibitors, limited to the geographical region controlled by the subcompany from which they rented machines, faced similar territorial restrictions. Although Howe was not the only such exhibitor in his territory, the number was probably no more than a handful.[35] The Ohio Phonograph Company, for example, estimated that its territory only supported four phonograph exhibitors. These territorial restrictions were consistent with the localism and regionalism of American cultural life, which continued despite the emergence of a national market and the growing number of touring theatrical troupes.

Localism was notably triumphant during Howe's first season as an independent phonograph exhibitor. Since the subcompanies viewed the phonograph primarily as a business machine, few recordings were available for purchase. Howe, therefore, had to rely heavily on local talent and his own resources. By the 1891–1892 season the showman was able to acquire a wider selection of records from subcompanies that had begun to make a specialty of selling prerecorded cylinders. Yet he continued to present his recordings of the Scranton and Allentown bands. Friendly rivalry and curiosity about their neighbors' musical groups boosted attendance, attracting amateur musicians and their supporters. At a concert in Gettysburg (1890 population: 3,221), he made recordings of local college students giving their class yell and class song, which were promptly added to his collection and played in other towns.[36]

Despite his purchase of prerecorded cylinders, localism continued to dominate many aspects of Howe's concerts. Presented under a group's auspices, the exhibition was locally organized. In smaller towns such as Gettysburg or Shippensburg, these concerts drew a substantial portion of the community. Even in cities such as Scranton, a high percentage of the sponsoring congregation attended, thereby maintaining the sense of a collective endeavor. Audiences were composed of people who knew each other, the sponsors and those who performed for the phonograph.

Although these exhibitions differed from later forms of more impersonal mass culture, they must also be contrasted with the many live concerts then being given by church groups and YMCAs. While Howe and Haddock were exhibiting their phonograph in Scranton, the local chapter of the

Epworth League, a national organization affiliated with the Methodist Episcopal Church, presented an evening's entertainment of solos, recitations, music, and readings.[37] Such live concerts depended on performers from the immediate locality, although occasionally an outside guest, usually from the region, participated. During the late nineteenth century, this type of entertainment constituted a major cultural activity for middle-class groups. Phonograph exhibitions mimicked its form even as they reduced (but did not yet eliminate) its participatory nature.

By late 1891 Howe was balancing his recordings of local performances with cylinders of artists from the principal eastern cities. His program at the Welsh Congregational Church in Scranton "consisted of solos, vocal and instrumental, and recitations by organizations and persons high in musical and literary circles":

PART 1.

Introductory Remarks .... By the Phonograph
Cornet Solo "L'elegant" .... Damar
            William Kennedy, Washington, D. C.
Reception Medley ....
                    Manhattan Quartette.
Piccolo Solo—"The Warbler" ....
                    Geo. Twinefest, Boston
Comic Song—"Laughing"... Dudley
                Geo. W Johnson, Philadelphia.
"Marion Schottisch" .... Missud
                    Allentown Band.
"The Fisherman and His Child" ....
                    Acme Trio.
"Fire Alarm" ....
                    New York Band.
Recitation—"Auction Sale of Household Furniture" ....
                W. O. Beckenbaugh, Baltimore, Md.
Cornet Solo—"Culver Polka" .... Steinhauser
                    John Martin, New York.

PART SECOND

Song—"The Jolly Farmer Boy" (comic) ....
                    Thomas West, Philadelphia.
"Loving Hearts Gavotte" .... Tobani
                    Gilmore's Band.
Vocal Selection (no imitation) .... Baby Cleveland
Chime Bells of Grace Church, New York—"The Changes" ....
Artistic Whistling—"Mocking Bird" ....Sep Winner
                J. Y. Atlee, Washington, D.C.

"The Prodigal Son" ....Parable
                    Rev T. C. Edwards, (now in Europe.)

"Beside My Mother's Knee" (new) ....Umstead
                    Arion Quartette.

Xylophone Solo—"Fire Fly Gossip" .... Ed. Strauss

Song—"Hot Corn" (comic) ....
                    John P. Hogan, New York.

Recitation—To be selected ....

Cornet Solo—Medley—"Old Folks at Home" and part of "Home Sweet
Home" ....
                    Jules Levy. [38]

Only two of the twenty-two selections—those by the Allentown Band and
the Reverend Edwards, a local Welsh minister—featured local or regional
people; approximately seventeen cylinders presented more or less well
known performers recorded by the subcompanies. Thus Howe's concerts
took their audiences on a whirlwind tour of the country's major cities. The
phonograph could annihilate not only time but space.

Howe's concerts can be retrospectively seen as a transitional phase toward a more modern cultural practice. Chief organizer of the entertainment, Howe was from outside the locale even if from the region. Although members of the community still participated, the principal
attractions were recordings of national entertainers such as Jules Levy or
Gilmore's Band. Howe's position found him mediating among local, regional, and national levels of cultural activity and between active and
passive participation in cultural production.

Howe also built on an ideological stance implicit in the repertoire of
these church-sponsored gatherings. Claiming to cultivate his audiences'
more refined musical tastes, he actually appealed to their desire for "fun"
with selections that made few demands on the listener. Concerts consisted
largely of band music. Patrick Gilmore, the nation's foremost band leader,
performed for one of the recordings and embodied the dominant musical
sensibility. Gilmore's own concerts provided listeners with a pastiche of
marches, patriotic airs, operatic medleys, instrumental solos, and popular
songs. [39] Around a similar conglomeration, Howe wrapped selections of
church chimes, the recitation of an Old Testament parable, and a brief
sermon and topped it off with the necessary "educational" commentary.
Thus he presented a package that won the hearty endorsement of church
fathers. The music was popular, commercial, and certainly secular but
easily distinguishable from two quite antithetical sensibilities. The sym-
phonic and operatic music favored by cultivated elites and championed by
conductor Theodore Thomas would have been too demanding and so fragmented the community rather than united it. Likewise, the sentimental
ballads and love songs that were sung in variety or vaudeville espoused a

worldliness that was perhaps even more unacceptable. Howe did not draw
from either repertoire. His was a cultural tact that did not offend. Rather
it complimented his audience and gratified his pocketbook.

Success as a phonograph exhibitor rested on the mastery of the many fac-
ets of showmanship. Howe's approach paralleled guidelines offered by
M. C. Sullivan:

> [The exhibitor] should not only aim to exploit the phonograph in such a
> way that all the points are brought out, but he should fully understand that
> he and his phonograph are there simply to please the audience, and he must
> not rest content with simply "feeding" cylinders to the machine as constitut-
> ing his part of the entertainment. . . .
>
> Monotony is the bugbear of the phonograph. In order to escape it, tact
> must be exercised, and all the inventive powers of which the exhibitor is
> possessed should be used to vary the selections as they follow one another.
> The entire exhibition should be an animated, shifting kaleidoscope, present-
> ing new features at every turn, as variety secures the powerful effect of con-
> trast. Not only should the above apply to the selections, but the exhibitor,
> in his own action and manipulation, should aim to follow out the same law,
> and every move that he makes should be finished and complete.
>
> It is not to be supposed that the man who exhibits the phonograph is a
> finished actor; on the other hand, the more he can learn as to effective stage
> presence the greater his success will be. When the phonograph is placed on
> a platform for the edification of an audience, some little consideration should
> be given to what is known as staging. Probably the best way to illustrate this
> is to be governed by the well-known laws of dramatic practice. Every dra-
> matic creation, as is well known, must have not only the best of plot and be
> conveyed in effective form, but it must be staged properly. In the case of the
> phonograph care must not only be taken that the selections of the material
> be good, but it must be presented in the most effective way.
>
> As the amount of action will differ greatly with the character of the selec-
> tion, set rules cannot very well be formulated, and the best guide in this
> direction is to "feel" the audience. Serious incidents should be of short du-
> ration and made powerful. Comic incidents should be numerous and carefully
> mingled with the serious. The transition from humor to pathos should not be
> too rapid, each cylinder should be made a separate element and every effort
> should be made by the exhibitor to cluster about it a single central animated
> idea.
>
> Suspense is one of the most important means of creating interest. Repro-
> ductions that are well known and have a special significance for the audience
> are best presented by alluding to them in some manner that will prepare for
> what is coming. A phonograph exhibition should be full of climaxes from
> beginning to end, but not in the nature of harsh, jerky surprises. As the

climax is heightened by the action of the exhibitor, he should put himself *en rapport* with every cylinder he is to use. He, however, must be careful that he does not overdo it, and thereby attract the interest that is intended for the machine, to himself.[40]

Howe's personal form of showmanship can be traced through the reviews. His public manner, his occasionally awkward but always "charming personality," was one of his most valuable assets.[41] The ability to create an entertaining and informative exhibition out of limited resources was just as important.

Howe established the educational value of his concerts at the start of each program. The introductory remarks, delivered by "Mr. Phonograph," explained how the mechanism worked. For a while the audacious exhibitor claimed that the voice and comments were Thomas Edison's. Audiences, as they had with Barnum, sometimes questioned such humbug. He eventually took the safer course and simply identified the voice as "Mr. Phonograph."[42] However, the showman's desire to embellish remained. In some of his concerts, Howe offered a dubious but colorful anecdote about the invention of the phonograph: "Edison and assistant were in the laboratory trying to connect some wires when they heard sounds, which proved to be their own voices, the words they had been speaking reproduced. Both were astonished and the assistant fainted."[43] Such Barnumesque stories created fertile ground for popular myths to flourish.

Once the educational prestige of each exhibition was established, Howe could entertain his audience in the name of science. In this regard, novelties played a valuable role. Since audiences expected to hear music and speeches in a theatrical setting, he amused patrons with "Songs Familiar on the Farm" which included "roosters crowing, ducks quacking, turkeys gobbling and a colored girl laughing at it."[44] These sounds succeeded precisely because they struck audiences as incongruous and unexpected in a lecture hall. The ephemeral was captured and made timeless. Sound that normally was little more than background ambience was foregrounded. The ordinary was made monumental. Such transformations testified to the power of the new technology.

Howe's recordings reveal a fascination with the quotidian which, as Barbara Kirshenblatt-Gimblett suggests, was a striking aspect of late nineteenth-century culture.[45] Everyday sounds, such as a baby's cry, found regular approval. At one exhibition "several mothers sighed audibly and said 'ah' it cried so naturally."[46] They heard a baby's cry while knowing it did not reflect an infant's customary unhappiness. Since they could feel aesthetic distance rather than concern or anxiety, this disjunction could spark amusement. Howe kept the cylinder in his repertoire for several years but refined his introduction. "Prof. Howe announced that the next

number would be a very common vocal selection which would doubtless
be familiar to all," one reviewer reported. "Many thought of Annie Roo-
ney and Comrades, but when it proved to be the crying of a young child
as though its heart would break the laughter of the audience knew no
bounds."[47] Here the relatively simple sounds of an unhappy baby could
not only surprise but satisfy audiences more readily than the singing of an
opera aria, for the latter was more likely to exceed the limited capacities
of the phonograph and encounter the more rigorous listening standards of
music aficionados. Later Howe offered a more elaborate rendition of the
same idea. Audiences not only heard the crying of the baby but the mother's lullaby and the father's impatient voice.[48]

The phonograph was sometimes ascribed a power it did not deserve, as
when Howe conjured up appealing if bogus recording circumstances. Although recordings had to be made under carefully controlled conditions,
he informed one audience that a quartet of Negro vocalists was caught
singing "Down in the Cornfield" on a Mississippi riverboat. The ringing
of steamer bells in the background was called upon to authenticate this
claim. But the recording was almost certainly made in the studio.[49] Other
times Howe depended on quick-witted excuses to help himself out of a
jam. In one instance, the acoustics of the halls were blamed for poor recordings of the local band when the problem might have more honestly
been attributed to the faulty adjustment or limitations of Howe's machine.[50] The name of "professor" emphasized the showman's special
knowledge and gave him greater opportunity to manipulate it for his own
ends. If, as Albert F. McLean, Jr., argues, scientifically based knowledge
was often perceived as a new kind of magic, such sleight of hand merely
increased its mystery.[51]

Howe, following "the well-known laws of dramatic practice," built his
exhibitions around those climactic moments when he recorded the local
band or a prominent member of the audience. A full revelation of the
phonograph's technological capacities functioned as the evening's high
point. At a concert in Lebanon, after the exhibitor had finished playing
his prerecorded selections, the local Perseverance Band "rendered two of
their choice selections, and these were caught up by the phonograph and
reproduced to the audience in so faithful a manner as to cause the greatest
applause."[52] In Hazleton, "the selections played by the Liberty Band were
faithfully reproduced and elicited rounds of applause."[53] If a full band was
unavailable, Howe usually found someone to play a cornet solo.[54] At
church entertainments, the assembled audience often sang hymns—
"Nearer My God to Thee" was the favorite—which were immediately
played back. The process always caused a certain amount of "consterna-
tion and amazement."[55]

Prior to the phonograph, the only way to mechanically record aural or visual stimuli was photography. It is interesting, then, that on at least one occasion Howe was called "a photographer of sounds."[56] Photography, however, lacked the ability to unfold over time, which cinematography would later introduce, and did not allow for immediate reproduction. Americans considered the phonograph to be a technological tour de force, even though they would take it for granted by the turn of the century. Not only did these concerts celebrate new technology, but they affirmed man's apparent ability to master it.

Showmanship demanded a complex array of talents and skills. Technical excellence was crucial for public exhibitions. Many musical cylinders could only be heard through earphones, failing entirely when they were reproduced through a horn. "Occasionally we get hold of very excellent pieces that will come out loud and clear, but not often," asserted Thomas Conynton.[57] Mr. Clancy of the Missouri Phonograph Company admitted, "There is a certain style of music of which we cannot get a loud reproduction. Of course, you cannot give a fine quartette selection that will be loud enough to be thrown in the hall."[58] Yet Howe was projecting precisely that kind of music. In the beginning he was helped by the Eastern Pennsylvania Phonograph Company, which improved the phonograph technology on its machines at a cost of $3,000. Beyond this, Howe depended on his personal virtuosity to make high-quality recordings and sound reproductions.

Showmanship was also linked to the exhibitor's promotional skills. Here, Howe also proved adept. Ministers were quick to boost events that benefited their church, fellow clergy, or affiliated institutions. One handbill went

To whom it concerns:

It gives me pleasure to state that I have twice heard Prof. Lyman H. Howe with his "Wonderful Phonograph," and I heartily commend his entertainment as pleasing and profitable, and worthy of the patronage of all friends of our Y.M.C.A.

F.W. Lockwood
Pastor, Baptist Church

After a private concert in Chambersburg (1890 population: 7,863), Howe convinced the town's leading citizens to endorse his program immediately before a public engagement at the local one-thousand-seat Rosedale Opera House.[59] These endorsements, printed in the local newspaper, publicized the event and increased patronage.

The size of Howe's audiences and his financial remuneration are difficult to judge. The number of attendees was rarely reported. When three hundred and fifty people filled the Methodist Episcopal Church in Kingston late in 1891, it was one of the largest crowds ever assembled at a

church entertainment in that area.[60] An earlier concert at the Christ
Church lecture room in York was attended by five hundred.[61] With an
admission charge of twenty-five cents, gross receipts for these two events
approximated $87.50 and $125.00 respectively. Howe thus received
$52.50 and $75.00 from which he had to deduct the cost of promotion,
travel, and equipment. Since both attendance figures were considered surprisingly large, typical attendance would have been smaller. Although
Howe generally enjoyed good patronage, his venues frequently had small
capacities. An exhibition in Marathon, New York, filled the Baptist
Church auditorium: it only netted $27.00 (a $67.50 gate, or 270 paying
customers). Another in Nunda, New York, netted a little over eighty dollars (just over 320 paying customers). One at the Susquehanna First
Methodist Church brought over fifty dollars in receipts.[62] Howe's contract
offers the best indication that sixty dollars in receipts or 240 paying customers was considered an excellent night.

THE NICKEL-IN-THE-SLOT PHONOGRAPH

Howe and other phonograph exhibitors were contending with the rival
coin-operated phonographs by 1891. For a nickel, these "slot machines"
played a cylinder that could be heard through earphones by a single individual. In large cities, the subcompanies sometimes set up "phonograph
parlors" devoted solely to automatic phonographs. The Ohio Phonograph
Company opened the first one in Cleveland on September 15, 1890, and
soon followed it with another in Cincinnati. Containing twelve automatic phonographs, the parlors were well patronized and remunerative
from the start.[63] These forerunners of the jukebox, however, were more
often placed individually in hotels, saloons, and railroad stations. In February or March 1891, the Eastern Pennsylvania Phonograph Company
installed twenty-five automatic machines, from which it generated income of $400 to $500 a month. By June, management was planning to
place twenty-five more. Of the approximately 3,200 phonographs or
graphophones then in use in the United States, almost 1,200 had nickel-
in-the-slot attachments.[64] Many of the subcompanies depended heavily
on income generated by this new exhibition mode.
    Coin-operated phonographs and phonograph concerts appealed to dif-
ferent kinds of audiences in different ways. The coin-operated machines
were routinely patronized by transient out-of-towners attracted to a particular selection by its titillating title. Their suggestions of private desire and
forbidden pleasures mobilized patron voyeurism in ways that were disturbing to guardians of public morality. Concerts were public, group activities
suitable for children, ladies and ministers—none of whom would step inside a saloon. Although phonograph parlors could also draw a more re-

3-2. Nickel-in-the-slot phonographs were often seen as pandering to aural voyeurism (ca. 1893).

spectable crowd, people who listened to the automatic machines in less supervised environments quickly found ways to cheat them. The Kentucky Phonograph Company's slot machines lost $4,000 to slugs and gunwads.[65] Most phonograph company executives found their dependency on such riffraff to be an undesirable commercial necessity.

The phonograph industry initially established two distinct though interrelated branches involving either practical uses, such as dictation, or entertainment, such as concerts. Concerts and slot machines represented a second division within the increasingly important cultural sector. The two different exhibition modes relied on opposing groups in American society. The church groups and YMCAs that sponsored Howe's evenings strove to keep young men away from the corrupting influences of the saloon—the very place that favored nickel-in-the-slot phonographs. Whenever possible, these religious groups tried to shut these establishments by preventing the renewal of their liquor licenses. Just as the phonographs made the saloons a more attractive place to visit, phonograph concerts proved to be an effective way to raise money for the very groups that were trying to close saloon doors. The phonograph industry was thus supported by two groups of self-proclaimed enemies. As Howe's advertising ex-

plained, *his* entertainment would be "Clean, Scientific, Amusing and Elevating—nothing like the Ordinary Phonograph that is seen on the
Streets, in Hotels and at the Fairs."[66] Phonograph company owners were
usually committed—emotionally and intellectually if not publicly—to the
kinds of entertainment offered by Howe, but much more money was in
the slot machines.

Howe's concerts and the automatic phonographs generally had in common such recordings as comic songs, cornet solos, and band music. Other
kinds of cylinders were unique to each situation. The professor presented
the Reverend T. C. Edward reading the 23d Psalm and telling the parable
of the Prodigal Son.[67] Howe also regularly recorded local preachers and
other respected figures for immediate playback.[68] In Bellefonte (1890 population: 3,946), a minister's reading of scripture was followed by Judge
Furst making a humorous judicial pronouncement. Speaking to the phonograph, he ordered salt scattered all over Bellefonte's streets in order to
keep the cows on the roads, "because they were very ornamental to the
town."[69] Audiences laughed uproariously and Howe assured the crowd
that he intended to play the cylinder throughout the state. In contrast,
racy stories with profanity might be quietly placed onto a coin-operated
phonograph.[70] Newspapers also reported the threat of infectious diseases
transmitted via the earphones. Again, such issues never arose with concerts. Morally and physically the slot machines were considered dirty and
the concerts clean.

Both the automatic phonograph and the phonograph concert were patronized by people with some disposable income. If both forms of exhibition relied heavily on middle-class patronage, the nature of these "middle
classes" was quite different. Salesmen and ministers, for example, generally held radically opposing attitudes toward desire. The former, who often
played off desire in their sales methods, enjoyed geographic mobility that
left them less fettered by societal strictures. They were heavy users of the
automatic phonograph as well as aficionados of vaudeville and burlesque.
In contrast, small-town ministers led many efforts to ban all kinds of
nickel-in-the-slot devices, including the automatic phonograph. Their
congregations commonly felt threatened by these and other new, impersonal forms of urban amusements. For them, Howe offered a sanitized alternative to the secular, popular culture coming out of large cities. Howe's
audiences were composed primarily of American-born, middle-class Protestants who felt comfortable singing "Nearer My God to Thee" and might
enjoy hearing the Gettysburg College cheer. At such events, Eastern European immigrants who worked in the coal fields or factories would have
felt awkwardly out of place.[71]

HOWE EXPANDS HIS FIELD OF OPERATIONS

Howe's phonograph activities underwent important changes during 1893. By the beginning of the year, the showman had developed an improved horn that increased the quality and strength of the sound. The number, length, and enthusiasm of Howe's reviews increased dramatically at this point, after having fallen off during 1892. All remarked on this new attachment, "a highly polished copper funnel with a diameter of about two feet at its widest end."[72] A critic in Shamokin (1890 population: 14,403) reported, "The phonograph stood in the middle of the stage and the sound, transmitted through a cone-shaped funnel of brass, about six feet in length, was wonderfully distinct. Solos, instrumental and vocal, dialogues and speeches were heard with telling success."[73] This superior sound was furthered by an improved diaphragm.[74] "This phonograph is a great stride toward perfection," another journalist remarked. "Its reproductions last night were the most successful demonstration of the kind ever attempted in this part of the State, and the quality of sound produced

HOWE'S EDISON'S IMPROVED PHONOGRAPH CONCERTS.

3-3. Howe and the phonograph horn that gave his concerts renewed popularity (1893).

was most life-like and natural."[75] Although the phonograph itself was ceasing to be a rarity, and the approaching depression would make it harder for a showman to survive, the horn and diaphragm brought new life to Howe's programs.

Shortly after introducing his improved phonograph, Howe expanded his circuit to include most of New York state. This move was facilitated by the New York Phonograph Company's decision to sell rather than lease its machine, a decision made earlier by most other subcompanies. Howe began to give exhibitions in cities such as Troy, Cohoes, Elmira, Albany, Gloversville, and Newburgh. Most of these places remained on his circuit in the years ahead. About this time he hired an advance representative, Clarence S. Weiss. Weiss booked Howe's phonograph, handled arrangements with local organizations, and generated advance publicity, enabling the professor to concentrate on his exhibitions. For the first time, a formal division of labor was introduced into Howe's exhibition practice. As a result, the showman went on more sustained tours, playing a different hall almost every day except Sunday during the theatrical season.[76] Howe's increased commitment to the phonograph was emphasized by his decision to stop exhibiting the miniature coal breaker, which he later claimed to have sold to the Reading Railroad for display at the Chicago World's Columbian Exposition.[77]

While he spent some of the summer at home, recuperating from his more strenuous schedule, he pursued two projects. The first, a phonograph concert at the Pennsylvania Chautauqua, underscored his success among devout, middle-class Protestants. The Chautauqua movement, started by Lewis Miller, Thomas Edison's father-in-law, had begun by training Sunday-school teachers at its summer institute in Chautauqua, New York. Soon it included many summer resorts combining religion with education and relaxation. To celebrate Independence Day in 1893, more than three thousand Chautauquans gathered to hear Governor Robert E. Pattison speak at the auditorium in Mount Gretna. The governor failed to appear, but Howe, assisted by his technical improvements, provided what he claimed was "the largest phonographic concert ever given in America."[78] After playing several cylinders, he recorded and reproduced a selection by the Iroquois Band and a doxology recited by the audience. The concert, perhaps the high point of Howe's career as a phonograph showman, was so well received that he returned the following year and performed immediately after several prominent politicians gave their election-year speeches.[79]

Howe's second project centered on the kinetoscope, Edison's latest invention. A peephole device that showed twenty seconds of moving pictures to an individual spectator, the kinetoscope was modeled after the coin-in-the-slot phonograph. Edison called it "an instrument which does for the Eye what the phonograph does for the Ear, which is the recording and reproduction of things in motion, and in such a form as to be both Cheap practical and convenient."[80] The kinetoscope was to be unveiled at the Chicago World's Columbian Exposition. Its upcoming debut was widely publicized and prominently mentioned in the phonograph industry's trade journal, *The Phonogram*.[81] Howe and many other phonograph devotees were naturally interested in this newest invention.

Preparing to attend the World's Fair, Howe wrote to the Edison works to inquire about purchasing a kinetoscope. Alfred O. Tate, Edison's business manager, told him that several kinetoscopes, then being made for the exposition, might be sold after the fair had ended.[82] Howe, like many others, hoped to project these films—just as he gave phonograph concerts rather than exploited the coin-operated phonograph. Although he subsequently claimed to have seen the kinetoscope at the World's Fair, it never reached the exposition. It is highly unlikely that Howe personally

3-4. Poster (ca. 1893).

assessed the new invention until its commercial introduction in 1894, when he must have realized that the peephole machine could not be readily converted to theatrical use. The kinetoscope presented a continually moving band of film, using a shutter mechanism that exposed it to the viewer's eye for a fraction of a second. Lacking an "intermittent" mechanism to stop each frame of film in front of the light source, the viewer could not be readily adapted for projection. Such a mechanism would not be introduced until late 1895. Until then, projection seemed a distant, even unrealizable, proposition.

Although temporarily frustrated, Howe did not lose interest in moving pictures. Changes within the phonograph industry itself made the move into motion picture exhibition increasingly desirable. By 1893 Emile Berliner was selling his version of the phonograph, which used discs instead of cylinders and had no recording capabilities. It did not run on electricity but relied on a spring motor, making it inexpensive to buy and easy to run. Although the spring motor produced results technically inferior to the phonograph's, Berliner's gramophone was practical for home use. As Edison commented in June 1893, "A very large number of machines go into private homes for amusement purposes."[83] The American Graphophone Company and the Columbia Phonograph Company soon followed Berliner into the nascent consumer market, selling new record players with spring motors for $10 to $20.[84] Since the North American Phonograph Company had begun to sell its electrically powered machines, these were becoming more plentiful, too. Such developments were harming the phonograph concert business. For instance, residents of Franklin, Pennsylvania, enjoyed free daily phonograph concerts one week in April 1894.[85]

Howe's technical skills and showmanship aided his survival from 1893 to 1896. This "very agreeable and entertaining gentleman" found new ways to entertain his patrons.[86] In Warsaw, New York (1890 population: 3,120), the local paper announced, "One of our citizens will give a short talk to the phonograph before the entertainment and the audience will have the pleasure of guessing his identity when the machine reproduces it."[87] In Rome, New York (1890 population: 14,991), Howe played several cylinders at different speeds and found that this "curious effort of increasing or decreasing the rate of speed was much enjoyed."[88] He again expanded his territory, exhibiting in New Hampshire during October 1894 and touring Ohio and Michigan towns during much of 1895.

Howe's creative and technical skills were necessary but not sufficient for his continued success. In the face of adverse conditions, church sponsorship helped to sustain him economically. The Chautauqua concerts strengthened already existing ties. In the months after his record-breaking concert, Howe regularly played the doxology he recorded in the Mount

COME AND HEAR THE FAMOUS

GILMORE'S BAND

- AND SOME OF THE -

GREATEST SINGERS

IN ∘ THE ∘ WORLD?

It would cost you many dollars to hear them sing in the large cities. Here you can hear them as truly as if they were to sing in your presence, for a mere pittance. Every quality of their rare and phenomenal voices is reproduced, causing the visitor to be awed by mystery and admiration. Come and hear and see for yourself. Don't lose this opportunity of being satisfied and seeing this world-famed wonder in its triumphant state of perfection.

No Ear-Tubes Used! The Sounds Reproduced are Loud Enough to Entertain an Audience of over Three Thousand People at One Time.

The Programme WILL INCLUDE GILMORE'S FAMOUS BAND, also selections played by the Great U. S. MARINE BAND of Washington, D. C.; BALDWIN'S CADET BAND of Boston; JULES LEVY and WALTER EMERSON, the world renowned Cornetists. Also Piccolo, Banjo, Clarionet, Flute and Xylophone Solos; Songs and Quartetts by eminent musical artists. There will also be Sounds From Nature made by animals, birds, etc.

Facts are Stubborn things.   -   Come and be Convinced.
AN ENTERTAINMENT TRULY STARTLING.

Clean, Scientific, Amusing and Elevating!
There is No Other Entertainment Like It!

IT EXCELS ALL PREVIOUS ATTEMPTS, not only in a more perfect Phonograph, but the quality of musical selections are of a higher order, rendered by musicians and singers of world-wide fame, secured at a great expense and never before reproduced by a Phonograph.   .   .   .   .

A Dollar Concert at a Popular Price.

3-5. Page from a Howe program (late 1894).

Gretna auditorium. Audiences found it "grand and impressive, though the music seemed to come a distance, like the echoes from Paradise."[89] For patrons, Howe's concerts achieved a double purpose. They supported the local church while being morally uplifting and enjoyable. Church members were pleased to aid the improvement fund of the First Baptist Church in Troy and the Young People's Baptist Union at the First Baptist Church in Jamestown, New York; the Young People's Society of Christian Endeavor of the Central Presbyterian Church in Erie, the Stone Church Epworth League in Meadville, and the Corinthian Circle of the First Presbyterian Church in New Castle, Pennsylvania; and the Methodist Episcopal Church in Saginaw, Michigan.[90] As a Mechanicsburg, Pennsylvania, newspaper reported,

> The thanks of the Bible and Tract Society are tendered to the people of the town and community for their kindness and encouragement. The attendance at the concert was phenomenally large and the members of the Society feel that the wish of all was to help on the work of providing good literature for our people. The assistance rendered is warmly appreciated and we trust the pleasure is mutual.[91]

Groups eager to raise funds for themselves made money for Howe, too.

The phonograph, however, was becoming a consumer product. Stores hoping to attract purchasers increasingly gave free concerts. Local amateurs or semiprofessionals often gave sponsored concerts similar to Howe's. It was time for the professor and others to move on. In April 1896, Edison followed his competitors' lead and introduced a spring-motor phonograph for home entertainment.[92] April was also the month that "Edison's Vitascope" premiered at Koster and Bial's Music Hall in New York City, inaugurating a new era of projected moving pictures within the United States. Even before then, Howe was again exploring the possibilities of adding motion pictures to his programs.

4

* *

Lifelike Pictures:
Howe's Animotiscope,
1896-1897

* * *

What the phonograph is to the ear, the animotiscope is to the eye.
Wilkes-Barre Record, January 5, 1897

THE ADDITION of projected motion pictures to Howe's programs did not at first appear to be a radical break from previous practice. The new technology had been conceived as an extension of the phonograph, and only over a three-year period did Howe gradually supplant the old with the new. This shift, however, spawned far-reaching changes in Howe's program. Motion pictures, for example, curtailed the operational aesthetic of his previous shows. Howe may have explained the principles of motion picture projection, but he was no longer able to demonstrate the complete process of filmmaking, since he lacked production capabilities. Nevertheless, his creative opportunities in the actual act of exhibition—the arrangement of images and their juxtaposition with sound—increased.

"EDISON'S VITASCOPE"

While many kinds of showmen hoped to acquire exhibition rights for the vitascope, America's first commercially available "modern" motion picture projector, the most eager group consisted of phonograph and kinetoscope exhibitors. This fraternity included Thomas L. Tally, who had a phonograph and kinetoscope parlor in Los Angeles; the Holland Brothers of Ottawa, Canada; Robert Fischer, who had several phonographs and kinetoscopes in Great Falls, Montana; and Howe.[1] Some, like the Holland Brothers and Fischer, negotiated successfully for such rights. Others, like Tally and Howe, did not.

Although the vitascope was invented by C. Francis Jenkins and Thomas Armat, the actual projectors were built by the Edison Manufacturing Company (owned by the famed inventor).[2] Norman Raff and Frank

Gammon, sole agents for the machine, astutely if questionably won permission to promote it as "Edison's Vitascope." They then marketed it by
selling exhibition rights on a territorial or "states rights" basis. Hoping to
acquire vitascope rights for Pennsylvania, Howe contacted Raff and Gammon in mid-February 1896, but the promoters wanted $5,000 for the ex-
clusive rights to Pennsylvania, a sum Howe could neither afford nor raise.[3]
Pennsylvania, moreover, proved a popular territory. On February 25, Raff
and Gammon announced that the rights for Philadelphia and Pittsburgh
had been acquired. They then offered to sell Howe the exhibition rights
to the rest of the state for $1,500 and 10 percent of net profits. In addition,
Howe would rent a projector for twenty-five dollars a month and buy the
necessary films.[4] Howe quickly expressed his interest in the territory (if
not the terms) but could not visit their offices until late March because he
was giving daily concerts in upstate New York.[5]

A group of Philadelphia businessmen, led by Allen F. Rieser, also
wanted the exhibition rights to the rest of Pennsylvania. Their American
Publishing Association mounted phonograph concerts for libraries—so
the libraries could generate money to buy its books. They saw the vitascope as a new, potent attraction in their entertainment repertoire. Although Raff and Gammon preferred to sell the rights to Howe and tried
to interest Rieser in other territory, the Philadelphian was adamant.[6]

Raff and Gammon finally obliged Rieser and informed Howe that the
rights had been sold.[7] When the dejected showman wrote back, Raff and
Gammon urged him to acquire some other territory:

> We regret that any act of ours should have "cost you pain," but we certainly
> gave you every opportunity to secure this territory, and even made conces-
> sions; but several parties were ready to pay us the money for the territory, and
> your last letter left the matter in doubt as to whether you would take it at all
> or not. Hence we were compelled, out of justice to our Company, to close
> the matter.
>
> If you will mention any other territory which you would like to negotiate
> for, we will promptly make you our lowest price on it, as we appreciate your
> ability, and the high plane on which you keep your exhibitions, and really
> would have preferred that you would have owned the exclusive rights to the
> State of Pennsylvania.[8]

The phonograph exhibitor declined to take advantage of their offer. The
era of projected motion picture entertainment began without Howe.

In the United States, projected motion pictures first appeared in the
arena of popular, urban amusement. The vitascope opened at New York's
Koster and Bial's Music Hall on April 23, 1896, and at Keith's Philadelphia vaudeville house on May 25. In France, for example, the Lumières
first projected their films before educated and refined audiences before

launching a more commercial strategy, but American advocates of church-based and refined culture generally lacked the intensity of interest, the necessary competitive instincts, or the financial resources of their rivals in the amusement world. Contrasting the vitascope's first appearances with the more genteel initial exploitation of the phonograph in 1878 underscores the changing balance of forces within America's cultural realm.

Although oft-repeated legend designates Lyman H. Howe as the first person to project moving pictures in Wilkes-Barre, that honor belongs to O. E. Jones, business manager for two commercial theaters in northeastern Pennsylvania.[9] He subleased vitascope rights for Luzerne and Lackawanna counties from Rieser and first presented the screen novelty at his 1,544-seat Frothingham Theater in Scranton (1900 population: 102,026) from June 22 to June 27. The exhibition, "augmented by John L. Kennedy, the popular comedian, and a high class vaudeville show," drew large crowds.[10]

The vaudeville show moved to Wilkes-Barre's 1,200-seat Grand Opera House for another week-long run beginning June 29. Shows were given twice a day. Prices were ten cents, twenty cents, and thirty cents in the evenings; for matinees, children paid ten cents and adults twenty cents. Although many working-class residents could attend if they were prepared to sit in the gallery, reviews looked more carefully at those in the orchestra. "The vitascope is doing a remarkably good business at the Grand this week, considering the warm weather, and the audiences are made up of the city's best people," the *Wilkes-Barre Times* announced. Turning to the exhibition itself, the reporter made a series of unusually astute observations:

> There is an unsteadiness of movement which is far from natural, though it is understood that Mr. Edison will have this remedied in a comparatively short time. The apparatus in use is somewhat crude, due no doubt to the hurried manner in which it has been prepared. The material which surrounds the machinery should be of sufficient thickness to prevent the light escaping and to a certain extent illuminating the room, for to get good results from the vitascope there must be absolute darkness in the house.[11]

Were the thoughts of a disgruntled Howe behind such criticisms? He must have attended several performances and may have shared his opinions with the local reviewer. Nonetheless, the vitascope drew well throughout its run.[12]

Despite the vitascope's preliminary success, Howe's failure to purchase rights proved fortuitous. The machine was ill suited for traveling showmen. The Holland brothers, who controlled Canadian vitascope rights, struggled with the problems that Howe would have faced. As they complained,

We are face to face with the fact that we cannot get a week's engagement in any other town [except Toronto] where we can get direct current without heavy expense to electricians for reducing the 500 volt current. To enable us to make money we have to so remodel the machine that it can be worked with hand power when we cannot get electricity, and construct new travelling cases so that the breakable parts can be safely and rapidly packed for shipment. I believe there is plenty of business to be obtained in the country once we are prepared to work it, but it is worse than folly undertaking it in our small towns until we are ready to meet a three night's business and then pack up and get out to the next town.[13]

Ultimately the capable Holland brothers lost several hundred dollars and concluded that their exhibition possibilities were unprofitable.[14] Competition from companies with comparable or superior equipment quickly undermined the vitascope's position.

COMPETING MACHINES: HOWE BUILDS
HIS OWN PROJECTOR

The popularity of motion pictures encouraged the construction and manufacture of rival projectors. C. Francis Jenkins joined forces with the Columbia Phonograph Company and began to market his version of the vitascope, called the "phantoscope," in May 1896. Since projection technology was not very complicated, numerous mechanics and aspiring exhibitors set about designing their own machines, and many enjoyed a degree of success. Each design had its own name, and the diversity of names from that first year of exhibition testifies to the breadth of American (as well as English and French) mechanical ingenuity. Chicago-based Edward Amet offered his magniscope for sale in September. The cinographoscope and centograph were being marketed by October, and several other projectors were for sale by the end of the year.[15] In some cases, exhibitors simply constructed projectors for their own use and sold a few models if the opportunity arose, as was the case with the Zooscope.

Lyman H. Howe was one showman who built rather than bought his own projector. After completing his circuit of phonograph concerts in the spring of 1896, Howe returned to Wilkes-Barre with sketches for his "mechanism." Convinced that his experience with the phonograph would enable him to solve the technical problems associated with projection, he constructed a model from which several local machinists built a machine.[16] These efforts were unsuccessful, perhaps because Howe's design lacked the crucial intermittent mechanism conceptually foreign to the phonograph. This inventive breakthrough had been a stumbling block for many prior to Howe, including Edison and his motion picture expert William Kennedy Laurie Dickson. Whatever the problem, Howe had to remodel his projector completely. In the fall, it was announced that he "has formed a film company and has called upon the services of electrician Fred Cosman, who has been in town for the past two weeks to aid Mr. Howe in his experiments."[17] Finally, perhaps after receiving advice from New York experts, he succeeded in building a "crude homemade machine" that he called the "animotiscope."

Howe's animotiscope differed from the vitascope in several respects. The vitascope, like the kinetoscope, showed a twenty-second loop of film spliced end-to-end and threaded on a bank of rollers. Raff and Gammon recommended that each endless band of film be shown continuously for four or five minutes.[18] Even if we assume briefer projection times, a single motion picture subject was shown many times at each screening. With one projector, there were two-minute waits between pictures as one film was taken off and another threaded on the machine. Vitascope technology thus made the effective juxtaposition of images difficult or impossible. "Lifelike" motion in conjunction with "lifelike" photography plus a "life-sized" image provided a new level of verisimilitude and the basis for cinema's initial entertainment value.

The animotiscope did not use film loops. Even before the vitascope's premiere, Howe was envisioning alternative exhibition methods. Re-

4-1. Howe's homemade animotiscope (ca. 1896). Note the reel for holding film.

sponding to Howe's questions about the vitascope, Raff and Gammon assured the exhibitor that he did not have to utilize the endless-band method of projection: "Your films can be joined together with a piece of blank film inserted between them and in this manner you can stop your machine when you have exhibited one film and immediately start again. There is no difficulty in accomplishing what you suggest whatever."[19] Other exhibitors, for example, the Lumières, did not use loops but showed films only once at an exhibition, running each film off individually into a bin. From the beginning, Howe spliced his films together and wound them onto a reel. The film strand unspooled from one reel, passed through his animotiscope projector, and was wound onto a take-up reel. Among the first to use reels for film projection, Howe developed the technology because he wanted to combine short films into more complex sequences.[20] Such strategies were apparent in his first programs.

THE ANIMOTISCOPE'S PREMIERE

When Howe added motion pictures to his programs, he also added an employee to handle the projector, Edwin J. Hadley. Hadley had been employed during 1894–1896 by J. B. Colt and Company, a New York firm specializing in the manufacture of electrical apparatus and active in the early motion picture business. As a Colt employee, he had installed an arc lamp on the Lumière cinématographe that appeared at Keith's Union Square Theater during the summer of 1896.[21] His knowledge of motion picture projection and electricity was key, since each exhibition site posed its own peculiar problems. By hiring Hadley, Howe elaborated on the division of labor and hierarchy begun when he employed Clarence Weiss. Now the division was within the exhibition process itself.

After holding a private screening for friends, Howe decided he was ready for a public premiere. In late November, as he purchased additional films from the Edison Manufacturing Company, the *Wilkes-Barre Record* announced the animotiscope's commercial debut:

A COMING EVENT

On Friday evening next will be the first public exhibition of Lyman H. Howe's new marvel, the animotiscope. This is the latest machine for reproducing animated living scenes from real life with all their varied movements and activity. Although the machine is a New York invention, our townsman, Mr. Howe, has added many improvements and overcome the bad features and defects so noticeable in other machines of this kind. Its work is now most astonishing, and will reproduce a steady, lifelike picture of animated life and objects in motion that it will be hard for the beholder to realize that the scene reproduced is not an actual reality.

The phonograph will be used in conjunction with it, and what the animotiscope conveys to sight the phonograph will do to the ear.

The first exhibition will be given in Y.M.C.A. hall on Friday evening,
Dec. 4, under the auspices of the Bible Study Club of the First Baptist Church
of this city.[22]

The sponsoring Bible Study Club was using its share of the proceeds for
"the erection of a new church building for the First Baptist Church congregation."[23] General admission remained twenty-five cents, the standard
charge for Howe's phonograph exhibitions, but reserved seating was increased to fifty cents.

Howe's program followed the basic format of his earlier phonograph
concerts but with some added selections of moving pictures. As the Holland brothers had already remarked, a motion picture program was too
short to realistically provide an evening's worth of entertainment. For
Howe, motion pictures added new dramatic climaxes for his two-hour entertainments. His first program included the following films:

First Series

1. Bowling Green. New York city.
2. The Haymakers at Work.
3. Mounted Police Charge in Central Park, New York city.
4. Runaway Horse, Central Park, New York city.
5. Boys Chased Off Dock in Hudson River and Rescued.
6. The Morning Bath.
7. Irwin-Rice Kissing Scene.

Second Series

1. Feeding the Doves.
2. Tub Race.
3. Responding to the alarm of fire.
4. Fireman at work, the rescue.
5. Burning stables and rescue of horses.
6. Watermelon contest.
7. Lone Fisherman.
8. Old Ocean off Manhattan Beach after a severe storm.[24]

Several of these—including the fire rescue, the kissing scene and the
ocean after a storm—had been seen at the Wilkes-Barre vitascope premiere in June.

Howe's organization of these films relied on sophisticated editorial strategies. The first two films contrasted life in the city with life in the country.
The two films of police in Central Park were grouped together, emphasizing a similarity of place and subject matter. The last two shots of the ocean
were likewise grouped together by location. Howe followed a scene of boys
in a river with a shot of a baby in a bath, suggesting an association by

a. *Runaway Horse, Central Park, New York City* (*Runaway in the Park,* 1896).

b. *The Morning Bath* (1896).

c. *Irwin-Rice Kissing Scene* (*May Irwin Kiss,* 1896).

d. *Feeding the Doves* (1896).

4-2. Some of the films shown in Howe's first program (1896). The original Edison titles are given in parentheses when they differ from those used by Howe.

analogy. In the second series, three films of a fire rescue were grouped together, creating a rudimentary narrative on a subject commonly found in the era's popular culture. Howe, making use of his experience as a phonograph exhibitor, sprinkled his program with a few humorous interludes to keep his audience amused, including one scene of children in a tub race and another of a watermelon-eating contest. The first preceded the excitement of the fire rescue narrative, the latter immediately followed it. This symmetry may have been suggested by the latter film's portrayal of African-Americans as childlike. Both "series" ended with popular hits of the first, novelty season of projected motion pictures: the May Irwin–John C. Rice kiss, an excerpt from the popular musical comedy *The Widow*

e. *Responding to the Alarm of Fire* (*Going to Fire,* 1896: one of several films that might have been used).

f. *Firemen at work—Rescue* (*Fire Rescue Scene,* 1894).

g. *Burning Stables and Rescue of Horses* (*The Burning Stable,* 1896).

h. *Watermelon Contest* (1896).

Jones, and waves breaking on the shore, a subject shown to popular acclaim at many local vitascope premieres.

In his selection and organization of films, Howe had created what we can call a cinema of reassurance. The city bustles with activity and energy while the country reaps a bountiful harvest. The tensions articulated by midwestern populism are submerged. Police and firemen courageously rescue women and children. African-Americans happily eat watermelon, and boys exude boundless energy in their play. The widow finds a lover. Nothing critical enters this view of America. All is right within a screen world where all fill their designated roles.

The everyday was emphasized even more than in Howe's earlier pho-

nograph concerts—and so was his ability to transform it. All the films demonstrated some aspect of the cinema's visual resources. With *Surf at Long Branch* (the original title for the closing ocean scene), the exhibitor "was glad to be able to bring the ocean to those who could not go to see it."[25] As Howe had earlier done with the phonograph, the outside world was brought inside and audiences saw one distant place after another transported before their eyes, new significance given to the ordinary. Recalling earlier phonograph recordings, a baby cries in *The Morning Bath*, the image reprising the incongruous luxury of witnessing without responsibility. Such contradictions between everyday impulses and theatrical experience once again provide catalysts for laughter, allowing the humor to appear spontaneous.

Howe's program differed from others that featured dancers and vaudeville stars, foregrounding urban amusements. His images generally possessed, as Erik Barnouw has noted, a documentary impulse.[26] Police scenes could be deemed educational. The three-part fire rescue provided an opportunity for Howe to show process and reassert the operational aesthetic. *The May Irwin Kiss* (as the picture was generally titled) was the only one on his bill that took some preexisting piece of amusement as its subject. Its use of a relative closeup, however, revealed details of the "luscious osculation" that eluded the theatrical spectator. Furthermore, in contrast to Howe's customary phonograph selections, the show lacked any overt religious imagery.

That a conservative Protestant group would willingly embrace such an entirely secular offering is testimony to the challenge of commercial amusements, to Howe's ability to shape and mediate the evening, and to the motion picture novelty's appeal across cultural divisions. The very intensity of cinema's new realism seems to have inured spectators to the ideological implications of what they were seeing. As a local critic remarked,

> Galloping horses, flying birds, running water, gliding cars, moving, living beings were the order at the Y.M.C.A. auditorium last evening. The occasion was the introduction to the public of the animotoscope [sic], the new marvel which Lyman H. Howe of Wilkes-Barre exhibited for the first time.
>
> Mr. Howe certainly has a winner in this wonderful machine and need not be afraid to exhibit where any of its earlier rivals have been seen. The pictures shown are various and perfect.[27]

The films' very brevity conveyed a jewel-like intensity. For the program sponsors, the novelty of the cinematic experience and the emphasis on technological achievement through the transformation of the quotidian, obscured the extent to which Howe was actually smuggling urban amusement into the inner sanctums of resistant religious groups. Having dis-

armed their conscious resistance, Howe began to engage their more unconscious desire with such films as *The May Irwin Kiss*.

Several moving pictures made spectators uneasy as the filmed subjects
seemed about to cross the proscenium arch. According to the *Wilkes-Barre
Record*, "one of the best [scenes] was of a squadron of mounted police at
Central Park charging at full speed from a distance to the direct foreground of the picture and seeming as if they would step out upon the
platform."[28] These early films did more than simply "reproduce" a scene;
they offered subjects that had been selected and photographed in ways
that induced a visceral, emotional reaction in the audience. The thrill
and anxiety they created, not unlike what people experienced on a Coney
Island roller coaster, made the overarching message of reassurance that
much more powerful. Such a dialectic would provide the key organizing
principle of Howe's programs throughout his career.

4-3. Broadside (ca. 1896).

AFTER his Wilkes-Barre success, Howe toured the small cities and towns of Pennsylvania and New York state. He was the first to introduce motion pictures in many localities. On December 11, Howe exhibited at the Opera House in Port Jervis, New York (1900 population: 9,385). Local headlines declared, "The Latest Marvel. Miracles Enacted at the Opera House Last Night. Greatest Invention of the Century. Life and Motion Reproduced With Startling Semblance of Reality by Prof. Lyman H. Howe—The Audience Delighted."[29] Over one thousand people attended, and the sponsoring Baptist Church cleared between seventy-five and one hundred dollars. The town's evening newspaper claimed that "the only persons who are disappointed are those who did not attend the entertainment."[30] Later that month Howe gave the first motion picture exhibitions in Danville, Pennsylvania (1900 population: 8,042). Again local reviews were ecstatic. As one paper reported, "The audience was enthusiastic in their applause and their astonishment could not be expressed in language."[31] When inclement weather prevented many from viewing the novelty, the show was held over for an extra night.

By March virgin territory had become hard to find. Among the few unvisited towns was Owego, New York (1900 population: 5,039), where Howe showed films for the first time on March 22, 1897. The exhibition was given at the eight-hundred-seat Wilson Opera House under the auspices of the Women's Catholic Temperance Union. Advanced newspaper publicity featured the endorsement of a local townsman who had already seen the Lumière cinématographe at Keith's Union Square Theater in New York and intended to bring his entire family to see the animotiscope at the Wilson.[32] The theater was full. Perhaps a fifth of the town was present. Receipts were $240, of which the sponsoring group received $100.

HOWE AND HIS RIVALS

In the 1890s and early 1900s, commercial methods of exhibiting projected motion pictures tended to assume two distinct forms, which might be called *exhibition services* and *traveling exhibitions*. Exhibition services provided a projector, a projectionist, and a group of films for a fixed, weekly fee and were usually hired by amusement entrepreneurs in large urban centers. Their most important customers were vaudeville theaters, where a turn of motion pictures, lasting about twenty minutes, was frequently one of many acts on the bill. As the novelty era began, vaudeville managers paid exhibition fees in the hundreds of dollars for these attractions. A successful exhibition service stayed many weeks in the same location and added unfamiliar films each week to keep returning customers amused.

Traveling exhibitors, in contrast, usually provided a complete entertainment—not only films, projector, and projectionist, but people to create sound accompaniment, the advance man, and promotional materials. Their income was usually based on gross receipts. In some cases they rented a space such as a theater, hall, or storefront, or pitched a tent and kept all income after expenses. More often they shared a percentage of the gate with the local opera-house manager or a sponsoring group that provided the space and helped to promote the show. These showmen generally operated in smaller cities and towns and stayed in one location for brief periods of time—sometimes a single evening, rarely more than a week. They relied less on changing films to entertain returning customers than on attracting new customers by moving from town to town. The different requirements of these two types of exhibition practice encouraged most exhibitors to specialize, but some showmen moved back and forth between the two methods, selling their services in large cities and then working on a percentage basis in smaller population centers or when arrangements could be made with a sponsoring organization. As Germain Lacasse has shown, this was the case with the d'Hauterives, who seemed to make the shift with little difficulty.[33] Organizations such as American Vitagraph eventually became large enough to have multiple units pursuing one or the other type of exhibition.

Since early motion picture programs were too brief to provide a full evening's entertainment, traveling exhibitors could make the cinema only part of their show. Company managers frequently hired or divided receipts with other acts to complement their motion picture feature. Sometimes, they formed variety companies that offered modest versions of big-city vaudeville programs. Just as often touring amusement managers added motion pictures to their already established shows. Either option was often beyond the means of exhibitors with very little capital. They became little more than "operators" (i.e. projectionists) who, for a set wage, hired out their goods and services to larger road shows, whether touring repertory companies, carnivals, or minstrel shows. Exhibition arrangements indeed varied but generally revolved around these two poles.[34] From the outset, Howe committed himself exclusively to the role of traveling exhibitor in its most characteristic form.

ONE common way to examine the initial diffusion of motion pictures is to concentrate on a large geographical area rather than a single locality. Howe's home state of Pennsylvania, with two major cities as well as many small towns and rural areas, is well suited for such a review. Philadelphia and Pittsburgh followed patterns broadly resembling those of other metropolitan centers.[35] Films appeared on vaudeville programs, at summer parks, and in storefront theaters. The vitascope, the Lumière cinématographe, and the American Mutoscope Company's biograph service had all appeared in both cities by late September 1896. Although the vitascope's popularity had faded by fall, the other exhibition services enjoyed long runs during the 1896–1897 season. Various other screen machines—notably the magniscope—appeared during the novelty year. Pittsburgh vaudeville impresario Harry Davis, for example, promoted the zinematographe, which played at his Avenue Theater and then in Philadelphia. At points during the year, residents of either city could see films in as many as three different theaters.

Although motion pictures were made and initially screened in large cities, they flourished in less populated areas as well. Initial showings catered to those seeking amusement, but the major urban exhibition companies could claim only limited credit for these screenings. The vitascope was easily most visible. As we have already seen, the O. E. Jones vitascope stormed Scranton and Wilkes-Barre in June and early July and may have subsequently visited other Pennsylvania towns during the summer months as well. More generally, the Rieser consortium ignored its vitascope rights to most of Pennsylvania and exhibited in Cleveland for the summer. Their Edison's Vitascope and Concert Company played Ohio and western Pennsylvania in November and early December before visiting several cities in eastern Pennsylvania. The company played Wilkes-Barre's Music Hall for three days in January.

The Lumière and Biograph companies played much less prominent roles. The Cinematograph Novelty Company (apparently with a Lumière machine) appeared briefly in such Pennsylvania towns as Irwin (1900 population: 2,452), Mauch Chunk (1900 population: 4,029), Freeland (1900 population: 5,254), and Easton (1900 population: 14,481) during December. The cinématographe never reached many other Pennsylvania localities, including Wilkes-Barre. Correspondingly, the American Mutoscope Company's biograph kept its exhibition service in Pennsylvania's two largest cities, where it could negotiate protracted runs.

Theatrical repertory companies provided Pennsylvanians with one of their principal ways to see motion pictures during the 1896–1897 theatrical season. Typically staying in a town for one or two weeks, they presented a different play at every performance. Since they usually acquired the rights to produce plays on a state-by-state basis, their activities were restricted to specified areas. Several troupes purchased a projector to show moving pictures between acts. The Waite Comedy Company probably acquired its animatograph from Robert Paul in England. Prominently advertising its new specialty, the company showed moving pictures in Altoona (1900 population: 38,973) for two weeks during October; in Reading (1900 population: 78,961) and Allentown (1900 population: 35,416) during November; in Lancaster (1900 population: 41,459) and Harrisburg

(1900 population: 50,167) during December; and in Wilkes-Barre and Scranton during January. The animatograph was the first motion picture machine to visit many of these cities. Spreading out its modest supply of films to avoid repetition, the Waite Comedy Company showed only a few pictures each evening and supplemented them with an array of magic lantern slides.[36]

The Spooner Repertory Company got its newly purchased magniscope projector in late December while playing at the thousand-seat Park Theater in Butler, Pennsylvania (1900 population: 10,853).[37] The magniscope, built by Edward Amet of Waukegan, Illinois and especially designed for touring shows, was used by many traveling exhibitors. After leaving Butler, the Spooners visited Beaver Falls (1900 population: 10,054), Titusville (1900 population: 8,244), New Castle (1900 population: 28,339), Bradford (1900 population: 15,029), and Carbondale (1900 population: 13,536). In all cases they enjoyed large patronage. The Spooners were to continue to show moving pictures between acts of their plays as long as they remained on the road. Even after the company settled in Brooklyn, New York, commencing February 1901, films remained on its bill.[38]

Kitty Rhoades and her company showed "Edison's Cinematographe" between play acts in Bethlehem (1900 population: 7,932) in mid-December and in other Pennsylvania towns in the next two months. Himmelein's Ideals, another repertory company, acquired an Edison projectoscope in March 1897 after careful inquiry.[39]

Besides these repertory companies, several well-established theatrical companies that toured throughout the United States acquired motion picture capabilities. These included Hopkins' Trans-Oceanics, a burlesque group that exhibited its kinematographe in Williamsport, Pennsylvania (1900 population: 28,757), for two days in early December.[40] Hi Henry's Minstrels featured a motograph when it played Bethlehem in February.[41] As with the vitascope and cinématographe exhibitors, these companies found the greatest recompense in larger cities and had little impact on less populated areas. For both companies and the above-mentioned repertory troupes, motion pictures were not essential to their success. Films merely enhanced their established popularity. In many instances they disposed of their projectors once the novelty season ended.[42]

Many small enterprises were created specifically to show motion pictures. Several acquired the Edison projectoscope or projecting kinetoscope, built by the Edison Manufacturing Company after the inventor severed his ties with Raff and Gammon's Vitascope Company in the fall of 1896. An experimental model was tested by G. J. Weller at the Bijou Theater in Harrisburg, Pennsylvania, during November and December— the first time films were shown in that city. The *Harrisburg Daily Telegraph* was "prepared to state that the invention will do until the greatest inventor of the age [i.e., Edison] springs something new and still more startling in its effects on an amusement-loving public."[43] The projectoscope was shown with various vaudeville bills and theatrical comedies. During the third week, the Bijou manager found his hit attraction competing against the Waite Comedy Company and its animatograph at the nearby Grand Opera House. In response, he arranged for the Edison Manufacturing Company to take a series of local views, including *Market Square, Harrisburg, Pa.*, "with all the holiday shoppers, electric cars, Commonwealth hotel and many familiar figures and faces passing by," and *First Sleigh Ride,* "taken after the first fall of snow and shows an exciting race along the river road."[44] These may have been intended to compete with the animatograph but were not ready in time. When the Bijou manager failed to bring the showman back for a quick return date, a competitor acquired another experimental projectoscope and most of the local views, which were shown at the rival Grand Opera House in mid-January amidst lawsuits and recriminations in the press.

E. M. Sharp and J. G. Elliot gave film debuts with a projectoscope in Chambersburg (1900 population: 7,863) and Hanover, Pennsylvania (1900 population: 5,302), in mid-January. Moving pictures were interspersed with magic lantern views to give the programs length.[45] By the time the Edison Company formally offered the projectoscope for sale in February of 1897, various versions of the machine had appeared in over a dozen Pennsylvania towns and cities. The manager of the 675-seat Hanover Opera House, impressed by the large crowds that attended the projectoscope programs at his theater, became business manager for the American Cineograph Company, named after the cineograph projector purchased from Sigmund Lubin in Philadelphia. The company proceeded to show Lubin's filmed reenactment of the Corbett-Fitzsimmons fight in the spring of 1897.[46] Towns such as Hanover were visited several times by amusement entrepreneurs who offered moving pictures as part of their entertainment.

One or two other Pennsylvanians followed a path similar to Howe's and built their own projectors. Will B. Wood of Shamokin (1900 population: 18,202) constructed the Woodoscope, "a machine somewhat on the principle of the Lumiere Cinematographe,"[47] which was shown publicly in his hometown on November 26, nearly two weeks before Howe's Wilkes-Barre debut. Although Wood may have had a few additional screenings, he had difficulty exploiting the machine. In February, when the initial craze for motion pictures was at its height, he tried to interest John A. Himmelein, head of the Ideals Repertory Company, in using his machine, but Himmelein opted for an Edison projectoscope instead. Zickrick's cinemetroscope was another machine that apparently had local origins.

Zickrick may have opened in Butler (1900 population: 10,853) on No-vember 25. His scheduled mid-January screening at Minersville (1900 population: 4,815), however, was canceled, and the company was reor-ganized during February. By April Zickrick was actively exhibiting in New York state.[48]

Somewhat similar patterns of motion picture exhibition occurred in the eastern and midwestern portions of the United States. Vitascopes, phan-toscopes, cinematographes, magniscopes, projectoscopes, and other ma-chines appeared in small-town opera houses with surprising frequency. A few of these itinerant showmen later became important figures in the mo-tion picture industry. Charles Urban, who had earlier run a phonograph and kinetoscope parlor in Detroit, traveled through Ohio with a cin-ematoscope, presenting films in Mansfield, Ohio (1900 population: 17,640), for a week in March. William T. Rock toured his vitascope through Louisiana. Companies even worked the southern and Rocky Mountain states where the theatrical business was less developed. The Buckman Farce Comedy Company played Phoenix and Tuscon, Arizona, in May 1897.[49] A pair of traveling showmen toured smaller Arizona pop-ulation centers that summer.[50] The Maryland Projectoscope Company toured North Carolina, presenting films in Wilmington (1900 population: 20,976), Raleigh (1900 population: 13,643), Goldsboro (1900 popula-tion: 5,877), Charlotte (1900 population: 18,091), and other towns.[51]

Motion pictures made their first appearances in most places as an ad-junct to urban commercial amusement. When Howe first entered the new field, his church-oriented exhibition was a notable exception. By the spring of 1897, however, competition between projector manufacturers had lowered the prices of machines to one hundred dollars, and many were subsequently purchased by exhibitors ready to give screenings for church groups and on the Lyceum circuit. Albert E. Smith and J. Stuart Black-ton, who later formed American Vitagraph, bought an Edison projecting kinetoscope in February 1897 and immediately embarked on such activi-ties. Since such "nontheatrical" shows received scanty attention in trade journals and newspapers, Howe's scrapbooks present a uniquely thorough source of information. If more seasoned and respected than many of his competitors, he was, nonetheless, only one of many exhibitors catering to Protestant cultural organizations.

SOUND AND IMAGE

Many traveling exhibitors besides Howe provided an evening's entertain-ment by alternating moving pictures and phonograph recordings. Lock-wood advertised his show as Edison's Wonderful Magniscope and Concert Phonograph. A reviewer in Geneva, New York (1900 population:

10,433), found the phonograph portion of his program somewhat disappointing: "There is a certain scratching tone that destroys the effect. And
the voices of singers are somewhat marred, probably by sounding through
the large brass trumpet, making a brassy tone."[52] An Animatoscope and
Phonograph Company, unrelated to Howe's activities, showed films and
played cylinders of "the very latest and most popular of music."[53] The
company's "Micro-Phonograph," however, apparently could only play
back prerecorded music.

Several showmen used the phonograph to add sound effects to their
moving pictures. Lockwood accompanied his films with sound: "Not only
could the observer see the moving pictures, but by some contrivance entirely new here, the sound of the horses' feet while running upon the pavement and the whistle of the Black Diamond Express could be distinctly
heard."[54] The American Cineograph relied on a graphophone to provide
realistic sound effects.[55] Wood's Woodoscope probably did so as well.[56]
While many isolated instances of this practice can be located, a developing interplay of sound and image can be most readily traced with Lyman
H. Howe.

Howe did not accompany his first motion picture programs with any
sound. After the animotiscope's debut, the *Wilkes-Barre Record* commented that "the realism is wonderful and one involuntarily waits for the
clamor of the fire bells or the clatter of horses' hoofs as the pictures move
upon the curtain."[57] In fact, the first vitascope screenings in Wilkes-Barre
and Scranton had been accompanied by theatrical sound effects added
from behind the screen.[58] This created a baseline of expectation for at
least some of Howe's audiences. The showman's real goal was "the task of
combining the phonograph, the kinetoscope and vitascope into one machine, so that the student will be enabled in a very short time to not only
see the moving figures but be entertained by their voices."[59] One week
after his Wilkes-Barre debut, as Howe took his animotiscope on the road
for the first time, many of the scenes "were accompanied by the phonograph which reproduced the sounds suitable to the movements in the pictures."[60] When the fire scenes were shown, "the smoke was seen to suddenly escape in a volley as the door of the burning building was opened"
and "the fire engine rattled by."[61] Throughout his first two seasons of
motion pictures, Howe continued to create sound effects with the
phonograph.

The Wilkes-Barre exhibitor featured both the phonograph and the animotiscope until the end of the 1898–1899 season. Throughout this three-
year period, the phonograph played a steadily decreasing role. For the first
month, with only fifteen films in Howe's collection, the phonograph did
the bulk of his entertaining. Initially Howe began with an hour of phonographic recordings, followed by the first series of films, then more recordings, and the second group of films. Within a few weeks he was spac-

ing the motion pictures throughout his program to punctuate the phonograph presentations. When Howe was again reviewed by Wilkes-Barre newspapers in October 1897, the *Record* reported that "Mr. Howe has made many improvements since last season tending to make the entertainment more interesting, chief of which is the rendering of selections on the phonograph between each moving picture scene. This is a good idea, as it rests the eye."[62] It also helped to reduce embarrassing delays when a film jumped its sprockets. Like other exhibitors, Howe had no reframing device. While the operator stopped the projector and rethreaded the film, the unscheduled interval could be filled with a recording.

Howe varied his mix of recordings and films according to his audience. When playing at the YMCA in Mahanoy City, Pennsylvania (1900 population: 13,504), he ended the program with a recording of "Praise God from Whom All Blessings Flow."[63] A week later, at the Danville Opera House, under the auspices of the local fire department, "the performance closed with a view of the ocean, the swelling breakers rolling in to the shore, carrying with them all the awe and sublimity of the original."[64] At first, Howe continued to record musicians and local luminaries. In Port Jervis, the local Peerless Mandolin Club played a selection that was immediately reproduced to the audience's enjoyment. But these live demonstrations stopped as the Howe's motion picture collection expanded in size.

Adding to his collection of fifteen films, Howe acquired Edison's *The Black Diamond Express* in early January. The Black Diamond Express train, which ran between New York City and Buffalo on the Lehigh Valley Railroad, stopped in Wilkes-Barre. Called "the finest train in the world," the express had its inaugural run on May 18, 1896, as people gathered along its route to cheer the technological triumph.[65] Over the following months, local newspapers reported its accomplishments, particularly whenever it broke a new speed record. At the time of Howe's Wilkes-Barre debut, the local papers were publishing reports about the Edison Company's successful efforts to film the express as it passed Lake Cayuga to the north. Since Wilkes-Barre and its suburb of Kingston (1900 population: 3,846) were jointly known as the Black Diamond City, *The Black Diamond Express* was considered a local view and its presentation attracted considerable excitement. Howe showed the film for the first time at Kingston's Nelson Memorial Hall, a four-hundred-seat chapel connected with Wyoming Seminary; Methodist and Presbyterian church meetings were let out early so people could attend.[66]

Prior to the Kingston screening, Howe recorded an approaching train with his phonograph. Then, when the film was projected, he played the cylinder to provide the appropriate sound effects. When sound and image were shown together, "it seemed as if the train were dashing down upon

4-4. *The Black Diamond Express*, taken by the Edison Manufacturing Company in December 1896.

the audience, the rushing of the steam, the ringing of the bells and the roar of the wheels making the scene a startlingly realistic one."[67] During the following months, *The Black Diamond Express* was the most popular film in Howe's collection as sound effects intensified the film's use of space and depth. In Rome, New York (1900 population: 15,343), audiences insisted that Howe repeat the scene. "The train is seen in the distance and the warning whistle is heard," reported the local reviewer. "Track hands at work on the road step to one side and wave their caps at the train. On comes the iron horse straight toward the audience at the rate of nearly 60 miles an hour, and just as it seems about to plunge off the front of the stage it passes from view."[68] Many found the illusion of reality so intense that "involuntarily you scramble to get out of the way of the train."[69] One spectator "thinking he had so few rides, decided he would jump on board but when on it came with a roar and rumble, the noise being simultaneously produced by the phonograph, he was one of the first to dodge out of the way."[70] The film remained in Howe's program for more than a year.

Howe regularly added to his collection of films to compete effectively with rival exhibitors. His programs included scenes of Niagara Falls by February and views of Buffalo stockyards and Coney Island chutes by April. In May Howe had added a fourth picture to his fire sequence and could exhibit about thirty-five different subjects. By mid-June 1897, he owned nearly forty views, including scenes of President McKinley's inauguration and the 71st New York Regiment. He even acquired a picture of Annabelle Whitford doing a serpentine dance. All were apparently made by the Edison Company. Howe was rapidly making the shift from phonograph to motion picture exhibitor.

Strategies for Success

"Survival of the fittest," one of the favorite phrases of turn-of-the-century American capitalism, applied to the competitive nature of motion picture exhibition. By early 1897 motion picture exhibitors seldom stumbled across a town of any size that had not already hosted a picture show. The failure to be first was made worse by the limited variety of available subjects. Almost every exhibitor had scenes of a fire company racing down the street, the May Irwin kiss, the Black Diamond Express, and dancing girls. Under these circumstances the novelty quickly faded. Some towns had never been very receptive to this new form of entertainment. When moving pictures were shown for the first time at the nine-hundred-seat Smith's Opera House in Geneva, New York (1900 population: 10,433), attendance was only fair. Later in the month, Lockwood's Magniscope and Phonograph Company mounted a highly praised exhibition but met with only a small audience.[71] As spring approached, the novelty of moving pictures was exhausted, and many found it wise to look elsewhere for profitable employment.

Edwin Hadley later claimed that Howe was "the right man in the right place and territory at the right time."[72] Yet even he did little more than survive the first motion picture season.[73] Start-up expenses were high, and his season lasted approximately half its normal length. Many of his first screenings were poorly attended. One complimentary review concluded, "It is a matter of regret that the audience did not swell to a packed house, not only for financial reasons but because of the merit of the entertainment."[74] After Howe's first screening in Port Jervis, New York, a local newspaper promised a much larger audience if he returned.[75]

Several factors favored Howe's survival. The commercial methods and network he had developed as a phonograph exhibitor held him in good stead. Remaining largely outside the system of opera houses proved advantageous. In Cohoes, New York (1900 population: 23,910), his exhibition was preceded by a company using an Edison projectoscope. The rival entertainment, extolled by the local critic, occurred at the city's only commercial theater.[76] Two weeks later, Howe presented his animotiscope and phonograph at National Bank Hall under the auspices of the Epworth League of the Remsen Street Methodist Episcopal Church. Admission was

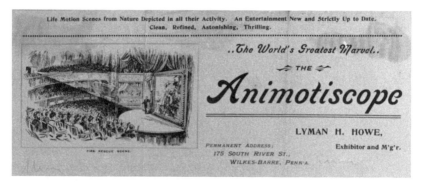

Life Motion Scenes from Nature Depicted in all their Activity.   An Entertainment New and Strictly Up to Date.
Clean, Refined, Astonishing, Thrilling.

..*The World's Greatest Marvel*..

☞ THE ☜

Animotiscope

LYMAN H. HOWE,

PERMANENT ADDRESS: Exhibitor and M'g'r.
175 SOUTH RIVER ST.,
WILKES-BARRE, PENN'A

4–5. Letterhead (1896–1897).

twenty-five cents, more than the highest-priced seat at the projectoscope exhibition. But the sponsoring group generated much more newspaper publicity than had the projectoscope company. Long reviews from other newspapers ran for several days prior to Howe's screening. The Epworth League also called upon its members and friends. Since Methodists were opposed to amusements, few had attended the projectoscope showings in any case. Howe tapped a new constituency with his "educational" program, and, not surprisingly, the hall was well filled. Spectators were enthusiastic, and Howe's show was extended for another night.[77]

Howe's concern for technical excellence also worked to his advantage. Whenever preceded by a rival exhibitor, he usually compared favorably. An exhibition at the First Congregational Church in Middletown, New York (1900 population: 14,522), was declared "the best of its kind ever given in this city."[78] As a result, the local hospital organized a benefit showing for later in the week.[79] When the animotiscope returned a few months later, "its popularity as an entertainment was shown by the increased size of the audience (which entirely filled the church), the frequent applause and the expressions of delight and wonder."[80] In Albany, New York (1900 population: 94,151), where the animotiscope was shown in a Baptist church, one critic declared that "the picture machine, which . . . has been seen in this city before under the names of the biograph and the vitascope, is the most perfect of its kind."[81] When the animotiscope was exhibited in Danbury, Connecticut (1900 population: 19,474), at the end of the 1896–1897 theatrical season, patronage was somewhat disappointing, although "the pictures were by far the best that have been seen in this city."[82] When Howe returned to Danbury the following season, so many people wanted to see the films that hundreds were turned away and his stay was extended.[83] Howe thus survived the first year of projected motion pictures, a period that saw the bitter disappointment of many showmen who dreamed of making a quick fortune.

5

****

Culture in Conflict:
Howe Moves into the Opera Houses,
1897-1899

* * *

> The War-graph entertainment given last evening under the auspices
> of the Ladies Aid of the St. James church was a perfect success. . . .
> The ladies wish to take the opportunity of thanking the public for
> their patronage and for the patience shown under the unavoidable
> confusion. And they also wish to thank the members of the police
> and the fire department for their attendance.
>
> *Cohoes Republican*, March 4, 1898, p. 1

BY THE 1897–1898 theatrical season, traveling exhibitors usually directed
their efforts to one of three distinct cultural groupings: church-oriented,
moralistic conservatives, overwhelmingly Protestant; lovers of urban,
commercial, popular culture; or advocates of a refined, elite culture. Although the initial novelty of motion pictures had transcended many class
and cultural divisions,[1] these distinctions were soon reasserting themselves in the motion picture field. This is evident in our survey of motion
picture exhibitions in the U.S. and Canada (excluding major urban centers) for the fall of 1897.[2] (See Appendix B.) The most popular motion
picture program listed was the veriscope's presentation of the heavyweight
championship fight in which Robert Fitzsimmons defeated the reigning
champion, James Corbett, on March 17, 1897, in Carson City, Nevada.
Opposition to prizefighting was strong, particularly among Protestant
church groups and other conservative institutions. The *Wilkes-Barre Record* denounced Nevada's sanction of the fight:

> This is a spectacle not before witnessed in this country. Heretofore when a
> brutal prizefight was arranged some out-of-the-way place had to be selected
> and the greatest care observed to escape the minions of the law. By act of the
> Nevada legislature, approved by the governor, that State has become the
> paradise of the pugilistic ruffians of the land.
>   There under the protection of the law, the prizefighters can pummel, and
> maim, and even kill each other with perfect immunity. All who care to wit-

ness such exhibitions of brutality can attend with every assurance that they
are in no danger of being arrested and held as participants, as they would be
in almost any other state in the Union. At Carson City, the coming prizefight will be an open, lawful exhibition, the same as though it were a theatrical performance or concert.[3]

Immediately after the bout, serious attempts were made in the legislatures
of several states, including Pennsylvania and Massachusetts, to ban the
exhibition of prizefight films.[4] These efforts, however, did not succeed—
perhaps because they did not have the full support of urban elites.

The Corbett-Fitzsimmons Fight premiered at New York City's Academy
of Music on May 22 and appeared in the leading theaters of every major
city during the following months.[5] Although male sports enthusiasts predictably flocked to the screenings, leisure-class women formed a large and
unexpected part of the audience. Normally restricted to the milieu of refined culture, they were anxious to see the all-male world of blood sports.[6]
By fall, more than ten companies were touring the fight program, which
appeared in virtually every town of consequence on the North American
continent. These exhibition units generally carried a prominent sporting-
world personality giving a running commentary as the films were projected. When a company appeared at Wilkes-Barre's Grand Opera House
on September 10 and 11, large crowds cheered as the two heavyweights
exchanged ferocious blows:

THE GREAT FIGHT AT HOME

   The warm weather did not prevent great crowds from attending the exhibition at the Grand Opera House yesterday. The Corbett-Fitzsimmons fight
was shown by means of the veriscope just as it occurred at Carson City, the
17th of last March. The moving pictures were thrown upon a canvas that
took up the entire stage, and every detail of the great contest was shown,
including the scene for five minutes before and after the fight. The various
rounds were plainly shown and the scenes between the rounds were also
given. In fact the whole thing was shown just as it occurred. The audience
was divided into Corbett and Fitzsimmons favorites and they at times applauded the specially severe punches. The knockout blow and the effort of
Corbett to get at Fitzsimmons after the fight were seen by the audience. The
exhibition will be continued this afternoon and this evening.[7]

The fears of ministers and editorial writers were fulfilled; the boxing ring
in Nevada had been transported, via motion pictures, to their local theater.

Differing practices and sensibilities clearly existed even within cultural
groupings. The veriscope and subsequent fight films were only the most
abrasive form of commercial amusement. Films shown between acts of a
melodrama appealed to the same amusement-goers, but their subject mat-

ter was usually acceptable to other groups as well, particularly when placed in a different institutional context.

Church Sponsorship and Cultural Mediation

Our *New York Dramatic Mirror* survey suggests ways in which motion picture exhibition changed once cinema's novelty had faded. The number of playdates for fall 1897 increased slightly over the previous spring, from almost ninety to over one hundred, but of these 105 play dates, ninety were for veriscope exhibitions. The number of exhibition companies appearing in commercial theaters fell from thirty-eight to twenty-three, eleven of which were sent out by the Veriscope Company. Among the remaining twelve companies and fifteen playdates, Howe's animotiscope appeared only once. But independent, traveling exhibitors had not all but disappeared. While some had withdrawn from the motion picture field, others had entered it for the first time. As with Howe, their activities often went unreported as they exhibited in churches and what the modern industry now calls "noncommercial" or "nontheatrical" outlets. Church groups considered the moving picture projector an updated magic lantern or stereopticon, forerunners of the modern slide projector. Stereopticon shows, like phonograph concerts, had long provided popular church entertainments and provided a precedent for Howe and many after him.

The kinds of sponsorship Howe enjoyed are evident in a survey based on information for forty engagements during the 1896–1897 and 1897–1898 theatrical seasons, a small fraction of his play dates. Howe exhibited in thirteen opera houses or local theaters, thirteen churches, thirteen halls (e.g., YMCAS, or town halls), and one unknown site. His exhibitions were sponsored by twenty-five church groups (e.g., eight Methodist Episcopal including five Epworth Leagues, seven Baptist, three Congregational, two Lutheran, and two Presbyterian), six religious social organizations (e.g., four YMCAS, and one temperance group), six civic groups (two lodges, a baseball club, a hospital, the local high school, and a fire company), and three under no auspices or auspices unknown.

As Howe returned to a town over a period of years, sponsorship usually rotated among different groups, encouraging reciprocity between local organizations and larger audiences. Under some circumstances, a stable relationship developed. In April 1894, Howe had given a phonograph concert at the First Baptist Church in Albany, New York. Almost three years later he returned to the same church with his animotiscope-phonograph program.[8] He gave a phonograph concert at the First Methodist Episcopal Church in Rome, New York (1900 pop: 15,343), in December 1893; in May 1897, his exhibition at Rome's opera house was sponsored by the Epworth League of the same church.[9] Sponsoring organizations used their

influence to sell tickets and acquire donated services from theater managers, newspaper publishers, and so on.

Methodists, the most frequent sponsors of Howe's exhibitions, were
strongly opposed to amusement in any form. When the general conference of the Methodist Episcopal Church met in May 1896, old church law
was affirmed: anyone attending theaters, horse races, circuses, or indulg-
ing in other popular amusements "shall be expelled from the church unless
the offender exhibits real humiliation."[10] Church-sponsored events were
among the few ways Methodists could find legitimate entertainment. Although they could not attend the theater and see May Irwin in *The Widow
Jones*, they could see an excerpt of the musical in their own church.
Church officials generally allowed Howe to show everything from *The
May Irwin Kiss* to a Spanish bullfight and found "nothing to offend any
taste or opinion."[11] There was the occasional exception. In one instance,
Methodist leaders required Howe to eliminate the bullfight before a second exhibition could proceed.[12] On only one known occasion did sponsorship per se encounter serious opposition within a local church. The
exhibition, sponsored by the Epworth League of Ellenville, New York
(1900 population: 2,879), nonetheless went forward and was declared a
success by the sympathetic local newspaper.[13]

Howe operated within a cultural context that inevitably confronted
Americans' conflicting relations to desire, a relationship that was aptly
depicted in Theodore Dreiser's *Sister Carrie* (1900). Sister Carrie embraced pleasure and ignored traditional moral standards upheld by the
church. Carrie's sister, in contrast, rigorously repressed even the possibility of sensual enjoyment or frivolity in favor of a grim respectability. She
disdained the theatrical indulgences that Sister Carrie eventually embraced. Certainly the two attitudes toward amusement represented by Sister Carrie and Carrie's sister were apparent in Howe's hometown of
Wilkes-Barre.

Traditionally the church had been the center of American community
life. As this ceased to hold true in the face of industrialization, the YMCA,
Epworth League, and other religious social organizations were formed.[14]
To counter the hedonistic threat posed by the revolution in secular amusement, these groups incorporated some of its elements into their programs.
The Wilkes-Barre YMCA, for example, with a hall almost the size of the
1,200-seat Grand Opera House, provided an array of services, including
classes, athletic facilities, and a series of entertainments that featured Polk
Miller ("a delineator of negro character and negro dialect"), Alexander
Black's "picture play" *Miss Jerry* (a play-like lantern show for which Black
mimicked the various roles from his post behind the lectern), and a lecture
by Thomas Dixon, Jr. (minister and future author of *The Clansman*).

Wilkes-Barre's cultural life continued to a remarkable extent under the sponsorship of community and religious groups. Commercial theatrical entertainment centered around the 1,500-seat Music Hall and the Grand Opera House, which hosted theatrical road companies that usually originated in New York. There was also the Wonderland Theatre, a small and financially marginal "museum" that specialized in curios and other novelties. Occasionally amusement enterprises appeared in makeshift storefronts for brief periods of time. By 1897 the Music Hall had virtually closed. The city's leading newspaper asserted, "There are people living almost under the shadow of the Grand who have almost forgotten its existence. These only go to plays of good standing and as they come only once in a while they forget to even turn out when they come along."[15] In fact, the *Wilkes-Barre Record* devoted much more attention to cultural events sponsored by church and civic groups than to amusements offered by commercial theaters.

In some areas of the country, a tenuous equilibrium evolved between church-sponsored and commercial popular culture; for many people the two were part of a continuum. Much of Howe's success rested on his ability to mediate between these two groups by selecting and organizing materials produced by urban popular culture in ways that church groups found enjoyable and beneficial. The same kind of accommodations were made by other exhibitors like Daniel W. Robertson, John P. Dibble, and Frank Percy, who are briefly profiled later in this chapter. Yet Howe adapted his business to the shifting power of these two cultural nexuses in ways that the other exhibitors did not. His need to distance himself, however slightly, from the churches was underscored by the opening of the Nesbitt Theater in Wilkes-Barre in October 1897.[16] This first-class theater, with 1,258 seats and a standing-room-only capacity of close to fourteen hundred, offered a more attractive and potentially more profitable setting than the thousand-seat YMCA where he had played from 1896 to June 1898. That such an upward move could be accomplished was effectively demonstrated by *The Passion Play of Oberammergau.*

Three exhibitions of *The Passion Play of Oberammergau* were given at the Nesbitt Theater in April 1898. The program, produced by the Eden Musee in New York City, was a free adaptation of the religious play performed every ten years in Oberammergau, Germany. Filmed in New York City late in 1897, its twenty-three scenes yielded approximately nineteen minutes of screen time. Incorporated into an illustrated lecture along with an array of lantern slides, they made a two-hour entertainment.[17] Efforts to produce a live, theatrical presentation of the *Passion Play* had provoked vituperative attacks from the country's clergy. Considering it sacrilegious for a human being to play the role of Christ, they successfully blocked its New York opening in 1880. Stereopticon programs devoted to the Oberammergau *Passion Play*, however, had found wide acceptance among these

5-1a. "The Last Supper," from *The Passion Play of Oberammergau* (1898).

5-1b. "The Ascension," from *The Passion Play of Oberammergau* (1898).

same groups. As the *Passion Play* opened at the Eden Musee on 23d Street in New York City on January 31, 1898, the reaction from church groups could not be predicted. Would it be praised like the stereopticon shows or condemned like earlier theater performances? Consensus quickly emerged and favored the Musee.[18]

Throughout the first months of 1898, the Eden Musee was heavily patronized by ministers and churchgoers. Clergymen brought their Sunday-school classes and extended public endorsements. "Everyone should see it," declared the Reverend H. M. Warren of the Pastor Central Park Baptist Church. "I would advise all Christian people to go and take their friends whom they desire to see leading a Christian life, for here they will get a vivid portrayal of the life and sufferings of the world's Redeemer, and at the same time hear the story of the Gospel given in a most striking and convincing manner, which certainly must leave a lasting impression for good."[19] That March several companies toured the Northeast but showed the Musee's *Passion Play* in commercial theaters rather than in churches or YMCA halls. Methodist ministers watched helplessly as these "dens of iniquity" flaunted their most sacred story. And they had to accept it with good grace. Not only had New York ministers already applauded the effort, but the Reverend N. B. Thompson toured with the company that stopped in Wilkes-Barre and delivered the descriptive lecture. Here a specific subject with demonstrable appeal transcended antagonism between religion and amusement. Howe achieved a similar reconciliation, but on a more sustained basis and without relying on religious subject matter.

Howe's move to the Nesbitt in September 1898 proved justified when all seats were sold and additional spectators stood through the evening exhibition.[20] Thus Howe began to depart from the general practices of his contemporaries by moving his exhibitions into commercial "theatrical" situations in cities of 20,000 to 100,000 people. In Scranton, Howe moved from the Simpson Methodist Episcopal Church, where he showed films in April 1897, to the Lyceum Theatre (1,544 seats). Both the Lyceum and Nesbitt were booked by theatrical managers Burgunder and Reis. Early in 1899, perhaps as a result of these successes, Howe won an engagement at John D. Mishler's Academy of Music (1,475 seats) in Reading (1900 population: 78,961), his first date in that city. In all three cities, Howe made arrangements directly with the theater and did not exhibit under any group's auspices. Nonetheless, ministers and church people continued to attend.[21]

Howe carefully avoided a sharp break with religious institutions. Although rarely relying on local sponsors in Wilkes-Barre after 1898, he did so in nearby towns. Shortly after his Nesbitt screening, he exhibited in Kingston under the auspices of the local Epworth League and in nearby Nanticoke with the help of the Moriah Church.[22] In Amsterdam, New York (1900 population: 20,929), he appeared at the Second Presbyterian

Church in March 1898; that fall he moved to the local Academy of Music but remained under the auspices of the Second Presbyterian Church.[23] Not until approximately 1900 did he exhibit at the Academy of Music on a strictly commercial basis.

Howe continued to use sponsors when they opened up new opportunities. He made his local debut in Troy, New York (1900 population: 60,651), in March 1899 at YMCA Hall (1,100 seats) under the auspices of the Ladies Aid Society of the Fifth Avenue Church. He regularly relied on local Troy sponsorship until the spring of 1905, his beneficiaries gradually becoming more secular. The exhibitor showed under religious sponsorship until 1900, when he provided a benefit for an orphanage. In 1901 his program was backed by a fraternal organization. From 1902 to 1904 he appeared under the auspices of a beneficial association designed to help employees from one of the town's largest manufacturers. As nonreligious groups played an increasingly prominent role in the social and cultural life of these cities, Howe turned to them with greater frequency.[24]

During the last months of 1898, Howe assumed a unique position in the motion picture field, as is apparent from our survey of traveling exhibitors. For that fall we located only thirty-one theatrical engagements by approximately thirteen exhibition companies. Howe was responsible for thirteen of these dates while two veriscope units were booked for four others. The remaining fourteen engagements, given by ten different companies, were scattered across the United States, from Albany, Georgia, to Exeter, New Hampshire, to Boise, Idaho. These listings represented isolated theatrical engagements by companies that otherwise played churches, YMCAs, schoolhouses, and lecture halls. Their number will never be exactly known but easily exceeded twenty full-time companies. Let us now look at five of these exhibitors, ones with whom Howe had contact or direct rivalry.

The company run by John P. Dibble had its first season in 1897–1898. Dibble was born in Meriden, Connecticut, and spent his adult life in New Haven. In the mid-1890s he managed a fancy goods store specializing in art novelties. When the store's owner, J. M. Dibble, died, the store closed and John P. Dibble began a career as a traveling showman.[25] He became a successful purveyor of moving pictures in New York, New England, and as far west as Ohio. At his first appearance in Hartford, Connecticut (population: 79,850), in March 1898, Dibble exhibited "Edison's picturescope" along with a phonograph and stereopticon:

EDISON'S PICTURESCOPE

*Fine Exhibition of Moving Pictures
and Stereopticon Views*

The exhibition of Edison's picturescope, and the attendant musical wonder, a phonograph which was very insistent, at Unity Hall yesterday and last evening was an attractive show of moving pictures shown by the ordinary stereopticon, and there were large audiences to enjoy the entertainment. The familiar express train and military and cavalry movements were shown and the moving picture that attracted so much attention at the first exhibition of the cinematograph in this city, the French cavalry crossing the river on the backs of their horses, was seen again and had lost none of its charm. Other water views were successfully produced, but the flicker of the film does not seem to vanish with the further improvements of the machinery. The still pictures were handsome and there were many of them, including large portraits of many well-known actresses, views of the Klondike region, of Cuba, both Spanish and insurgent soldiers, the latter being cheered, while the boys in the gallery insisted in a loud voice that the former were "no good."

There were pictures of nearly all of the ironclads of the navy including a fine one of the Maine and of her crew, which was cheered with three big hurrahs. Consul-General Lee's portrait was welcomed with a big cheer. The exhibition was a most generous one, over 200 pictures being shown, and there was much that was instructive as well as entertaining about it.[26]

The theater space, Unity Hall, was usually reserved for recitals, lectures, and other refined events.[27] Claiming that his machine exceeded both the biograph and cinématographe, Dibble stayed for a week and gave two shows a day. Adults were charged twenty cents and children a dime. Dibble had longer runs than Howe, regular matinees, and lower admission fees, and he relied less on local, particularly religious, sponsorship. Although Howe never played Hartford in the 1890s or early 1900s, he and Dibble were competing for patrons in some of the same towns.

Daniel W. Robertson ran an Edison Projectoscope Company from New York City. He began his entertainment career as a musician in Brooklyn during the mid-1880s. Within a few years he had formed the Brooklyn Entertainment Bureau, which entertained church groups and Lyceum audiences. By 1890 Robertson had opened an office in lower Manhattan and renamed his company the New York and Brooklyn Entertainment Bureau.[28] Moving pictures were easily incorporated into his shows. During 1897–1898, his first season of motion pictures, Robertson claimed 247 engagements. He supplemented films with illustrated songs and a few comic interludes. Although exhibiting primarily for church groups, his company also toured a circuit of small Long Island opera houses not covered by theatrical journals. During the summer of 1898 he visited a score of regional Chautauqua assemblies in Kansas, Missouri, Minnesota, South Dakota, Iowa, Indiana, Illinois, Michigan, Wisconsin, Ohio, and Maryland. This tour of 10,500 miles concluded in a two-day engagement at the originating assembly in Chautauqua, New York.[29]

Charles H. Oxenham joined the ranks of itinerant motion picture exhibitors as the Spanish-American War spurred demand for film programs and increased the likelihood of attractive profits. Based in Brooklyn, he had previously given phonograph concerts and claimed to be the inventor of "the Duplex horn, which doubles the ordinary powers of the phonograph."[30] The accomplished electrician had also exhibited the Edison-Roentgen X-rays around 1896 and boasted some added expertise as a magician.[31] His first programs heavily favored war films, which were not organized into easily discernible narrative sequences.[32] The phonograph was retained to provide songs accompanied with lantern slides and possibly films. Oxenham's greatest strength lay in his technological expertise rather than creative organization of materials or ballyhoo. He sometimes called his machine "Edison's phantagraph" or "Edison's photoscope," but the names never stuck. More often he simply exhibited as Edison's "wargraph." Likewise, his company was frequently assigned new names during these early years. Initially he traveled across New York state—Spring Valley (1900 population: 1,992), Sherburne (1900 population: 899), and Niagara Falls (1900 population: 19,457)—and into eastern Ohio. Later he played throughout the Northeast and Midwest but never established a well-organized circuit. Oxenham occasionally appeared on vaudeville programs, hiring himself out as an exhibition service. More often he made arrangements with the manager of a hall or, particularly as the popularity of war films faded, exhibited under the auspices of church groups. By the turn of the century, he was performing at regional Chautauquas during the summer months.

Frank T. Percy, who lived in Sodus, New York (1900 population: 5,228), between Rochester and Syracuse, is a particularly intriguing figure. Percy bought one of Howe's phonographs in the spring of 1897. Perhaps Howe viewed him as an undesired competitor even then, for he surreptitiously replaced its sensitive diaphragm before turning the machine over to the new owner.[33] Percy modeled his exhibitions after Howe's and presented both moving pictures with sound effects and phonograph recordings in western and northern New York state. He even labeled his show "the animotiscope." By July 1897 Percy was appearing at the Methodist Episcopal Church in Baldwinville (1900 population: 2,992). Other engagements followed at the First Presbyterian Church in Oswego (1900 population: 22,199), at the Methodist Episcopal and Presbyterian churches in Syracuse (1900 population: 108,374), and for the local seminary in Cazenovia (1900 population: 1,819). He also performed in hospitals, hotels, and small-town opera houses. The latter included Waverly (1900 population: 4,465), Waterville (1900 population: 1,571), and Trumansburg (1900 population: 1,225). The confusion over projector and company names, however convenient for Percy, must have irritated Howe. Nonetheless, such generic names were common—there was more than one Edison Projectoscope Company—and Percy never posed a serious threat to Howe's commercial supremacy. While some of their territory overlapped, Percy generally played smaller venues.[34]

Edwin Hadley left Howe's employ at the end of the 1896–1897 season and started his own exhibition company. Howe had been anxious to sell one of his phonographs in the spring of 1897 and sought Hadley's aid by hinting at a commission. Although Hadley had urged Frank Percy to buy the machine, Hadley's reward failed to materialize, and the angry operator left.[35] The Hadley Kinetoscope Concert Company offered "animated pictures," illustrated songs, and a concert phonograph. Over the next two years Hadley relied on several men to present specialty numbers between film selections. These included Charles E. Phillips, a musical eccentric, mimic, mandolin virtuoso, and palm whistler; Alonzo Hatch, an operatic tenor and balladist who had once sung on the vaudeville circuit; and Norman Howe (the stage name for Arthur Lane), a "good lecturer, monologue artist and singer."[36] Hadley exhibited films in Warrensburg, New York (1900 population: 2,352), in August 1897 and Glens Falls, New York (1900 population: 12,349), the following year. Eventually he moved west to the Indiana-Illinois area in search of more profitable territory.[37]

THE BROOKLYN INSTITUTE AND BURTON HOLMES

We have examined motion pictures as they were used either for popular amusement or to entertain religious groups. A more elite group of showmen catered primarily to people seeking refined culture. Occasionally presenting their programs at local YMCAs or town halls, this group found its principal institutional support in large cities. One of the leading institutions of this type was the Brooklyn Institute of Arts and Science, which provided a variety of cultural events for its members: musical concerts and recitals, dramatic readings of Shakespeare, Tennyson, Lowell and Longfellow, public lectures, and a variety of courses from its departments of philology, fine arts, political science, and law. Travel lectures, usually illustrated with lantern slides, were particularly popular. Alexander Black, who had come to enjoy considerable fame with his lantern-slide "picture plays," was an Institute favorite. He bridged the gulf between church-sponsored and genteel culture.

The Brooklyn Institute, which had hosted Edison's first public demonstration of his peephole kinetoscope in 1893, began to show films during the 1896–1897 season. Projection had sparked new interest in motion pictures and induced Institute trustees to arrange screenings under their auspices. A late November screening of the Lumière cinématographe and color photographic lantern slides was their initial undertaking. The films were organized in a variety format and their presentation interrupted by a

lecture on glaciers using the slides. Alexander Black was scheduled to
show the films but was taken ill, and the Institute found a substitute lecturer to accompany the films.[38] When Black finally gave his lecture, it was
not reviewed but apparently integrated the films into his stereopticon
lecture.

Black was followed by another institute regular, Henry Evans Northrop
of the Brooklyn Polytechnic. In April 1896 Northrop had given an illustrated lecture using tinted photographic slides taken the previous summer
when he and a group of "Poly boys" had traveled through Europe. "The
accompanying lantern views were of great beauty and were so numerous
that they presented the kaleidoscopic effect of scenery seen from a rapidly
moving train."[39] These were now combined with cinematographic scenes
into a unified, single-subject program alternately called *An Evening With
the Cinematograph* and *A Bicycle Trip Through Europe.*[40] Although Northrop's speaking ability was sometimes questioned, the program was suffi-
ciently popular to be repeated many times. In January 1898, it was retitled
A Bicycle Tour with the New Cinematographe. Starting out with London
and moving on to Paris, Frankfurt, and Berlin, the talk was illustrated "by
lantern slides and cinematograph views, shown alternately in the ratio of
one moving picture to five or six photographs, by this method securing for
the eyes of the audience a grateful rest from the always trying quiver of the
rapidly moving cinematograph films."[41]

For the 1897–1898 season, a number of traveling lecturers included
moving pictures in their programs when they visited the Institute. Miss
Esther Lyons, on a speaking tour of the country, was billed as "the first
white woman to cross Chilcoot Pass." She discussed the hardships of the
Alaskan Gold Rush using 147 colored lantern photos. During an intermission relevant moving pictures were shown by a cinematoscope as she
changed into her "Klondike costume." In keeping with the operational
aesthetic, she then gave a demonstration on how to pan for gold.[42] Miss
Lyons's popular talk was reengaged three more times by the Institute.
Early in the season, Alexander Black unveiled his newest lantern-slide
drama, *Miss America.* He returned with *A Capital Courtship*, his most popular picture play, in April and presented it with newly photographed
scenes and fourteen cinematographe views pertinent to the Spanish-
American War.[43] For Black and Northrop, programs were not fixed but
constantly subject to creative reworking. Neither was responsible for the
films, yet both embedded these within a narrative of their own creation.
Precinematic narratives and genres were adapted so that patrons of genteel
culture could experience moving pictures without ever having to enter a
vaudeville house. In doing so, these associates of the Brooklyn Institute
were clearly precocious. Exclusive frequenters of elite culture in the rest

of the country usually had to wait for a visit from Burton Holmes before they saw projected motion pictures.

E. Burton Holmes showed films at the Brooklyn Institute during the spring of 1898. His appearance was facilitated by the retirement of renowned travel lecturer John Stoddard, who designated Homes as his successor, at the end of the previous season. Holmes, the eccentric son of a Chicago banker, was born in 1870 and gave his first amateur stereopticon lecture before the Chicago Camera Club in December 1891. Two years later he became a professional and presented two illustrated lectures on Japan. Drawing his audience chiefly from the "refined" upper class of which he was a part, Holmes quickly established himself in the large cities of the Midwest. "The audience was largely made up of society people and the most intelligent classes," remarked one arbiter of taste. "His lecture was characterized by beautiful, chaste diction and apt figures of illustration. The views which he presented were wonderfully lifelike and picturesque, the coloring of the scenes and the contrasts of lights and shade being exquisitely artistic."[44] By 1895, the world traveler had developed a lecture course consisting of five different presentations delivered at the rate of one per week. During each five-week period, he gave several courses by traveling a circuit of neighboring cities, and then he moved on to new territory. During the summer months he traveled to distant lands to gather firsthand accounts and make slides for the following season's lectures.

In the fall of 1897, Holmes concluded his travel lectures with a selection of moving pictures taken by his projectionist, Oscar Depue, during their recently completed summer travels. Depue's chronomatograph, purchased from Gaumont in Paris, used an uncommonly large gauge, 60 mm film that yielded a high-quality image. The views varied for each program and were unrelated to the lecture. Each group of seven to nine films was organized around two or three subjects. Like Howe, Holmes was an experienced exhibitor who at first simply added a selection of films to his already established programs.

Before his appearance at the Brooklyn Institute, Holmes made his Manhattan debut with a series of "Lenten lectures" at Daly's Theatre. His first lecture, *The Wonders of Thessaly,* focused on the monasteries situated on Greek mountaintops. The *New York Tribune* praised the "elevated" presentation and declared itself delighted with Stoddard's choice of a successor while surprised by the enthusiasm that greeted the concluding motion pictures: "Motion pictures seemed to be an entire novelty to a large part of the audience, in spite of the fact that such pictures have been on constant exhibition for the last year and a half and more in the music halls and continuous-performance theatres, and have been used for advertising purposes in the streets."[45] Holmes had tapped an audience that eschewed the world of commercial amusement not for religious reasons but because they insisted on cultural elitism.

In Brooklyn, Institute members were also happy with Stoddard's successor and found Holmes's deportment unusually appealing:

> You see before you a well groomed young man in his later twenties, tall and muscularly built, with a high bred and clear featured countenance, the lower part of which is adorned by a comely French beard. His voice is not raised more than sufficiently to be heard in all parts of the hall, his tone that of the refined if not particularly profound or serious observer save when occasionally he touches on the solemn and mysterious side of the old civilizations. Then he rises to something like eloquence. Whatever wit is imparted to the discourse is unforced, and the felicity of the verbal description and phrasing is often striking.[46]

Although films were nothing new to this group, Holmes had clearly won its approval as well.

Even though Northrop and Black had given individual lectures,

5-2. Traveling exhibitor Burton Holmes often appeared in costume when lecturing next to the screen.

Holmes was quick to boast that he was using motion pictures "for the first time in connection with a *course* of illustrated lectures."[47] Even in the world of refined culture, a showman had to rely on subtle linguistic distinctions to make claims that seemed to say more than they actually did. For most audiences, of course, Holmes provided the first opportunity to see films connected with a lecture in any shape or form. The "connection," however was too tenuous to satisfy everyone. Although audiences were delighted with Holmes's films, more knowledgeable reviewers complained of "miscellaneous subjects for which there was no excuse."[48] Perhaps in response to such criticisms, Holmes made an effort to coordinate lecture and film subjects the following year. After his lecture on *The Hawaiian Islands*, "a special series of Motion Pictures illustrates Hawaiian life and customs and the visit of the United States Manila Expedition to Honolulu."[49]

During the following 1898–1899 season, Henry Northrop and Alexander Black ceased to exhibit films and reverted to simple lantern-slide programs. Films had never become a regular part of their exhibitions outside of Brooklyn, and the difficulties and expense of such an undertaking probably outweighed its advantages, particularly once the cinema's novelty had faded. Few other lecturers were ready to take their place. One exception was Dwight Elmendorf, who not only showed films but integrated them into his programs.[50] His principal effort, *The Santiago Campaign*, recounted his experiences with the Ninth Regular Infantry in Cuba during the Spanish-American War.[51] Among the other travel lectures for his four-course series, *Old Mexico and Her Pageants* included a long film of a Mexican bullfight. Unlike Holmes, Elmendorf did not have the capability to take his own films but used pictures that were available from American producers and sales agents.

By the 1897–1898 season, traveling exhibitors were offering films to three quite different types of audiences. Inevitably these groups were not rigorously delineated: spectators attending commercial amusements might well go to a local hall or church to see an evening of films. A devotee of refined entertainment might indulge his secret taste for pugilistic gore. Even among ministers there were rare, controversial defenses of this "manly sport." Yet real distinctions and barriers existed. Members of conservative Protestant denominations were unlikely to attend melodrama and see films between acts of the play. Working-class Catholics were unlikely to attend an event at the local YMCA hall with its militant Protestants. Exhibitors situated themselves among these different groups. The films they showed, the locations they selected, the groups with which they worked, and the nature of their publicity and presentations all told potential patrons and spectators where they stood. Howe and Robertson had the closest ties with church-related groups. Dibble and Hadley seemed to lean more toward urban amusement even though they were careful to avoid that forbidden term. Their exhibitions were clean and safe and could appeal to women and children with the necessary degree of propriety.

Howe's Second Season of Moving Pictures

Having situated Howe and other exhibitors within their cultural milieu, we will turn to Howe's actual programs. The Wilkes-Barre showman prepared for the 1897–1898 season with limited financial resources. He purchased few new subjects, for films cost between twenty and thirty cents per foot: thus a hundred-foot film, which lasted less than a minute on the

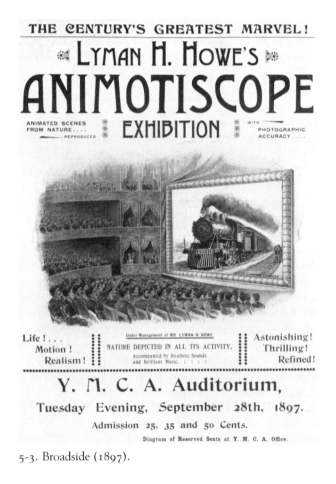

5-3. Broadside (1897).

screen, could cost thirty dollars.[52] His new subjects included a scene of Thomas Edison at work in his laboratory (actually staged in Edison's Black Maria film studio in West Orange, New Jersey). This scene began many of Howe's programs, taking the place once occupied by his cylinder of Mr. Phonograph (a.k.a. the voice of Edison). Lumière films of Milan and of French military maneuvers, probably purchased from Maguire and Baucus, a New York-based film agency, also entertained spectators. "At the cavalry charge as the horses came nearer to the foreground several children in the front seats cried out in their terror lest they should be trampled under the hoofs," observed one reporter.[53]

A bullfight, added in October 1897, became one of Howe's more controversial subjects. When projected at the Opera House in Carbondale (1900 population: 13,536): "People sat in breathless silence while they watched the furious charges of the maddened animal on its tormentors. Horses are gored and thrown, and dragged from the ring, the populace rise in their excitement as the sport grows fast and furious, and the staid Americans in the opera chairs are no less excited and interested than the Spaniards [sic] in the pictures seem to be."[54] After the sinking of the U.S. battleship *Maine* and the United States' declaration of war on Spain, the bullfight was offered as evidence of Spanish barbarity. One reviewer remarked that "the cruelty of the sport was carried home with full force and added to the repugnance entertained for the brutal Spaniard."[55]

Animotiscope exhibitions in fall 1897 still included *The May Irwin Kiss*, *Watermelon Contest*, and other films from Howe's first program.[56] Howe, therefore, tried to maintain interest with new techniques: "A novel feature was the reversing of some of the films, which, causing all the movements to be made backwards, excited a great deal of merriment. This was particularly true of a bathing scene, in which the swimmers appeared to be projected back from the water to the diving boards, and the artillery practice, when the horses and men advanced backwards and the smoke of the discharged pieces was seen to be drawn back into the cannons again."[57] This practice was also followed by one of Howe's English contemporaries, Cecil Hepworth, who later recalled that "it required considerable ingenuity to spin the material out into an evening's entertainment. I showed the films forwards in the ordinary way and then showed some of them backwards. I stopped them in the middle and argued with them, called out to the little girl who was standing in the forefront of the picture to stand aside which she immediately did. That required careful timing but was very effective."[58] Able to rely on the phonograph to supplement his supply of motion pictures, Howe did not have to go to such extremes. Like other successful nineteenth-century exhibitors, however, he had to actively form his programs.

When looking at early motion pictures, today's spectators must remind

themselves that no single individual then existed whom we can retrospectively call "the filmmaker," unless it was Burton Holmes who produced
the films he showed. Early programs did involve considerable creative effort, but what would now be considered the filmmaker's responsibilities
were then divided between the production company and the exhibitor.
The production company selected or created subject matter and took the
scenes. The exhibitor was responsible for what is now called postproduction. From a range of possible scenes, the exhibitor chose certain shots (in
the 1890s, a film, a scene, and a shot were usually the same) and combined
them into sequences or alternated them for purposes of variety. In performing this editorial function, the exhibitor drew on a range of strategies.
From his first program onward, Howe utilized principles of variety, contrast, and surprise on the one hand and principles of narrative continuity,
spatial or temporal relations between shots, and similarity on the other.
Howe also held complete responsibility for what is now the sound track.
He delivered a running commentary on the films that he either wrote or
delivered extemporaneously.[59] His contribution to the cinematic experience was at least comparable to that of the motion picture photographer,
and audiences knew it. What was important to the nineteenth-century
patron was not who made the film but who was showing it. The exhibitor
was the guarantor of excellence.

Evidence of Howe's increased popularity is plentiful. His exhibitions at
the Second Presbyterian Church in Amsterdam, New York, were attended
by twelve hundred patrons even as another four hundred were turned
away. The sponsors, who had oversold the show, informed shut-out ticket
holders that they would be admitted the following evening without any
additional charge![60] Although other exhibitions were better organized,
hundreds of people were also turned away in Wilkes-Barre and Danbury.
Under such circumstances, a night's receipts must have exceeded three
hundred dollars and Howe's share more than two hundred dollars.[61] In
many places Howe's exhibitions were so well attended that he gave additional performances the next evening. In North Adams, Massachusetts,
and Danbury, Connecticut, Howe advertised new films and recordings for
the second night so that people attending on the first night would be encouraged to return.[62]

THE WAR-GRAPH

The 1898–1899 season was dominated by the Spanish-American War,
which had proved a boon to motion picture producers and exhibitors. In
the large cities, many vaudeville houses began to show war-related films
in late February or March 1898, shortly after the sinking of the *Maine*.
Outside these population centers, Americans generally saw war films after

the fighting had ended but before the euphoria of victory had dissipated. To express their patriotic sentiments and promote their popular pictures, Howe, Dibble, and many other traveling showmen renamed their machines and companies the "War-graph."[63] The term was adopted by two New York exhibition services, Eberhard Schneider's German-American Cinematograph Company and J. Stuart Blackton and Albert Smith's American Vitagraph Company. To avoid losing his identity, the Wilkes-Barre showman called his show "Howe's War-graph" whenever possible. In some respects this was preferable to the old term "animotiscope," which had been compromised by Percy and perhaps others.

The war-graph sparked important changes in many exhibitors' methods of production and representation. Showmen like Howe began to organize films into more complex programs, not only because they wanted to treat a single important subject in detail but because this desire was facilitated by new technology: a combination motion picture-slide projector, which appeared in November 1897. The device enabled the projectionist to change rapidly between slides and films. With war films only available from a few sources, the selection was limited, particularly if views of hometown troops were desired.[64] Almost every exhibitor showed slides along with films to increase his choice of subject matter and lower his costs.

Although Dibble and other exhibitors had used slides from the beginning, Howe prided himself on avoiding this inexpensive filler, using records instead. Once he accepted the need to show stereopticon slides, however, he again tried out his new approach on a friendly, local audience. For one group of war films, he introduced still pictures of the wreck of the *Maine*. These "awoke an enthusiastic patriotic feeling." At another point in the program,

> A lot of Cuban war pictures were then shown and the audience was kept almost continually applauding. They were not moving pictures. Among them were portraits of the prominent army and naval officers. The pictures of Sampson and Schley were enthusiastically received, but when the picture of Dewey appeared the audience burst out in a long continued demonstration. Pictures of Pittston Co. H at Mt Gretna, Maj. John S. Harding on horseback, a company of recruits, the newspaper correspondents from Wilkes-Barre were faithfully pictured.[65]

Images such as these were unavailable in motion pictures and may have been acquired from one of the local newspapers, a practice adopted by other exhibitors.[66] When Howe displayed slides of the American flag, the audience sang "America the Beautiful." As in other American cities, the theater became a place in which people expressed their patriotism.

During his summer hiatus, Howe acquired additional war films. His fall program listed individual motion picture subjects and indicated the two points at which groups of lantern slides were shown. "The display of pictures," wrote one reviewer, "is separated into groups with brief waits between groups for necessary explanations and to rest the eyes, thus affording a relief that is fully appreciated."[67]

Howe offered a narrative account of the war, not once but twice, and from different perspectives. The first group followed the land war, troops parading before leaving for the front, going to their Florida staging areas, landing in Cuba, and fighting to defend the flag. The second group focused on the sea and began earlier than the land series, with the *Maine* (in fact its sister ship) leaving New York Harbor. It continued with a highly emotional catalyst—the explosion of the *Maine* (a Méliès reenactment)—and then detailed the resulting defense of American honor. Howe's audiences thus had the pleasure of savoring America's victory twice in one evening. Not surprisingly, this elaborate program pleased audiences everywhere. At the same time, the war was presented as if it were a process to be broken down, analyzed, and objectively presented.

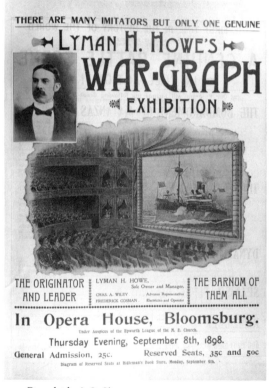

5-4. Broadside (1898).

PROGRAMME
....OF....
LYMAN H. HOWE'S
.~~ GREAT ~~.
...War-Graph Exhibition...
▼▼

STORMING A WALL.
THE QUEEN'S LANCERS.
REGENT STREET, LONDON.
SEA BATHING.
MOUNTED DRAGOONS Leaping over Obstacles.
CHICKEN THIEVES (Humorous).
BLIND MAN'S BUFF.
SWIMMING BATHS OF MILAN, ITALY.
THE SLEEPING COACHMAN.

Spanish-American War Pictures.

THE 71ST REGIMENT OF NEW YORK Parade before leav-
   ing for the Front.
ARRIVAL OF TROOPS at Tampa, Fla.
MORNING WASH IN CAMP.
BLANKET COURT MARTIAL.
TROOPS EMBARKING FOR CUBA.
TROOPS LANDING AT CARNEGIE PIER.
TROOPS LANDING AT BAIQUIRI, CUBA.
PACKING AMMUNITION ON MULES.
PACK TRAINS ENROUTE.
SPANISH SOLDIERS Capturing and Shooting Insurgents.

1st Series—Incidents and Men of the Hour.

WAGON TRAIN with Supplies En Route.
THRILLING WAR SCENE, "Defending the Flag."

2nd Series—Incidents and Men of the Hour.

BATTLESHIP MAINE, before leaving New York Harbor for
   Havana.
EXPLOSION OF THE "MAINE."
U. S. CRUISER, "CINCINNATI."
U. S. CRUISER, "NASHVILLE."
U. S. BATTLESHIP, "IOWA."
THE FLYING SQUADRON.
THE FLAGSHIP NEW YORK Bombarding Cabanas Fortress.
THE DYNAMITE CRUISER, "VESUVIOUS," in Action.
THE BOMBARDMENT OF MATANZAS by the Flagship
   "New York," and Monitor "Puritan."
                OLD GLORY.

5-5. Howe program
(1898).

The various stages in the process of defeating the enemy were each represented by a single scene. Even the double land and sea narrative allowed
for more careful analyses of what were essentially two separate operations.
The operational sensibility remained influential.

Since the program was shown after the war's conclusion, Howe did not
perform the jingoistic, overtly propagandistic role of earlier exhibitors in
the vaudeville houses. Howe's show allowed Americans to savor their
achievement and appreciate their country's new international power. Like

Sousa's marches, it projected American self-confidence. Images of bur-
geoning Yankee imperialism, the films were closely linked to Howe's philosophy of reassurance.

As Howe's organization of images shifted, so did his use of sound. During the previous year and a half, the showman had relied on the phonograph for sound effects. Although it was impossible to synchronize picture
and sound perfectly, generic effects for which precise timing was unnecessary could be effectively executed, but not gunshots and other specific
sounds, no doubt a serious failing with war films.[68] To overcome this lim-
itation, Howe adopted the practice of providing live sound effects from
behind the stage. In June 1898, the *Wilkes-Barre Times* informed its
readers:

> Mr. Howe has gone several steps beyond other exhibitors who have appeared
> here with the moving pictures. Some time ago, realizing that while Edison
> perfected an appliance which enabled reproduction of life-like and natural
> movement, he had not provided such noises as would be a natural accompa-
> niment of such movement. For instance, the spectator sees a train swiftly
> passing, but he fails to hear the usual rumble and racket made by the cars and
> engine; he sees a cannon fired, but hears no report; he sees the beach but he
> fails to detect the swish of the water. But Mr. Howe has begun where Edison
> left off and in an ingenious manner, probably known only to himself, he has
> supplied the missing noises.[69]

Live sound effects had been used with magic lantern shows and in the
theater;[70] now Howe became a leading advocate of the technique for motion pictures. Demanding realistic sounds to accompany the image, Howe
steadily added to his repertoire of sound-making devices, including "the
rattle of musketry" early in 1899.[71] In the process, the phonograph's role
was reduced to filling a few quiet interludes between films.

Live sound effects led to a further decline in Howe's operational aes-

5-6. Letterhead (1898–1899).

thetic. Since the phonograph must have been near the speaker's platform, the process of synchronizing recordings and projected images was revealed to the audience, emphasizing the exhibitor's intervention. By shifting the creation of synchronous sound behind the screen, Howe concealed the process of producing effects from the viewer. This change may have intensified the immediate, visceral illusion of reality, but it further obscured the workings of motion picture technology.

Live sound required Howe to hire additional personnel. The most important new employee was Stewart Maxwell Walkinshaw, who soon established himself as Howe's closest associate and eventually became his partner. Born in Buffalo, New York, on April 27, 1873, Walkinshaw grew up in St. Catherines, Ontario.[72] When Howe met him, Walkinshaw was a "drummer," a salesman, with a talent for the piano that he had acquired from his mother, a music teacher. Howe later recalled their first meeting in the lobby of a Connecticut hotel:

> After the meal and before going to the theater where the [phonograph] concert was to be given, [Howe] was impressed by the piano playing of a young man in the parlor—also a temporary guest. He invited him to come to the theater and assist him by accompanying the phonograph. Mr. Walkinshaw complied, and Mr. Howe suggested afterward that if he, Mr. Walkinshaw, happened to be in town the next night, he should come to the theater again, i.e. if he had nothing better to do. Mr. Walkinshaw complied. The extra money looked good as the drummer was cleaning up about $10 a week and had been much of a soldier of fortune. Mr. Howe then went his way and Mr. Walkinshaw in another direction. The following year, however, they again met in a Connecticut town and both were doing the same thing. Mr. Howe suggested that Walkinshaw sign a year's contract with him for $10 a week and the latter agreed.[73]

Walkinshaw's contract commenced September 1 and lasted for ten months, with Howe paying for hotel and travel expenses. To ensure Walkinshaw's fidelity, Howe held back three dollars of his salary each week until fifty dollars had accumulated as a guarantee.[74] Similar contractual arrangements were undoubtedly made with Howe's operator. It seemed the best way to deter tired or disgruntled employees from leaving in midseason.

Howe's organization had significantly expanded by September 8, 1898, when the showman opened his third season of motion pictures at the Opera House in Bloomsburg, Pennsylvania (1900 population: 6,170).[75] Max Walkinshaw made his first appearance as musical director and accompanied the films on the piano. Howe's advance man Charles Wiley had replaced Clarence Weiss. Howe had also expanded and updated the contract he gave to sponsoring organizations. In two years, Howe had ceased to be a solitary showman traveling with his machine. He had become the

●●●● SEASON 1898-'99. ●●●●

LYMAN H. HOWE'S ◢

High Class Exhibition of

Moving War Pictures.

Permanent Address :

LYMAN H. HOWE,

175 SOUTH RIVER STREET,
WILKES-BARRE, PA.

SHARING CONTRACT.

This Agreement, Made and entered into this_____day of_____189_.

between the LYMAN H. HOWE MOVING PICTURE COMPANY, party of the first part, and_____

_____party of the second part.

Witnesseth : That the said party of the second part, in consideration of one dollar, the receipt of which is

hereby acknowledged, agrees to play the party of the first part in_____

_____a period of _____and

_____matinee ____, commencing _____ 189___

and agrees to furnish in this contract the_____ Opera House,
well lighted, cleaned and heated, with all the requisite attaches, both in rear and before the curtain, including 4 stage
hands ; all licenses and special war taxes ; stage furniture ; piano in orchestra ; properties, scenery, and equipments
in accordance with plots furnished ; if the house is not supplied with electricity, to run wires supplying electric current from city mains into building to place where machine will be operated ; house programs ; coupon tickets ; all
bill posting ; bill boards, distributing and hanging ; and advertise usual squares one week in advance of opening with
local notices in each issue of each local paper, and to continue the same throughout the entire engagement ; and to
receive all baggage and properties on the arrival of the Company, at the stage door, and to carefully carry the same
to all property and dressing rooms and stage ; and to take the same from property and dressing rooms and stage,
and deliver outside of stage door immediately after last performance ending same engagement FREE. The stage
to be kept lighted after the final performance for the removal of this Company's baggage and properties.

And Further Agrees not to play any other similar show ten days prior, or five days after the date of this performance, and to allow no bills or lithographs posted over the lithographs or other paper of this show, advertising any
other show, until after the expiration of this contract.

The party of the first part agrees to furnish in this contract the entire stage representation, perishable properties,
all transportation, express, freight and baggage charges for their Company, advance printing, and_____

_____

_____

It is also understood and agreed that the prices for the above entertainment shall be as follows :_____

_____

In consideration of which the party or parties of the second part agree to give the party of the first part

_____

of the gross receipts of each and every performance during the above named time ; said receipts shall be determined
both from the ticket seller's statement, which is to be furnished previous to counting the boxes, and the box count.
The party of the first part to have full control of complimentaries. Settlements shall be made in full during or at

close of each performance_____

_____

The key of ticket boxes to remain in the hands of the party of the first part during the entire engagement.

It is further agreed, that during this engagement, no performance or rehearsal other than herein stipulated shal
take place in the above mentioned building without the consent of the said party of the first part.

It is further understood and agreed that, if by reason of sickness or accident, or from any other cause, reason
or unforseen event, the party of the first part is not able to meet this engagement, he shall not be held liable for any
damages of any name or nature.

Witness our hands and seals the day and year first above written.

_____[L. S.]

_____[L. S.]

☞IF THE TERMS OF THIS CONTRACT ARE NOT SATISFACTORY, PLEASE RETURN WITHOUT ERASURE.

5-7. Contract, 1898–1899.

head of a small company. His organization now paralleled those of Dibble and Robertson, who also relied on several assistants to entertain patrons and keep their companies functioning.

The changes and additional expense were justified. Packed houses were the rule throughout Howe's circuit and return engagements were frequently demanded by theater managers. (See Appendix G, Document 1.) After showing the war-graph on October 3, 1898, at Scranton's Lyceum Theatre, Howe returned with essentially the same program on January 19–20, 1899. In Reading, where Eberhard Schneider had already shown his war-graph for six weeks at a short-lived vaudeville house, over three thousand people saw Howe's program at the Academy of Music on Tuesday and Wednesday, January 17 and 18, 1899. There was standing room only at these two evening performances, and receipts came to $771.45.[76] The *Reading Eagle* reported that Howe presented "the best exhibition of animated pictures ever given in the Academy."[77] Howe later returned for three days in April and gave five shows, including two matinees. Receipts were still an impressive $761.40. Howe's exhibitions were so successful that he could introduce still further changes in his organization the following year.

Howe had been among the first motion picture showmen to cater to a religiously devout clientele. But he was also among the first to see the possibility of creating programs that appealed across rival cultural groupings. Having established a strong rapport with conservative Protestant groups such as the Methodist Episcopal church, he broadened his appeal and wooed those who prefered less righteous and ideologically constrained forms of diversion. The Spanish-American War gave him this opportunity. The war evoked a patriotic response that transcended conflicting attitudes manifested in the motion picture field during the previous year. The immense popularity of war pictures provided a logic for moving his screenings from churches and YMCAs to more accommodating and neutral facilities. Having constructed cultural coalitions within these communities, however fragile and limited, Howe now needed to nurture and sustain them in the years ahead. With these groups often seeing fundamentally different solutions to the nation's ills, elaborating on his cinema of reassurance was a logical way for Howe to proceed.

6

✳ ✳ ✳ ✳ ✳ ✳ ✳ ✳ ✳ ✳ ✳ ✳ ✳ ✳ ✳ ✳ ✳ ✳ ✳ ✳

Hard Times for the Roadmen:
Lyman H. Howe, the Premier
Traveling Exhibitor, 1899-1902

✳ ✳ ✳

At this late date of modern entertainments moving pictures, unless
presented in a new and novel manner, together with all the realistic
sounds, are far from satisfactory.

"Satisfactory Moving Pictures," *Cohoes Republican,*
January 22, 1900

HOWE ASSUMED a unique role in American cinema between 1899 and
1902. Although not the only traveling exhibitor, as he would sometimes
claim, he was the only one to play commercial opera houses on a consistent basis. His new position can be most profitably understood within a
broader context of exhibition. Differences between exhibition services
and traveling exhibitors had increased by the turn of the century. At first
both had offered motion picture programs of similar length, less than
twenty minutes. By 1899, some traveling showmen were presenting an
evening's entertainment composed almost entirely of films. In contrast,
urban exhibitors continued to provide a one-reel, twenty-minute presentation that remained one of many turns on a vaudeville bill.[1] By 1900 the
fee paid to an exhibition service was typically forty to sixty dollars a week
(more for Biograph's 70 mm format). A successful traveling showman,
who operated on a percentage of receipts, could gross more in a single
night than an exhibition service received in a month—but the venture
was also riskier and more demanding. For this reason successful exhibition
services routinely managed multiple units, while Howe and his colleagues
ran only single-unit companies.

During 1899 several 35 mm exhibition services established long-term
relations with specific vaudeville entrepreneurs: in New York City, American Vitagraph with Tony Pastor, William Paley's Kalatechnoscope Company with F. F. Proctor, and Percival Waters' Kinetograph Company with
Huber's Museum. In Philadelphia, Lubin's cineograph service became a
permanent fixture at Bradenburgh's Ninth and Arch Street Dime Mu-

seum.[2] These exhibitors had previously been hired for relatively short runs—some of only a week—and were forced to constantly scramble for new contracts. Now they gave shows in the same theater, season after season. The certainty of long-term contracts not only permitted but required them to reorganize their companies. Perhaps most importantly, the heads of these services assumed increased managerial functions while they delegated the responsibilities for actual exhibitions, the general execution of their plans, to employees.

Vaudeville theaters that made long-term arrangements with urban exhibition services expected a different program every week. To satisfy this constant demand for new subjects, leading urban exhibitors had to rely on their own production capabilities. They filmed fires, parades, sporting events, and other newsworthy happenings. Their programs were often conceived of as a "visual newspaper." Human-interest subjects also had newspaper counterparts, and short comedies were the equivalent of the comics. In contrast, traveling showmen changed programs far less often than their urban counterparts. Dibble, who visited a city only once during a theatrical season, kept the same basic program throughout the year. Howe, who usually made semiannual stops, had two program changes a year by 1899–1900. These men avoided ephemeral subjects of purely local interest; rather, their longer format favored a more elaborate treatment of important subjects, more like an illustrated monthly rather than the daily newspaper.

Few traveling motion picture exhibitors enjoyed commercial advantages in any way comparable to the long-term contracts of leading exhibition services. A handful developed circuits of theaters or halls that they visited on a regular basis. Howe stands out as the only one with a circuit of commerical theaters. This is evident in our *Dramatic Mirror* survey for fall 1899 (Appendix B): thirty-five percent of the thirty-three motion picture exhibitions are Howe's. The remaining twenty-one dates were filled by fourteen different companies. Although the number of opera-house exhibitions was increased to eighty-three for the following spring by Biograph's *The Jeffries-Sharkey Fight*, only thirteen exhibition companies, responsible for twenty-seven exhibitions, were showing nonfight films. Of the twenty-seven exhibitions, Howe was responsible for almost half. Thus his regular, semiannual visits to theaters in middle-sized cities were the only equivalent to the long-term contracts enjoyed by exhibition services.

Out on his own, Edwin Hadley discovered that traveling motion picture exhibition remained a treacherous undertaking. As he wrote Howe from the Midwest in September 1899:

I am going to try very hard to make a little money this year, as I am head over heels in debt. I must have slipped a cog somewhere last season as everything went wrong from the start. Had two solid weeks of rain to begin with, and all kinds of competition. Then societies out here are not like those in the east. They won't hustle and sell tickets, no matter how you boom things and $100 houses are very rare.

Then again every detail of the show rested on my shoulders. I was mgr, operator, baggageman, typewriter, etc. I will try the game once more, and if I don't succeed, I'll drop it.[3]

Hadley's situation did not improve. By October he had decided to close his picture exhibition and find employment as an operator. He even hinted to Howe that he would be happy to return to his old position.[4]

Howe's success as a motion picture showman distinguished him from many. After his 1898–1899 season, he reorganized his business by separating the planning and execution stages of his exhibitions. Over the previous two years, his presence on stage had become less and less essential. The phonograph had assumed a minor role, and, as one reviewer remarked, "There is little for him to do any more, as most of the titles are projected on the canvas before the picture is shown."[5] Howe therefore stopped traveling with his company, based himself in Wilkes-Barre, and concentrated on the business aspects of the enterprise. Max Walkinshaw was given the role of company manager, musical director, and general assistant. For the next two seasons he was paid twenty dollars per week, double his previous salary.[6] By the fall of 1899, Howe had assumed a level of commercial stability and organizational complexity comparable to that of many of the leading urban exhibition services.

With Howe no longer on the road, the phonograph was retired. To entertain audiences between reels of films and to comment on the subjects, Howe advertised for a monologist: "Wanted: Lecturer for Moving Picture Exhibition. Must have fine stage presence and good voice. Monologuist preferred. Ten months' engagement at ten dollars per week and all expenses. Must be clean morals and strictly temperate."[7] Edwin Hadley took this opportunity to reestablish contact with Howe, recommending Arthur Lane, "a perfect gentleman, refined, a Presbyterian."[8] Using the stage name of Arthur Howe (an obvious attempt to borrow Lyman H. Howe's prestige), Lane had lectured for Hadley during part of the 1898–1899 season, until Hadley could no longer afford his services. In the interim, Lane had returned to his home in Providence, Rhode Island, and made his vaudeville debut at the local Keith theater under the stage name of George Channing Darling. His specialty was "smoke pictures and chalk sketches."[9] Howe, perhaps attracted by a fellow Presbyterian, accepted Hadley's recommendation and hired Darling, who not only introduced and commented on the pictures but gave "chalk talks" between reels of film. Darling delivered a breezy verbal patter as he illustrated "scenes from

6-1. George Channing Darling (Arthur Lane) and his clay modeling act (ca. 1899).

James Whitcomb Riley's stories, the 'way down' people of a Maine village, portraits of prominent men, etc."[10]

Howe continued to develop his sound-effects department. During the 1899–1900 season, his show sometimes had "three men behind the scenes to produce the noise effects."[11] Their effects covered a wide range and "startled the audience . . . with all the realism of sound." When Howe showed a fire rescue, the fireman's "call for a ladder, with smoke so thick that nothing could be seen, was distinctly heard, with the sound of his breaking the window as he carried first the baby and then the mother through the perilous flame."[12] Howe had at least five people producing the show: pianist/manager, projectionist, monologist (who doubled as a sound-effects artist), and two locally hired effects-makers. In addition, the company had to support an advance man and Howe himself.

Howe became an executive no longer involved in the day-to-day process of exhibition. He provided the films and the general framework within which "department heads" brought their specific talents to bear, but he did not exercise rigorous control over all the details. Once on the road, his employees were expected to refine their program in response to audience reaction.[13] The absent Howe asserted his claim to authorship by renaming the show "Lyman H. Howe's High Class Exhibition of Moving Pictures," his physical presence replaced by the presence of his name.

Howe's decision to settle down came at the age of forty-three. Life on the road must have been losing its appeal; his return to a more sedentary life must have had its rewards but also its difficulties. Though he was successful and financially secure, his family life grew complicated. After more than ten years of marriage, Lyman and Alice Howe still had no children. Perhaps it was not unrelated that Howe began a liaison with the maid, the evidence of which was a boy born on May 23, 1901, and promptly adopted by the Howes.

By this time the motion picture exhibitor had achieved some renown and stature within the Wilkes-Barre community. This was manifested in several minor yet revealing ways. In Wilkes-Barre, prior to the 1899–1900 season, Howe had charged his standard twenty-five, thirty-five, and fifty cents admission. After he retired from personally presenting the films, Howe raised the top admission price in his hometown to seventy-five cents. Furthermore, he declined to appear on the Nesbitt stage after the show. His status had been elevated above that of the common performer.[14] Howe's new standing was emphasized by newspaper reports of a three-month European trip, a luxury only the well-to-do could afford. After traveling the small towns of Pennsylvania, Howe was finally touring the capitals of Europe.

Howe's trip to Europe during the 1899 summer was motivated by business more than pleasure. Like other exhibitors, he was looking for films.

6-2. Letterhead (1899–1900).

The popularity of war films was fading, and much American production was disrupted by Edison's many lawsuits for patent infringement. European pictures, particularly trick films made by Georges Méliès of the Théâtre Robert-Houdin in Paris, were popular with American audiences but difficult to acquire in the United States. Those available through the Edison and Lubin companies were "dupes" (films made from duplicate negatives and therefore of lesser photographic quality). To acquire top-quality prints, an exhibitor had to go directly to the producer in Europe. Howe did precisely this and purchased a selection of Méliès trick films and several European scenes, a trip up the Eiffel Tower and an English rugby match. The last was purchased from the Warwick Trading Company, an English production and distribution company owned by Maguire and Baucus and headed by an American, the former traveling exhibitor Charles Urban.[15] According to the *Wilkes-Barre Times*, Howe's visit had "enabled him to familiarize himself with the very latest ideas pertaining to animated picture shows for his entertainment last night was as far ahead of those formerly given by him as the latter were in advance of his old-time phonograph or miniature coal-breaker."[16]

Howe used his freedom from day-to-day operations effectively and built relations with those New York producers who were still in business. From them, he acquired the most popular films in his fall show, those of the September celebration in New York City honoring Admiral George Dewey for his naval victory in Manila Bay during the Spanish-American War.[17] Some of Howe's Dewey pictures were not in general distribution and may have been acquired directly from American Vitagraph. Howe organized these into a narrative account of the festivities:

> The series of pictures of the Dewey celebration showed Admiral Dewey on board the Olympia receiving the governor and staff, the departure of the Washington committee from the Olympia, the admiral leading the land parade, Governor Roosevelt and staff in the parade, the 10th Pennsylvania, a view of the Olympia from all sides, the camera being on a boat that made a circuit of the big warship, the great guns sticking ominously from the sides and deck of the vessel; also several other pictures of the celebration. The pictures were true to life. The marching men, the crowds waving hats, handkerchiefs, umbrellas, etc., the dense throng swaying to and fro, made up a scene as realistic as it is possible to portray. The pictures showing the admiral on board of his ship gave an excellent likeness of the noted man. His erect figure, his quick and precise manner of walking, his active and alert spirit were all faithfully reproduced and the audience showed its enthusiasm by repeated cheers.[18]

Darling commented on the pictures while "a most realistic tramp of feet and the clatter caused by the contact of hoofs with cobbles" were added.[19]

Audiences were impressed by Howe's up-to-date subjects. For his

Wilkes-Barre screening, the showman added films of the recently ended America's Cup races. Other pictures were reenactments of American fighting in the Philippines. Such timeliness was typical of exhibition services playing large-city vaudeville theaters, not of exhibitions offered by traveling showmen. The Méliès films were predictably popular. "The pictures showed almost impossible feats of magic on an extensive scale, including some of a humorous turn. The latter created no end of merriment, especially among the little ones. The pictures were clear and distinct and among the best of the evening."[20] "The audience was agreeably surprised by the completeness of the entertainment," noted one reporter.[21] Many agreed that the exhibition was "by far the best in the moving picture line ever seen in these parts."[22]

The triumphant procession collapsed when Howe suffered the misfortune feared by every motion picture exhibitor—fire. This danger was ever present because nitrate film stock was highly flammable. None of the many American mishaps was on the scale of the 1897 Charity Bazaar Fire in Paris, in which many lives were lost, but some came close.[23] In the summer of 1897, a traveling exhibitor burned down the Newark YMCA and lost $3,000 worth of equipment.[24] Even a small fire could seriously damage an exhibitor's reputation and career. Howe's fire occurred at the Wilson Opera House in Owego, New York, on November 8, 1899:

WILSON OPERA HOUSE BURNED

Wilson Opera House was partially destroyed by fire about five o'clock yesterday afternoon. The origin of the fire is a mystery, suffice to say that it was indirectly caused by an explosion of a number of films belonging to the Howe Moving Picture Company, which was booked to give an exhibition in the Opera House last evening for the benefit of the First Methodist Church. . . .

The machine was set up yesterday, near the main entrance to the Opera House. Nearly 5,000 feet of celluloid film were rolled on cylinders and laying in a trunk. There were no persons in the Opera House at the time of the fire, except a few employes of the Opera House and the "moving picture" company, who were all on the stage, with the exception of one who was playing the piano. They were startled by a hissing sound, which came from the picture machine in the rear of the hall. They rushed to it, and found one of the long films, which was on the machine, on fire. In an instant the sparks had fallen in the trunk, where the other films were stored. There was a loud report and the concussion knocked down a few of them, who were standing near the machine. Flames filled the rear part of the house. The employes escaped through the back exit. An alarm was sent in, and the fire department quickly responded. After about an hour's fight the fire was put out. It was found that the fire and the water had almost completely ruined the Opera House. The rear part of the hall, near the entrance, was almost completely destroyed. The left gallery and box were also damaged, the fire extending down the hall on that side to the stage, badly scorching the piano. Fortunately the scenery did not catch fire, or the whole building would have probably been destroyed. L. S. Leonard's store, under the Opera House, was badly damaged by water.

It was fortunate that the fire did not happen four hours later, as the disaster would be appalling. Nearly every seat down stairs and in the gallery had been sold and as the fire shut off the main exit the loss of life would have been terrible.

Mr. Howe's picture machine was uninsured and his loss is estimated to be over $2,000. The building is owned by Mrs. Caroline Wilson, and is insured with G. S. Leonard for $3,000 which will probably cover the loss sustained. L. S. Leonard's stock is insured with G. S. Leonard for $500. Steevens & Chapman's store, adjoining Mr. Leonard's was also slightly damaged by water. Holders of tickets for the entertainment last night may receive their money back on presentation of the ticket at the grocery store of W. W. Andross, North avenue.

There are all kinds of reports as to what caused the fire but so far nothing definite has been ascertained. As the electric light company had not turned on the arc current, it was impossible for an electric spark to have caused the fire. A cigarette or cigar stub may have been the cause. Chief Sweeney deserves great credit for the masterly manner in which the fire was handled.[25]

According to one story passed on to later Howe employees, the operator was smoking while setting up the machine, and a cinder fell on the nitrate film, which burst into flames. After the disaster, Walkinshaw telegraphed Howe, who rushed from Wilkes-Barre to Owego. Nothing could be done. The following two weeks of screenings were canceled.

Howe immediately began to rebuild his show. He fired the projectionist and reengaged Edwin Hadley. Howe needed an experienced motion picture operator to minimize the possibility of another mishap and Hadley, who needed a job, filled the bill. Their tearful reconciliation may have been facilitated by common experiences of misfortune. Howe purchased a new projector and prints in New York City. Some films, for instance those of the Dewey celebration, merely replaced those lost in the fire. Three pictures related to the Boer War in South Africa were new and proved especially popular. When these were screened in Troy, the audience "went wild and cheered the Dutch fellows to the echo" even though the films were probably taken by English companies from a pro-British perspective.[26] Generally, Howe's replacement program emphasized variety: a Boston horseless fire department, a sham battle of a herd of elephants, and a trip across the Brooklyn Bridge. He acquired Blackton and Smith's recently completed comedy-trick film, *A Visit to the Spiritualist*. The Vitagraph partners may have sold films to Howe at reduced cost in exchange for the showman's lost play dates. Certainly, Vitagraph filled several engagements on which Howe had defaulted.[27] The result was a new program that Howe could present when he went back to the towns he had visited during September and October.

OCT.	1899 NOV.	GROSS % NET
SUN. 29		
MON. 30	Williamsport Pa	City Hotel
TUES. 31	Clearfield "	Windsor Hotel
WED. 1	Olean Ny	Imperial Hotel
THURS. 2	Du Bois Pa	National Hotel
FRI. 3	Olean Ny	Imperial Hotel
SAT. 4	Jamestown "	Everett House
TOTALS		
SUN. 5		
MON. 6	Bradford Pa	Bay State Hotel
TUES. 7	Election Day Wellsville Ny	New Church House
WED. 8	Owego "	Awaga House
THURS. 9	Corning "	Everything at Owego destroyed by Fire Nov. 5 Cancelled
FRI. 10	Binghamton "	
SAT. 11	Cooperstown "	
TOTALS		

6-3. Max Walkinshaw noted the film fire and subsequent cancellation in his date book (1899).

THE BARNUM OF THEM ALL

Howe's showmanship, sense of self-promotion, and sharp business practices enabled him to maximize his opportunities. He promoted his moving
picture show as "the best in America" and himself as "the Barnum of them
all."[28] To succeed, Howe had to persuade local sponsoring societies to
push his programs. He exhorted one society officer:

Madame:

Now is your most valuable time to boom our concert, keep the newspapers
talking, push the sales of tickets. Have it announced in all the different
churches next Sunday, etc. We are going to bring you the greatest, most
successful and satisfactory exhibition in the country and we hope you will
have the town there to enjoy it. You might just as well all roll up your sleeves
and thoroughly work this up and make a paying sum as to allow it to go by
default and realize only a small amount. Hard work means big returns so go
in and leave no stone unturned necessary to make it a big affair. Set your
minds on booming it until you are sure you are sure it will be. My outfit is the

most elaborate and expensive on the road and we are going to give you the highest development of this new marvel that has yet been attained.[29]

When possible, Howe ballyhooed endorsements of prominent local citizens. A Howe leaflet for Corning, New York, quoted one matron ("it has been given here twice with the greatest satisfaction, has been attended by the best people of the place, and the last time every seat in the opera house was sold before the entertainment"), a doctor of divinity ("a clean, popular and profitable entertainment"), and a medical doctor ("do not fail to see it"). Howe thought up slogans such as "While the oldest in years, yet it has the newest things out, and keeps fully abreast of the times," "An entertainment for every member of every family," and "Character and reputation unexcelled."

Howe used to a variety of promotional practices and often took advantage of his church-oriented reputation. In Winfield, New York (1900 population: 1,475), he advertised on the local trolley at a cost of four complimentary tickets. Its four cars, pulled by poverty-stricken mules, had banners on each side advertising Howe's show. Such modest publicity was particularly notable since his show was "the only attraction that plays

6-4. A horse trolley in Winfield, New York, advertising Howe's program circa 1900.

Winfield that can use those cars, as the president of the road hates a 'Play Actor' and says: I would not hang an oil painting of Maude Adams in my car barn."[30] Since successful promotions generated more money for Howe to reinvest in his show, they were a crucial aspect of the business.

Howe was a religious man who believed himself "greatly blessed." Hadley suggested that Howe felt himself freed of certain ethical restraints and able to act selfishly, on his own behalf, as when he sold Frank Percy a phonograph after switching its diaphragm with a less effective one.[31] Similarly, in late 1899, he was quick to reassure Wilkes-Barre residents that an accidental fire could not happen during a regular exhibition, although Howe and anyone familiar with motion pictures knew that such reassurance was not warranted.[32] Howe emerges as a shrewd businessman who did not let moral principles unduly interfere with his commercial self-interest.

Although the fire cost Howe several thousand dollars in destroyed materials and lost revenue, it was only a temporary setback. During the normally slow Easter week, Howe's company made a brief tour through Ohio, stopping in five cities including Youngstown (1900 population: 44,885), Ashtabula (1900 population: 4,087), and Lisbon (1900 population: 3,330). It also played Wheeling, West Virginia (1900 population: 38,878), for the first time, opening at the Grand Opera House (1,100 seats) for two days. The *Wheeling Register* reported:

> The exhibition was the best ever given in Wheeling by a moving picture machine. Not only is this true of the quality of the pictures, but of the pictures themselves. The subjects cover a wide range and all are intensely interesting. The South African and Philippine war views were excellent. The reproduction of the tricks of a celebrated French magician were marvellous and kept the audience applauding during each intermission. The chalk pictures introduced during a wait furnished a very pleasing interruption.[33]

Although the show was only greeted by a fair-sized audience on its first day, the newspaper assumed that good notices would produce large audiences on the second.

AN AMERICAN'S VIEW OF EUROPE

Howe's fall 1900 program offered a multidimensional view of Europe through a series of parallels and oppositions. To prepare, Howe again returned to Europe and increased his purchases. Boer War subjects, scenes of European royalty, and views of English life were primarily acquired from the Warwick Trading Company in London. Trick films, notably *The One Man Band* (*L'Homme Orchestre*) which had been made that spring, were purchased from Georges Méliès. At the Paris 1900 Exposition Howe appeared unobtrusively in several scenes of the "moving sidewalk" taken by Edison cameraman James White. Only a few pictures in his fall show, for instance Blackton and Smith's *Weary Willie Takes His Annual Bath* and *Weary Willie Causes a Sensation,* were taken in the United States. Howe also replaced Arthur Lane with a new monologist/lecturer known as Ackland Lord Boyle.

PROGRAM

1. A London Street Scene.
2. After the Storm.
3. Lord Roberts accompanied by Lady Roberts leaving Southampton for South Africa.
4. Sir Geo. White, the hero of Ladysmith.
5. The Interrupted Bridal Trip. France.

In the Presence of Royalty

1. Emperor William of Germany and his Ministers and Army Officers arriving at Settin.
2. Emperor William of Germany and Francis Joseph of Austria with members of the Royal Families, Ministers and Body Guards.
3. Edward VII, King of England and Emperor of India.
4. The Late Queen Victoria.
   A Scene in Legation Street, Shanghai, China.
   A Street Scene and Market Place in Algiers.
   A Scene at an English Railroad Lunch Counter, also showing the same in reversed motion.

OVERTURE

The Paris Exposition

1. Panoramic View of Champ de Mars, showing the base of the Eiffel Tower.
2. The same showing a close view of Palace of Electricity.
3. Ascending Eiffel Tower, 1000 feet high.
4. Esplanade des Invalides with a view of the new Alexander III Bridge.
5. A view looking over Alexander III Bridge.
6. A View of the Moving Sidewalk.
7. A Panoramic View from the Moving Sidewalk.
8. A scene in the Swiss Village, Paris Exposition.

Mr. Ackland Lord Boyle (Von Boyle) in Monologue

In Mid-Ocean with Deep Sea Fisherman

1. A Cricket Match during a Heavy Sea.
2. Cycling under difficulties.
3. Launching a Yawl.

A Film Over 5000 feet long showing the Review of Lord George
Sanger's Circus at Windsor Castle
by her Majesty Queen Victoria.

1. A Street Scene in Pekin, China.
2. A Scene on an Ostrich Farm, South Africa.
3. The Inheritance.
4. An Interesting Study at an English Derby.
5. Why the Cow Left Home.

OVERTURE

The Boer-British War—South Africa

1. Troops leaving Southampton for South Africa.
2. Pastime on Shipboard en route for South Africa.
3. Arrival of British Troops at Port Elizabeth.
4. A War Train conveying Troops and Ammunition to the Interior.
5. A Novel Ride on Board a War Train Crossing the Veldt.
6. Lord Roberts and Kitchener with Army en-route to Bloemfontein.
7. Conveying Heavy Artillery to the Front—A Scene on the Vet River.
8. A Reproduction of Major Wilson's Last Stand.
9. Boer Prisoners under Escort.
10. Scene in Camp. Washing a Boer Prisoner.

Mr Ackland Lord Boyle (Von Boyle)
in a Character Sketch

1. Weary Willie takes his Annual Bath.
2. Weary Willie causes a Sensation.
3. Oriental Magic, or the Mysteries of the Brahmin.
4. The Mysterious Knight.
5. Always Room for One More.
6. M. Mouliere, the great French Lightning Change Artist, twenty characters in two minutes.
7. The Cook's Troubles, or Discord in the Kitchen.
8. The One-Man Band.

Good-Night. [34]

The structure of the program was quite elaborate. Howe organized his views of the Paris Exposition to emphasize the spatial relations between shots. The first two scenes were panoramas of the Champs de Mars; the fourth and fifth scenes both contained views of the Alexander III bridge. The sixth and seventh scenes showed reverse angles of a "moving side-walk": spectators first saw the sidewalk and then saw the view taken from it. The sidewalk then took the spectator to a different part of the Exposition, the Swiss Village. By situating spectators within a spatial world, the sequence of shots heightened their sense of actually being there. Boyle

6-5a,b,c. The 1900 Paris Exposition. Howe showed a scene of the "moving boardwalk" and then one taken from it. Howe appeared in several of the films.

acted as a tour guide: "The various government buildings and places of interest were pointed out as they were shown. A general idea of the magnitude of the exposition and the beauty of the general effect was made apparent through the pictures. In several of them Mr. Howe is plainly seen."[35] These scenes provided evidence of Howe's visit, proclaimed his status as a world traveler, and suggested his involvement in film production. They also gave him a presence within his exhibition although he no longer traveled with the show.

The Boer War films, like his earlier Spanish-American War program, were sequenced into a clear narrative line. Troops embarked in England, spent time on board ship, landed in South Africa, traveled by train into the interior, fought, and escorted Boer prisoners back to camp. Although this sequence came near the end of the program, Howe provided a foretaste of the war scenes by showing scenes of Lord Roberts and Sir George White near the beginning. The entire program was constructed around these two sets of films. Howe evoked the Boer war when showing royalty, juxtaposing scenes of Emperor William of Germany, a Boer sympathizer, with views of England's King Edward VII and the late Queen Victoria. The program's overall structure generally contrasted the serious world of British-German international affairs with the celebratory tone of the French Exposition and Méliès trick films. Yet the self-confident internationalism of the exposition remained at Western civilization's center while war was relegated to its periphery. Although Howe offered a world view in which the United States had no place (except perhaps as a tourist or voyeur), it was one in which Americans could rest easily.

Howe's sophisticated program was matched by improved projection technology. It not only offered "an almost entire absence of flickering that is so annoying and hard on the eyes," but the pictures were "clear and distinct" and "larger than ever before, they being thrown upon a canvas twenty feet square."[36] Hadley later claimed credit for a number of these improvements: "I advised the use of better lens, the making of larger pictures, reconstructing the resistance to do better work on alternating currents than it had ever done in the past, made the arc lamp improvement, a successful and decided one."[37] The result was another record-breaking season. The *Wilkes-Barre Record* reported that "everywhere he has played to crowded houses and in many places people have been turned away. The audiences have been especially delighted with the series of the Paris exposition and the Boer War pictures, some of which are thrilling as well as interesting."[38]

Not all programs had the balance and complexity of this fall selection. When Howe offered a new program in the spring, variety took precedence over the sustained treatment of a particular subject. Two films remained from the previous program: scenes of England's late Queen Victoria and the new regent, Edward VII. Otherwise, the Howe exhibition included new scenes of Russia, Paris, Niagara Falls, Atlantic City, American Indians, India, and China, which were interspersed with comedies. If the selection and arrangement were uninspired, the presentation was up to Howe's standard. Praising the program, one reviewer contended, "Judged from an artistic standpoint, too much praise of the exhibition cannot be given. The program throughout is refined; it is presented in a thoroughly intelligent way and what adds more to the enjoyment of those who witness it, is the fact that the usual arts of the average showman are in no way employed in an effort to make attendants believe they are seeing more than they really are."[39] Howe knew his audience and how to please them even when his subjects were relatively pedestrian.

LOCAL VIEWS

By the turn of the century, local views were a well-tested method of boosting the popularity of a motion picture show. As early as December 1896, the Edison Company had taken local scenes of Harrisburg, Pennsylvania, later shown to enthusiastic crowds at the city's theaters. In April 1897, the Biograph Company shot a series of films in Hartford, Connecticut, for local exhibition.[40] In fact, such films became a standard element of Biograph's commercial repertoire. William Paley, whose kalatechnoscope service operated in Proctor's vaudeville theaters, also took local views. When he showed them at the Park vaudeville theater in Worcester, Massachusetts, during the spring of 1900, they drew "as it was the first time anything of the kind had been attempted here."[41]

Local views were not taken by traveling exhibitors in the late 1890s and early 1900s. Their single-unit companies could not readily support the costs of a camera and additional paraphernalia. When Howe enticed fellow Wilkes-Barreans to his exhibitions in the spring of 1901 with promises of hometown views, it was a highly unusual announcement. According to advance publicity, "Among the views to be shown at the coming exhibition will be several street scenes from our own town which were taken several weeks ago. These views were taken on Public Square and North and South Main streets and East and West Market streets and should prove interesting."[42] Since Howe did not have his own production capabilities, he must have hired an outside cameraman, probably either the Edison Company's James White or American Vitagraph's Blackton and Smith. These pictures were not incorporated into his standard program but were intended for his single Wilkes-Barre screening. Howe could afford this expense because he charged more for his exhibitions in Wilkes-Barre than in other towns. Perhaps more importantly, presenting exclusive films of Wilkes-Barre, like presenting views of himself at the Paris

Exposition, was a way for the showman to enhance his standing within his own community. Reviews, however, failed to mention the pictures, so it is possible that the project was aborted.

Howe did not acquire another local view until his fall 1902 tour. This film was made in Troy, New York, where his new advance representative, Charles H. King, had grown up.[43] King was helping Howe to enhance his position in that city, moving his screenings from YMCA Hall to the Music Hall, the city's largest theater; the picture may have been part of these efforts.[44] The exhibition was sponsored by the Cluett, Peabody, and Company Beneficial Association, an organization that aided employees of one of the city's leading makers of collars, cuffs, and shirts. The beneficial society and Howe modeled *Employees Leaving the Factory of Cluett, Peabody & Co., Troy, N.Y.* after similar views made by various companies originating with the 1895 view of workers leaving the Lumière factory. Seats for the Music Hall performances on October 21 and 22 were on sale at Cluett and Sons Music Store. Residents could also see the films at Powers Opera House in Upper Troy on October 23. "The picture representing the employees of Cluett, Peabody & Co. leaving the factory was so distinct that many in the audience recognized friends as they passed along the sidewalk," wrote one commentator.[45] As a result, Trojans poured into the theaters.

Howe's local Troy view was an isolated effort. By early 1901, the motion picture industry was entering a period of commercial retrenchment. Although motion pictures had become a permanent feature in many vaudeville theaters, they were often called "chasers." Films were generally shown at the bottom of the bill, and many patrons did not remain to see them. Urban exhibition services were burdened by a lack of appealing subject matter and a shortage of new productions. By this time Thomas Edison had sued virtually all domestic film producers for infringing on his motion picture patents. Several companies had retired from business or ceased production. Others only continued as Edison licensees. When Edison revoked Vitagraph's license in January 1901, Blackton and Smith ceased making films. In July 1901 Edison won a court victory over the American Mutoscope and Biograph Company. The judge's decision recognized the inventor's patents and gave him a virtual monopoly in motion picture production. Although the decision was reversed on appeal in March 1902, allowing producers to make films once again, the threat of legal action did not disappear. Edison simply revised his patents and resumed his litigious efforts to gain control of the industry. Meanwhile, other court cases involving copyright practice and projection patents further impeded the industry. In vaudeville, exhibition services were forced to keep the same films on the bill for several weeks or to repeat those from earlier programs. When a popular new film came out, it often appeared in many theaters simultaneously and was soon played to death.

Howe was a frustrated film producer, but one unwilling to take undue risks. Asked to give his occupation in May 1901, he wrote "picture producer." Yet he chose to avoid the world of patent litigation. After relations between Thomas Edison and American Vitagraph soured, the despairing Vitagraph partners offered to sell their business to Howe. But he declined.[46] The threat of legal prosecution deterred regional exhibitors like Howe from entering production at the turn of the century. The American situation contrasted sharply with circumstances in Europe, particularly in England, where traveling showmen such as Walter Haggar and Frank Mottershaw produced films for their own use and for sale through London-based agents.[47] In the United States, as an aspiring motion picture producer who did not really make films, Howe was typical.

The difficulties in vaudeville had some parallels in the traveling exhibition field. Our survey shows a significant decline in the number of exhibitions in local opera houses. By the fall 1900 survey, two-thirds of the eighteen engagements were Howe's while the remainder were given by six different companies. Figures virtually identical to the fall 1900 survey appear again in the fall of 1902 with slightly higher frequencies in the interim. (See Appendix B.) From the fall of 1899 through the fall of 1902, the traveling exhibition field was in a decided slump. Howe's enterprise stood out as a rare exception.

The McKinley Films

The period of retrenchment and despair had its upbeat moments for motion picture showmen. One ironically involved the death of President William McKinley at the Pan-American Exposition in Buffalo, New York. Edison cameramen, who had taken many films of the exposition during the spring of 1901, returned in the late summer to document President McKinley's tour of the grounds. They filmed his speech and several related scenes on September 5. The President remained at the exposition on September 6 and shook hands with well-wishers inside the Temple of Music building. The Edison crew was outside when word spread that he had been shot. The cameramen promptly photographed the anxious crowd. When the President died a week later, Edison crews filmed the funeral ceremonies in Buffalo, Washington, D.C., and McKinley's hometown of Canton, Ohio.

Exhibitors from all over the country purchased Pan-American–McKinley subjects from the Edison Company. Howe gradually acquired many of these films, as they came out. Even before the assassination he showed *A Complete Trip Around the Pan-American Exposition Grounds*, taken from the front of a launch as it meandered through the exposition's extensive network of canals.[48] In this 625-foot, ten-minute film, the seated spectator assumed the role of passenger and the lecturer the role of tourguide. Howe had already used this viewer-as-passenger convention as he placed his audiences on the front of a train or on a moving sidewalk, but never for such a sustained period of time. Such a technique, which pulled audiences into the space they appeared to be moving through, was becoming a hallmark of Howe's exhibitions. In mid-October, as other McKinley films became available, the Pan-American–McKinley films became his featured subject.[49] When Howe's company reached Wilkes-Barre on November 22, his program listed this eight-film sequence:

A COMPLETE TRIP AROUND THE PAN AMERICAN
EXPOSITION GROUNDS.

A series of scenes taken in connection with President McKinley's visit to
Buffalo, the assassination and the funeral obsequies at Buffalo,
Washington and Canton:

1. President McKinley at the Pan American making his last speech.
2. President McKinley reviewing the troops at the Pan American.
3. A view of the mob outside the Temple of Music taken just after the shooting occurred.
4. Arrival of Funeral Cortege at the City Hall, Buffalo.
5. Crowds standing in the rain waiting to see the remains.
6. The funeral Cortege at Washington.
7. Scene at Canton, President Roosevelt.[50]

The rest of the program, consisting of travel scenes and short comedies, was arranged in a variety format.

Many exhibitors adopted the idea of constructing a narrative out of the Pan-American–McKinley pictures. Because they had considerable freedom in their editorial arrangement of films, their live commentary, and their musical and sound accompaniment, each program was different. The Searchlight Theatre in Tacoma, Washington, for instance, offered this combination of films:

N.B.—These highly valuable educational and historical scenes reproduce the following:
McKinley Funeral at Buffalo, arrival at City Hall.
The cortege at Washington, D.C.
President Roosevelt at Canton.
Arrival of McKinley's Body at Canton.
Leaving the McKinley Home.
Funeral at Westlawn Cemetery, and other scenes of interest.[51]

Although these various programs were organized within somewhat narrow parameters, each had its own unique qualities.

6-6. Films in Howe's fall 1901 program.

a. A complete trip around the Pan-American Exposition grounds.

b. A complete trip around the Pan-American Exposition grounds.

c. President McKinley at the Pan-American making his last speech.

d. A view of the mob outside the Temple of Music taken just after the shooting occurred.

e. The funeral cortege at Washington.

f. Scene at Canton, President Roosevelt.

By late 1901 fundamental changes in the film industry were beginning
to affect the traveling exhibitor's status as a creative contributor. Production companies—the Edison Company in the United States and many
European companies from abroad—were gradually assuming greater editorial responsibility for their productions. Their films were usually longer
than the films they had sold in the 1890s and routinely consisted of more
than one shot. Although many exhibitors continued to select and arrange
these somewhat larger units into extended narrative structures, the producing companies were gaining control over this level of cinematic organization as well. The Edison Company, for example, offered to sell a pre-
arranged selection of seven McKinley funeral films as a package, with
dissolves between each film.[52] This was desirable for the producer since it
was more efficient to make copies of a few long films than many short
films. Moreover, many exhibitors had little experience in arranging films
into a satisfactory program and were ready, even anxious, to defer to the
producer's expertise.

Although some exhibitors undoubtedly chose the Edison Company's
package of McKinley films, Howe chose to offer his own programs, to
maintain a meaningful claim to authorship. While editorial control generally shifted from exhibitor to producer within the industry, Howe resisted the process.[53] This resistance was possible with documentary subjects such as the McKinley assassination. It was more difficult with
fictional story films. A few comedies on Howe's 1901 program already had
comparatively complex editorial structures. *Grandma's Reading Glass*,
made by G. A. Smith in England, intercut an establishing shot of a child
looking through a reading glass with close-ups of people, animals and objects at which the child was purportedly looking. In filmmaking such as
this, editorial control gave producers a repertoire of techniques that enabled them to make innovative, entertaining pictures. This was not so
necessary with actuality subjects. The producer of news films did not control activities in front of the camera. Travel scenes did not rely on complex temporal or spatial relations. Above all they lacked the kind of narrative specificity that compelled the producer to exercise such control.

To enrich his fall program of McKinley films, Howe acquired a new
performer. Whether he wanted a new act each year or the entertainers
thought one year was enough is unclear. Whatever the case, he hired
P. Kendall, a "clever entertainer," to give a sketch from *Dr. Jekyll and Mr.
Hyde* between acts.[54] Although his performance received applause, Howe
soon began to look for a replacement. With the theatrical season already
under way, Howe's options were limited. He ended up hiring Jay P. Kern,
the son of a Wilkes-Barre saloon keeper, who had formerly worked as an
artist for the *Wilkes-Barre Record*.[55] Under the stage name of Jay Paige, he
entertained audiences with rapid clay modeling.

6-7. Advertisement in *New York Clipper*, September 14, 1901.

6-8. The Ninth Regiment Armory in Wilkes-Barre (ca. 1901).

Howe's program drew huge, enthusiastic crowds throughout October and early November.[56] Howe had several choices for his Wilkes-Barre exhibition: he might have had several showings at the Nesbitt Theater, but instead, decided to have one exhibition at the Ninth Regiment Armory, which had a seating capacity of close to three thousand. In what was probably a calculated publicity stunt, the showman set a record, or so he claimed, for a single performance of moving pictures with over 2590 admissions and ticket sales of $1384.50.[57]

More people wanted to see the films than could be accommodated. After noting that "No such scene has ever been witnessed in Wilkes-Barre as occurred last night," the *Wilkes-Barre Times* concluded,

> To describe last night's scenes is a difficult task, suffice it to say that the crowd in front of the Armory formed a solid surging mass that extended nearly to the pavement on the opposite side of Main street. The crowd pushed and shoved, pulled and hauled, and some of the women in it had a sorry time of it. One of them fainted and fell into the arms of her husband, who after considerable trouble succeeded in getting her out of the surging

6-9. Account sheet for Howe's exhibition of November 22, 1901.

mass and into the alley below the building. Then it became necessary to close the big iron gates, when the crowd settled down and something like order prevailed. Four officers were on duty and in order to facilitate matters one of the gates was opened just wide enough to allow one person to pass at a time, but only those who had tickets were allowed to enter.[58]

Newspapers would inflate attendance figures to almost four thousand. Howe had staged the kind of event that was legendary among showmen (see Appendix G, Document 2).

In Reading, at the Academy of Music, where Howe's moving pictures had become "the only entertainment of the kind that Manager Mishler will allow to be exhibited," receipts for Monday and Tuesday, December 17 and 18, were $714.10, a comparatively modest figure, perhaps because the Bennett and Moulton Repertory Company had presented a group of McKinley films between play acts a month earlier. Overall, it was an exceedingly profitable year, both for Howe and at least some of his fellow roadmen.[59]

HOWE AND THE SEMIANNUAL TOUR

Through an astute use of promotional materials, Howe was developing his mythic persona. By the early 1900s Howe's company regularly distributed large sheets of press comments, which were routinely published in local newspapers to puff upcoming shows. The veteran promoter presented several dozen ways to tell local newspaper readers that "there are moving picture shows galore but Mr. Howe's is the king of them all, as everything about it is right up to the times, and it leads all competitors just like the Barnum show leads all circuses."[60] As the *Reading Eagle* remarked, prompted by Howe's publicity, "While most other exhibitors content themselves with showing cheap and unimportant pictures, Mr. Howe secures the pick of the market, regardless of the cost, and puts them on in a manner that challenges admiration."[61] Thus the fiscally conservative Howe cultivated a reputation for extravagance that must have annoyed his employees, whose salaries were quite modest.

Unlike most small-time exhibitors, Howe had developed an established circuit. Twice a year, at approximately the same time, he visited the same towns. This regularity was made explicit in the 1901–1902 season by the formal introduction of the "semiannual tour." The 1901 fall program was called the fourteenth semiannual tour, while the 1902 spring selection was the fifteenth. Howe's numerical designation of these tours was largely arbitrary since, projecting backwards, the animotiscope's debut might have qualified as Howe's fourth semi-annual tour though certainly not his first. And if Howe's phonograph concerts had been included in the calculations, the number of semiannual tours would have been higher.[62] In a

world with few certainties, in which entertainment was particularly fad-
dish, such regularity redoubled Howe's theme of reassurance for his faithful aficionados. As with Sousa's annual appearances at Manhattan Beach
in New York and Willow Park outside of Philadelphia, Howe's reappear-
ances marked the passing years and changing seasons.[63]

By his fourteenth semiannual tour, suffering from a bad knee and on
crutches, Howe had become heavily dependent on Max Walkinshaw.
Walkinshaw's increased authority was recognized by a new contract with
a salary of thirty-five dollars a week.[64] Although the company manager
provided needed continuity, Howe experienced difficulties with his society entertainers who performed during reel changes. In late October,
newly hired Jay Paige accidentally shot Walkinshaw in the eye with a
blank cartridge (the gun was used for sound effects). Medical specialists

6-10. A drawing by Jay Paige sketched shortly after
he shot Walkinshaw in the eye with a blank (1901).
Paige is hanging. From left to right: Walkinshaw,
Howe, King, and Hadley.

were called in, and Lyman Howe hobbled up to Chatham, New York (1900 population: 2,018), where the accident occurred.[65] Walkinshaw recovered, but by early April 1902, Paige had been replaced by E. George Hedden of Allentown.[66] Hedden introduced the films and served as stage manager, supervising the production of sound effects from behind the screen. He did not perform between reels of film, and his name did not appear in newspaper advertisements, as had been the case with Darling, von Boyle, and Paige. Henceforth, the only name appearing in the ads was that of Lyman H. Howe. For the first time, Howe's entertainment consisted exclusively of moving pictures, with only brief introductory remarks and musical interludes between reels of film.

Howe's fifteenth semiannual tour featured scenes of mountain climbing in the Swiss Alps (acquired from the Warwick Trading Company in London) and several pictures of Germany's Prince Henry visiting the United States (taken by the Edison Manufacturing Company). In addition, Howe offered the usual Houdin (Méliès) magic films, a selection of comedies, and miscellaneous travel subjects. When exhibiting in Wilkes-Barre, he returned to the Nesbitt, giving screenings on Friday and Saturday nights as well as a Saturday matinee. Seating capacity totaled 3,750—more than the armory could hold in a single seating and over three and a half times the capacity of his single YMCA screening four years earlier. In Reading he gave three shows in one weekend, netting $1,131.95, an increase of almost sixty percent over earlier visits.

Howe's sixteenth semiannual tour, in the fall of 1902, again built on his earlier successes. The coronation of England's King Edward VII was his main subject. Méliès's "reenactment" *Coronation of King Edward in Westminster Abbey* had been made long before the ceremony occurred and was shown in New York City theaters only a few days after the actual event. While this staged production entertained urban audiences during much of August and early September, competing exhibition services acquired films of the actual pageantry and rushed them across the Atlantic. By mid-September, these films had replaced the Méliès subject in vaudeville houses. Howe's efforts at least equaled those of his urban colleagues. During his annual summer trip to Europe, he made special arrangements to acquire coronation pictures from Charles Urban of the Warwick Trading Company. By September 9, Howe was presenting an elaborate series of coronation views that "if shown alone would have provided an evening of excellent and profitable amusement."[67]

Unlike vaudeville exhibition services, which usually showed first the Méliès reenactment and then replaced it with the actualities of the pageantry, Howe combined all the films into an elaborate, unified account of the ceremony. Audiences were impressed. One reviewer observed:

6-11. Patrons for Howe show gathering outside the
Casino Theater (1902).

Mr. Howe has every reason to feel complimented over the warm reception
accorded both himself and his pictures. Perhaps his best film was that of the
coronation of Prince Edward. By means of this are shown the decorations of
Westminster Bridge, House of Parliament, White Hall, the Canadian and
Italian arches, looking from the Abbey, Royal Exchange, the Bank of England, the Mansion House and others. Then followed the review of the Indian regiments in London, procession to the Abbey, a fitting climax to which
was the anointing of the Prince, the crowning and inthronization, the two
latter being especially well presented. It seems almost incredible to believe
that the photographer's art has reached a point where the detail work of such
an important event as the coronation of a king can be so faithfully reproduced
as is done by means of the Howe pictures. For instance even the fibre of the
beautiful and delicate draperies, the handsome costumes of the ladies, the
elaborate decorations, are easily discernible. The parade to the Abbey with

its richly caparisoned horses, mounted on which were dignified men. Then were heard the clatter of the horses' hoofs on the pavement, the metallic clatter of sabres, and all that goes to contribute toward making up a magnificent military equestrian parade was reproduced in a most realistic way.[68]

In Reading, Howe's Friday and Saturday presentations, including two matinees, grossed $1,436.90—over $350.00 a performance. In Troy, Howe took in $559.25 and $555.75 on successive nights. In Wilkes-Barre, the *Record* reported that "there was standing room only last evening, and not much of that. Not only in Wilkes-Barre, but everywhere else, the same conditions prevail, for he has come to be recognized as the most enterprising and most successful moving picture exhibitor in America."[69]

Success and Failure on the Road

Within somewhat more limited parameters, John P. Dibble also thrived. When he was at Hartford's Unity Hall during the spring of 1900, his pictures were received with much applause and laughter. In many instances the auditorium was so full that people could not find room to enter. As a result, the show was held over an extra week, and thereafter played Hartford for two weeks each spring.[70] Dibble also gave regular week-long exhibitions in Utica, New York (1900 population: 56,383), which Howe did not frequent. In October 1901 he showed "scenes at the Pan-American and the Midway, President McKinley's last speech and funeral ceremonies, a trip through Niagara gorge, Montreal Fire Department in winter on runners, the latest Boston fire boat in action, and many new comic and magical scenes."[71] By the time he visited Hartford in April 1902, Dibble had added a few recent news films of Prince Henry's visit to the United States.[72] To accompany these films, the show manager employed a phonograph for sound effects or musical accompaniment, a practice he continued until at least 1903.

Dibble developed a particular form of local sponsorship that effectively utilized his own background as a store manager. He made arrangements with local merchants, advertising their stores in his shows with lantern slides made especially for these occasions. As a result, "a commercial tone is given to the show by advertisements of local firms, which are thrown on the screen."[73] He may have also convinced these merchants to buy tickets at a discount so that participating stores offered a limited number of complimentary tickets to customers.

Dibble and Howe sometimes competed in the same cities and occasionally even went head to head. In North Adams, Massachusetts (1900 population: 24,200), Dibble's Moving Pictures played from March 14 to 16, 1901, at the Columbia Theater. On the last day of Dibble's engagement,

Howe gave a single performance at nearby Odd Fellows' Hall.[74] Dibble
showed films and illustrated songs in Elmira, New York (1900 population:
35,672), a regular part of Howe's circuit, for a week in March 1902. He
charged only twenty cents for adults and ten cents for children, making
his show less expensive than Howe's entertainment. Moreover, Dibble's
pictures were called "the finest that have been shown in Elmira, and . . .
wonderfully clear and realistic."[75] Yet Howe showed for one night in a
town's large commercial theater while Dibble used smaller exhibition sites
and remained for longer periods of time. Thus Howe covered more territory and made greater profits.

D. W. Robertson continued his one-night stands in churches and small-
town auditoriums. Easthampton, New York (1900 population: 3,746),
was a regular stop on his circuit. There he presented a program in August
1899, perhaps hoping to attract vacationers as well as local residents. His
advertisements promoted scenic views of the western United States and
new illustrated songs. In addition, Robertson performed "his popular
sleigh bell solos."[76]

This handful of prosperous showmen must be contrasted to a much
larger group. By 1900 Chicago mail-order businesses were selling the op-
tigraph projector for as little as thirty-five dollars, and even marginal
showmen could buy machines if they had a streak of good luck. Staying in
business was another matter. Charles G. Pfeiffer, the Young brothers, and
Professor Trites are names that briefly surface, then seem to disappear.[77]
Frank J. Howard, a Boston-area exhibitor who doubled as a local selling
agent for films and projectors, offered one explanation:

> His customers came principally from shoe workers, grocers, textile hands,
> and others from the mill towns, who, hearing of the new moving pictures,
> came to Boston, bought an outfit with a couple of films, and started in the
> show business. Ninety per cent of these ventures were failures. Principally
> from the fact that the men had no knowledge of electricity, knew nothing of
> the moving picture machine, were in total ignorance of the show business,
> and in fact, were totally unfitted for promoting any amusement enterprise.[78]

Making a living in film exhibition continued to be a difficult undertaking
for those without experience and good fortune.

Between the successes of Howe and Dibble on the one hand and the
failure of Hadley and others on the other, some exhibitors earned a modest
but respectable living. Many played at fairs and with carnivals rather than
churches or opera houses. The Bonheur brothers are particularly intriguing for the outlandish nature of their promotional schemes, documented
by a constant stream of correspondence to the *New York Clipper* and *Billboard*. The three brothers, who had a tent show that traveled through the
midwest and plains states, had an imatoscope projector by 1897.[79] Au-

6-12. Howe's company spoofs its rivals.

thorship of their modest show was not enough, for J. R. Bonheur claimed to have provided Edison with the idea of motion pictures in January 1886.[80] In fact, he claimed to be on quite intimate terms with the inventor. In Homestead, Oklahoma, on November 2, 1901, the Bonheurs were struck by a wind storm. While people were seeking safety in nearby hotels,

Mr. J. R. Bonheur thought of his pet Humanograph, made especially for him by Mr. Edison. It is an exact duplicate of the machine made by the great inventor for his own private use at his elegant home in Orange, N. J. In getting the Humanograph from amidst the flying poles and canvas, Mr. Bonheur's trousers were torn almost into rags. A heavy quarter pole fell across the pedestal an instant after he seized the machine, which was still running when he put it down in a place of safety. It uttered indistinctly, "There is no North or South to-day" as he let go of it. This machine was made to synchro-

nize musical records with film pictures in illustrated songs, forming a combination of pictured melodies with which Mr. Bonheur is making a great hit.[81]

A week later, still in Oklahoma, they had reorganized their company for
a southern tour during the winter months. Without blinking an eye, the
Bonheurs discarded their Edison connection and announced they were
using "Kinodrome motion pictures" of the McKinley obsequies and America's Cup Races.[82]

Ireland's Pan-American Electric Carnival traveled with a tent although
it played in a variety of venues. Featuring moving pictures, the troupe
was more peripatetic than most. In October it was reported,

> Ireland's Pan-American Electric Theater was one of the principal attractions
> at the Grand Rapids (Mich.) Himeod Fall Festival and Street Fair last week
> and did an immense business, pleasing all its patrons with McKinley's Fu-
> neral, International Yacht Race and the Pan-American Scenes and Midway.
> With the company is G. H. Ireland, E. L. Ireland, Charles Law, Angus Frazer
> and Prof. John C. Green, the Wizard, as "Spieler." They were at the Indiana
> State Fair at Indianapolis last week. From there they go south for the
> winter.[83]

In April, it played theaters in Vicksburg and in Yazoo City, Mississippi.
By October 1902, it was at an amusement park in Montreal, Canada,
showing reenactments of the eruption of Mount Pelee and the coronation
of Edward VII.[84]

By the early 1900s traveling motion picture shows were likely to be
named for their manager or owner, a development with which Howe was
again in the vanguard. Dibble's name did not even appear in his Hartford
ads until the spring of 1900. Even then he billed himself as manager and
called his show "Edison Moving Pictures."[85] It was not until 1903 that he
advertised as "Dibble's Moving Pictures." Others made the shift somewhat

6-13. Letterhead (1901).

earlier. For example, Sherman's Moving Pictures presented films of Queen Victoria's funeral in Canadian theaters during the spring of 1901. During the 1901–1902 season Britton's Moving Pictures showed in Iowa and Illinois and the Beatty Brothers in North Dakota and the Far West while the Rodaker Brothers began in Waseca, Minnesota, and toured the state. McKinley Moving Pictures toured Ohio. Lewis's, Drake's and Oxenham's companies toured Pennsylvania, New York, and New England. Although the exhibitors used their names to make claims of authorship, they never enjoyed well-developed public personas.

Burton Holmes became a well-known and esteemed personality even as he operated largely within the long-established parameters of the illustrated lecture. By the turn of the century, he was ensconced as a worthy successor to John Stoddard even as he established his own distinctive tone and "look." For the 1899–1900 season, he integrated films into his illustrated lectures rather than showing them at the close of the program. To patrons, he explained that this integration had had to await "the solving of certain mechanical problems and the possession of a complete series of views pertinent to each subject." In the future, Holmes's films were to "be projected during the lecture at moments when movement is essential to complete and vivify the impressions produced by the spoken words and colored illustrations."[86] For example, in his lecture on Japan, Holmes devoted a section to the geisha:

> Photographs of some of the girls were shown and demonstrated instantly their right to the claim of beauty and fascination that is made for them by so many travelers. Then in motion pictures they went through many of their dances for the express edification of the motion picture machine and the audiences which it was to reach. Always they were graceful, always picturesque and quaint, always there was about them an atmosphere of unreality as if they were characters out of a fairy story and not real persons dancing in a real [world] and before a real camera.[87]

Given Holmes's own filmmaking capabilities and his prestige on the lecture circuit, he was perhaps justified in claiming that "this innovation marks the beginning of a new epoch in the treatment of the illustrated lecture."[88]

Other Holmes lectures on Hawaii and the Philippines presented America's new colonies to the ruling elites. The world traveler informed his audiences that during his stay in the Hawaiian Islands "annexation with America was the chief enthusiastic topic of the hour." He showed the island's beautiful scenery but explained that "the original Hawaiian is fast disappearing, the natives decreasing, while the energetic Japanese and economical Chinese are gradually taking possession of their fertile lands, the Americans supplying the brains, while the Portuguese, Chinese and

Japanese do the work."[89] In the Philippines, where the U.S. Army was putting down an insurrection, he found conditions to be both primitive and miserable. The only "civilized" quarters Holmes could locate were run by the U.S. Army. The colony was declared in desperate need of American know-how and energy.[90] Holmes's success depended in large part on his presence and personality (during production as well as at the exhibitions) in ways that Howe's did not. These differences help to explain why Holmes continued as a solitary lecturer while Howe could begin to create additional companies.

Between 1899 and 1902, during a period of disarray within the film industry, Howe solidified his preeminent position in the field of traveling motion picture exhibition with entertainment that provided a common ground for diverse cultural groups—for churchgoers and theatergoers alike. Taking advantage of this unique situation, he withdrew from the day-to-day presentations of pictures, oversaw operations, and developed valuable ties with European and American producers. Howe luxuriated in this new image of himself as an accomplished, secure businessman who operated at the apex of a far-flung business enterprise. While striving for the highest levels of technical perfection in his exhibitions, he kept his programs up-to-date, planned publicity stunts, and furthered his cinema of reassurance both through the content and organization of his programs. He offered a view of the world in which Europe was the center of power and cultural achievement—but Howe was at home in that center. Before his company could claim scarcely three cycles of twice-a-year visits along a circuit of theaters, he introduced the mythology of semiannual tours, which promoted his programs as pillars of refinement and reliability. His approach had succeeded, and with the commencement of 1903, Howe started a second company.

7

* *

The Proliferation of Traveling
Exhibitors: Howe Forms
Multiple Companies, 1903-1905

* * *

Do not let my success worry you, but be glad to work for a man that
is a winner.

Lyman H. Howe to Edwin Hadley, draft letter, 1903

THE MOTION PICTURE field enjoyed renewed prosperity by the end of
1903. Not only was the number of vaudeville theaters rising, but the percentage of such theaters showing films was increasing dramatically. This
expansion was facilitated by changing methods of film distribution and
exhibition. The Miles brothers and the Kinetograph Company had begun
to rent films directly to vaudeville theaters, which bought a projector,
trained their electrician to run it, and simply rented a new reel of films
each week. The old exhibition services that had once provided projector,
projectionist, and films became renters. This commercial innovation lowered the cost of showing films and helped to pave the way for the era of
specialized motion picture theaters.

One of the most distinctive aspects of the 1903–1905 period was the
growing number of traveling motion picture showmen. Our survey dis-
closes that approximately fourteen companies gave forty-nine exhibitions
in the spring of 1903. That fall, nineteen different companies gave seventy-five different engagements. These figures increased to thirty-two
companies and 112 engagements during the spring of 1904. Unfortunately, the *New York Dramatic Mirror* then stopped reporting these screenings in its "correspondence" section. This is understandable insofar as
some theaters were reporting film showings as often as legitimate theatrical engagements. As a trade journal primarily for the "legitimate theater,"
the *Dramatic Mirror* suppressed this information. If it had continued to
report film exhibitions as before, evidence would have pointed to yet another large increase in motion picture activity in the fall of 1904. Traveling picture shows had become "one of the best money makers on the

theatrical circuits."[1] By 1905 scores of traveling showmen were making comfortable livings presenting films. Howe's intimate knowledge of the business enabled him to anticipate this new opportunity.

HOWE FORMS A SECOND COMPANY

Building on the base he had established in cities such as Reading and Troy, Howe began to form a second company at the end of 1902. Although his company had toured Ohio in the spring of 1900, the Wilkes-Barre exhibitor could not incorporate this territory into his regular circuit with only one unit. Now western Pennsylvania, Ohio, Michigan, Indiana, Illinois, West Virginia, and Kentucky could be reached. Howe was operating from a secure financial base that made the potential payoff of

7-1. Howe's companies traveled by rail. Mrs. Walkinshaw sees off her husband, his exhibition company, and its equipment (ca. 1902).

7-2. S. M. Walkinshaw's business card (ca. 1903).

the second unit far outweigh the risks. The possibility of increased reve-
nues was further enhanced by economies of scale. Howe's many fixed expenses—his annual European visit, his own managership, and general
overhead—could now be spread over both companies.

Howe hired Fred Willson (often misspelled "Wilson") as manager and
lecturer for his second company and Willson's wife as the company's pianist and musical director. Fred Willson was born in Towanda, Pennsylvania, northwest of Wilkes-Barre, in 1873. The son of a singing evangel-
ist, he married Daisy Hall of Scranton. The couple settled in Wilkes-Barre
and opened a music studio, while he also worked as a carpenter and telegraph operator. With their musical careers going badly, the Willsons were
ready to join Howe, presumably at a modest salary.[2]

In early January 1903 Fred Willson traveled with Walkinshaw and the
first company in order to learn the business. Long-standing tensions between Hadley and Howe erupted when Hadley learned that Howe intended to assign a new projectionist to the first company while he was to
lend his experience to the second. Hadley, already feeling slighted by
Howe's failure to select him as the new manager, refused to cooperate.
Eventually he agreed to Howe's plan, provided his salary was raised seven
dollars per week. As he explained, "I am not at all desirous of practically
having the responsibility of a new show in new territory on my shoulders
. . . as I know well what it means to travel with a green manager who has
no knowledge at all of the show-business, or of our particular line. Compared to my work at present it would be a continual performance of 'on
the jump.' The few new towns we played this season, amply demonstrated

that fact."[3] Howe reminded Hadley of their contract. Hadley, arguing that he had signed the contract assuming there was only one company, tried to justify his seven-dollar demand:

> I felt that a proper presentation of a first class performance would rest on my shoulders, and my work on the door, and knowledge of the business would have been to you, valuable.
>
> There would be no lost dates, through any cause of mine, and I would be practically . . . a #3 manager for the #2 Co. It seems, you look at the subject in a different light, thereby causing a difference of opinion. Mr. Wilson is just beginning to realize that his hands will be more than full with work. In some towns Max does not finish his settlement till after midnight. Mr. Wilson might take a longer time, and then who would pack up his stage outfit? Why I would, and cheerfully at that. At the finish of my proposed tour with Wilson, I would probably be a fit occupant for the Danville Sanitorium. You also lose sight of the fact, that the pianist is a woman and there will be only two men with the show, who will have more work, and more difficulties to contend with than the three men, now with the present show.[4]

Rather than pay the salary increase, Howe allowed Hadley to stay with the first company.

Hadley was convinced that his loyalty and contributions to Howe's enterprise had gone unappreciated. He reminded Howe of one incident in particular. When Thomas Armat had sued Howe for infringing on the Armat-Jenkins patents in 1901–1902, Armat had asked Hadley for help and promised to provide him with many future benefits. But Hadley had refused to cooperate. The operator also claimed to have declined other more profitable situations. When Hadley suggested that his employer might wish to give him two weeks notice, Howe replied with a lecture that revealed much about his own approach to work and life:

> Ed:
>
> Your letter from Norwich read and I will only say it indicated a mutinous and inharmonious state of mind. History is repeating itself. Have you forgotten that you went through this same thing with me once before? Your outlook then was brighter than it possibly can be now and yet you know what happened. . . .
>
> Now Ed these thoughts are leading you on to trouble. If your head is being swelled because you have had some flattering offers from other parties do you think your troubles are going to end if you go with them? Do you think if I should send you off that your future would be surer, better or more permanent than where you now are? Can you see into the future and be sure that you will improve your condition, are you willing to exchange an uncertainty for a certainty? Have you forgotten that old saying that you know to be so true that "A bird in hand is worth two in the bush."
>
> I will not answer your disrespectful letter in the spirit that you sent it but will . . . write this kindly sincere letter hoping it will appeal to the good that

is in you and trust that this effort to restore peace and harmony will find a ready response in your heart.

You have a good sure thing now and Ed get these foolish things out of your head and stop brooding just as quick as you can. Get some sunshine into your heart, think pleasant images, stop thinking that you have been wronged and insulted. Try and think something good in others, have a little faith in me, and develop a loyal true blue feeling that will strengthen your manhood and my love for you.

Do not let my success worry you, but rather be glad to work for a man that is a winner.[5]

After the two met face to face, matters only became worse. In May an embittered Hadley resorted to ethnic slurs when he complained to Harry Manhart, Howe's secretary, "Can you wonder when the crushed worm turns at last? Can you wonder at my feeling toward such a man? . . . I doubt if any Jew would have treated me worse."[6] Within a month Hadley resigned and readied his own show. Animosity between the two only increased when Howe refused to return his former operator's fifty-dollar guarantee for breach of contract.

While Hadley and Howe sparred, the second company began its initial tour, exhibiting the program shown by Howe's first company during the past fall. When the new troupe played Chambersburg, Pennsylvania (1900 population: 8,864), in mid-February, it was called "the best of its kind ever shown here."[7] The company then moved on to Martinsburg, West Virginia (1900 population: 7,564), and Clearfield, Pennsylvania (1900 population: 5,081). After showing films to good-sized crowds in Ohio, the new company traveled through Michigan and into Indiana. Most of these towns had between five and ten thousand residents.[8]

Meanwhile, Howe's first company made its customary tour of mid-Atlantic and New England theaters. Its leading feature was an Egyptian series, acquired from Charles Urban, which took spectators on a tour from Cairo to Khartoum:

SCENES AND INCIDENTS EN ROUTE FROM
CAIRO TO KHARTOUM

A Cairo Street Scene showing a picturesque Arab Wedding procession passing the Continental Hotel.
The Kasa-en Nil Bridge, showing the Nile Boats passing through the open draw.

The Picturesque Nile Shores of Upper Egypt.
Leading Tourists From a Nile Steamer.
An Arab Vegetable Market.

An Ancient Egyptian Water Wheel—an apparatus exceeding twenty feet in diameter, operated by Buffalo.

Panorama of the Temple of Kom Ombo.
A Panoramic View of the Sphinx and Pyramids.

Climbing the great Pyramids of Gizeh.
A Tug of War.

The Great Dam of the Nile at Assouan

A Panorama from a train at the base of the Dam, showing the extensive
nature of this wonderful piece of engineering.
Irrigating the soil along the Nile Banks by means of the "Shaduf."
Arabs scrambling for Bakshish (coins) at Edfu.

The Temple of Horus at Edfu

Begun by Ptolemy in 237 B.C. The best preserved ruin in Egypt.
A Characteristic Street Scene, Khartoum.[9]

The series contrasted the exotic primitiveness of Egyptian life with the
technological prowess of the English. An Arab wedding procession passed
in front of a British hotel. An ancient Egyptian water wheel and traditional irrigation system were counterposed to Aswan Dam as shown from
a moving train. One review suggested the impact of *From Cairo to Khartoum*:

> The Sphinx loomed up in all its grandeur with the Pyramids in the back-
> ground, and the various temples and ruins were brought before the audience
> better than any photograph could attempt to do. A wonderful bit of engi-
> neering skill was shown in a picture of the immense dam built at the base of
> the Dau which has just been completed. A solid stone wall over a hundred
> feet high and wide enough at the top for two horsemen to ride abreast shows
> the magnitude of the undertaking. This dam is three miles long and was built
> by the natives under the direction of English engineers.[10]

Although also a monument like the pyramids, the dam served a utilitarian
purpose. Obviously, the British had not only replaced the pharaohs as
master builders; they offered a superior form of civilization. Egyptians were
shown to benefit from the British presence, while European civilization
enjoyed the otherness of Africa, made safe for tourists by colonial rule.
The camera both confirmed colonial rule and extended it, subjugating the
Egyptian countryside, transforming it into a commodity that Europeans
and Americans could enjoy and consume. Through selection, narration,
and cinematic organization, these images were made to tell a tale of English glory. These were British possessions, photographed by Englishmen,
and presented by an Anglophile.

The same theme was apparent in *The Coronation Durbar at Delhi, India*,
also shown by the first company. Program notes informed readers that this
coronation of Edward VII as emperor of India was "the most gorgeous
pageant of Oriental splendor ever witnessed in modern times. Hundreds
of magnificently caparisoned elephants decorated with the wealth of India
including jewels and precious stones are seen in this grand procession of
barbaric splendor."[11] Such films placed Howe in the long-standing debate

over imperialism and isolationism that preoccupied the American people and Congress up through World War II. Howe was an admirer of President Theodore Roosevelt and his activist, interventionist foreign policy. For both men, England provided a model of internationalist vigor. This ideological perspective, which can be traced back to earlier programs on the Spanish-American War, became steadily more pronounced in Howe's programs, reaching its height in his pre–World War I exhibitions.

Howe's representations of the British colonies (including an Edison view of native women loading bananas onto a ship in Jamaica) were interspersed throughout a program designed to reassure his audience. The barbarians had been domesticated, and western culture reigned triumphant. A few scenic views of the United States lacked the exoticism of distant locales, but *A Canoe Flotilla on the Charles River near Boston* evoked the easy self-confidence of a warm afternoon. *Snoqueline Falls, Near Seattle* emphasized the country's size and natural grandeur. All was well with the world as it went about its daily activities, whether sheep farming in Scotland, yacht racing on the ocean, or pole-vaulting at Columbia. Lest reassurance evoke boredom, short comedies such as *A Non-Union Paper Hanger* (the incompetent paperhanger does a terrible job) and *The Burglar-Proof Bed* (when a burglar breaks into a bedroom, the potential victim converts his bed into a heavily-gunned fortress and literally blows the thief into oblivion) provided relief. Thrills were provided by *The Georgetown Loop, Colorado* ("Look out for the curves. Hold fast."), along with the assurance that danger always had its happy ending (*A Thrilling Rescue Scene at Atlantic City*). Science and magic films (*In the Realm of Mystery—Visible Phenomenal Growth* and *The Human Fly*) tested the spectators' sense of limits and affirmed the powers of technology, particularly that of motion pictures. Nothing was allowed to interfere with this comfortable, white, middle-class view, which found pleasure in the world's diversity and its certainty. The program was well received and financially rewarding.

FALL 1903: THE HADLEY-HOWE RIVALRY

Howe's staff assumed a new shape with Hadley's defection. For the fall 1903 tour, Howe found an experienced operator to take Hadley's place and now had two: Will C. Smith, who had previously run projecting machines for traveling road shows, and Russell Blake, who would remain with Howe longer than any other projectionist.[12] When lecturer and effects specialist E. George Hedden exited with Hadley, LeRoy Carleton was the replacement. Carleton became an important part of Howe's organization, for he "at once showed remarkable ability in infusing life and realism in every scene and incident depicted on the screen. . . . His native wit and ingenuity enabled him to recognize the possibilities of imparting life instantly to every picture, and this originality combined with his rare skill in imitations made him distinctly a master of his chosen profession."[13] Earlier, Walkinshaw's contract had been renewed for the 1903–1904 and 1904–1905 seasons at a salary of sixty dollars per week.[14]

Howe also acquired improved projectors from Charles Urban, who had left the Warwick Trading Company in early 1903 and formed the London-based Charles Urban Trading Company. One of the new company's innovations was the Urban bioscope projector with a three-blade shutter that dramatically reduced the flicker that plagued early motion picture exhibitions. Many of Howe's new films were in hand-tinted color. They were twice as expensive as black-and-white films, but the showman could justify the cost by amortizing the purchases over two semiannual tours.

Howe's new fall program favored longer story films, which had become very popular and were being adopted by urban exhibition services:[15]

Presenting the **Most Marvelous Moving Pictures in the World.**

Not One Dull Minute | **An Entirely New Program**

OUR NEW MECHANISM

IS A REVELATION IN PROJECTING MACHINES

NO FLICKER!
NO VIBRATION!

After years of experience we are now able to present an exhibition that is without a peer.

An Absolutely New Feature.

MOVING PICTURES

IN THE COLORS OF NATURE.

LYMAN H. HOWE,	Sole Owner and Mgr.
F. E. WILLSON	Business Mgr.
D. B. WILLSON	Musical Director
WILL C. SMITH	Electrician and Operator
C. R. BOSWORTH	Booking Agent

For Information regarding Engagements, Dates, Terms, Etc., Address,
LYMAN H. HOWE,
PERMANENT ADDRESS 387 SOUTH RIVER ST.,
WILKES-BARRE, PA.

7-3. From a program (fall 1903).

As we are constantly adding new pictures of notable events whenever they occur, this program is subject to change.

A Scene at England's Coney Island—(Brighton).

Branding Colts in Colorado.

Scenes at Midnight with the Aid of a Policeman's Dark Lantern.

King Edward of England and President Loubet of France—*Entering their Carriage at Vincennes.*

A French Compartment Car Episode—"No Smoking Allowed."

Acrobatic Burglars and Policemen.

Panorama of the Exterior, Interior and Shrines of the "Shwe" Dagon— *The Most Sacred Pagoda in Burma, India.*

Man's Best Friend—*Prize Winners at the New York Dog Show.*

One of Uncle Sam's Formidable Arguments.

The Queen's Musketeers.

Battle with Snow Balls.

How Willie was Jammed.

A Sensational Ride on the Front of an Express Train—*Through the Picturesque Frazer River Canon, Rocky Mountains.*

OVERTURE

A GRAND HISTORICAL SERIES IN COLORS

THE RISE AND FALL OF NAPOLEON THE GREAT.

Scene   1. Napoleon at the Military School.
  "   2. The Battle of the Bridge of Arcola.
  "   3. Napoleon in Egypt.
  "   4. Crossing the Alps.—The Great St. Bernard.
  "   5. Napoleon at Home.—The Summer Fete at the Chateau of Malmaison.
  "   6. The Coronation of Napoleon and Marie Louise.
  "   7. The Battle of Austerlitz.—Napoleon Watching the Battle.
  "   8. The Sentinel Asleep.
  "   9. Napoleon Wounded at the Battle of Ratisbon.
  "   10. The Emperor's Library. The Infant King of Rome.
  "   11. The Great Fire of Moscow.
  "   12. The Departure from Fontainebleau.
  "   13. Battle of Waterloo.—The Fall of the Eagle.
  "   14. St. Helena.—Death of the Emperor.
  "   15. Grand Allegorical Apotheosis.—The Past and Future. Universal Peace!

Scenes in a Canadian logging camp.

Reception of Naval and Military officers and diplomats at Algiers.

The refractory collar—(*The sterner sex will appreciate this.*)

Rube and Cynthia seeing the sights of Coney Island.

The poachers.

OVERTURE.

THE MYSTERIOUS BOX.

The giants and pigmies—*Or the land of the Lilliputians.*
Novel coasting—*Rounding the Curve, also the Dangerous Pastime of Jump-*
  ing into space from a Raised Platform.
"I want my dinner."
Well! Well! Well!—*The Magic well.*
Comedy in an enchanted bed chamber.
                                      Goodnight. [16]

Howe's featured subject was Pathé's historical drama *The Rise and Fall of
Napoleon*, which lasted over twenty minutes. "The Napoleon series," one
critic wrote, "is intensely interesting to the student of history." [17] *Rube and
Cynthia Seeing the Sights of Coney Island* (original title: *Rube and Mandy's
Visit to Coney Island*) showed fictional characters moving through the
landscape of the nation's foremost amusement park. One is struck that
Methodist church groups so readily accepted this long (725-foot) subject
that so effectively promoted what they were actively forbidding. One selection, *The Poachers* (made in England and originally titled *A Desperate
Poaching Affray*), was filled with sensationalistic violence completely un-
characteristic of Howe's usual bill of fare. Perhaps because it was one of
the cinema's first chase films, it proved an irresistible choice. Its exterior
locations may have also given it a documentary feel. Shorter films like
Biograph's *I Want My Dinner*, showing a screaming child in his highchair,
recalled Howe's recording of a crying baby that proved so popular in the
early 1890s. The only real news film, *King Edward of England and President
Loubet of France*, was hand-tinted but only two minutes long. [18] The headline attraction on Napoleon thus reinforced Howe's image of respectability while less advertised subjects provided the spice.

   The response to Howe's program, as evidenced by fragmentary information, was somewhat less impressive than in the past. [19] Howe's first company suffered slight box-office declines, caused primarily by increased
competition from rival exhibitors. His second company, however, had become more popular and profitable on its second tour even though it relied
on previously used films. Many selections were from the first company's
newly retired repertoire but others were from at least four earlier programs.
In addition, Howe assigned the company a handful of new pictures that
were being used by showmen like Edwin Hadley, who was directly competing with the first unit. [20]

EDWIN HADLEY'S UNEXCELLED HIGH-CLASS
MOVING PICTURES

Hadley was one of the main reasons for the first company's difficulties.
Although Howe had predicted that his former operator would encounter

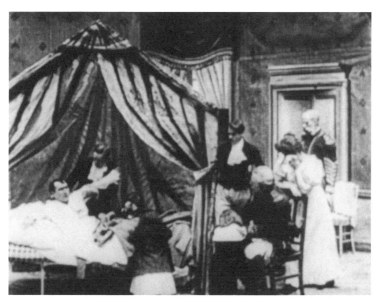

7-4a,b. *Rise and Fall of Napoleon the Great* (1903).

7-5a,b. *Rube and Cynthia Seeing the Sights at Coney Island* (1903). Despite Howe's new title, they do not simply "see the sights," they enthusiastically participate in the discovery of this unfamiliar amusement world.

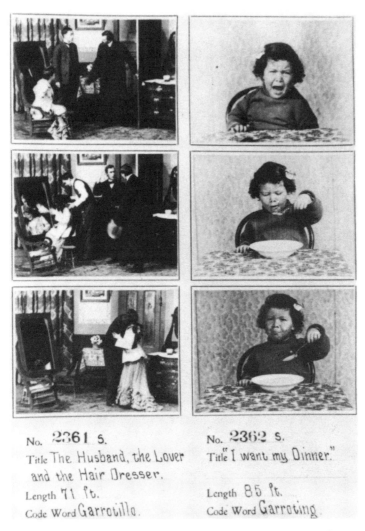

No. 2361 s.
Title The Husband, the Lover and the Hair Dresser.
Length 71 ft.
Code Word Garrotille.

No. 2362 s.
Title "I want my Dinner."
Length 85 ft.
Code Word Garroting.

7-6. Biograph's *I Want My Dinner* (1903) provided continuity of subject matter from Howe's days as a phonograph exhibitor, when a baby's cry amused audiences. The other film pictured here is the kind that Howe never showed.

only trouble if he started his own show, Hadley's timing proved to be perfect. In a manner reminiscent of Frank Percy, Hadley not only modeled his shows after Howe's, he tried to assume his identity. He sought to convince his clientele that Howe's exhibitions had really been his—and featured ex-Howe personnel to strengthen his contention. He hired away E. George Hedden and billed him as a "Society Entertainer and Lecturer," while Clarance S. Weiss, Howe's first advance representative, assumed the same role for Hadley. Hadley's choice of films was similar to Howe's and were often accompanied with realistic sound effects.[21]

Vicious and often petty battles erupted between the two exhibitors. During the 1903–1904 season, Hadley's promotional material and ads emphasized his former connection with Howe. As someone informed Howe, "He uses your name in his advertisements to increase his box office receipts and he knows it, as he has his name 'Hadley' in small type and your name in large type to deceive. We all know that when a person glances at a lithograph or card with your name in large attractive type, and the Hadley name hidden to a certain extent that it is liable to make one think the original Howe show is billed."[22] Hadley even paid for column space in a Pennsylvania newspaper to taunt his former employer:

7-7. A poster advertising Edwin S. Hadley's show in Wilkes-Barre, October 7, 1903.

Asks Comparison
Claims His Moving Picture Show Has No Equal

A certain exhibitor revelled for a number of years in the thought that he had a monopoly of the moving picture business. This he practically had because Edwin J. Hadley, the expert, was associated with him, but now his monopoly is a shattered idol, as the man whose experience stamps him as the acknowledged pioneer, is no longer associated with him, but presents his own America's Greatest moving picture exhibition.

Mr. Hadley defies Lyman H. Howe to prove that he (Mr. Hadley) is not doing business legitimately, and the only use he has for Lyman H. Howe's name is to establish the fact that for many years he was the one upon whose abilities the success or failure of satisfactory exhibitions depended.[23]

Howe responded by advertising his own program as "America's Greatest Exhibition of Moving Pictures" and declaring that "all others are dull tiresome imitations."[24]

Hadley not only played the same towns as Howe but whenever possible preceded his former employer. He exhibited at the Music Hall in Troy, New York, under the auspices of the Troy Police Beneficial and Protective Association on September 18; Howe did not not appear there until October 29.[25] Having beaten Howe to Gloversville, New York, Hadley gleefully wrote his former employer,

Dear Sir:

I am assisting you in advertising that Lyman H. Howe's exhibition will appear later.

The best advertisement I ever had.

Yours Truly,
Edwin J. Hadley[26]

Many theater managers who regularly presented Howe's exhibitions at first refused to cooperate with Hadley. When Hadley showed films in Johnstown, Pennsylvania (1900 population: 35,936), on December 7, he did so at the high school. Howe appeared there two weeks later but at his traditional venue, the local commercial theater.

When Hadley invaded Wilkes-Barre itself, on October 7, he beat his former employer by over a month. Unable to play the Nesbitt, Hadley performed at the Armory under the auspices of John Knox Commandry, Knights of Malta, recreating the circumstances of Howe's record-breaking 1901 exhibition.[27] According to the program, Hadley's show was "the most perfect exhibition" of "unexcelled high-class moving pictures from the most perfect and costly machine ever constructed."[28] The *Wilkes-Barre News* reported, "Hadley's exhibition of moving pictures at the Armory Wednesday evening surpassed the rosiest anticipations of the management. The drill-room floor was completely filled by a refined, cultured and appreciative audience. Each number was received with well-deserved applause."[29] Even the *Wilkes-Barre Record* declared Hadley's exhibition to be "well worth seeing."[30] Although Hadley was soon playing in the same theaters as Howe, theatrical manangers often insisted that he follow rather than precede his former employer. Thus Hadley exhibited at Reading's Academy of Music in May 1904—exactly a month after Howe had been there.[31] By March 1906, Hadley was playing even Wilkes-Barre's Nesbitt Theater.

Hadley, like Howe, had adopted the three-blade shutter for his projector, sharply reducing the flicker that plagued early motion picture exhibitions. In towns where he exhibited prior to Howe, Hadley received the credit for introducing this important innovation and could therefore cite many reviews declaring his exhibitions superior to Howe's, at least in this one respect. According to the *Amsterdam Recorder*, "Last evening the Hadley Moving Picture Company gave a performance of a most satisfactory nature. Mr. Hadley was formerly in charge of Mr. Howe's machine when he exhibited here, but in the almost complete oblivation of that ceaseless blur as the result of a new improvement on his machine, Mr. Hadley has succeeded in going Mr. Howe one better." In Warren, Pennsylvania (1900 population: 8,043), the local paper simply called Hadley's moving picture show "the best."[32] Introducing this innovation was invaluable in helping Hadley establish his show on a profitable basis.

Vengeful feelings toward Howe often spurred Hadley's activities. Hadley sought to harm or inconvenience his former employer by purchasing a hand-tinted copy of *The Rise and Fall of Napoleon*. Howe was forced to make up an alternate reel of subjects that could be substituted wherever Hadley's show had preceded his own.[33] Although Hadley's determined effort to imitate both Howe's programs and his exhibition circuit inconvenienced Howe and hurt him financially, it hardly ruined him. Yet neither man typified the new breed of showmen who came to the fore in the 1903 period.

Archie Shepard and the New Picture Shows

As the traveling exhibition field rapidly expanded during 1903–1905, most new shows catered to people who enjoyed commercial, urban, popular amusement. In this respect Archie L. Shepard, who put a moving picture show on the road in the fall of 1903, quickly became the leading figure. He was the only showman to rival Howe in scope and ambition over the following five years. During the 1901–1902 and 1902–1903 seasons, Shepard traveled with the Maude Hillman Stock Company and presented motion pictures between acts of plays.[34] When Shepard struck out on his own, he took Franklin A. Batie, another member of Maude Hillman's company, with him. Shepard began by building a circuit in eastern Massachusetts, Connecticut, Rhode Island, New Hampshire, and Maine. He and Howe often showed in the same town, but their styles of exhibition were quite different.

Shepard did not have formal semiannual tours like Howe. He bought films as quickly as they came out and added them to his exhibitions. A fall 1903 program featured Méliès's *A Trip to the Moon* and *Little Red Riding Hood*, Edison's *Life of an American Fireman*, Biograph's *Rip Van Winkle*, scenes of the Durbar in Delhi, and travel films of Egypt, China, Japan, and Italy. Lubin's *The Holy City* was shown with "Franklyn A. Batie, California's Greatest Baritone," singing in accompaniment.[35] By late 1903, Shepard had added Edison's *The Great Train Robbery* to his collection.[36] Within a few months he claimed to have over twenty thousand feet of film and a completely new program that included *Jack Shepard; or, the Stage Coach Robbery*, *Marie Antoinette; or, the Fall of the Bastille*, *The Salmon Fishing Industry*, *A Week with a Honey Bee*, and *Hiawatha*, performed by the Ojibway Tribe.[37] Edison's *Buster Brown Series* and *Life Savers at Work* were added to his repertoire in March 1904, shortly after their release. When he remained in town for several days, Shepard often rotated the films in his collection. Exhibiting in Lewiston, Maine (1900 population: 23,761), he presented afternoon matinees for children with special films such as *Gulliver's Travels*, *Fairyland*, and *Beauty and the Beast*. For his two evening performances, he presented more recent headline attractions.[38]

Shepard situated himself in the mainstream of urban, commercialized, popular culture. Although he offered actualities, Shepard increasingly featured the kinds of sensational, melodramatic films that were to appear in the first nickelodeons. From the beginning he showed in commercial theaters and did not rely on sponsorship by local organizations. He gave Sunday concerts, which Howe had always avoided lest he alienate local churches. Between reels of films, Shepard offered illustrated songs rather than piano overtures. Evening admission to his two-hour show was also more modest: ten, twenty, and thirty cents. Occasionally the best seats went for fifty cents, but Shepard's High-Class Moving Pictures were geared toward a somewhat different audience than Howe's. Patrons were more likely to be working class and less constrained by religious scruples in their enjoyment of amusement.

Shepard's High-Class Moving Pictures visited towns more frequently than Howe's companies. During the first three months of 1904, Shepard made three separate visits to the Empire Theater (1,480 seats) in Lewiston, Maine, and gave fourteen shows over seven days.[39] Once he had established himself in a town, it was hard for rivals to exhibit without repeating many of the same subjects. Shepard's methods proved so successful that he added a second company in late January 1904 and a third in February. Throughout the 1903–1904 season, however, Shepard continued to travel with his first company. Within a few months he had more units on the road than Howe.

Other exhibitors addressed similar kinds of audiences but maintained single-company road shows. Morgan and Hoyt's Moving Picture Company may have played clubs and nontheatrical venues for several years prior to 1903. Then it claimed to have "broken away from all the old-time traditions of the picture business and introduced some decided innovations. Among the first was the addition of a ladies' band and orchestra; then followed the engaging of Rose Katherine Hawkins, America's gifted whistling soloist; G. Theo. Girard and Little Willie Kelly in the latest illustrated songs are a recent acquisition."[40] The company gave frequent Sunday concerts and exhibited without local sponsorship. Primarily active in New York State and New England, it was managed by A. S. Anthony, a long-standing purveyor of amusements.[41]

England's Moving Pictures, which started out in the fall of 1903, was owned by F. M. Hook and James G. England of Zanesville, Ohio (1900 population: 23,538). England managed the local Weller's Theatre and Schultz Opera House. Neither man traveled with the show but rather sent it out under the direction of Fred Hilton.[42] Exhibiting in New York, Ohio and neighboring states, the company featured *The Great Train Robbery* early in 1904.[43] The fall 1904 program was called an "Indoor Circus" and included

> the elephants shooting the chutes, the diving and boxing horses, with a third horse for the referee, and the ride on a phantom train, seated on the cow-catcher of the engine, where you are whirled dizzily and enchantingly through the most picturesque territory in Uncle Sam's domain. Then too, as an eminently proper relief from the circus views, Nick Russell, the human pianola, as he is known here and in the east, gives a 'musical stunt' that was never excelled. Tonight's performance was arranged for the especial benefit of business men and clerks.[44]

In the Midwest numerous motion picture showmen became active. Ben and Myrtle Huntley left Oshkosh, Wisconsin, in 1903 to start what soon became known as the Huntley Entertainers.[45] The show toured Wisconsin, Minnesota, and Iowa, stopping each time for a few days at places like Hilbert (1900 population: 497), Hortonville (1900 population: 913), Waupaca (1900 population: 2,912), and Marshfield (1900 population: 5,240).[46] During the summer of 1904, the Huntleys purchased a copy of Lubin's *The Great Train Robbery*, an imitation of Edison's popular hit of the same title. Its cost of sixty-six dollars compared favorably with the Edison Company's 110-dollar price tag. Huntley was pleased, informing

Lubin, "I do not regret the investment a moment, as the Film draws the crowd."[47] During the spring of 1906 they featured *San Francisco Earthquake* (1906) and a lecture on the Panama Canal.[48]

Ben Huntley operated the projectors while Myrtle Huntley sang illustrated songs. Their company included two or three other performers, for example Donald Ax Jonson, who received board plus $1 a day. Admission was a dime. During 1906 the Huntleys made between $70.50 and $251.50 a week, though most weeks fell in the 110-160 dollar range. A fair day's gate was twenty-five to thirty dollars. Even on the best of nights, they never brought in more than fifty dollars—except on July 4 ($112.40) and Christmas ($59.75). Money was often tight and financial reserves small. Writing her ill mother, Myrtle explained:

> I will send $5.00 but you need only say you received the $2.00. I have some of my own from Songbooks. And I know you will need it. Ben would send more but this town is a total loss rain every night is raining now. And he got himself two pair of shoes, one pair pattent leather for stage and the

7-8a. Ben Huntley at the projector (ca. 1905).

7-8b. Myrtle Huntley, a soubrette, sang illustrated songs between reels of film (ca. 1905).

other pair for St.—But any time you need money or want to come wire us and you will get it quick.

Had about three doz prints of kodak films made here and some large photos printed here that we must pay for. Exp[ense] of box Ben made painting trunks, etc : all counts up. $5.00 per day board here for Co. So you will understand Mamma we are not "stingy" Have $100 in my little sack yet that we don't want to touch if we can help it.[49]

Their total financial reserves were less than the cost of a single reel of new film.

The Dodge-Bowman Amusement Company originated from Quincy, Illinois, and operated on a somewhat more luxurious scale. Active by early 1904, the group interspersed a few small vaudeville acts between films and traveled through Iowa, Illinois, and Indiana. Their films included *The Great Train Robbery, The Gambler's Crime, The Corbett-McGovern Prize Fight,* and *Personal,* a popular Biograph comedy in which a horde of American working-class women answer a "personal ad" placed by a French count who wants a rich American bride. The women chase the small fellow over fields and streams in the hopes of marrying a titled gentleman. The Dodge-Bowman company gave frequent Sunday shows; their ten- to thirty-cent admission fee would have encouraged a working-class clientele.[50]

Many other companies were on the road, seeking to satisfy the growing desire for moving pictures. The Ireland Brothers, who had been in Canada in late 1903, offered vaudeville and moving pictures to residents of Iowa and Illinois during the following spring. As the field became more crowded, they took their show to South America.[51] Sherman's Moving Pictures, which played in New England from 1903 to 1905, and the Colonial Moving Picture Company, which toured the Midwest, had been around since at least 1901. Newcomers who started business in the Northeast in 1904 were usually relegated to quite small towns. Raymond's Moving Pictures was exhibiting in Pennsylvania localities like Emmanus (1900 population: 1,464), Downington (1900 population: 2,133) and Pottstown (population: 13,696). These companies helped to establish the audiences that later frequented the small, storefront motion picture theaters where one or two reels of film could be seen for a nickel.

Not every exhibitor benefited from the boom; those failing to adjust to rapidly changing circumstances often experienced unexpected trouble. Dibble, who avoided ladies' orchestras and *The Great Train Robbery,* encountered particular difficulties. Nor did he concern himself with technological improvements like the three-blade shutter. (At least his advertisements and promotional blurbs did not mention a new flickerless image.) In Hartford, he was confronted by S. Z. Poli's new vaudeville house, which opened in September 1903 and regularly featured motion pictures on its bill. In addition, two other Hartford theaters began to offer Sunday motion picture concerts. Although Dibble's former two-week engagements had become outmoded and inappropriate, he nevertheless returned to Hartford in March 1904 for his customary two-week stand, with disastrous results. With Shepard and other showmen visiting cities more frequently, Dibble's single annual visits proved dismal failures. His annual program change had become inadequate. Many factors, therefore, caused Dibble's circuit to collapse at the end of his seventh, 1903–1904 season. Although he remained active as a show manager through at least 1910, he exhibited under more marginal circumstances.[52]

Those who continued to ply the Lyceum and church circuit were more insulated from these competitive pressures. D. W. Robertson took timely advantage of the increased interest in moving pictures by starting additional units that covered the same basic territory as his original company. Given the lack of documentation, it is impossible to trace the moment and methods he chose to form new companies, but his process must have paralleled Howe's and Shepard's. When one of his Edison Projectoscope companies played Norwalk, Connecticut (1900 population: 19,932), in the fall of 1904, Robertson was no longer traveling with it. The company was also more elaborate, consisting of four men: "John Forsman, the great comedian entertainer, vocalist and dancer, with Harry Willard, America's greatest piccolo-banjoist and mandolinist; Howard D. Argoe, musical director and accompanist," and a projectionist.[53] His headline attraction was either Biograph's hit comedy *The Escaped Lunatic* or an Edison imitation. Robertson's success suggests that the church-oriented sector continued to expand, although not with the gusto of shows presenting commercial amusement.

Expansion did not occur within the erudite-lecture field. During the 1903–1904 season at the Brooklyn Institute, only Elmendorf and Holmes illustrated their talks with moving pictures. Others relied solely on stereopticon slides, often from negatives they had taken themselves.[54]

HOWE RESPONDS TO COMPETITIVE PRESSURES

To maintain his distinct identity, Howe searched for subjects unlikely to be shown by his competitors. For his 1904 spring tour, his companies did not show Méliès's *The Fairyland* or Edison's *The Great Train Robbery*. Frequently acquired by other exhibitors, they would have disappointed many audience members who had already seen them. Howe instead favored films that were less available or less obviously popular. He selected Méliès' short magic films rather than his more ambitious fairy tales, and European subjects more often than domestic productions. Three European story films were shown by the first company on its spring program: *An Up-to-*

Date Elopement, made by British Gaumont and copyrighted in the United States as *A Runaway Match; Thrilling Incidents in the Capture of a Daring Highway Man*, originally sold by the Urban Trading Company as *Robbery of the Mail Coach*; and *The Deserter*.

Howe's spring 1904 tour moved away from the ideology of reassurance. Children outwit their parents and elope. Mail coaches are held up even if the culprit is finally captured. Even Howe's American-made "feature," *The Buster Brown Series*, titled by Howe *Buster Brown and His Dog*, reveal the persistent unsocialized behavior of a young boy. Howe wavered, uncertain about the identity (and authorship) of his shows. Although this detour into the world of sex and violence soon proved brief, it suggests the extent to which this new type of story film and the correspondingly new type of showman challenged his cinema of reassurance.

Howe's uncertainty was partially masked by his novel, headline attraction, *The Unseen World*, composed of four early science films acquired from the Charles Urban Trading Company, which had become Howe's principal film supplier:

THE UNSEEN WORLD
MAGNIFIED STUDIES IN NATURAL HISTORY

A Drop of Water

Taking test water from pond, examination in laboratory; wonderful microscopic study of a drop of water magnified 2,920,000 diameters.

Cheese Mites

The busy inhabitants of a speck of Stilton cheese magnified 2,000,000 diameters.

"The Busy Bee"

Capturing a swarm of Bees from a tree; Bees entering and flying about the hive; Bees drinking honey; Bees removing an obstruction in front of hive; smoking out bees from hive into basket; general view of the bee farm; Brood Comb, with Queen and workers busily engaged depositing honey into cells, etc.

The Frog's Dinner

A novel and interesting study of Reptile life.[55]

These films opened up "an entirely new field in the line of instructive entertainment" and astonished Howe's audiences.[56] Spectators saw a "toad as large as [an] elephant!"[57]

As happened with increasing frequency, Howe's company found itself with direct competition one evening in April 1904. The Chicago Novelty Company was featuring "Moving Pictures and High-Class Vaudeville" at Reading's 1,025-seat Temple Theater. The advertised attractions were

The Great Train Robbery and *Life of an American Fireman.* Announcements claimed that this latter film showed scenes of Pennsylvania fire departments—a false statement designed to woo customers.[58] Meanwhile, Howe was playing at his regular venue, the Academy of Music. Despite the competition, more than 2,100 people attended Howe's show on the first day, while income for his two-day stand totaled $973.45.[59] Not only did he outdraw the Chicago Novelty Company, but people who saw *The Great Train Robbery* on one day could attend Howe's show on the next and see completely different films. As the number of exhibitors continued to grow, so the film-going audience was increasing in size and frequency of attendance.

LOCAL VIEWS: HOWE ACQUIRES A CAMERA

As the traveling exhibition field became more profitable, yet more competitive, some exhibitors acquired their own cameras and took local views. Here again, Howe was in the vanguard. On his 1903 summer trip to Europe, the showman acquired "the pick of the world's best cameras."[60] The exhibition of *Employees Leaving the Factory of Cluett, Peabody & Co.* may have convinced him that production capabilities could be financially justified. The first account of actual filming appeared in March 1904, when Howe photographed floods engulfing the Wyoming Valley. On March 9 "Lyman Howe employed the Auto Machine Repair Co.'s large auto . . . and went up and down the street taking moving pictures of the flood."[61] By the time his company played at the Nesbitt on April 9, these films were in the program. Calling Wilkes-Barre the "Venice of America," Howe offered two views: "A Scene looking out Academy Street towards Carey Avenue," and "C. L. Davis and his big Automobile. A scene on South Street."[62] The morning newspaper devoted much of its review to detailing the scenes: "Two local scenes dealing with the late high water were shown. One was a view of South River street showing horses and carriages driving through the water up to the axles of the vehicles. The other was taken at Academy street, looking toward Carey avenue. This showed the men and boys in their wading boots with a number of boats and canoes taking the people from their houses to places of safety."[63] The views stayed on the program for the remainder of the company's tour; the flood was of general interest, having attracted ten thousand tourists from Scranton, Hazleton, and other sections of northeastern Pennsylvania.[64] In Reading the films were pronounced "especially fine."[65]

This filming pointed toward two interrelated developments in Howe's work. First, the showman reestablished his ability to make subjects of his choosing, which he had essentially surrendered when he gave up the phonograph six years earlier. This did not mean a return to the operational aesthetic, whereby the whole process of filmmaking was laid out for the spectator. Such an approach did not concern Howe, as it did some other traveling showmen. Rather, it enabled Howe to offer exclusive subjects and so gain a commercial advantage over his competitors. He developed this capacity, moreover, as established production companies, particularly in America, were concentrating more and more of their resources on fictional story films. These companies would have only filmed the flood on a commission basis, and the logistics would have made filming costly and perhaps impossible. With production capabilities, Howe could sharpen the distinction between his programming and the rising tide of sensational and risqué story films.

Second, production capabilities enabled Howe to present Wilkes-Barre to itself and to audiences in other cities. This gave Howe a new authority and enhanced his stature in the Wilkes-Barre business community as the city's goodwill ambassador, the man who made his hometown a visual reality. The Wilkes-Barre flood and the Baltimore fire both appeared on Howe's spring 1904 program with equivalent importance. Proven worthy of cinematic attention, Wilkes-Barre gained in prestige among its neighboring cities and towns. Wilkes-Barre citizens, anxious about their city's future, were given visual reassurances of a very particular kind.[66]

Howe took his next film, *The Wilkes-Barre, Pa., Crack Fire Department Responding to a General Alarm*, in September 1904. It was designed to "form a unique and forceful advertisement of Wilkes-Barre" with a heroic image of the entire city fire department racing down a prominent thoroughfare in fine frenzy. "The keen, alert, determined facial expression of every member—the wild dash of every steamer, truck and horse cart; the spick and span and sleek horses imbued with the same spirit, with the splendid background afforded by the fine trees and residences of South River street all contribute to what promises to be the finest moving picture of its kind ever taken anywhere."[67] It was characteristic of local views to present positive images that would attract, not alienate, paying hometown customers.[68]

Howe did not use local views as a systematic commercial strategy to spur patronage on his circuits, which were already well established. But in 1904 and 1905, at least two moving picture companies, both late arrivals in the field of traveling exhibition, made local views a central element in their programming. The most prominent was American Vitagraph, which had built a strong position in vaudeville exhibition.[69] As early as 1904, Vitagraph put four shows on the road, preceding each with a cameraman. This special "advanced representative" took local scenes and built up interest in the forthcoming exhibition.[70]

One of Vitagraph's road shows traveled through Connecticut. In Oc-

tober, just prior to a two-day exhibition in Norwalk, publicity announcements such as the following encouraged local residents to attend:

Moving Picture Show

"O wad the power some giftee gie us
To see ourselves as others see us."

When the great scotch poet wrote the above lines, he had no idea that his
wish would ever be gratified. Thanks, however, to the invention of the vitagraph, the impossible is now made possible. Realizing the popularity of local
scenes, the American Vitagraph company have fitted out a special photographic corps to take moving pictures in every town and city where the popular vitagraph concerts are being produced. You can see pictures of your very
own town, your very own fire department, and what is more, you can see
yourself in life motion pictures at the vitagraph concert, Friday and Saturday,
October 7 and 8 at Hoyt's Theatre.[71]

The cameraman did not reach New Britain, Connecticut (1900 population: 28,202), where Howe's company regularly presented its programs,
until late November. Prior to his arrival, the local theater manager announced that films would be taken of several familiar scenes. Town residents were then told, "If there are any other subjects in the New Britain
line which anyone may think would make a suitable moving picture, one
that would be novel and entertaining to other audiences, Manager Lynch
would be pleased to have it suggested to him before the expert comes."[72]
The making of the films became an event in which the whole community
happily participated. It was supervised by the theater manager and endorsed by city officials who posed for a scene:

Fire Department Pictures

Photographs Taken Today for Manager Lynch

The fire department was photographed today in Commercial street for the
purpose of having slides [sic] made for exhibition at the Russwin Lyceum.
Manager Lynch had the photographer in charge. Mayor Bassett, Chief Raw-
lings, City Clerk Thompson and other city officials appear in the picture.
Alderman Landers passed in his automobile and was caught in the picture.[73]

Scenes were modeled after subject types first popular in the 1890s: two
thousand employees leaving the P. and F. Corbin Hardware Factory at
noon-time, a fire run, students exiting the parochial school after hours,
and a fire drill at one of the public schools. Again, publicity urged residents to "see yourself as others see you."[74] If Vitagraph's intent was profit
oriented, its method was to encourage local residents to participate in all
phases of the film process. The advance sale for these exhibitions was
enormous, justifying a return date later that winter, at which Vitagraph
showed the same local views accompanied by a new group of pictures.[75]

For Vitagraph and Howe, community control over the production of local scenes was important. These pressures differed markedly from those on cameramen making travel films such as the Egyptian series or *The Wild Men of Borneo,* which appeared on Howe's spring 1904 program. Although Wilkes-Barreans did not formally sanction Howe to represent their city's daily life and newsworthy events, the assumption of this power by a native son, rather than by some outsider, served as a guarantee of sympathetic imagery. Only a fellow resident would have so carefully selected a wealthy neighborhood as background for a film of the fire department. In contrast, the Borneo films acquired through Charles Urban were intended to explain the operations of England's North Borneo Company and to show "in this entertaining way the beautiful scenery of North Borneo and its commercial riches."[76] Routinely celebrating western imperialism, such travel films were made by outsiders for outsiders. The point was not for Borneo natives to see themselves on the screen. Local views and travel views existed in dialectical opposition to each other, but within a single practice based in a few industrialized nations.

Howe Forms a Third Company

Howe failed to expand his business as rapidly as conditions warranted, perhaps not only because of his own conservative instincts but because of a sustained illness. Howe's knee problem did not improve. Even while forming his second company, he was not altogether well. In early February 1903 Hadley solicitously ended an otherwise argumentative letter, "Trusting again that the operation on your knee will be a success and that you will regain your health."[77] Howe had the operation later that month and remained at Philadelphia's Presbyterian Hospital into May.[78] He was back in the hospital by April 1904 for five more months of knee operations and henceforth endured a pronounced limp.[79]

In the spring of 1904, while still in the hospital, Howe began to form a third company. Walkinshaw, who had assumed the role of general manager and remained in Wilkes-Barre, advertised for a first-class press agent, distributor, piano player, operator and experienced business manager. The ad suggested that Howe would then have four companies, outshining Shepard.[80] Walkinshaw was preparing for the fall season, hoping to hire key personnel who might tour with an established company before taking responsibility for the new show. By September Howe had three active companies.[81]

The Howe Moving Picture Company had many new members. Certainly it is difficult to track these employees: their names, when they were hired, when they left, the positions they held, and the companies with which they worked. Yet even a tentative assessment provides insight into

WANTED, FOR

THE LYMAN H. HOWE

MOVING PICTURE CO.,

NORTHERN

EASTERN

SOUTHERN

WESTERN

EXPERIENCED

BUSINESS MANAGER

WHO CAN FURNISH BOND.

Must have fine stage presence and good voice, to give brief lectures. A capable, refined man, with ability, who is not afraid of work, and willing to accept a reasonable salary, with expenses, can obtain a three or five year engagement, with sure money.

WILL ALSO REQUIRE a First Class PRESS AGENT, DISTRIBUTOR, PIANO PLAYER and OPERATOR.

STATE SALARY, AGE AND FULL INFORMATION IN FIRST LETTER.

Address   S. M. WILKINSHAW, General Manager.

387 So. River Street, WILKESBARRE, PA.

7-9. Advertisement in the *New York Clipper*, May 7, 1904.

the company's activities and one small portion of the motion picture industry. By 1904–1905, Howe had an office staff of five. Harry Manhart had been his secretary for several years, perhaps since the exhibitor stopped touring with his show. Ralph W. Barber, the assistant secretary, had grown up in Wilkes-Barre. Jack Carleton, the office clerk, was LeRoy Carleton's brother. Wellington C. Pflueger had been hired as general booking agent. Originally from Allentown, Pflueger had toured the Far East for several years as a pianist for a theatrical company before returning to the United States in 1902.[82] Howe's enterprise was developing a layer of administrative management to coordinate the exhibitor's increasingly far-flung operations.

With Howe out of the hospital, Walkinshaw apparently returned to his old role as business manager and musical director for the first company. Russell Blake was the company's operator, LeRoy Carleton its impersonator and sound-effects artist, and Charles King its advance representative.[83] The second or midwestern company had Fred Willson for manager, Daisy Willson for musical director, and Will C. Smith for operator. Charles R. Bosworth, of nearby Pittston, Pennsylvania, was advance representative, and Edward C. Mayo, a former housepainter also from Pittston, was newly hired to provide voices and sounds from behind the screen.[84] The third or southern company included Robert Brackett as manager, Chester Stoutenberg as operator, and Paul Felton as musical director. Felton, like Fred Willson, was from Towanda, Pennsylvania. With

7-10. Howe and his employees (1904–1905 season). From left to right, front row: Lyman H. Howe (owner), Ralph W. Barber (assistant secretary), Harry Manhart (secretary); S. M. Walkinshaw (manager and musical director, no. 1 co.); second row: Robert Brackett (manager, no. 3 co.), Chester Stoutenberg (operator, no. 3 co.), LeRoy Carleton (impersonator, no. 1 co.); third row: Charles R. Bosworth (advance representative, no. 2 co.), Will C. Smith (operator, no. 2 co.), Wellington C. Pflueger (general booking agent), Paul Felton (musical director, no. 3 co.), Russell Blake (operator, no. 1. co.); fourth row: Fred Willson (manager, no. 2 co.), Daisy Willson (musical director, no. 2 co.), unidentified, Charles King (advance representative, no. 1 co.), Jack Carleton (office clerk).

the exception of Howe's operators, who came from all over the country and were hired for their prior experience, most of Howe's personnel came from northeastern Pennsylvania.[85] Several of these employees would have long careers with Howe's organization and eventually assume more important roles.

For the twentieth semiannual tour in the fall of 1904, Howe did not pass programs down from company to company. By this time too many traveling exhibitors were active to permit this cost-saving luxury. Programs for all three companies list *Man the Life Boats*, about the lifeboat service, and a group of Russo-Japanese War scenes as their principal subjects. Considerable variation, however, existed in the selection of additional films. The first two companies showed Urban's *The Making of a News-paper*, which commenced with the reporting of a sporting event and concluded with newsboys selling papers on the streets. Like many of Howe's longer nonfiction subjects, it traced a process with an emphasis on technology. The third, "southern" company offered a film series on winter sports: *Ice Boating, Tug of War on Ice, Skating Races, Obstacle Races, A Lively Snowball Fight, Thrilling Coasting Scenes, Exciting Hockey Games*, and *Dangerous Ski Contests*, presumably of special interest to people in parts of the country that rarely saw snow.

Variation was evident in the ways each company organized its films. For example, the first and third companies arranged their Russo-Japanese War scenes thus:

COMPANY No. 1:

A Regiment of the Japanese Imperial Guards and Engineer Corps off to the Front,—*a fine picture of Japanese troops—one of the most successful of the very few which have been so far secured in the far East.*

The Military Funeral of the Standard Bearer of the Yalu, *who was killed at the Battle of the Yalu while defending the colors. A quaint and highly interesting spectacle as the procession marches through the streets of Tokio.*

The War Correspondent and the Two Bear Cubs.

Attack of a Supply Train.

Japanese Devotees Going to the Temple of the God of Battle to Pray for Victory.

COMPANY No. 3:

Japanese Devotees Going to the Temple of the God of Battle to Pray for Victory.

A Reproduction of the Attack on a Russian Fortress.

The War Correspondent and the Two Bear Cubs.

Attack on a Supply Train.

A Regiment of the Japanese Imperial Guards and Engineer Corps off to the Front.

The Military Funeral of the Standard Bearer of the Yalu.[86]

The lectures and most films for these programs do not survive, so one can only guess the implications of these differing arrangements. Various connections between scenes could have been made by the narrators, but the third company's ordering suggests greater effort to provide a narrative account of the war.

Although Howe's companies enjoyed brisk business, all three faced intensifying competition. Howe's new, third company competed directly with Archie Shepard as both exhibitors sent companies to tour the southern states for the first time. The Howe show traveled in Shepard's wake. Shepard appeared in Sumter, South Carolina (1900 population: 5,673), and New Bern, North Carolina (1900 population: 9,090), in early October: Howe played both towns less than two weeks later.[87] Shepard, determined to establish himself in the southern states, sent another company to tour the region in November. In the end, Howe withdrew from the South, where his exhibitions would never be firmly established. His third company moved north and west, traveling through Indiana, Illinois, Iowa, Missouri, and Kansas. Nevertheless, it still occasionally found itself exhibiting shortly after an appearance by one of Shepard's companies. The Howe company played Quincy, Illinois (1900 population: 36,252), on February 22, 1905, one day after Shepard's show was in town. But Shepard was not the only rival. The Dodge-Bowman Amusement Company had had two recent engagements at the same 1,361-seat Empire Theater.

In New Britain, Connecticut, residents could see full-length motion picture shows on twenty different days during a ten-week period in 1905:

> January 7: Russwin Lyceum (1,264 seats), Edwin J. Hadley
> January 8: Majestic (1,600 seats), Moving Pictures (Sunday)
> January 13: Russwin Lyceum, Vitagraph Company of America
> January 14: Russwin Lyceum, Vitagraph Company of America
> January 15: Majestic, Moving Pictures (Sunday)
> January 21: Russwin Lyceum, Vitagraph Company of America
> January 22: Majestic, Moving Pictures (Sunday)
> January 23–28: Casino, vaudeville and Edison Kinetoscope (theater closed after one week)
> February 5: Majestic, Moving Pictures (Sunday)
> February 12: Majestic, Harstn's Moving Pictures (Sunday)
> February 18: Russwin Lyceum, Morgan and Hoyt's Life Motion Pictures
> February 19: Majestic, Moving Pictures (Sunday)
> February 25: Russwin Lyceum, Vitagraph Company of America
> February 26: Russwin Lyceum, Vitagraph Company of America (Sunday evening)
> Hanna's Armory, Robertson's Projectoscope Company
> March 5: Majestic Theater, P. J. Corcoran's Moving Pictures (Sunday)
> March 8: Russwin Lyceum, LYMAN H. HOWE
> March 12: Majestic, Harstn's Moving Pictures (Sunday)
> March 17: Russwin Lyceum, Archie Shepard
> March 18: Russwin Lyceum, Archie Shepard
> March 19: Majestic, Harstn's Moving Pictures (Sunday)
> March 26: Majestic, Harstn's Moving Pictures (Sunday)

The Sunday concerts charged a dime for general admission, a quarter for reserved seats. Hadley, Morgan and Hoyt, Shepard, Robertson, and Vitagraph all had ten, twenty, and thirty cent price schedules that were substantially lower than Howe's twenty-five, thirty-five and fifty cent scale.

Every exhibitor claimed that his show was "the best of its kind."[88] Howe not only claimed to present "The World's Greatest Exhibition of Moving

Pictures," he charged his patrons more for the privilege of seeing it. Potential patrons who wanted the best expected corresponding admission prices, and Howe's programs were generally well received. In Troy, New York, Howe grossed an astounding $753.25 for one date despite immediate competition from Sunday motion picture concerts.[89] In Reading, Howe grossed $1,277.75 in two days, a substantial increase over his previous three engagements. Howe's program notes declared, "Our cardinal characteristics have been to deserve the patronage of the best people by presenting unequaled quality, tone and superior excellence in every instance."[90] Behind this claim was a threatening reality. If his exhibitions were only as good as the others, they were not good enough. Where his reputation was already acknowledged, he might lose his edge. Where his companies were less well-known, his reputation might never become established.

Howe relied on state-of-the-art technology. Voices and sound effects from behind the screen continued to provide his shows with a distinctive quality. His greatest challenge was subject matter. His first and second companies received new films for the twenty-first semiannual tour, in the spring of 1905, as they had for the previous fall. Again, both companies showed many of the same titles. *From Christiania to North Cape* examined Laplanders "in their native habiliment and quaint domestic life;" *Egypt* offered new views of the pyramids; and *The Story of a Piece of Slate* detailed the process of extracting and refining slate in Wales. News pictures were provided by *The Recent Motor Races Across the English Channel* and *The Japanese-Russian War*, which reenacted the battle at Mukden. In mid-March, *Scenes and Incidents of the Inauguration Ceremonies at Washington, D.C., March 4, 1905* was added to these programs as the headline attraction. Howe also balanced these nonfiction subjects with a number of story films. Both the eastern and midwestern company presented Biograph's *The Waif,* "a pathetic story of real life in the big city." Howe's midwestern company began its spring tour with Biograph's *The Moonshiner,* which culminated in a sensational shootout between still operators and lawmen. By mid-May, this story film, much of which emphasized the quotidian, had been replaced by *The Suburbanite,* a more recent—and less violent—Biograph comedy.[91]

To promote his shows, Howe embraced a practice commonly employed by his rivals. He claimed authorship for films taken by established production companies. When *The Moonshiner* was shown in Wheeling, West Virginia, Charles Bosworth claimed that the subject was staged and photographed by the Howe company in Maysville, Kentucky. This claim formed the basis for an extensive newspaper story about a recent presentation in a remote town. During the screening, Bosworth's story went, a woman recognized her long-lost husband in the film. She stood up and

7-11. An informal moment with members of company number 1:
Charles King, Russell Blake, Jack Carleton, Howe, and Walkinshaw
(ca. 1905).

7-12. Letterhead (1902–1905).

denounced him as a criminal, only to learn he was an actor.[92] Later Howe asserted that the views of Roosevelt's inauguration were exclusively his and that "his efficient staff of special photographers made elaborate preparations to secure the most advantageous locations."[93] Operating within the long-standing tradition of the exhibitor's creative responsibility, Howe, like others, tried to exploit this perception for his commercial advantage.[94]

In the East and Midwest, Howe had gradually shifted his exhibitions from churches and small towns into the theaters of middle-sized cities. In the spring of 1905, Howe's companies made their first tentative moves into major urban centers. On Sunday, May 7, Howe's midwestern company gave a concert at the Grand Opera House in Detroit (1900 population: 285,704). On May 19, the same company played at Grays' Armory in Cleveland (1900 population: 381,768), with Howe billed as "America's greatest traveller and exhibitor." City dwellers had had frequent opportunities to see moving pictures in the 1890s and early 1900s, but such screenings had seldom exceeded 20 minutes. Now, after the technical quality of projection had improved and a wider assortment of films was available, these people could more readily enjoy a full evening of moving pictures. Although attendance in Detroit was small, the audience liked what it saw. Howe incorporated both cities into his circuit. Competition in the smaller urban localities had encouraged him to seek new venues in major cities.

Traveling motion picture exhibitors enjoyed a period of tumultuous growth between 1903 and 1905. While Howe caught the wave of prosperity and added two new companies, old competitors such as Dibble fell by the wayside, and new ones such as Archie Shepard emerged and displayed tremendous vitality. Former employee Edwin Hadley likewise set up his own company and challenged Howe's circuit in a bitter, often petty contest of wills. Charging a higher admission fee than any of his rivals, Howe sustained his image as *the* high-class motion picture exhibitor of the Northeast. Yet his first company's reduced profits, the third company's failure to establish itself in the South, his tentative and confused departure from a cinema of reassurance, and his own sustained illness all pointed toward an uncertain future even while the veteran showman boasted much larger operations and impressive income. New problems but also new opportunities had developed, and with the help of S. M. Walkinshaw Howe would minimize the former and maximize the latter in the years immediately ahead.

8

✳ ✳

The Nickelodeon Crisis:
Howe Moves into the Big Cities,
1905-1908

✳ ✳ ✳

Mr. Howe has succeeded in giving to the public a novel, somewhat
different entertainment in the moving picture line than ever before
seen here.

Boston Herald, October 6, 1905

BY 1905, MOTION PICTURES had filled established amusement formats—theaters, arcades, carnivals, summer parks—to the bursting point.
Vaudeville entrepreneurs and traveling showmen were intruding on each
other's turf. Vaudeville with moving pictures had opened in many cities
previously served only by traveling showmen. Howe, for example, had to
contend with it in Reading (the Orpheum), Troy (Proctor's Griswold
Theater), Gloversville (Family Theater), and Poughkeepsie (Family Theater), as well as in Wheeling, West Virginia (Bijou Theater). Special Sunday motion picture shows and penny arcades also appeared in many localities. Correspondingly, ambitious itinerant showmen were making
appearances in major cities.

Archie Shepard not only had as many as five companies on the road
during the 1905–1906 season but also started to provide regular Sunday
concerts.[1] By November he had Sunday venues in Washington, D.C., Fall
River and Lawrence, Massachusetts, and Atlantic City and Asbury Park,
New Jersey. Starting in December, Shepard's shows were given twice every Sunday at New York City's Fourteenth Street Theater.[2] By the following month, they were at New York's Majestic, West End, and Third Avenue theaters as well. Although Sunday concerts, featuring vaudeville and
usually including moving pictures, had been popular in New York City
since the 1890s, Shepard's entertainments notably presented only films
and illustrated songs.[3]

D. W. Robertson had five companies by the 1905–1906 season. One
played only New York and vicinity, while others toured his original circuit

in the Midwest and Mississippi valley. Conventional theatrical venues constituted but a small portion of his business. "My specialty," Robertson explained, "is not so much theaters but church and Y.M.C.A. entertainments. They want, of course, high class subjects. Travel pictures with accompanying lectures, or at least a little running talk being popular with them." Based in his New York office on Park Row during the theatrical year, Robertson took one company to more than forty Chautauquan meetings in the summer to renew contacts and make arrangements for the following year. "Yes," he assured a reporter, "the business is developing outside what you might call strictly 'show' lines."[4]

Shepard, Howe, and Robertson were unlike the more than a hundred traveling motion picture exhibitors who had single-unit companies. Although Hadley began to make appearances in major cities such as Philadelphia and to offer Sunday concerts, he believed in the single company concept and never ventured a second road show.[5] Sherman's Moving Pictures and the Beatty Brothers, who continued their exhibitions in the Far West, enjoyed their prosperity but did not seem anxious to alter their commercial practices in order to take advantage of new opportunities.[6] Most of these small companies were briefly mentioned in trade journals, then quickly faded from view. Among these were J. W. Randolph, based in Texas, W. B. Madison, with the Madison Monarch Picture Show in the South, and the Herber-Edson Picture and Concert Company, in Ohio.[7]

Many companies, like the Huntley Entertainers and the Missouri-based Murray and Murray's Cineograph and Vaudeville Company, were primarily family affairs. The latter company's roster included F. O. Murray, manager; Frankie Murray, treasurer; Charles A. Bradley, black-face comedian; Master Roy Murray, contortionist; Florence Murray, singing and dancing specialties; B. M. Day, pianist; Frankie Murray's troupe of educated birds; and the moving pictures.[8] Others, like Vernie Hackett's Moving Pictures and Harris and Tilley's Moving Picture Show, had begun with such modest capital that they could not break into population centers already frequented by Shepard's companies, and so rarely visited places with more than three thousand inhabitants. Hackett played Fayette (1900 population: 604), St. Francisville (1900 population: 1,059), and Gloster (1900 population: 1,661), Mississippi. At the same time Harris and Tilley were trekking through Alabama, stopping in Blockton (sharing 3,823 inhabitants with two other villages in 1900), Cottondale (1900 population: 1,990) and Tuscaloosa (1900 population: 5,094) as well as hamlets too small to be listed in the census.[9] Some of these small-time showmen associated themselves with carnivals or amusement parks during the summer and then played halls and rural opera houses during the winter.[10] Across the country, in even the smallest village, films were being shown.

HOWE SHOWS FILMS OF PORT ARTHUR

The 1905–1906 theatrical season brought several important personnel changes. Max Walkinshaw worked out of the home office in Wilkes-Barre. No longer traveling with a road company, Walkinshaw would soon take control of the day-to-day business operations and eventually become Howe's partner. By 1908, as Howe's chauffeur Lloyd Davey recalled, "Employees respected Howe but they didn't have much to do with him. He'd come in and be very friendly with the boys and so forth when they would come in from the road. But Max was the kingpin."[11] Walkinshaw's position as company manager was taken by Robert E. Gillaum, an opera house manager in Tiffin, Ohio. Leo Gertchester was hired as pianist and music director. Finally, Will C. Smith left Howe's employ to become part of a successful vaudeville team, Diamond and Smith.[12] Fred H. Rogers replaced Smith as operator.

The saturation of the market was the most immediate problem confronting Howe in 1905. He urgently needed distinctive subjects. In the summer of 1905, he thus acquired the Urban Trading Company's films of the Russo-Japanese war. He was reported to have secured

> for exclusive exhibition in America the most valuable series of moving pictures ever taken, the only authentic and genuine views of the siege and surrender of Port Arthur. The pictures were taken inside the firing lines and on account of the great risk assumed in securing them Mr. Howe was compelled to pay for the exclusive American rights an immense sum of money as the party who backed the enterprise and secured the pictures expended a fortune in doing so. Mr Howe does not expect to make much profit this season, even if he has crowded houses, as is the rule with his exhibitions, but he hopes to prove to the people that if they want to see the newest and the best in the moving picture line they must wait for him.[13]

The report was essentially correct, although Howe shared this "exclusivity" with Burton Holmes, who also had strong ties with Urban. (It is even possible that the two reached a joint agreement to share the costs.) Moreover, the article embellished the Howe legend by dwelling on Howe's extravagance and claiming that the showman valued his reputation more than his profits—as if the two were not interdependent. The myth concealed the fact that Howe's purchase was a coup precisely because he stood to make a substantial profit. He could amortize the costs among his several companies, an advantage most other traveling exhibitors did not share. Those exceptions like Shepard had neither the same connections nor the same degree of interest. Because he collected a percentage of the box-office receipts rather than a flat rental fee, Howe also had an advantage over film exchanges and American producers. In a unique position, the

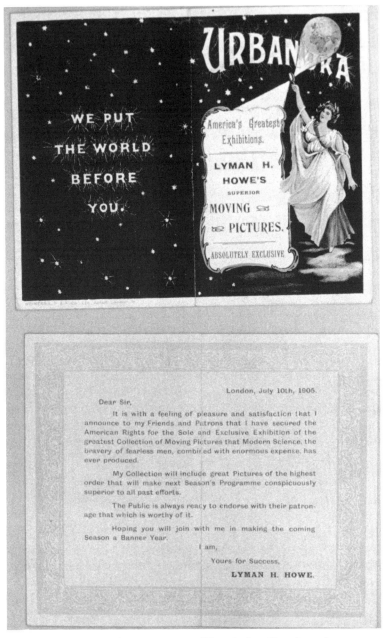

8-1. Howe announces his acquisition of Port Arthur films from the Urban Trading Company.

capable show manager acquired at least two sets of Urban's Russo-Japanese War films for his companies.

Howe and Walkinshaw made maximum use of their various resources. The Russo-Japanese War had captured American attention as President Theodore Roosevelt brought the two sides to the negotiating table and cajoled them into signing a peace treaty in early August. In mid-August, fresh from his diplomatic triumph, Roosevelt visited Howe's hometown and spoke at a mammoth temperance meeting sponsored by the Catholic Total Abstinence Union and the United Mine Workers. The national press devoted much attention to Roosevelt's visit; the *Wilkes-Barre Record* simply called it "the greatest day Wilkes-Barre had ever experienced."[14] Howe responded by photographing *Scenes and Incidents During the Visit of President Roosevelt at Wilkes-Barre, Pa., August 10th, 1905*. It showed "the President approaching the platform on the river common from his carriage through the mass of humanity; the President delivering his speech; shaking hands with Cardinal Gibbons after the speech; visit to the Wyoming monument; acceptance of bouquets from three children at the monument."[15] The film survives in incomplete form at the Library of Congress. The camera was well situated to show the action and capture the self-confident, energetic President. Although now suffering from slight nitrate deterioration, the image was sharp and well-developed, revealing excellent technical capabilities. It was a local subject that interested the whole country, in perfect counterpoint to Howe's Port Arthur films.[16]

These films were supplemented by two more subjects that originated with Howe. One of a Carnegie steel plant in operation showed "first how the iron ore was melted; then on through the various processes, until it comes out in a sheet through the rolls."[17] This depiction of process was screened by all his companies during the 1905–1906 season. The other film, of the Allentown fair, included scenes along the midway and at the race track: "Dan Patch was . . . seen breaking the world's record and having the 'Good Luck Horseshoe' placed around his neck by the president of the Lehigh County Agricultural Society, Hon. Jeremiah Roth."[18] The film was subsequently exhibited in selected towns and cities by Howe's first company. In addition, the showman acquired films of the well-publicized Gordon-Bennett Automobile Race in France.[19]

With exclusive subjects, Howe countered the competition posed by rival exhibitors and strengthened his circuits.[20] "For several seasons past Mr. Howe's moving picture show has been presented here," remarked the *Wheeling Register*, "but never before has it been on so pretentious a scale as last evening."[21] When Howe exhibited in Troy, Proctor's vaudeville theater was offering films of the city's police and fire departments. Headlining the bill, the local views attracted standing-room-only crowds and "elicited the greatest enthusiasm at each performance." If it had not been

8-2a,b. *Scenes and Incidents during the Visit of President Roosevelt at Wilkes-Barre, Pa., August 10th, 1905.*

for his extraordinary program, Howe undoubtedly would have suffered a drop in patronage. Instead, the advance sale for tickets was larger than usual and a sell-out was assumed.[22] Howe's program also did extremely well in eastern Pennsylvania, grossing almost six thousand dollars in eight consecutive playdates.[23]

Howe and Walkinshaw used the Port Arthur films as a wedge to open up further opportunities in large American cities. Howe first broke new ground in Boston (1910 population: 670,385), where his show ran for three days at the Tremont Temple. A Baptist church on Sunday, the Tremont Temple served as a theater during the week, regularly hosting stereopticon lectures and travel talks by prestigious figures, among them Burton Holmes. Since Holmes did not play Boston until the spring, Howe screened the Port Arthur films there first. Tickets for the three-day stand, October 5–7, were fifty cents, seventy-five cents and one dollar—higher than Howe normally charged but the price scale used by Holmes.[24] Matinees were slightly cheaper, with children admitted for twenty-five cents. The program was "a great success." Headlining its review "Moving Pictures of Superior Order Delight Crowds at Tremont Temple," the *Boston Herald* declared,

> Mr. Howe has succeeded in giving the public a novel, somewhat different entertainment in the moving picture line than ever before seen here. It is most instructive, too. Anyone seeing the Japanese-Russian war in such proximity will gather more real knowledge of it than by the reading of columns of dispatches. It should be of especial value to school children of all ages, as well as to students of the times in general.
>
> President Roosevelt's speech is most entertaining, so is the view of the Carnegie steel works in full swing, smelters, engineers and carters work in an ear-splitting din of pounding hammers, and white furnaces run in full blast. The audience was large and went away immensely pleased.[25]

Similar reviews in other Boston papers and good patronage gave Howe's company future playdates in that city.

Howe's second company returned to Detroit, where its Port Arthur films drew several thousand people. Declaring the war pictures "good," the *Detroit Journal* praised Howe's exhibition as "an example of the twentieth century inventive skill and enterprise put to novel uses."[26] In Milwaukee (1910 population: 373,857), Howe presented his Port Arthur films during late November, six weeks after Burton Holmes had given his illustrated lecture, *Port Arthur: Siege and Surrender*, at the same theater.

HOLMES AND HOWE: A COMPARISON

Holmes, like Howe, had previously addressed American interest in the Russo-Japanese War. In his course for the 1904–1905 season, he had in-

cluded two programs reworking material gathered on his visits to Japan in
the summer of 1899 and to Russia in the summer of 1901. In *Port Arthur:
Siege and Surrender*, Holmes used scenes from these trips and many of the
films also used in Howe's program. The results, according to one reviewer,
were impressive:

> Mr Holmes introduced a number of startling effects by means of contrasts in
> points of view, by breaking the continuity of his recital to show within two
> minutes what was being done at home and what was being accomplished at
> the front. By these means Mr. Holmes made a deep impression by showing
> us a Manchurian battlefield and immediately thereafter a view of the Emperor
> of Russia receiving the blessing of his high priest at home. Again a picture of
> the war was shown and again the speaker showed us a scene in St. Petersburg.
> These exhibitions of contrast made the recital all the more dramatic.[27]

Holmes used editorial techniques and narration to offer an explicit analysis and viewpoint. The entire two-hour program was devoted to one subject. In contrast, Howe limited the Port Arthur films to a half-hour seg-
ment of a program that relied on variety principles for its final structure.

Reviews in the *Milwaukee Sentinel* clarify some of the differences between the two men's programs (see Appendix G, Documents 3 and 4).
Holmes's illustrated lecture was called "a contribution of distinct literary
and historic value" and "gave insight to the marvelous scenes portrayed
by the pictures." The reviewer was inspired to quote Holmes's "brilliant
word descriptions" at length.[28] Howe's program did not give insight so
much as "refreshen the memory." Praising his sound effects, the reviewer
declared that Howe "brings the scene close to home until the spectator
fairly lives in the atmosphere and is translated in imagination to the spot
where history is being made."[29] Howe achieved a heightened sense of reality, a "faithful reproduction" that precluded the explicit intervention
practiced by Holmes. Using many of the same films and drawing from the
same repertoire of "postproduction" procedures, Holmes and Howe produced distinctly different results.

Holmes used the conflict between the European and Asian powers as an
opportunity to compare two national characters. Although both exhibitors showed films of the peace conference, Howe's Wilkes-Barre pictures
of the President further emphasized Theodore Roosevelt as an international hero who brought devastating warfare to a close. The showman
projected a cocky American optimism as he showed the triumphant
Rough Rider whose forceful personality tamed the bloodied antagonists.
The leader of the new world had done the old world an inestimable favor.
Pride in the accomplishments of the United States, a feeling of well-be-
ing, and security pervaded the program.

The sharing of subject matter and exhibition sites by Holmes and Howe

signaled a new dimension of Howe's activities. For the first time he was seriously appealing to a more erudite, elite audience, the kind of patrons who flocked to Holmes's lectures year after year. In fact, he was in the process of creating a new middle ground that would satisfy churchgoing traditionalists, amusement lovers, and believers in genteel cultivation. In many respects Howe located common ground that Sousa had already discovered in the musical realm by nudging his band closer to an orchestra. For many middle-class music lovers, as Neil Harris points out, the renowned conductor had thus bridged the gulf between the classical and the popular.[30] Now Howe was achieving a similar synthesis for the screen.

After Howe's twenty-second semiannual tour, his first and second companies acquired new scenes of mountain climbing in the Alps, naval maneuvers, insect life, and foreign travel, none apparently taken by Howe personnel.[31] When Howe's company returned to Boston in February for a six-day run, the *Boston Herald* labeled the exhibition "a good entertainment" but stopped short of earlier accolades.[32] The new program, lacking the exclusivity and topical interest of his Port Arthur pictures, may not have warranted such an extended playdate. His second company returned to Detroit's Light Guard Armory for two days with better success. One subject shown by the company was of the recently invented "aeroplane."[33]

Howe remained intent on exploiting the Port Arthur films which were turned over to his western company:

THE LIVING HISTORY OF THE TRAGEDY OF PORT ARTHUR

The following pictures, which are ABSOLUTELY AUTHENTIC, are the only animated views in existence of this historic event.

THE SIEGE

(a) A Regiment of the 3rd Division Imperial Japanese Troops Leaving Tokio for the Front.

(b) General Baron Oshima at Counsel with his Officers — *A splendid portrait of the famous Japanese General discussing plans of campaign with his subordinates. (The picture was taken just outside of the General's tent, showing those officers at a table inside the tent with front flaps thrown back.)*

(c) Ammunition Transport Proceeding Through a Mountain Pass.

(d) Advance of the Japanese Army. *This picture conveys an excellent idea of the nature of the country where the resources of two empires engaged in mighty conflict. It is in close proximity to 203 Metre Hill.*

(e) Cleaning and Inspecting Rifles in the Advance Trenches. *The alternate expression of determination and laughter on the faces of these warriors convey a good idea of the resolute yet happy disposition of the stoical Japanese soldiers.*

(f) Panoramic View of the Principal Fortifications of Port Arthur. *This unique picture was secured on Jan 3rd, after the capitulation of Port Arthur. (We show the picture at this stage in order that the public may by its exhibition, gain an accurate idea of the "theatre of war" in which the following events transpired.) It shows plainly the sapping operations and trenches where earth combated earth.*

(g) Field Gun in Action. *Showing one of the field guns operated by a squad of Artillerymen firing round after round from the gun, which rebounds up an incline after each shot. This photograph was taken during the assault on 203 Metre Hill.*

(h) Transporting an 11 inch Siege Gun. *Showing the manner in which these heavy Howitzer (17 ton) guns are transported from one position to another, requiring the united efforts of 1,000 troopers to move them.*

(i) The Battery of 11 Guns Pouring 500 lb. Shells into Port Arthur. *Showing four of these formidable Howitzers in action. Each shell cost $175.00. The cost of each discharge (with impelling powder) is $400.00. During the heavy bombardment each gun was fired every eight minutes and as each grand bombardment lasted about four hours, the cost of one such battery fire was $200,000, and for all the batteries in action approximately half a million for each 4 hours.*

(j) Blowing Up Erlingshan Fort, December 28th, 1904. *This affords a new phase of the unspeakable spectacle of war.*

(k) Erlingshan Fort after the Capture. *This is the shattered point of contact where the two great armies clashed with terrible sacrifices of human lives.*

THE SURRENDER

(a) Arrival of General Baron Nogi and Staff to Arrange Terms of Surrender.

(b) General Stoessel and Officers Leaving after Their Meeting with General Baron Nogi.

(c) General Baron Nogi Leaving after Arranging Terms for the Surrender of Port Arthur.

(d) Russian Prisoners leaving Port Arthur, January 8th. *Their faces present a curious study. All appear to feel keenly their humiliating position. While some appear resigned, others show signs of resentment. The men look well fed, but their faces show signs of the terrible physical strain which they have undergone. They seem resigned and glad indeed that the end has come.*

(e) Arrival of General Stroessel, Madame Stroessel and Orphan Children at the Railway Head.

(f) Train Bearing General Stroessel and Paroled Officers and Soldiers Leaving for Dalny.

(g) State Entry of the Japanese Army into Port Arthur, January 13th, 1905.

Naval Manoeuvres.

Ostriches Eating Oranges.

New Scenes at Niagara Falls.

The Sultan of Morocco and His Army. *Revealing the Personnel, Equip-
     ment, Tactics, Accoutrements, etc. of Military Life in this quaint Empire.*
Jean Valjean and the Bishop.
Impossible Wardrobe.
Scenes at the Carnegie Steel Works.
Yachting by Moonlight.
The Overhead Railway, Germany.
Drill of the Reedham Orphans.
With the Imperial Express in the Rocky Mountains.
Post no Bills.
Fire Cascades.

GOOD NIGHT[34]

In mid-May, the Port Arthur films enabled Howe to break into another
major American city, Baltimore (1910 population: 558,485). Ford's
Grand Opera House, the largest theater in the city, with a capacity of
2,250 seats, agreed to present his program for one week at the end of the
theatrical season. These exhibitions were billed as the first of a series of
semiannual lectures, indicating that Baltimore was now on Howe's circuit. At the last moment the showman added films of the San Francisco
earthquake to the program.[35] The timeliness of these films (the quake had
been in April), as well as memories of the 1904 Baltimore fire, led one
reviewer to call these views "even more interesting than those of Port
Arthur."[36] Their addition was fortuitous, for Baltimore's leading vaudeville theater also showed earthquake films for the first time that week.
Howe's week-long stand was a success and proved that he could play large
cities for a sustained run.

THE NICKELODEON ERA BEGINS

The nickelodeon era of storefront, specialized moving picture theaters was
well underway by the 1906–1907 theatrical season. This new form of exhibition, made possible by the still rapidly growing popularity of motion
pictures, overpowered all others. It is doubtful that nickelodeons offered
patrons lower per-minute costs than already established formats; by the
minute, a half-hour nickelodeon show for five cents was at least as expensive as a two-hour Sunday concert for ten or twenty-five cents. The earliest nickelodeons did appear in Pittsburgh and Chicago, where there were
no Sunday concerts, but the format quickly spread to cities like New York,
where the Sunday show was well established. The nickelodeons reached
audiences more quickly, easily, and effectively, allowing patrons to drop
in for a brief respite and then continue with their daily routine. The nickelodeons' regular, frequent changes of program decimated traveling
showmen, just as Archie Shepard's frequent visits to towns had earlier

undermined Dibble's circuit of annual visits. A nickelodeon manager could coordinate his programming more effectively than a diverse group of traveling showmen and avoid repeating films his patrons had already seen. Once the nickelodeon system was set up, the itinerant showman was virtually certain to be out-of-date.

This nickel madness had begun in Pittsburgh during the summer and fall of 1905. By March 1906, C. R. Jones had moved from Pittsburgh to Wilkes-Barre, where he showed moving pictures for five cents in a vacant storefront.[37] Boston's first motion picture theater, the Theater Comique, opened on August 30, 1906, and charged ten cents. It featured melodramas such as Edison's *Kathleen Mavourneen* and Biograph's *A Kentucky Feud,* comedies such as Vitagraph's *The Jail Bird and How He Flew,* and occasional actualities such as *Sights in a Great City.*[38] In Reading, a five-cent movie house had opened by late October.[39] Two months later, in Troy, New York (1910 population: 76,813), a penny arcade reopened as a nickelodeon. By March 1907, at least two other nickel theaters, including the five-hundred-seat Novelty, were entertaining Trojans. By early 1907, most good-sized towns in the Northeast and Midwest had one or more nickelodeons.[40]

As nickelodeons multiplied like cockroaches, Archie Shepard contributed to the infestation. In New Bedford, Massachusetts (1910 population: 96,652), he took control of a theater that closed in April 1906 after an unrewarding season of plays. By early May, it was showing moving pictures. When his road companies were stymied by newly opened nickelodeons, they informed Shepard of these developments. One company reached Lewiston, Maine (1910 population: 26,247), on March 6, 1907, and found its business preempted by the 1,254-seat Nickel, a picture theater run by the Keith organization. One month later, Shepard opened his own Lewiston nickelodeon, the five-hundred-seat Bijou. By then he had two picture houses in Meriden, Connecticut, one in Oswego, New York, and another in New Bedford, Massachusetts.[41] *Moving Picture World* reported that "Mr. Shepard is largely interested in the moving picture proposition, probably more so than any other promoter in the country. He has theaters all over the country, as well as picture shows on the road and dramatic companies as well."[42] Certainly, his exhibition practices were easily adapted to the opportunities offered by storefront theaters.

Other traveling showmen also settled down. By late 1906, England's moving pictures were established at the Bijou Theater in Binghamton, New York.[43] Charles Oxenham started the American Film Exchange from his Brooklyn base.[44] Thomas L. Tally, who had traveled through the Far West, returned to Los Angeles to open his own nickelodeon and a film exchange. William Swanson, who had shown motion pictures in a black top at street fairs and then traveled through the Midwest showing fight films, became an operator at one of the first nickelodeons in Chicago.[45] Within a year, he had opened up the Swanson Film Exchange. William Steiner gradually turned his Imperial Moving Picture Company into a film exchange. Many traveling exhibitors, particularly those already oriented toward popular urban amusements, adapted to the nickelodeon era quickly and often to good effect.

Howe did not follow the path of these contemporaries but sought to exploit potential differences from the nickelodeon system. Since film exchanges renting to nickelodeons avoided marginal practices in an effort to maximize efficiency and profits, they generally did not acquire news films. Topicals lost their rental value as their timeliness faded while other types of subject matter could be circulated until their prints wore out. Howe thus exploited this gap in their repertoire, showing what they avoided. His twenty-fourth semiannual tour, sometimes labeled "International Events 1906," showed *Wedding of King Alphonse (of Spain)*, *Olympic Games: Athens*, and *Eruption of Vesuvius*.[46]

Howe further distanced himself from the nickelodeons in his promotional practices. Although he had neither photographed any of the international events featured in his show nor traveled outside of Europe and America, Howe billed himself as "America's Greatest Traveler."[47] Howe thus appealed to people who enjoyed or wanted to enjoy vicariously this favorite pastime of the well-to-do. The program was also called "Howe's

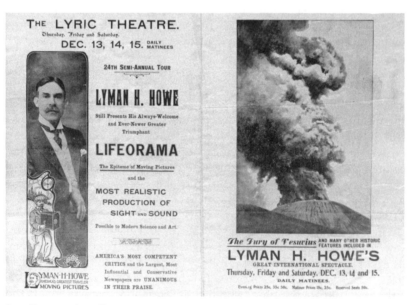

8-3. Program (1906).

Lifeorama" to emphasize the illusion of reality created by the mechanical, musical, and vocal effects as well as by the vibration-free, flickerless image. Nickelodeons, in contrast, operated on a shoestring, often using makeshift equipment, inexperienced operators, and prints damaged by previous users. Even the smell of these working-class venues could offend middle-class sensibilities. Howe's comparatively high admission fees—twenty-five cents to one dollar—and his location in prominent theaters emphasized the respectability of his shows and patrons. He catered to the better classes not only for their patronage but as a way to appeal to the less well-to-do—working as well as middle-class—with upwardly mobile aspirations.[48]

When Howe's companies returned to Boston and Milwaukee for three-day visits in the fall of 1906, recently opened nickelodeons may have encouraged and certainly did not harm attendance. According to the *Boston Herald*, "Lyman H. Howe's 'Lifeorama' . . . delighted a large and appreciative audience."[49] In both cities Howe appeared before Burton Holmes. Again the two presented similar subject matter. Of Holmes's five lectures, one was on Athens and the Olympic Games while another treated the eruption of Vesuvius. As before, Holmes devoted an entire program to each subject while Howe highlighted several events in a program that emphasized variety. Although Howe publicized these "high-class," news-

8-4. New, larger posters signaled Howe's increasing prominence (ca. 1907).

worthy events, he was also careful to lace them with short comedies. He clearly understood how to appeal both to his audiences' aspirations for sophistication and their desire to be amused. In contrast, Holmes's programs were truly part of the "documentary tradition" that some have seen beginning with Robert Flaherty.

With Americans of all classes and backgrounds increasingly interested in moving pictures, Howe was able to incorporate many of America's largest cities into his circuit. For his inaugural, January 1907 screening in Cincinnati, Howe gave a benefit for the Boys' Home. In newspaper interviews Howe asserted, "The day is not far distant when every schoolroom will have its moving picture machine, as it now has its globe of maps. . . . I have the same forecast from more than 500 teachers, who now realize the educational possibilities of the animated camera."[50] His pronouncements reassured parents that their children could attend his presentations without being exposed to the "immoral" pictures standard in the nickelodeons.[51]

A year later, in January 1908, Howe showed films for the first time in Pittsburgh (1910 population: 533,905), where the nickelodeon craze had begun. His two-day engagement was split between matinees at the prestigious 2,364-seat Nixon Theater and evening performances at Carnegie Music Hall. To attract Pittsburghers, Howe offered to "refund the price paid to anyone who does not find it the most interesting two hours of travel amusement he has ever seen AT ANY PRICE." Clearly, Howe was addressing those who regularly attended Burton Holmes's lectures, which also played at the Nixon and Carnegie Music Hall. In addition, he asked nickelodeon patrons "To Attend This Graduation of Pittsburgh From the Kindergarten Class of 'Picture Show'."[52] Once again Howe sought to transcend social and cultural divisions.

Howe's Pittsburgh team was headed by D. J. Tasker, a Pennsylvania newspaper editor who had joined Howe as company manager. The pianist was Arthur Martel, a former member of the Bijou Theater orchestra in Wheeling, West Virginia.[53] The two had probably replaced Fred and Daisy Willson, who settled in Wilkes-Barre and became established music teachers. Three impersonators were behind the screen: Edward C. Mayo, Fred C. Morgan, and LeRoy Carleton. Carleton moved from company to company, working the most important engagements and training new imitators.[54] Although the show "did not receive the patronage it deserved," approximately 3,000 people were at the four screenings.[55] The modest audience, however, was impressed. The Pittsburgh Post reported that "Lyman H. Howe's New Artistic Novelty Astonishes Audience at Matinee," while the Pittsburgh Dispatch headlined its review, "Howe Scores a Success."[56]

Howe's spring 1907, twenty-fifth semiannual tour included such travel and industrial subjects as The Perils of Whaling, Ireland and Her People, Climbing Untrodden Peaks, and The Making of a Locomotive; these were

shown for two days in Boston, Detroit, and Milwaukee. Howe also returned to Ford's Grand Opera House in Baltimore where advertisements
and advance publicity featured these titles along with *A Real Bullfight* and
Polar Bear Hunt (which may have proved controversial and been witheld
since they were not mentioned in reviews).[57] The week-long engagement
generated 15,367 paid admissions and grossed over five thousand dollars.[58]
Although Ford's closed for the summer after Howe's program, the exhibitor kept his companies on the road for several more weeks before closing
his road show.[59] This proved to be Howe's last summer hiatus for several
years. He was soon to make use of an exhibition practice pioneered by
Archie Shepard.

THE SUMMER SEASON

The theatrical season in the United States traditionally ran from late August or early September to May or June. During summer months enter-
tainment-goers sought outdoor amusements: sports, roof gardens, and
summer parks. Only in the large cities did a handful of theaters stay open
twelve months of the year. Elsewhere summer seasons proved unprofitable

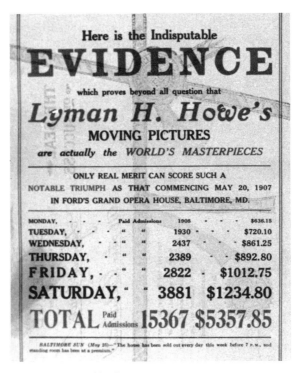

8-5. Promotional leaflet (ca. 1907).

and theaters stood empty. In one of his most successful ventures, Archie Shepard took advantage of this situation by placing motion picture shows in "legitimate" theaters during the summer months. Shepard enabled small-city opera houses to stay open year round. As noted above, he had experimented with this innovation during the summer of 1906 in New Bedford. The following year, the showman placed motion picture programs in nine theaters in Massachusetts, Vermont, Connecticut, Maine, and Delaware.[60] He also exhibited at the 750-seat Manhattan Theater on Broadway near 33rd Street in New York City.[61]

In Baltimore, Charles Ford recognized the value of a summer season. Perhaps he was encouraged and challenged by the success of Sigmund Lubin, the Philadelphia motion picture producer who had opened a nearby picture house. Lubin's Baltimore theater enjoyed excellent patronage during the summer months. Since Howe's May engagement had been so popular, Ford invited the experienced exhibitor to return for four weeks in August with a change of programs each week. Prices for the two-hour entertainment were twenty-five cents for adults and fifteen cents for children at matinees; and twenty-five, thirty-five, and fifty cents for evenings. Although Lubin offered forty-five-minute programs for a nickel, Howe was better patronized.

Faced with an unprecedented run, Howe played up the most distinctive element of his exhibitions—his use of actors behind the screen, in "The Crowning Triumph, Moving Pictures That Talk by Lyman H. Howe: The Only Perfect Exhibition of its Kind."[62] The response was electric and would have far-ranging ramifications for motion picture practice over the next several years. The *Baltimore Sun* felt that "the Howe 'realism' was apparent from the start and worked well. Behind the scenes there were trained assistants who yelled orders when the marines attacked the land force, made noises like the popping of guns and the booming of cannon, and helped the figures on the canvas to carry on the proper amount of conversation at suitable times."[63] "Talking Pictures" added much to the enjoyment of the program, and middle-class spectators were clearly willing to pay for the added expense of such techniques.

Howe's distinctive choice of subject matter became readily apparent as the showman introduced new programs each week. Military subjects, popular with audiences since the Lumières showed a squad of cavalry charging toward the camera, remained a staple, even in a period of relative world peace. *England's Naval Display* was the "pièce de resistance" of the first week:

> It begins with some good pictures of a gun drill by ships, followed by vivid reproductions of the maneuvers of torpedoboats and torpedoboat destroyers. The pictures were evidently taken from the stern of a swiftly moving vessel, and possess unusual scope. The boats are pictured tearing through the water

at a 25-knot gait, firing torpedoes in their wake. Some of the pictures show the path of the torpedoes through the water as they race toward the ship they are to attack.

The mollycoddle touch is given by a brief halt in the proceedings for Jack to say farewell to his sweetheart "just before the battle." There is the old millwheel, which has done duty in so many popular songs, and by the rippling waters Jack gets 101 kisses before the conflict that is to make him a hero and a husband.

The next scenes show several hundred Jacks trying to make a landing in the face of a deadly fire. They succeed, drive back the enemy, but ere long are themselves routed.[64]

The second week included *Servia and its Army*. The third featured *The Military Review at Aldershot*, which "gives one a capital idea of the discipline in the English army" and *Field Gun Drilling in the Navy*.[65] The final week reprised *Italian Cavalrymen* from an earlier program. Most of these films were acquired from Charles Urban. They favored the English, presenting them as the dominant imperial power.

Not unrelated to these military films were others showing the pastimes of European elites: stag hunts in France and a yacht race in England during the first week. The second week featured *Boar Hunt in France* and *Great English Derby*. *The Great London Horse Show* of the final week "shows several good pictures of King Edward, dressed in a new top coat, and a number of views of fine horses. Some of the ponies on view are owned by Mr. C. W. Watson of Baltimore; Mr. Ross Winona, of Baltimore and London; Mr. Ogden Armour, of Chicago, and Mr. Alfred Gwynne Vanderbilt, of New York."[66]

Howe offered a panoramic, complacent view of life among the rich in the years prior to World War I. World travel, one of their favorite forms of relaxation, was featured in *The Land of the Midnight Sun*, "a journey from Christiania to Trondhjem through the country of Ibsen."[67] During the second week, *London to Paris by Automobile* "displays some celebrated landmarks between the two cities" as patrons vicariously enjoyed the experience of motoring through Europe.[68] Likewise, *Southampton to Cape Town by Sea* "unfolds some of the innocent joys of a long sea voyage."[69] Other films featured the exoticism of distant colonies: *Darkest Africa*, *Teak Forest in India*, *Picturesque Java*, and *Fiji and South Sea Islands*. Hunts for exotic animals in remote locales recurred, whether the victims were whales, polar bears, or hippopotamuses. In *Hunting the Hippopotamus*, "The lazy hippo is enjoying a good bath when the huntsman puts a bullet into his thick hide and ends his career. The skinning and cutting winds up the expedition."[70]

The processes of hunting a wild animal or manufacturing industrial goods achieved a kind of equivalence in these programs. One showed how wealth was spent, the other how it was accumulated. These depictions of production processes pushed the workers and their milieu to the periphery. The concern was with representing and celebrating the world of the wealthy, of "people who mattered." Howe's programs entertained and informed in an uncritical manner. Showing the armed forces of various nations, Howe indirectly glorified the military buildup that preceded World War I. At least the transformation of military activities into spectacle effaced the serious implications of what was shown. Howe mediated between his chief source of supply, the British producer Charles Urban, and his American audience. As he exhibited them, the films cultivated a vicarious envy, a desire to emulate the grand imperialism of European power that many Americans shared with President Theodore Roosevelt.

Howe's selections struck a responsive chord as Ford's Theater filled to capacity despite sometimes trying weather. Among the throngs of patrons, Baltimore's Mayor Mahool came to see pictures of the Elks Parade in Philadelphia, including Baltimore's "Gallant 600" taken from Philadelphia Mayor Reyburn's viewing stand. *Billboard* found that "The audiences were noticeably out of the ordinary. There were many in attendance who, perhaps through their religious scruples would not enter a theatre on any other occasion. The audiences were mostly of an intellectual element. Many of the pictures were highly instructive as many views and scenes in foreign lands were thrown on the canvas. . . . The moving pictures as presented by Lyman H. Howe are *a worthy successor of the famous Stoddard lectures.*"[71]

Lovers of refined entertainment, Protestant proponents of moral enlightenment, aficionados of amusement all came. Lubin's decision to close and remodel his nearby theater suggests that Howe won away many of his regular, working-class patrons. Thus Howe overcame class barriers to a significant extent, appealing to working-class residents who could afford and wanted to emulate their economic betters. He tapped diverse elements of the urban classes and "established a precedent in point of large attendance."[72] The fragmentation of American culture that so distressed Woodrow Wilson seemed to have been countered.[73] A new common ground had emerged in, of all places, the movie theater.

Ford's Opera House was sold out twice each day in advance. Only standing room was available on the day of each performance. On the last day, Saturday, August 31, a third show was given, and this was sold out as well. "Hundreds were turned away loudly expressing their disappointment."[74] Howe played on this enthusiasm with an advertisement in the *Baltimore Sun*:

OPEN LETTER FROM LYMAN H. HOWE

Mr. Howe desires to express his appreciation of the patronage he has received during the past four weeks. Such a response coming from a hundred thousand people within the time is most gratifying to the originator of "moving pictures that talk" and of the embodiment of sound with sight. He feels that his illustrations of world travel have met your favor, and no effort will be spared to make his future visits to Ford's equally, if not more attractive.[75]

Howe, whose first efforts at showmanship had ended so unhappily in Baltimore more than twenty years before, had every right to be pleased. His Baltimore success was a turning point that enabled him to contract with first-class theaters in other big cities, not simply for a few days each tour but for weeks at a time.

Archie Shepard, perhaps annoyed that Howe had appropriated his idea of a summer season, opened at a prominent Baltimore theater just as Howe ended his run at Ford's. Shepard's "Famous Advanced Moving Pictures" were shown with sound effects at a cost of twenty-five cents for adults and fifteen cents for children—Howe's matinee fee. Films were typical nickelodeon fare, dramas and comedies such as Sigmund Lubin's *When Women Vote*, Edison's *A Winter's Strawride*, and Vitagraph's *The Boy, the Bust and the Bath*. Although his initial performances were sold out, Shepard inadequately distinguished his exhibitions from those at Lubin's and other picture houses where the admission fee was a nickel. After the third week his "indefinite" run was terminated.[76]

Howe approached his business methodically, never exploiting new possibilities as impetuously as Shepard. He used his Baltimore triumph and enhanced reputation to expand but not abruptly change his business activities. As the fall season began, Howe's companies were back on the road, making significant gains in the Midwest. Michigan's *Bay City Tribune* compared Howe's fall exhibition to previous visits: "At the first appearance two years ago the audience was exceedingly small; last year it was fair; this year excellent and the audience seemingly enjoyed itself as fully as it would with a dramatic attraction of high merit."[77] The elaborate use of sound effects and behind the screen dialogue aroused much favorable comment, particularly in Cincinnati, where Howe showed "Moving Pictures That Talk" for six days during Christmas week. Unlike the previous year, when a flood had discouraged attendance, Howe "attracted a surprisingly large and tremendously well-interested audience."[78] Despite a sharp though brief recession following a business panic in October 1907, Howe's companies were regularly greeted by large audiences throughout the 1907–1908 theatrical season.

THE DEMISE OF THE "OLD ROADMAN"

Howe's prosperity contrasted starkly with the experiences of most traveling exhibitors. By late 1907, motion picture theaters could be found in almost every town and city in the United States. As a result, many peripatetic companies, like the New Jersey-based International Moving Picture Company, simply closed down.[79] As Archie Shepard opened his nickelodeons, he gradually disbanded his companies, though some remained active into the summer of 1908. Robert Brackett left Howe's employ in mid-1906 and started his own road show, exhibiting in the midwestern territory he had traveled for Howe. Although he followed in Edwin Hadley's footsteps, his timing could not have been worse. With nickelodeons opening across Kansas, Brackett stayed on the road for only about a year.[80] Yet Howe continued to flourish and filled Brackett's vacated slots with Charles King as company manager and John (Jack) Carleton as an impersonator.[81]

Those traveling exhibitors who persevered soon found the industrial structure changed in ways that further interfered with their ability to operate. Early in 1908, leading American motion picture producers organized as the Association of Edison Licensees, so named because they recognized Thomas Edison's patent claims. By acknowledging Edison claims, these companies created a trade association that could impose advantageous commercial practices. The licensees, seeking to control the supply of films more effectively, only sold prints to selected exchanges. Traveling showmen could no longer acquire films from these companies. Ever tougher fire regulations that varied from town to town were also onerous for many itinerant exhibitors.

By the spring of 1908, *Moving Picture World* remarked, "The road show business in the moving picture line has pretty nearly dwindled to a minimum and with the opening of the next Fall and Winter season there will be less than half a dozen shows in existence in the United States. The moving picture theaters and store shows have put the road man on the retired list."[82] Perhaps the trade journal overstated the case. Some itinerant exhibitors moved to the margins of the industry where they lost contact with the trade press. The Huntley Entertainers continued to tour the upper Midwest with moving pictures until World War I.[83] Carnivals often continued to show films in their black tents. Others, like Hadley and Robertson, cultivated an educational slant, specializing in travel views and news topicals that appealed to church-affiliated groups and cultural conservatives.[84]

Not all peripatetic exhibitors were retrenching or retiring. Several travel lecturers finally emulated Burton Holmes and Dwight Elmendorf by adding motion pictures to their programs. For the 1906–1907 season at the Brooklyn Institute of Arts and Sciences, Frederick Monsen gave four lectures on California and the Southwest, illustrating them with stereopticon slides and films.[85] In subsequent years, he used the same combination. With slides and films Edward S. Curtis illustrated three special lectures on western Indians in spring 1907.[86] Garrett P. Serviss, who had

8-6. Travel lecturer Dwight Elmendorf (ca. 1907).

8-7. Announcement from the Brooklyn Institute of Arts and Sciences (1907).

lectured at the Institute and in the New York area since the 1890s, finally introduced moving pictures into his programs the following year.[87] Elmendorf also began to take his own films.[88] By the 1907–1908 season, two-thirds of the illustrated lectures featured in the Institute's leaflets included moving pictures.

The travel lecture emerged as the antithesis of the dominant film industry. The one appealed to a small elite seeking education and enlightenment, the other to a mass audience seeking amusement. While film production was rationalized and rigorously separated from exhibition in the mainstream industry, the lecturer usually took some or all of his films and photographs. Frederick Monsen even emphasized the fact that he had personally colored his own lantern slides.[89] Holmes appeared in many of his films; at other times he showed scenes through the eye of his camera. Since he was also present during the exhibition, lecturing on the films, Holmes gave audiences a unified, subjective view of his topic. Yet at the

same time, he and his colleagues worked within a genre that had norms
which changed very little. Here again they differed from the commercial,
popular cinema, which was being rapidly transformed in its production,
representational, and commercial methods.

Changes in the commercial structure of the film industry may have actually helped Howe. He had acquired very few of his recent films from the
Edison-licensed manufacturers. The Urban Trading Company, for example, remained outside the Edison association. Furthermore, exchanges
leasing Edison-licensed films could not acquire films from other manufacturers, and licensed manufacturers concentrated almost all their resources
on the production of story films. This made it very easy indeed for Howe
to show the kinds of subjects that people could not see in regular picture
houses.

The most successful of these subjects was *A Ride on a Runaway Train*,
which Max Walkinshaw acquired in Europe and the Howe organization
first showed late in the summer of 1908. For this film, a camera was placed
on the front of a train traveling through the mountains. The camera was
undercranked so that the motion accelerated when projected on the
screen. One Philadelphia reviewer reported that spectators "were genu-
inely thrilled by the sight of the train dashing down steep grades and skirt-
ing yawning chasms at terrific speed. Death it seemed, had his hand upon
the throttle, and, since moving pictures were first seen in Philadelphia,
few have been so applauded."[90] As with other films that Howe showed in
the past, the spectator "feels that he is moving, so realistic is the picture,
and the excitement is intense." The subject culminated with "a plunge
into a tunnel and a suggestion of destruction in a terrific accompanying
crash."[91] Many "found themselves clutching the seats in front of them."[92]
Lloyd Davey remembered that Howe's employees used to "see how many
wet seats you'd find out there. That's what the fellows use to bet each

8-8. Letterhead (1905–1908).

other, how many wet seats they'd find."[93] This terrifying, roller-coaster-like thrill balanced or rather inverted the reassurances offered by other kinds of images.

In the summer of 1908, many big-city theaters offered moving pictures. The recession had marred their business, forcing them to stay open if there was any chance of recouping their losses. Although Shepard had demonstrated the profitability of a summer season of moving pictures, most theatrical managers now found it more advantageous simply to rent films from exchanges rather than divide the box office with an exhibitor. Since Shepard showed the same pictures as the nickelodeons, he had little special to offer. (His attempt to play a summer season in Wilkes-Barre, for example, proved short-lived.)[94] Howe, in contrast, offered legitimate theaters an upscale alternative to nickelodeon fare and so could appeal to their winter patrons. High-toned theaters could maintain a respectable image yet reap financial rewards from showing films. In Baltimore, Howe not only exhibited at Ford's Opera House for two weeks in May 1908 but returned in August for another five. In Cincinnati, he opened at the Lyric Theater for two weeks in early June and reappeared for two more in early September.

While Ford's Grand Opera House and the Lyric were run by local independent theatrical entrepreneurs, Howe also established a fruitful connection with Nixon and Zimmerman, a theatrical organization that controlled several theaters in Philadelphia and Pittsburgh and invited Howe to return to their Pittsburgh house, the Nixon, at the end of June. The sweltering theater was made more bearable by an apparatus for regulating the temperature.[95] Initial expectations were for a two-week run but it was quickly increased to three. "Tremendous patronage" eventually extended the engagement to a total of six weeks.[96] Even on a Monday night, "an audience . . . comfortably filled the playhouse . . . and was constantly evincing its appreciation."[97] Well before Howe's engagement ended, it was announced that "more people have seen [Howe's] entertainment than have ever attended any summer amusement in Pittsburgh."[98] Having impressed Nixon and Zimmerman, Howe played their 1,516-seat Philadelphia theater, the Garrick, for three weeks in September, perhaps delaying its customary fall opening of legitimate entertainment. Thus a relationship was inaugurated that would endure for the next ten years.

By early August 1908 Howe had three companies presenting summer programs in Pittsburgh, Baltimore, and Trenton, New Jersey. In August the Pittsburgh company moved to Cleveland's Opera House for a three-week run. At a time when many of Cleveland's sixty-seven motion picture theaters were defying the city's attempts to license and regulate their premises in order to reduce the danger of fire, the Opera House arranged for off-duty members of the city's fire department to be entertained by

Howe's program and see a "gymnasium drill of the French firemen."[99] Such promotional techniques distinguished Howe from the suspect nickelodeon owners by simultaneously emphasizing his public-spiritedness and the educational value of his pictures.

Pictures That Talk

"Talking Pictures," one of the least examined aspects of cinema before 1915, owed its initial impetus largely to Lyman H. Howe. Many theaters followed his example and presented "pictures that talk" during 1908 and 1909, and to a lesser extent into the 1910s. As one observer remarked, "Since the advent of the moving picture as an amusement feature no phase of the industry has ever become so popular as the talking picture."[100] The popularity of these exhibition methods, however, must be understood as one aspect of a more general crisis in cinema's representational techniques at this time.

Prior to the nickelodeon era, three fundamentally different ways existed for the audience to understand and appreciate a film. First, many films used stories that the audience already knew: spectators therefore had a pre-existing framework for understanding the films. Second, many films had simple story lines that were easily understood and appreciated without any special advance knowledge. In isolated instances producers even provided intertitles to aid the spectator. Finally, exhibitors often assisted the viewer by clarifying the narrative through a lecture or by introducing other sound cues, notably dialogue behind the screen.

With the nickelodeon boom, these representational approaches broke down. Familiar stories no longer existed in sufficient quantity to accommodate the production of many more films. Moreover, the increased diversity of nickelodeon audiences meant that even fewer stories were known in advance by most moviegoers. Simple stories or stories that reworked the same premise from scene to scene lacked sufficient diversity to satisfy audiences. Demand existed for complex narratives, but the problem was how to make them understood. Ultimately, producers learned to present a self-sufficient narrative. This approach emerged gradually over several years. The resulting mode of representation involved a strict linear narrative structure; previous narrative structures had never made it certain if a shot presented a scene that began prior to, simultaneously with, or after the conclusion of the preceding one. Film producers also relied heavily on intertitles to clarify the story told in pictures. This 'modern' form of cinematic expression did not appear overnight. For a period, the exhibitor's intervention provided an effective though expensive form of clarification and enjoyment. Thus trade journals frequently made passing

references to the renaissance of the showman's lecture and more particularly to the popularity of talking pictures.

By 1908, at least a dozen businesses were supplying talking pictures using actors behind the screen. Many other theater managers simply impro-
vised on the idea with the limited resources at their disposal.[101] In almost
every city that Howe frequented during the summer of 1908, other leading
theaters were using actors behind the screen.[102] During Howe's May engagement in Baltimore, Lubin's Theater presented "Talking Moving Pictures" in its lower hall for five cents. At the Maryland Theater, Keith's
Picture Vaudeville showed films and illustrated songs. Specialties included
Mr. and Mrs. Edward H. Kemp lecturing on the Grand Canyon and, the
following week, John C. Bowker lecturing on Russia. Kemp only showed
stereopticon slides but Bowker showed slides and film. After Howe's departure, the Maryland added "Humanova talking pictures" presented by a
traveling troupe of actors organized by Adolph Zukor.[103] In Cincinnati,
the Columbia Theater presented a summer season of moving pictures with
a company of actors delivering dialogue from behind the screen. With the
beginning of the run's third week, the *Cincinnati Commercial Tribune*
reported,

> The daring idea of having human beings imitate the various sounds which
> the moving pictures call for and the dialogue to portray each story has made

8-9. Creating sound effects from behind the screen (1908).

an impression on Columbia audiences and the new name of "advanced pictorial vaudeville" has been coined for the Columbia summer shows. The
company of demonstrators behind the scenes, but close enough to make the
figures appear human, are all thoroughly trained in the work and they are all
thoroughly acquainted with the pictures before they are presented. This work
has injected new life in the picture show. The pictorial demonstrator must be
a character artist and impersonator, a versatile vocalist and able to delineate
all the sounds which are supposed to emanate from the action on the sheets.
Under his magic spell the picture is no longer a picture for it becomes real
life. There are eight of these, both men and women, at work behind the
Columbia pictures.[104]

For its talking and singing pictures, a summer theater at Cincinnati's
Chester Park hired its actors from the same organization as the Columbia.[105] Pittsburgh's Fifth Avenue Theater presented *Rip Van Winkle* and
other films as talking moving pictures; they "proved a factor of great drawing power."[106] Smaller theaters not mentioned in the newspapers, undoubtedly, offered more modest versions of the same idea.

Howe's companies routinely outperformed their rivals. In Pittsburgh,

The "noise" portion of the show—the use of stage effects to make the pictures
more like real—is the best that has ever been used in Pittsburgh. Conversations of the subjects in the pictures, expressing every emotion as depicted on
the faces in the pictures: whirr of machinery, rumble of railroad trains, swish
of water in marine scenes, and various other things that help the onlooker to
imagine that he is witnessing the real thing instead of a counterfeit present-
ment—were in evidence.[107]

To achieve this elaborate sound, the company rehearsed its programs in
advance, in the mornings or afternoons when there were no matinees. But
even Howe's staff sometimes failed to perform adequately. One critic chas-
tised a Howe company because "the volume of sound back of the stage
accompanying the picture was not sufficient to give a truely realistic effect,
and some of the noises were not produced promptly enough."[108]

Competition from other talking picture companies required Howe to
expand his staff of behind-the-screen performers. Maude Anderson joined
Howe's midwestern (Pittsburgh) company in August, while it was exhibiting at the Cleveland Opera House. She provided a badly needed female
voice, and her stature as an actress earned her an interview in the city's
leading paper:

One of the hidden performers with Lyman Howe's moving picture entertainment is Miss Maude Anderson, a legitimate actress who has had a broad
experience in the dramatic field. For the past two seasons she was connected
with Robert Mantell and played small roles. For several years previous she
served in character parts with Maude Adams.
Her appearance here with the Howe show is significant, since it shows

recognition of the importance of having talented artists to carry on the dialogue and unseen acting behind the curtain. If the scene represented is in France, Miss Anderson has a sufficient smattering of the language to carry on the dialogue in that tongue, and so with other lands and their people. Her knowledge of the stage is helpful and often she makes up extemporaneous speeches to go with the pictures as they are shown on the sheet. However, most of the time these behind the curtain actors have daily rehearsals to become familiar with the pictures so that they can make them seem lifelike. "I really like the work," said Miss Anderson yesterday, "for there is no jealousy in the company which is so often the case in dramatic companies, and I don't have to bother with any make-up."[109]

The degree of elaboration varied according to the city and the length of the company's run. Outside large cities, the road shows traveled with only one impersonator, who hired a small group of local children as assistants. When one company arrived at Topeka's Grand Opera House in April 1907, Jack Carleton went to a nearby school and convinced a teacher to let a group of her students perform effects behind the stage.[110] In Scranton, ten-year-old Edward Plottle and one other boy were hired to help out with the sound effects at the local Lyceum Theater. They had previously worked as supernumeraries for a few plays that came through town. Hired for twenty-five or fifty cents a performance, they were rehearsed by Howe's stage director in the morning, then all the boys and the adult stage manager gave matinee and evening performances. The boys were good enough that the following year they were hired to perform in Wilkes-Barre as well as Scranton.[111]

Although the same basic arrangements occurred in the large cities, two or more additional skilled impersonators were brought in for these shows. Thus for Howe's Pittsburgh visit in the summer of 1908, D. J. Tasker, Fred Morgan, E. C. Mayo and Jack Carleton were behind the screen.[112] They were aided by large numbers of children. "On the floor, squatting like a bunch of young Turks, are thirty men and children with a little fox terrier named Buster as an added starter," reported one behind-the-scenes visitor.[113] After some queries, he discovered that some of the children "are paid for their labor, while others are willing to work simply for the privilege of seeing the pictures." Howe's talking pictures relied heavily on inexpensive child labor—but labor that was provided enthusiastically and allowed children to participate in the creation of an elaborate production.[114] For this small group, the operational aesthetic remained in effect. For paying customers, "pictures that talk" effaced the exhibition process while emphasizing spectacle and the audience's visceral involvement.

Although Howe's companies generally outperformed their rivals, the widespread nature of these exhibition practices preempted the Wilkes-Barre showman's entrance into several major markets. Henry Lee, who had headlined many vaudeville bills as a mimic and impersonator, presented his "Mimic World" at Chicago's prestigious Auditorium Theater. It was immediately hailed by the critics. Burns Mantle of the *Chicago Tribune* wrote:

> The moving picture moves; and having moved, begins to talk. In Henry Lee's "Mimic World" entertainment introduced in the Auditorium yesterday afternoon.
>
> Mr. Lee has sought to perfect the moving picture show. He offers two kinds—the pictured play, and the pictured experience of interest. The pictured play is either a drama or a farce, and the story of this is told by the actor (Joseph Kilgour), who stands at the side of the screen, while practically every action displayed on the screen is audibly duplicated back of the screen on the stage.
>
> The pictured incidents may deal with sports in Australia or the shipment of ice from Norway to England, or, perhaps, the singing of several songs by a music hall soubrette in London. The element of realism is the same as that introduced in the plays.
>
> Some thirty people assist Mr. Lee, including two organists, Arthur Dunham and Arthur Keller. The other twenty-eight are variously employed. All have been rehearsed with the pictures. Whenever a lady falls down a hill in the picture an alert person back of the screen makes a noise like a lady falling down hill. If there is a wood chopping scene, as there is, several industrious young men with hatchets, each watching his particular chopper on the screen, hacks away at a tree trunk in time with the photographed chopper. There is a long table devoted to horses, with an assortment of cocoanut shells for pavement trotting, and rubber cups for galloping over the turf. The wind and rain machines are numerous, and the practiced clog dancers seldom miss a tap with their hands that the pictured dancers should make with their shoes.[115]

Lee worked in conjunction with George Kleine, America's major importer of foreign films. Kleine, who had not joined the Edison licensees, was agent for films produced by the Urban Trading Company and other Howe sources. The mix of fiction and documentary subjects, the reliance on a single keyboard instrument, the elaborate stage effects, and actors behind the screen made Lee's program virtually indistinguishable from Howe's.[116] Talking pictures played in many New York theaters. As the 1908 summer season began, the *New York Clipper* reported that Loew's People's Vaudeville Circuit "is using talking pictures in all its theatres. These are put on in a more elaborate style than is usual, using the best dramatic talent available and meeting with great success."[117]

The nickelodeon boom destroyed the economic basis for most traveling exhibitors by usurping their audiences. Most showmen changed with the times by starting permanent theaters, forming distribution companies, or retreating to the nation's backwaters where towns were too small to support a regular picture house. Lyman H. Howe, in contrast, responded by moving into the large cities and offering a selection of films that was fundamentally different from the fare being screened by the movie houses. After wavering, uncertain of his future course, he returned to a cinema of reassurance, sharply distinguished from the cinema of desire that dominated the nickelodeons. He further buttressed his exhibitions by featuring exclusive subjects that he had either taken himself or, as with scenes of the Russo-Japanese War, purchased on a restricted basis. His method of exhibition, elaborate behind-the-screen effects and dialogue, further distinguished his shows from the average storefront. Moving pictures were growing in popularity among all Americans, including members of the middle and elite classes who felt uncomfortable visiting dingy picture shows and sitting next to a sweaty day laborer on the way home from his job. The middle classes were Howe's principal clientele; when the working class attended, they dressed up in their Sunday best. Showmen and motion picture entrepreneurs across the country again paid Howe the highest compliment—in whole or in part they imitated his programs. Although these imitators blocked Howe's entrance into the two largest markets, other developments soon enabled Howe to have a gala premiere in New York City and eventually exhibit in Chicago as well.

9

★ ★

Motion Pictures under Attack:
Howe Provides a Model Cinema,
1908-1911

★ ★ ★

Every exhibitor ought to make time and spend a Sunday evening at
Lyman Howe's model moving picture entertainment.
                        Clipping, ca. February 1909, Paul Felton scrapbook

REFORMERS, ministers, and cultural guardians questioned the cinema's
social role with unprecedented urgency in the new era of nickelodeon
theaters. Local officials often found the picture houses unsafe. In this respect Wilkes-Barre was not unusual. When a building inspector rummaged
through its four nickelodeons in late November 1907, he concluded they
were firetraps. The Dreamland had red lights indicating exits where none
actually existed. The Empire, owned by the same firm, had unmarked fire
exits that were locked and debris in the alleyway outside. Across the
street, the Star Theater had an unmarked exit almost completely blocked
by the canvas screen. Audiences at the Unique would have had to burst
through the screen to reach the fire escape.[1] The *Wilkes-Barre Record* applauded the crackdown, remarking, "The moving picture exhibition furnishes cheap entertainment to many people, but the safety of the people
should be the first consideration."[2] As city after city mandated new regulations, many nickelodeon owners complied only reluctantly, while others
even resisted.[3]

Religious conservatives saw the physical dangers posed by nickelodeons
as the external manifestation of a more insidious corruption. Serious opposition to the nickelodeon phenomenon had already developed by 1906,
when Chicago clergymen waged war against motion picture theaters because "they inflame the minds of the younger generation, seriously divert-
ing their moral senses and awakening prurient thoughts which prepare the
way for future sin."[4] Some influential spokesmen urged that motion picture shows be abolished. Many cities exercised informal censorship. In
April 1907, the mayor of Worcester, Massachusetts, banned showings of

Sigmund Lubin's *The Unwritten Law* for its salacious depiction of relations between Stanford White and Evelyn Nesbitt.[5] The Huntley Entertainers, who exhibited the same film along their route, also encountered opposition from community leaders. Large attendance, however, more than compensated for the annoyance.[6] Later that year, Cleveland police arrested the proprietor of the Lyric for showing *A Lust for Gold* because it showed a murder and debased the public's morals.[7] Other vicinities, including Chicago, Detroit, and St. Joseph, Missouri, required that films be censored by local authorities.[8] Many cities previously allowing Sunday shows either passed ordinances that prohibited them or began to enforce old Sunday blue laws.

New York City (1910 population: 4,766,883) was the center of much anti-motion picture agitation led by Protestant clergy, many of whom had long doubted the value of any form of theatrical amusement. One of Brooklyn's most active opponents was Canon William Sheafe Chase. At a talk to an association of charity workers, Chase discussed "Protecting Children from Demoralizing Influences of the Theater." His speech praised "a bill introduced last year and defeated in the [New York State] Senate, prohibiting the admission of children to theatrical and other entertainments calculated to injure their morals. . . . He said that the work against the operation of the demoralizing picture exhibition was just a phase of it."[9] Yet two days later, Howe presented moving pictures under the auspices of the YMCA at its Brooklyn Auditorium.[10] This was only symptomatic of Howe's continuing ability to attract church-based support. Although the Methodist Episcopal Church reaffirmed its opposition to theatrical amusement in May 1908, Howe continued to present his "educational" programs under the auspices of their affiliates.[11]

Throughout 1907 and 1908, a war was waged in New York City around the issue of the Sunday show. Managers were arrested and convicted, only to have their convictions overruled by a higher court.[12] When Sunday shows were completely banned in December 1907, working-class residents held a protest.[13] Theatrical managers were equally distressed. Many vaudeville theaters would have difficulty showing a profit without the aid of Sunday concerts.[14] Although amusement managers finally won that battle, Mayor George Brinton McClellan renewed the war a year later, when he held public hearings on the desirability of Sunday picture shows and on the physical safety of nickelodeon theaters. Ministers testified and condemned motion pictures as morally degenerate. One reverend asked, "Is a man at liberty to make money from the morals of people? Is he to profit from the corruption of the minds of children?"[15] Dr. E. Fellows Jenkins of the Society for the Prevention of Cruelty to Children declared, "The darkened rooms, combined with the influence of pictures projected on the screens, have given opportunities for a new form of degeneracy."[16]

A member of the Bureau of Licenses, who had surveyed New York's nick-elodeons, found them to be unsafe. The following day, Christmas Eve, Mayor McClellan revoked the licenses of all the city's "common shows"—its small nickelodeons—and refused to issue or renew licenses to any the-ater that did not promise to stay closed on Sunday. Although his action was soon declared illegal by Judge William J. Gaynor of the Supreme Court in Kings County (Brooklyn), almost all the shows were closed on Christmas when theatrical attendance was normally at its height.

The day after Christmas, Police Commissioner Theodore Alfred Bing-ham brought the managers of large theaters, those operating under a $500 a year license, into his office. He handed them the statute covering Sun-day shows and indicated that it would be rigidly and broadly enforced. This law prohibited "any moving picture given in a play or a part of a play" but allowed "moving pictures illustrating lectures of an instructive or educational character."[17] According to Terry Ramsaye, theaters show-ing a film like *The Great Train Robbery* then used a lecturer to inform patrons, "These are railroad tracks. More railroad tracks."[18] Yet managers could not simply undermine the statute's intent: that might soon lead to still more rigorous restrictions. In the fight for the Sunday show, theater managers had to prove that Sunday programs were not indecent in and of themselves, to demonstrate the cinema's real potential for instruction and elevation. Howe proved a useful ally in the achievement of this goal.

While ministers and reformers decried the degenerative influences of motion pictures, they regularly applauded Howe's programs for their edi-fying value. As one Pittsburgh critic noted, "Not one [patron] left the pretty playhouse without feeling benefited materially as the result of seeing the pictures. The program is a liberal education in itself, covering as it does nearly the entire earth, and showing much that could not be learned from books."[19] Another in Cincinnati found that, "These Howe views are excellently selected to begin with, imparting the dignity of truth and the distinction of educational subjects to an entertainment that has been made cheap, in most exhibitions of similar kind, by an overabundance of the frivolous or unimportant."[20] By the summer of 1908 Howe was emerg-ing as the foremost representative of what "responsible" people thought the cinema should be.

HOWE AT THE NEW YORK HIPPODROME

In the context of the debate over moving pictures, Howe's Sunday exhi-bitions at the New York Hippodrome in January and February 1909 took on unusual significance. The 5,200-seat Hippodrome was "perhaps the largest and grandest staged playhouse in the world."[21] Managers Lee Shu-bert and Max Anderson gave few Sunday programs, and then only of the

9-1. Poster (1909).

most prestigious kind.[22] Howe's evening exhibition on Sunday, January 31, 1909, thus focused maximum attention on a kind of entertainment that was already controversial. Scenes of the recent earthquake in Sicily, the first to be projected in New York, provided the headline attraction. "Messina was shown in all its natural beauty before the disaster. Then in lieu of the earthquake, a Gatling gun and stage lightning represented the destructive forces of nature, and the beautiful city was shown in ruins with rescuers working over the injured."[23] The program also included films of Egypt, France, Russia, the Wrights' airplane, and A Runaway Train. "Lyman Howe gave New York the best example of what a high class moving picture entertainment ought to be that it has ever had," exclaimed the Dramatic Mirror. "It was a moving picture show pure and simple, but it was presented in such an intelligent manner, with appropriate stage and light effects, and the programme was so well selected, that the large au-

9-2 The Hippodrome in New York City (early 1909).

dience recorded its warm approval by repeated and hearty applause."[24]
The Howe organization made a special effort to induce Shubert and Anderson to see the show.[25] They attended and were impressed. In a public
letter of endorsement, the managers declared that the attraction had exceeded their "most sanguine expectations" and demonstrated "the real
possibilities of animated photography, in a way that was a revelation to
the vast audience."[26]

Howe's prestigious New York debut was followed by two more Sunday
concerts at the Hippodrome. Programs for each screening detailed a variety of instructive subjects:

> A Carriage Drive Through Rome.—*A personally conducted tour of the
> ancient and historic city with a competent and experienced guide. The most
> memorable ruins of Rome at the zenith of her power are passed and in-
> spected en route.*
>
> The Fountains of Rome.—*A wealth of sculptured art, beauty and grace are
> represented by the famous fountains of the city.*
>
> Physical Phenomena.—*Kaleidoscopic effects; weird positive and negative
> electrical discharges; Smoke Vortices; Story of a Soap Bubble. Exceedingly
> interesting experiments photographed for the first time in moving pictures.*

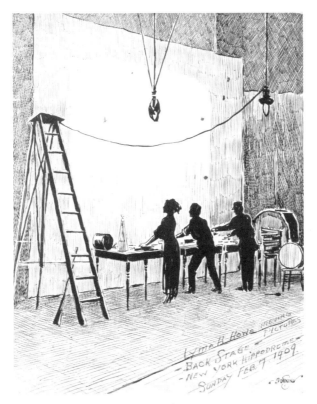

9-3. Sound-effects artists at work.

Trooping the Colors.—*The most Brilliant Military Review in England. A magnificent spectacle at Buckingham Palace, London, attended by King Edward VII and the Royal Family.*

The India of To-day and Yesterday.

Photographed by Special Authority of the Indian Government and the Secretary of State for India.

(1) *Busy Life in Bombay and Environs.*

(2) *Cosmopolitan Calcutta—The Viceroy and Staff leaving for Simla.*

(3) *Market scenes in Darjeeling on a Sunday morning.*

(4) *Ancient Benares viewed from the Sacred Ganges; A panorama of ruins is unrolled which is indescribable. It forms a mute but eloquent tribute to a mighty past. Countless millions for thousands of years have deified the river and worshipped in this temple-burdened city.*

(5) *A devotee Doing Penance—Lying on a bed of nails for seven years— a typical illustration of religious devotion.*

(6) *The Monkey Temple—The abode of five hundred Monkeys worshipped as divine by the Hindus.*

(7) *Primitive Irrigation.*

Niagara Falls in Winter.
*Nothing could be more pleasing than these scenes of picturesque splendor.
Niagara Falls encompassed by immense fantastic masses of ice and robed
in snow presents a scene of sublime grandeur.*
Animal and Bird Sagacity.
*Strange and unusual friendships. Unique, quaint and intensely humorous ep-
isodes. Sagacious conduct of animals hitherto regarded as stupid, and mis-
chievous scenes in a Central African forest.*
Through Savoy (France) by Automobile.
*A superb reproduction of the beauties of nature. The scenes depicted range
from the idyllic to the majestic, from placid river scenes through swirling,
foaming torrents to snow-capped Alpine heights, and abound throughout in
glorious perspectives.*
The Lightning Post Card Artist.
*A delightfully whimsical series combining genuine humor, magic and mystery
executed with consummate art.*
New Scenes of the Sicily Disaster.
*These views are now enroute to New York and will arrive here the end of the
week. Mr. Howe guarantees that they will positively be entirely different
from the Sicily Earthquake scenes which he exhibited here last Sunday
night, and will be a complete series in detail of the latest phase of Sicily's
tragic fate.*
A Thrilling 10-mile Steeplechase in England.
*The most startling series of steeplechasing ever photographed, Crowded with
incidents and accidents, hair-breadth escapes and marvelous riding from
start to finish, it proves conclusively that the riders, by their pluck and
daring, richly earn the big fees paid them.*
The Reedham Orphans in their Annual Drill.
(1908)—Displaying new and elaborate evolutions.
Modern Sculptors.
A poem in color, sculpture and art. [27]

Only a discreet notice at the bottom announced that several comedies
unmentioned in the program would also be shown. They were carefully
censored to avoid offending even the most moralistic tastes. As Lloyd
Davey recalled, "These films were mostly French and they had a lot of
different ideas about virtue over there than we did. And Howe was giving
shows with the Ladies' Aid Society and the Missionary Society and so
forth. So we just cut, cut, cut, cut. It's a wonder there was anything
left!"[28] The showman publicized the educational and appeared to offer
comedy as a quick respite before more instruction. He thus refuted the
extremist statements of conservatives like Archbishop Joseph Murphy Farley who delivered a sermon at St. Patrick's Cathedral on the second Sunday of Howe's run. Farley lambasted modern theatrical amusement: "We
see to-day men and women—old men and old women—who ought to
know better bring the young to these orgies of obscenity."[29] Such blanket

condemnations appeared ludicrous in light of Howe's Hippodrome shows (see Appendix G, Document 5).

The kinds of people who attended the Hippodrome concerts were as important as what was shown and how it was presented. With tickets priced from twenty-five cents to one dollar, the Sunday shows attracted well-to-do patrons who would not otherwise attend motion picture programs. One trade journalist ecstatically remarked,

> Who was there? A fine, big and pleased audience, not unlike any that ever crowded the Gay White Way at the midnight hour. There was a generous sprinkling of silk hats and opera gowns, and no very few automobiles took cargoes from this moving picture show. It was such an audience that made one sit back for a moment and close his eyes and think back a few years; the natural question followed, "Who would have thought it would be thus?" Sitting very near the writer were two clergymen, and he took a keen, almost fiendish delight in the pleasure which it was apparent they were deriving from the entertainment. The writer wished that he could have seen there every foe of picturedom, to show them what the ideal moving picture entertainment looks like, and to gloat over their inevitable admission that it deserves more of their aid than condemnation. As reel after reel was run off on the big sheet, the moving picture was soaring high above the appellation "amusement for the masses" and other phrases of more or less lowly designation.[30]

In a time of crisis, when the city's cultural fabric was badly frayed, Howe's shows reduced tensions and reassured all parties involved in the dispute. But one demonstration of a model cinema could not resolve the crisis over cinema's role in society. Howe's shows had symbolic significance, but his approach was incompatible with dominant motion picture practices. The idea of an exhibitor meticulously selecting a film program when programs were customarily changed every day was unrealistic. In any case, nickelodeon patrons were generally attracted to the sensational, the spectacular and the melodramatic—the kinds of films reformers opposed and Howe avoided. In the end, a very different resolution was found. In February 1909, industry leaders and various New York reformers set up what soon became the National Board of Censorship. The board passed judgement on films prior to their release, requiring the removal of offending scenes in some cases while banning entire subjects in rare instances. The board brought more liberal reformers into the approval process and made sweeping denunciations more difficult or less credible. Although the cinema frequently came under attack in succeeding years, protests never reached the proportions of the period just prior to Howe's Hippodrome appearance.

Despite their critical success, the Hippodrome triumphs did not give Howe new commercial opportunities in New York. Terry Ramsaye has suggested that motion picture audiences and amusement entrepreneurs

developed strong negative associations to the notion of "educational" programming in reaction to Mayor McCellan's attempts at censorship.[31] Although the Howe organization periodically contemplated a return to a
major New York theater, it never could arrange acceptable terms.[32]

LYMAN H. HOWE'S NEW YORK HIPPODROME
TRAVEL FESTIVAL

Howe's New York debut coincided with a fundamental commercial reor-
ganization of the motion picture industry. The Edison and Biograph companies patched up their differences and formed the Motion Picture Patents
Company. This organization, activated on March 1, included the Edison
and Biograph companies, all the former Edison licensees, and George
Kleine, who was allowed to import European subjects produced by Charles
Urban's Urban-Eclipse Company and Gaumont. The Patents Company
not only licensed producers but film exchanges and theaters. As Howe had
done during the previous year, he survived by *not* being a licensed exhibitor. His very success depended on showing what could not be seen in a
regular picture house. Although the Motion Picture Patents Company
sued producers like Carl Laemmle, they did not pursue Howe, Burton
Holmes, or other illustrated lecturers. The Patents Company, publicly
committed to uplifting the cinema, did not wish to bring adverse publicity
on itself and felt little threatened by these alternate practices. Howe's
ability to acquire films from Charles Urban and Gaumont went uncur-
tailed.[33] Howe was thus able to reap the full benefits of his Hippodrome
screenings outside New York City.

The Hippodrome success enabled Howe to solidify ties with the Shuberts' growing theatrical empire. In early March, J. J. Shubert asked
Howe, "As we are closing our season about the first of May, we could
arrange to put pictures in our various houses throughout the country. Does
a proposition of this kind interest you? Kindly let me know."[34] The Shuberts, battling the theatrical trust led by Klaw and Erlanger, were seeking
reputable attractions for the summer months. Pflueger responded by offering unbooked time for Howe's several companies to the Shuberts. He also
offered terms that the Howe organization made for similar engagements:
"50/50—no orchestra—the house to pay the regular bill-posting and
newspaper advertising, but the extra bill-posting and newspaper advertising to be mutually agreed upon and shared pro rata."[35] J. J. Shubert found
these terms "quite unsatisfactory." He wanted a fifty-fifty split with Howe
assuming all promotional and advertising costs. He also wanted the companies in his theaters by mid-May or June 1. If Howe balked, he indicated
that he had offers from several other picture concerns.

A compromise was reached wherein Shubert picked up at least some of
the advertising costs, and Howe formed a fourth and then a fifth company

so his enterprise could work with established customers and still play Shubert theaters. Paul Felton, who had played the piano for Howe's Hippodrome showings, was made a company manager. So was H. J. Bayley.[36]
Hired as impersonators were Fred R. Wrenn and his wife Marie Carleton
Wrenn, another member of LeRoy and Jack Carleton's family.[37] Howe
opened at the Shuberts' 1,241-seat Garrick Theater in St Louis on May 9
and remained for five weeks. A week later another company appeared in
Kansas City for the first time, at the 1,603-seat Shubert, and remained for
five weeks. Howe had a third five-week run at the Shuberts' 1,469-seat
Royal Alexandria Theater in Toronto, Canada. Opening on May 3, the
exhibitor "came and conquered,"[38] then moved to the Shuberts' 2,021-
seat Teck Theater in Buffalo for an additional three weeks.

Howe, advertising his shows as "Lyman H. Howe's New York Hippodrome Travel Festival," found still further opportunities. A Howe company appeared for the first time in Washington, D.C. (1910 population:
331,069). Since "the city is a little too far south and too warm to expect
big business during these months," a protracted summer run was deemed
undesirable.[39] Instead, Howe's Baltimore-based unit commuted to the
capital's 1,450-seat Columbia Theater for three Sunday showings in August while a fourth, mid-September date was incorporated into the regular
fall tour. The Washington exhibitions proved so successful that this policy
of Sunday showings was extended in future seasons.[40] Unlike most promoters of Sunday concerts, Howe did not seek long-term venues for his
programs. Like Burton Holmes, who gave a series of Sunday lectures in
February and March 1909, Howe offered a brief "season" and then moved
on.[41]

The year 1909 was a high point for Howe. In many cities his shows
enjoyed longer runs than in any prior or subsequent year. In Cincinnati,
record-breaking crowds jammed the Lyric to capacity, and one Sunday
afternoon show drew "the largest crowd ever in the Lyric."[42] Howe's engagement at Nixon and Zimmerman's Garrick Theater in Philadelphia
lasted twelve weeks and was the longest continuous run his shows ever
enjoyed. Companies remained in Pittsburgh for eight weeks and in Boston
for five—his only summer season in that city.[43] His five-week summer season in Baltimore might except for his limited number of
companies. The New York Hippodrome Travel Festival combined prestige, reputation, and novelty. This and a lack of direct competition
yielded extraordinary box-office results.

LYMAN H. HOWE, THE MASTER
NEWSPAPER PUFFER

The possibilities for puffing a traveling picture show were probably never
more fully realized than in Cleveland where Howe enjoyed a ten-week run

9-4. Howe and family, with Lloyd Davies (ca. 1909).

at B. F. Keith's 3,000-seat Hippodrome during the summer of 1909. The combined Keith-Howe publicity machine elaborated on Howe's biographical legend as it placed an impressive stream of promotional pieces in the local papers. During Howe's first week, an attention-gathering blurb appeared in the *Cleveland Plain Dealer* almost every day. One item informed readers that Howe was depositing a copy of *Sicily Before and After the Earthquake* in the cornerstone of the Wilkes-Barre city hall.[44] The next day, it was reported that the popularity of Howe's shows had made him a millionaire in less than ten years.[45] (None of these claims appear to be true.) Howe then came to town and was interviewed, observing:

> From the way business has started out, it is evident that Cleveland will maintain its high place on our books. The pictures I show will always attract big crowds of foreign born citizens and this is especially true of Cleveland. People

read the papers keenly here and when a list of the foreign lands depicted are announced I can always see people of those nationalities which the pictures represent coming up to the box office. For instance, this week I have noted the great number of Russians and Italians attracted by the announcements of views of Russia and Italy, while I have been astonished to note that there are so many people of French extraction here who come to see the scenes of Paris and of France. Next week I will attract an entirely different set of nationalities. The Americanized foreigner looks upon these pictures as a quick, economical and pleasant means of reviving memories and details of the fatherland.[46]

In addition, announcements of forthcoming films and a review appeared in the *Plain Dealer* over the course of every week.

The publicity continued relentlessly, as articles in several local papers featured members of the Howe company. A brief biography of LeRoy Carleton described his job coaching "young imitators" [impersonators and sound-effects artists] who were "studying for important places with other Howe shows."[47] When pianist Emilie Mather left to visit her mother in mid-July, company manager Paul Felton resumed his old role as piano player, providing an excuse for another piece. After "explaining" that Felton learned to play the piano so he could get a job with Howe, the article reported that Howe went into the motion picture business after seeing "the first moving picture machine brought to this country" at Keith's theater in Philadelphia. For added dramatic effect, Howe's state at the time was described as penniless. The run at Keith's Hippodrome was thus depicted as a reunion of sorts.[48] (Again, none of this appears to have been true.) One portrait in the *Plain Dealer* showed six company imitators who worked behind the screen. Another article in the Sunday magazine section was devoted to imitators Mr. and Mrs. Wrenn and their efforts to train the fox terrier Trixie to bark on cue. By the end of the Howe run, every member of the Howe company had been profiled.

An entirely different type of article emphasized Howe's public-spiritedness and the educational value of his films. Perhaps his biggest coup was a front-page news item in the *Plain Dealer*:

"Church picnics are no good," says Rev. G. F. Williams, of the Church of the Ascension, Lakewood. "They're a thing of the past."

Williams put his ideas into practical effect yesterday afternoon when he took 150 of his Sunday school children to Keith's Hippodrome to see the Lyman H. Howe moving pictures. The trip to the theater was a substitute for the old time picnic.

"Instead of taking a crowd of children, packing them into stuffy trains, shaking them up for fifty to 100 miles, landing them at a 'park' at which they ate rich and unhealthful meals, and then bringing them home half asleep

9-5. A drawing by Paul Felton (1909).

after having lost one or more by drowning, we take them to the theater once each year.

"I believe in sending children—and grown folks, too—to the theater, provided that the shows are of the right sort. Every Sunday morning I announce from the pulpit the names of the good plays in town, and I advise my parishioners to attend."[49]

Another newspaper detailed a free morning screening for newsboys.[50]

In one interview, Howe told of the many opportunities he had of making money when proprietors of foreign hotels, theaters, and restaurants tried to bribe his cameramen to take pictures of their businesses. But he reassured readers, "Fortunately we are in a position where such offers have no allurements for us, and yet the sums are not trivial, but highly substantial. We would not bother our audiences by thrusting an advertisement before them, even though it was so carefully veiled that the spectators

9-6. Noisemakers at work (July 1909).

would be unconscious of the trick."[51] Although such temptations were entirely mythical, these assurances served to emphasize Howe's integrity.

The educational value of another group of films, then playing at the Hippodrome, was dramatized in a fanciful interview with Max Walkinshaw. The general manager suggested that he and two Howe cameramen had shot the scenes in India and Ceylon. Assistance, he claimed, was provided by Professor Mowskowski and Professor Delenka of the Berlin Academy of Sciences.

> I received an invitation from these gentlemen to form a party with them to take pictures of the daily life and habits of an aboriginal race of Veddahs in Ceylon. . . . We went to Ceylon and secured some excellent views of this ancient people. They are one of the oldest and most primitive races still extant; but they are fast disappearing and now number less than 2,000. Of course we intended to use the pictures for general exhibition purposes but the scientists attach great ethnological value to the films and a roll will be deposited as an historic asset in the vaults of the academy. A request for a copy has also been received from the trustees of the British museum.[52]

In another interview, Walkinshaw remarked that Europeans believed in cinema's scientific value and used it as "a practical means of conveying important information in commercial enterprises and as a means for modern education."[53] Additional publicity claimed that Howe's moving pictures were of great value to the United States government. Men considering enlistment in the navy were being given free passes to Howe's shows. "The navy department feels that applicants and wavering candidates for positions in the navy will be readily won over by this method of thoroughly exploiting the wonders and beauties of foreign travel such as are offered in an enlistment in the navy."[54] If the pictures could inspire a man to join the navy for three years, certainly others would enjoy them as well.

Newspaper puff frequently exaggerated the scope of the Howe organization. Not only was Walkinshaw's trip to India bogus, but one news blurb announced that Howe had taken several excellent films of Cleveland and screened them for the Hippodrome staff. Elaborate developing tanks were said to fill the backstage area.[55] Yet a public screening of these films never followed, in Cleveland or anywhere else. This same article, moreover, indicated that Howe planned to show the films in Europe that fall. Such a business venture was never seriously considered and certainly never occurred.[56] Yet it effectively fostered an image of Howe as an international entrepreneur who worked both sides of the Atlantic.

The Howe Organization and Its Programming

To attract diverse social and cultural groups, Howe's publicity was complemented by carefully balanced programs. "In subject matter they are just heavy enough to attract the serious minded and yet light enough for those seeking amusement only," a Howe associate explained to J. J. Shubert.[57] The balancing even extended to the name of his exhibitions, called a "travel festival" instead of "travel lectures."

Howe turned increasingly to the depiction of the U.S. military, appealing to American patriotism in ways that had effectively transcend cultural differences in the past. *War Games*, initially featured during his 1910 spring tour, proved particularly popular. The previous summer, American armed forces had conducted "war games" in the Boston area amidst extensive front-page coverage in the country's newspapers.[58] Howe personnel subsequently photographed an array of military activities "for which Mr. Howe was granted a special permit from the government through the good offices of congressman Henry W. Palmer and attorney Andrew Hourigan."[59] The *Baltimore Sun*, one of several newspapers to give the series prominent attention, explained,

> The government, anxious to promote a greater interest in the service, gave the exhibitor every facility to produce his "United States War Game," the first animated reproduction of the fighting forces of a great nation. More than 10,000 soldiers, midshipmen at Annapolis, cadets at West Point and officers posed for the scenes. The wonderful trick cavalry at Fort Myer display their ability, land mines explode, crack companies of the army make record time

in scaling walls, there is a musical manual drill by colored troopers and the colored regiment that led the charge at San Juan Hill with Colonel Roosevelt demonstrate their present efficiency on horse and foot.

The building and destruction of a pontoon bridge by engineers with an attack, repulse and retreat of a thousand men, is an interesting part of the spectacle. For the first time human eyes see the actual impact of a giant projectile hurled from the largest gun in the service against the [armored plate of a battleship. The photographer] was within 40 feet of the plate and the reproduction is remarkably clean. Admiral Dewey and Rear-Admiral Schley are included in the scenes.[60]

In the past, Howe's presentations in this genre had been confined primarily to the European armed forces. *War Games*, therefore, inaugurated a significant new development in Howe's programming. A new sense of America's international role emerged even as this display of American power was intended to demonstrate the value of a larger military.

Some spectators saw America's new relationship with Europe epitomized in *The Funeral of King Edward*, which documented the pomp surrounding the death of England's monarch. In Cincinnati, Howe patrons were "held in silent admiration as the great parade moved along, breaking out in applause only occasionally as some feature of particular interest excited attention. The life-like figures of the many kings in the procession following the royal catafalque were the occasion of much comment while the appearance of Colonel Roosevelt, minus any pretentious decorations of the others, brought spontaneous applause."[61] Through contrasts and parallels, the film alluded to an Anglo-American alliance. The English King symbolized the British empire while the simply dressed Roosevelt embodied America's imperial adventures. On the one hand there was tradition and ceremony, on the other iconoclasm and youthful vigor. *The Funeral of King Edward*, Howe's principal feature during the 1910 fall tour, was implicitly related to *War Games*.

Howe rarely produced films between 1908 and 1910. One of his few efforts focused on the showman's continuing interest in the relation of sound and image. *Wild Animals' Impression of Music*, taken at the Washington Zoo in September 1909, claimed to document a scientific experiment regarding the listening preferences of various mammals.[62] His crew filmed animals responding to different phonographic recordings of music. Although the film enhanced Howe's programs during the following year, the showman avoided extensive filmmaking at a time when the Motion Picture Patents Company was busily suing Carl Laemmle and other independent producers for patent infringement. By 1911, as the independent movement gained momentum, less caution was required, and Howe's need for his own distinctive subjects had increased. Not only were travel lecturers freely making their own productions, but several large companies

9-7a,b. *The Funeral of King Edward* (1910). Roosevelt walks modestly in the lower right corner of the image.

had moved into the travel film field. Howe responded to these threats and
to more sweeping changes in motion picture practices by expanding his
production capabilities.

HOWE INCREASES HIS FILMMAKING ACTIVITIES

In Europe, where Howe and Walkinshaw made frequent visits, the newsreel enjoyed wide popularity by mid-1910. Such achievement may have
encouraged Howe to pursue a somewhat similar course in the United
States, where the newsreel had not yet been established. Early in 1911 he
hired the English cameraman H. A. Crowhurst and brought him to the
United States. Shortly after his arrival, one newspaper detailed Crowhurst's background: "He has taken pictures all thru the United Kingdom
and in every country in Europe. He has recorded the life of the Parisians,
the military manoeuvres of the Italian cavalry, the gymnastic exhibitions
in Belgrade, the capital of Servia, the life of Russians in St. Petersburg
and Moscow. He has recorded the movements of monarchs and crowned
princes and has defied authority in obtaining the photographs which afterwards delighted thousands of people."[63] Crowhurst was teamed with
Charles Bosworth, one of Howe's advance representatives, who now assumed the role of producer.

Howe's two-man crew traveled around the United States taking local
scenes and news films. In February 1911 Crowhurst and Bosworth arrived
in Duluth, Minnesota (1910 population: 78,466), to make what one local
newspaper called "the first moving pictures of this part of the United
States":

> The skee tournament will be the big feature of the series of pictures to be
> made. Excellent positions from which the advantages of the local hill will be
> demonstrated and striking scenes of the biggest jumps made have been re-
> served for the moving picture camera. The contestants are keenly alive to
> the international reputation coming from the tiny films to be exposed and
> they have promised their best efforts. A panorama of the crowd and some
> close pictures of some of those attending will also be made.
>
> Another part of the arrangements is the reproduction of a ride on an ice
> boat. The camera will be taken on one of the biggest local ice boats and a
> record flight photographed. It is planned to take a picture of the ride down
> the traction car incline at Seventh avenue west with a sweeping view of the
> harbor. This is one of the points of Duluth that is generally reproduced in
> newspapers and magazines and Mr Howe is anxious to make it a good part of
> his series.[64]

Among the scenes at the ski tournament, they took John Rudd doing a
double somersault on skis.[65]

Three sound effects specialists—D. J. Tasker, Fred C. Morgan and John

Carleton—were on hand to "record" the sound for later reproduction. According to a local report,

> A novel part of the picture taking will be the presence of the three Howe imitators. They will not appear in the pictures but their work will be an important feature of the reproduction of the films in the four Howe organizations which appear in the leading theaters of the United States and Canada. These men "listen" to the events photographed. It is their business to build for stage presentation behind the screens on which the pictures are to be flashed mechanical apparatus that will exactly reproduce the sounds of the things depicted. Records of exclamations, charactertistic conversations, etc., are also made for the reproductions. [66]

Howe's concern for accurate sound reproduction was carrying over from his early film showings, when the phonograph provided appropriate effects.

The films of Duluth were first presented at the city's 1,500-seat Lyceum Theater on March 4 and 5 when Howe's travel festival made its regular, semiannual appearance. Shortly before the exhibition, Howe wrote the Lyceum manager, puffing the local views. He insisted that the scenes would not only be of great local interest but would be a big advertisement for Duluth when exhibited all over the United States and Europe. Using a promotional angle he would employ many times in the future, Howe contended that residents should patronize the show and see themselves as others would see them.

The ski tournament scenes were shown by Howe's companies in other cities, but the films of Duluth were apparently only for local consumption. Similar local views were taken and shown in Cleveland, Ithaca (1910 population: 14,802), and other cities over the next year. [67] In both Duluth and Ithaca, Howe gave credit for the idea to the local theater manager and enlisted local business groups to assist in the filming. [68] Hometown elites approved and actively participated in the filmmaking, assuring maximum community interest in the pictures. As one astute reviewer remarked, "Many expressions of approval were heard as the audience passed out of the theater, but we, with our mercenary minds wondered casually just how much of the box-office receipts could be credited to the local pictures and if an advance photographer a week or two ahead would fill the theaters in every town." [69] In many respects, Howe elaborated on methods developed by the Vitagraph Company six years earlier. [70]

A month after taking the Duluth films, Howe's camera crew photographed the construction and dedication of Roosevelt Dam outside of Phoenix, Arizona. Although this was hardly a major news event (appearing on page sixteen of the *New York Times*), Howe was anxious to film Theodore Roosevelt, who was at the dedication. [71] "After an inspection at

LYMAN H. HOWE IN CENTRAL AFRICA.

"WHERE ROOSEVELT HUNTS," NIXON THIS WEEK.

9-8. Roosevelt was assigned a key role in many of
Howe's programs (1909).

close range of the huge pile of masonry the film shows Mr. Roosevelt delivering the dedication speech."[72] Less than a month later, the film was
shown in Washington, D.C. Although speech from behind the screen was
usually felt to add to a picture's realism, Howe's impersonators decided
that Roosevelt's voice was either too well known or too sacred to permit
imitation. Thus, "the invisible performers, who supplied dialogue for the
other pictures, gave over at this scene, and Col. Roosevelt was left to
deliver an impassioned address in pantomime."[73] After filming the dedication of the dam, Howe's camera crew went on to photograph the Black
Canyon in northern Colorado from the front end of a moving train. "The
ride through the canyon follows the winding of the river, and as the train
rounds each curve new scenic vistas and wild rock formations are
shown."[74] Views were also taken of the Shoshone Falls in Idaho.[75]

Howe's most popular film of 1911 was A Thrilling Ride with Lincoln
Beachy over Wilkes-Barre. Lincoln Beachy, one of America's pioneer aviators, had switched from piloting a dirigible balloon to flying an airplane.

9-9. Teddy Roosevelt at the dedication of Roosevelt Dam (March 1910). Frame enlargement from the Howe film.

By 1911, he was winning competitions and performing stunts at fairs and amusement parks. When he flew at the Wilkes-Barre air show from May 29 to June 4, Beachy was still seeking to establish his fame. Helping Howe make a film was one of several gambits that brought him recognition that year.

> At first it was the intention to have Mr. H. A. Crowhurst, one of Mr. Howe's photographers, make the flights with Beachy and operate the camera, but after careful consideration this plan could not be followed. Then special appliances were devised to fasten and adjust the delicate motion picture camera to the aeroplane in such a way that . . . would allow Beachy to operate it readily with one hand while steering the aeroplane with the other. All this was imperative, but was finally accomplished very satisfactorily. Then Beachy familiarized himself thoroughly with the mechanism of the camera itself and rehearsed the operation. Without all these precautions, Mr. Howe realized no reasonable success could be expected. But even after arranging for all details so thoroughly, Beachy never would have succeeded were it not for his wonderful skill both as a mechanic and expertness [sic] in adapting himself so quickly to manipulating a camera with one hand while simultaneously operating the steering wheel of the aeroplane with the other.[76]

The idea for placing a camera in an aeroplane owed much to the head-line attraction for Howe's 1911 spring tour, *In a Dirigible Balloon*, which gave audiences the sensation of riding in an airship. This convention, in

9-10. Lincoln Beachy (1911).

which the spectator assumed the role of passenger, had been central for
Howe since the 1890s.[77] A surviving print of *A Thrilling Ride with Lincoln
Beachy* confirms its continued success. As the *Wilkes-Barre Journal of Trade*
remarked, "All these efforts were richly rewarded by a series of animated
scenes which shows every spectator just what Beachy saw. They are so
sharp and clear that they impart the same exhilarating sensation he felt
while flying high over the city, and they show just how the city, its streets,
parks, notable buildings, railroads, etc. look as seen from the clouds."[78]
The manner in which the film was exhibited intensified this illusion:

> The picture opens with a view of Beachy starting his flight and shows the
> camera being strapped into his seat. A few views of the ascent are followed
> by a reversal of the picture system. The airship is no longer in view. Now the
> earth is seen far below, swaying, receding, staggering in reverse complement
> to the pitching of the airship. The illusion needs no verbal encouragement.

Chapter Nine

9-11. *A Thrilling Ride with Lincoln Beachy* (1911).
a. Attaching camera.
b. Beachy taking off.
c. Wilkes-Barre from the air.

One immediately feels that he is seated with the flyer and unconsciously grips the arms of the chair and settles to the motion of the biplane.

Over the city, across a river, over the tops of trees and high above undulating fields and farms sweeps the airship, carrying the audience with it. Now it dips low and boats and tiny men and women are perceptible as the plane trembles above a wide river. Up she goes once more until the composite tree-tops of a forest look like a bunch of ferns on a dining room table.

Through it all the low whir of the camera and the loud ratchet of the airship rumble on incessantly. No effect is missing. The theater is so dark that one cannot see anything except the faraway earth as it reels drunkenly below. [79]

The new, dynamic technology of airplanes was synthesized with that of Howe's motion pictures.

The popularity of the Beachy film was enhanced by the pilot's activities during the summer. On June 27 he flew through the gorge at Niagara Falls. [80] Then, on August 5, Beachy won the first long-distance cross-country air race ever held in the United States, traveling from New York to Philadelphia in less than two and a half hours, a feat reported on the front page of many newspapers. [81] On August 20, in Los Angeles, Beachy flew his plane 11,642 feet above sea level, setting an altitude record. [82] From that summer until he died in a plane crash at the San Francisco Exposition in March 1915, Beachy was considered the foremost exhibition pilot of his day. Howe and Beachy had furthered each other's ambitions and fame.

Max Walkinshaw, Howe's partner, traveled to London and hired several cameramen to photograph *The Coronation of King George* in late June. [83] American rivals, anxious to be the first to market the subject in the United States, acquired films of the opening day's festivities and then left. Their coronation pictures were being shown during the first week of July. In Baltimore, they were the leading feature at two theaters, one offering vaudeville and another presenting a full program of travel films. [84] Walkinshaw operated with a different commercial imperative, since Howe's travel festival did not even open in Baltimore until July 24. He remained behind and shot subsequent portions of the ceremonies. "It so happened in the programme of events of the coronation that the king and queen were in a closed carriage the first day of the celebration. The following days gave the opportunities for picture taking that Howe wanted. The royal pair then appeared in a open carriage." [85] This raw footage was developed on board ship and edited into sequences that created the maximum impact. [86]

The most popular pictures in Howe's 1911 repertoire were of Wilkes-Barre from Beachy's airplane, King George's coronation, and the devastation of a flood in Austin, Pennsylvania. Crowhurst and Bosworth filmed this last subject shortly after a dam broke and the cascading water de-

stroyed the village on September 30. The camera crew reached the remote
locale before other members of the media "and planted their cameras in the
very center of the narrow little valley. From this point they photographed
panoramic views showing the magnitude of the awful destruction caused
by the irresistible wall of water 50 feet high, and the houses stranded by it
in every conceivable position on the hillsides."[87] The pictures, shown only
a few days after the disaster, made "hundreds of eyes glisten with tears"[88]
and were closely related to Howe's two other hits. Howe could not place
his camera on the wave itself, but the visceral thrill of potential danger
that Howe generated by metaphorically placing his audiences on a runaway train or an airplane implied the possibility of such devastation as an
endpoint. Likewise this spectacle of destruction inverted the spectacle of
coronation. It fused, intensified, and manipulated those feelings of thrill,
awe, and reassurance that Howe's programs regularly evoked.

The expansion of Howe's production activities was matched by exten-
Animation was another area of production developed by Howe's company. For several years, Paul Felton had drawn humorous scenes on lantern slides projected between individual film subjects. By 1911 he had
begun to make short animated films to serve a similar purpose. Precisely
when these animations were first produced is uncertain. *Winsor McCay's
Drawings*, released in April 1911, may have served as an inspiration.[89] In
any case, by the following fall, animations were in Howe's programs. One
reviewer noted that "the novelty of seeing a caricature of a woman's hat
break up into small pieces, fly about and finally form the sentence: 'Ladies
will please remove their hats,' puts the audience in a happy state of expec-
tancy right at the very beginning."[90] Such scenes increasingly supplanted
the brief comedies in Howe's programs.

The expansion of Howe's production activities was matched by extensive new facilities. By late 1911 or early 1912, Howe had built a new
headquarters with offices and studios at 175 West River Street in Wilkes-
Barre.

> The first floor is occupied by the booking, advertising, auditing and mailing
> departments. The second floor is devoted to the private offices of Messers.
> Howe and Walkinshaw, a comfortable private auditorium, and other rooms
> for the technical processes and handling of films.
>
> Those who have only vague ideas of moving pictures in the making, would
> probably find the third floor of surpassing interest. Here are a series of dark
> rooms, "trick photography" rooms, "printing" rooms, drying rooms, etc.,
> each designed for a special purpose. This maze of tiny rooms is the first objec-
> tive point of all of Mr. Howe's photographers when they return to Wilkes-
> Barre after having traveled thousands of miles to photograph scenes through-
> out the world. Not until they get here can they ascertain positively whether
> their weeks of labor were in vain or not.[91]

The array of rooms reflected the organization's increasingly elaborate division of labor.

With five companies on the road, Howe had generated a substantial organization. Company managers were Paul Felton, Robert Gillaum, Charles King, D. J. Tasker, and H. J. Bayley. In 1910, however, Howe's organization suffered a major loss: LeRoy Carleton, the showman's leading impersonator, died abruptly of blood poisoning in April, at only thirty years of age. An obituary declared, "Everywhere his work commanded the admiration of the press and public. Managers and attaches who saw him work behind the scenes recognized in him a real artist—or rather, truly a genius in the art of illusion. His career was full of promise and his death is lamented by a legion of friends throughout the theatrical profession."[92] At this time two young men were working in Howe's home office. Bob Jones, a former student at the Wyoming Seminary, became the mechanical expert, fixing everything from projectors to cars. He sometimes served as Howe's camera operator on local subjects.[93] Linn Hallet, a young boy who had run away from an orphanage, ended up on Max Walkinshaw's doorstep. Walkinshaw, who had no children, gave him odd jobs and a place to live. Hallet would eventually tour with the road shows; his long, close relationship with his benefactor would be reflected in his decision to name his son Max Walkinshaw Hallet.[94] A general optimism infused Howe's staff.

HOWE'S THEATRICAL ENGAGEMENTS

Howe prospered during 1910 and 1911, although his travel festival seldom enjoyed runs longer than six weeks. The Shuberts favored the enterprise with substantial bookings. At their Kansas City theater Howe's programs ran for six weeks in 1910 and five weeks in 1911. The shows enjoyed "good business and pleased immensely."[95] In St. Louis Howe's runs were cut back to three and four weeks respectively. When Howe encountered difficulties with the Keith organization in Cleveland, the Shuberts enabled him to play their affiliated Colonial Theater (1,470 seats) for four weeks in 1911. Another company returned to the Shubert's Toronto theater for three weeks during May 1911 and then moved on to Montreal where Howe exhibited for the first time.[96]

Relations with the Shuberts were not always smooth. In 1911, Howe's Travel Festival had its Chicago (1910 population: 2,185,283) debut at their 1,289-seat Garrick Theater on June 4. The initial audience numbered only two hundred people, and the Shuberts backed off, forcing Howe to pay for all outdoor advertising. During the first week this included:

Billposting	$96
Lithographing	60
Stretchers	35
Electric Sign	15
Advertising Boxes	10
total	$216

Many of these expenses continued for the second week: billposting cost Howe $83.20, and the electric sign remained at $15.00. Posters and other promotional materials routinely supplied by Howe were not included in this breakdown. Extra newspaper advertising was expected to be $120 a week, for which J. J. Shubert finally agreed to contribute fifty dollars.[97] With favorable newspaper reviews and good word of mouth, business picked up, and the three-week run was extended to seven weeks, closing with newly arrived scenes of the Coronation. By the last week there was standing room only in the afternoon and evenings; the final week's gross was $3,800, while 1,500 people were turned away from the last two programs. Howe executives naturally were anxious to extend the run, but the Shuberts refused.[98]

Howe maintained good relations with independent theater managers. In 1910 and 1911, he played Charles Ford's Grand Opera House in Baltimore for six weeks and Cincinnati's Lyric Theater for five. One critic remarked that "the hold that these Howe exhibitions of motion photography have upon the people is beyond explanation. Were the Lyric twice its size there would still be hundreds turned away on many occasions."[99] With the Chicago and Montreal debuts and good patronage at established locales, the year 1911 was particularly good for Howe. His operations were at their peak, not only in production but in exhibition.

Yet 1911 also burdened Howe with a new wave of competition. After witnessing Howe's extraordinary success in their theaters, Nixon and Zimmerman moved into motion picture exhibition. Frank G. Zimmerman formed the International Amusement Company, which showed "The World's Travel Pictures."[100] These opened at their Philadelphia Garrick Theater on May 28, 1911. Claiming to feature the "Greatest of Sound Effects," Zimmerman used "a little company behind the canvas . . . for purposes of human dialogue, the cries of animals and the sounds of inanimate objects."[101] The exhibition company balanced its programs of travel films and comedies just as Howe did. Many subjects were the same as Howe's, including films of King George's coronation. "The World's Travel Pictures" ran in Philadelphia throughout the summer, played at Nixon and Zimmerman's Pittsburgh theater for four weeks, and had a brief run in Baltimore.[102] Howe's relations with Nixon and Zimmerman were strained but not severed. At their Pittsburgh venue, he preceded the

World's Travel Pictures with a five-week run. In Philadelphia he found alternate outlets at two other theaters. Thanks to his established reputation and exclusive subjects, Howe competed effectively with his rival in both cities. Once Zimmerman found the picture field to be less profitable than expected, he abandoned the endeavor. In 1912, Howe was again at the Garrick.

Similar problems emerged in Cleveland, where Keith executives sabotaged his 1910 engagement. In contrast to the previous year, his presence was totally ignored by the press. The Keith management then replaced Howe with Van C. Lee, a well-known lecturer who programmed similar kinds of films.[103] Lee lasted three weeks, and then manager Harry Daniels instituted "Keith's Motion Pictures" for the remainder of the summer. The following year Keith's offered "Perfect Travelogue Picture Tours," featuring *President Diaz and the Mexican Army in Action* and *1911 Carnival of Roses, Pasadena.* Howe meanwhile had relocated at the Shubert's Colonial Theater. During their head-to-head competition, both groups showed films of King Edward's funeral and an expedition to the South Pole.[104] Even after Howe's four-week run, Keith's continued to show travel pictures. The Keith organization's hostility was hardly surprising; this major theater owner and motion picture exhibitor must have seen Howe as a competitor more than an ally. Yet neither "The World's Travel Pictures" nor "Perfect Travelogue Picture Tours" could effectively challenge Howe's organization and reputation.

THE THREAT OF KINEMACOLOR

Kinemacolor proved to be Howe's most successful and persistent rival in the early 1910s. Kinemacolor emulated many of Howe's long-established practices, but a crucial innovation, the first commercial system of color cinematography, gave the newcomer its own identity. The process consisted of shooting panchromatic black-and-white film with alternating frames exposed through red and green filters. These filters were also alternated in the projection process, with the eye synthesizing the images to form a color spectrum. The technique originated with Charles Urban's organization in England and was first marketed in the United States by the Kinemacolor Company of America, based in Allentown, Pennsylvania. Despite technical imperfections, Kinemacolor proved commercially viable, particularly when utilized in exhibition circumstances similar to Howe's. The two exhibitors hungered for the same legitimate theatrical venues and, in the end, the same middle-class audiences. Competition was intensified by further parallels. Since both organizations acquired films from Charles Urban, their programming shared similar types of subjects. Kinemacolor, like Howe, emphasized a complete and accurate reproduction of the world. Howe employed sound effects and often tinted images to achieve this simulacrum. The Kinemacolor Company emphasized the scientific nature of its cinematographic processes for the same end.

The Kinemacolor Company of America launched its first commercial showing at the Nixon, Nixon and Zimmerman's Pittsburgh theater. Its debut came immediately after Howe's 1910 summer season and probably reduced the length of his Pittsburgh stay. Advance notices puffed the new process,[105] and reviewers found that it lived up to this advance billing:

> The "kinemacolor" pictures, the latest departure in moving picture repro-
> duction, faithfully and accurately presenting in all the varied hues and tints
> of nature, were first presented in America last evening in the Nixon Theater.
> A large and enthusiastic crowd applauded every scene, for the effects were
> wonderful and something entirely new.
> The program included a wide range, landscapes, seascapes, flowers, ani-
> mals, harvest scenes and the funeral pageant of the late King Edward.[106]

The same program was later shown in Philadelphia. Although the praise was more restrained, it was evident that Kinemacolor could provide Howe with serious competition over the coming year.[107]

Howe did not give way to Kinemacolor's claims. He boosted his hand-tinted films, which were superior in many respects to Kinemacolor's two-color process. One of Howe's promotional columns, reprinted in various newspapers, quoted a hypothetical viewer who claimed, "The golden rays of the sun shine so brightly; the rich green of the leaves seem so inviting; the colors of the distant landscape unrolled to the gaze are all so true and real that one forgets entirely that it is a picture not the living reality." The column asserted that *A Journey through Indo-China* "is especially remark-able for its exquisite Oriental color. The rich bluish-green of the Mekong River at high tide flowing along banks covered with a dense jungle of tropical vegetation in hues of green ranging from the most delicate to the deepest—gives the spectator a profound impression of the actuality."[108]

The underfinanced Kinemacolor Company encountered commercial difficulty and was reorganized early in 1911. Substantial funds were pro-vided by a prominent Wall Street trust company as well as New York and Chicago capitalists. John Murdock, a well-known vaudeville impresario who had been involved with the motion picture industry for several years, oversaw the new company's activities. Murdock wanted "to supply legiti-mate theaters with entire programmes"[109] and realized that Kinemacolor's *Coronation of King George V* was well-suited for these designs. These ex-hibitions, handled by a separate enterprise headed by George S. McLeish, commenced in North America only one week after Howe premiered his black-and-white coronation films. Both openings took place at the Prin-cess Theater in Montreal, where Howe was enjoying a successful six-week run. Buoyed by his coronation pictures, Howe would have remained even longer if McLeish had not previously booked the house for the week of July 17. In fact, the Shuberts tried to extend Howe's stay, but McLeish took them to court and won an injunction that required Howe to vacate the theater. Montreal critics were impressed by the Kinemacolor system. "The pictures of a week ago were striking and impressive. These colored scenes, however, possess a vividness, a compelling fascination the plain black and white views must of necessity lack," declared one writer. "The gorgeousness of regimental uniforms of East Indian attire, the ever-moving, ever-varying kaleidoscope of brilliant colors, make the panorama even more memorable than its historical significance."[110]

Preceding Kinemacolor was clearly a commercial necessity for Howe if he was to receive much value from his coronation films. Fortunately for him, his entrenched organization successfully reached most major cities before the Kinemacolor Company could open. In Baltimore, St. Louis, and Philadelphia, Kinemacolor immediately followed Howe's Travel Festival, even moving into the same theaters.[111] In Cincinnati, when Kinemacolor opened one week, Howe closed the next. Only in large cities like Boston, where Howe lacked a summer season, or Cleveland, where Howe's run had ended before the subject was available, did Kinemacolor win the commercial confrontation.

Kinemacolor's coronation films did outmaneuver Howe's in important markets. In New York, the Kinemacolor Company opened its own theater where it showed the pictures for many months. A feature of the exhibition was "the exact reproduction of the words and music of the actual crowning ceremony in Westminster Abbey."[112] Its New York success may have harmed Howe's chances to reopen there. Significantly, as Kinemacolor toured the smaller cities and towns, it often appeared before Howe's semi-annual visit. Kinemacolor played both Wilkes-Barre and Ithaca in September, well before Howe arrived. Small-town critics were consistently delighted with Kinemacolor films. One declared, "They are to ordinary moving pictures what a human voice is to a phonograph. The views afforded of royalty are intimate and overpowering."[113]

HOWE'S NEW PUBLICITY SCHEMES

Howe, challenged by increasing competition, sought new ways to promote his programs. During 1908 and 1909, newspapers in many cities had run articles on Howe's behind-the-screen personnel. New, attractive publicity opportunities were more difficult to find the following year. Although the papers provided advance announcements, reviews, and mention of special showings, these did not draw sufficient attention to the exhibitions. When Howe gave free passes to orphans and deaf-mutes, the gesture was

briefly acknowledged in the *Cincinnati Commercial Tribune*.[114] When members of the Fourteenth Regiment attended *War Games* en masse in Pittsburgh, it received a short paragraph in the *Pittsburgh Post*.[115] While these reports made careful readers aware of Howe's public-spiritedness, they did not necessarily inspire potential patrons to attend.

Howe's publicity items in the St. Louis newspapers were among his most inventive, unsurprisingly, since many promotional schemes in the motion picture field had originated in St. Louis. In March 1910, St. Louis newspapers reported that Florence Lawrence, one of America's first film stars, was dead.[116] To reassure her distraught fans, Lawrence visited the city in April amidst considerable fanfare. Motion picture theaters in the St. Louis area thrived on giveaways. One promised to raffle a baby. Outraged people jammed the theater—and learned that the owner was giving away a baby pig.[117]

Howe started contests that were more in keeping with his image. In conjunction with his screening of *Wild Animals' Impression of Music*, the *St. Louis Times* sponsored a competition, asking children seventeen years or younger to answer the question "Which wild animal loves music most?" The fifty children with the best answers each received five box seats at Howe's show at the Century Theater.[118] In return for this giveaway, Howe received extensive newspaper coverage. Another arrangement was made with the *St. Louis Star*. To aid its circulation drive and promote Howe's show, an extra Saturday-morning screening was organized for poor, crippled children. The daily then invited "its readers to be a part of the spirit of good will that will bring joy to the hearts of many little ones that seldom, if ever, go to the theater. By sending *The Star*, the name of a deserving boy and girl in their neighborhood they will be doing something for someone who will never forget it."[119] Such columns incidentally detailed the attractive aspects of Howe's programs even as they emphasized his generosity. Correspondingly, the scheme helped the *Star* build its readership and presented the paper as a community-oriented, responsible publication.

The following year Howe, Walkinshaw, and the company managers developed several new schemes. The most often used was a newspaper contest that asked readers, "What kind of moving pictures do you like and why?" In August the *Cincinnati Post* ran the contest offering prizes of twenty-five, fifteen, and ten dollars for the best answers in fifty words or less. There were also five hundred free tickets as consolation prizes. Presumably these runners-up would bring along paying patrons. The *St. Louis Times* ran the same contest in early September with somewhat smaller prizes. The *Times* informed readers that "the exhibition will be really a demonstration of the tastes of St. Louis picture lovers as revealed in the majority of the statements sent to the moving picture editor." Participants, however, tended to be self-selected by the nature of the prize and indications of expected answers. "For those who have expressed a love of travel, Howe will show views of winter sports in Switzerland, a journey through old Japan—that part of the empire untouched by modern civilization—and the beauties of Japan's rapids and waterfalls."[120] The answers, at least those that won prizes, were always favorable to Howe.

The contests once again highlighted Howe's presentation of a model cinema. Answers selected for newspaper publication commonly distinguished Howe's programs from those in the nickelodeons.

> Moving Picture Editor: Melodramas and "senseless nonsense" in the moving picture circles are not to be tolerated. Melodramas are an evil influence to the growing generation, as has been proven, while the latter leaves a disagreeable "dark brown taste."
>
> Personally, I enjoy a Shakespearian scene, or something otherwise instructive, but there is such a great difference between nonsense and comedy that the latter is always desired.
>
> Victoria Callahan
> 1530 Race St.

Others simply favored certain kinds of films regularly found in Howe's programs.

> Moving Picture Editor: The pictures I like best are of travels that make us realize that the man of other countries, no matter how distant, or weird his customs, is our brother, with the same sorrows and joys we have. The pictures of travel that broaden and instruct are the pictures for me.
>
> Grace Cook
> 531 Clark St.[121]

These and other answers buttressed Howe's contention that "he has appealed to the majority of the public in offering travel pictures of worth and educational value"[122] even though the nickelodeons attracted a quite different and much larger clientele.

As calls for censoring and restricting the movies proliferated, Lyman H. Howe and his reputable programs emerged to play the role of model cinema on the national stage. The selection of subjects, the methods and sites of exhibition, and ticket price all offered a clear alternative to the nickelodeons, reassuring those who feared a descent into cultural barbarism. By demonstrating that the cinema could perform a "positive" social function, Howe earned the gratitude and respect of the motion picture industry then feeling under seige. This profile led to substantial exhibition opportunities in large Eastern and Midwestern cities, where he enjoyed extended summer runs in high-toned legitimate theaters. To meet this demand, Howe and Walkinshaw increased their number of exhibition units from three to five in 1909 and operated them year-round. In 1911 they hired a full-time, experienced cameraman to take films exclusively for their exhibitions. Their very success spawned a new group of competitors, some of which, notably the Kinemacolor Company, posed a serious commercial challenge. Between 1909 and 1911, however, the Howe organization reached its apex as a culturally prestigious and commercially lucrative enterprise.

10 * * * * * * * * * * * * * * * * * *

A New Generation of Roadmen:
Howe Faces Renewed Competition,
1911-1915

* * *

Those who are so fortunate as to see the Navy at work and at play, as
you have portrayed it, will have a high appreciation of its strength
and power. I wish every American citizen could see your pictures.
Their pride in their Navy and their country would be increased.

Secretary of the Navy Josephus Daniels to Lyman H. Howe,
23 February 1915

ALTHOUGH commentators had declared that the days of the old-time
traveling exhibitor were over, such did not prove to be entirely the case.
A few managed to survive at the margins of the film industry, while others
joined them. This modest revival was largely attributable to the automobile. In the past, most exhibitors had traveled by railway and only
screened in towns along the tracks. Now they could easily drive to out-of-
the-way places that were too small to support a picture house. The Heavens brothers of Cleveland took up traveling exhibition in 1911. They had
accumulated the necessary finances by running a successful picture house.
Significantly, an automobile-dependent show required "more capital than
. . . renting an ordinary store and calling it a theatre."[1]

The automobile is a steam car. It is the experience of the firm that better
speed regulation is obtainable with steam than with gas, and that the former
is more reliable. Upon a substantial platform behind the front seats is set a 5-
k. w. D. C. generator (dynamo), which derives its power from the engine of
the car. The dynamo furnishes electricity for lighting the hall, as well as for
the picture machine. This enables the management to dispense with the dangerous calcium gas ordinarily used by traveling shows. Also it makes them
independent of the town for general illumination, which in small places is
likely to be gas, or even coal-oil.

When the automobile reaches the hall there are doings on the outside of
the building which attract general attention, and are a good advertisement
in themselves. A pulley is attached to the driving-shaft of the car, which

operates a belt running to the pulley of the dynamo. Then a long piece of flexible duplex wire with incandescent lamps attached is run from the generating plant on the car into the hall. It is hung on gas fixtures or other convenient places, and gives all the light required. Another wire from the dynamo connects with the picture machine.[2]

The Heavens brothers finally solved a problem that had plagued itinerant motion picture exhibitors since 1896—a consistent power supply. They also revived the operational aesthetic. As a supplementary attraction, they demonstrated a wireless outfit to the audience "in everyday untechnical language." The Heavens' show thus descended from the telegraph and fire alarm demonstrations of the late 1840s.[3] Their portable generator allowed them to present the bright lights, recent technology, and cultural excitement of the city. Consistent with this spectacle of modernity, the Heavens' operator doubled as an advance man and dashed ahead to future towns on a motorcycle.

In 1911 the Heavens' show was still viewed as an experiment, but it was not an isolated one. Frank H. Thompson started Thompson's Pictures at about this time and also relied on the automobile. Touring such small Wisconsin towns as Trego, Spring Brook, Drummond, and Springfield, Thompson often used a tent.[4] His show remained in business throughout most of the teens. Such traveling showmanship continued throughout the silent era and beyond.

10-1. Frank H. Thompson's picture show in LaCrosse, Wisconsin, showing *The Birth of a Race* (ca. 1919).

Showmen had to "keep up with the times" or fail. Edwin Hadley, whose methods had changed little since 1903, survived until about 1912, but then records of his showings cease.[5] Such pressures were less pronounced in the area of church entertainments, a constituency that D. W. Robertson continued to supply.[6] The Huntley Entertainers, however, branched out into new areas. Ben Huntley opened a motion picture supply house in Winona, Wisconsin, and began to rent films and make colored lantern slides (with Myrtle Huntley often acting as a model). By 1913 he had acquired a camera and was taking films of local news.[7] His negatives of the Mississippi flood were picked up by national distributors such as Paramount.[8] In time the Huntleys made short fiction films, including some that burlesqued Charlie Chaplin. These were distributed through their rental bureau. For the veteran troupers, traveling exhibitions gave way, at least for a time, to a more sedentary lifestyle.

A New Generation of Roadmen

Another group of traveling showmen offered motion picture specialties that were unavailable to the nickelodeon system. All relied on trained personnel who were familiar with the films they exhibited, the antithesis of the nickelodeon system with its daily changes. As we have seen, at the very moment that old roadmen were forced to the periphery in 1907–1908, scores of talking-picture companies, with their carefully rehearsed actors and designated pictures, toured big-city theaters.[9] Fight films, which used a live announcer to comment on the action, continued to rely on road-show methods. Several companies went out with the *The Burns-Johnson Fight Pictures* during the summer of 1909.[10]

Certain types of motion picture entertainments exploited technology not found in regular nickelodeons. Several companies had developed complicated systems to coordinate films with synchronized recorded sound. Although a handful of these systems were purchased by theaters, most localities depended on road shows to see these experiments. The Cameraphone, perhaps the most successful early attempt at mechanical synchronization, was shown at Wilkes-Barre's Nesbitt Theater in February 1908 by an itinerant company (one of several then operating).[11] In the summer of 1913, the Edison Kinetophone Company managed as many as sixteen road shows, which exhibited Edison's talking-picture system. Initially, most netted between two hundred and six hundred dollars per week. The following March, twelve companies of "Edison Talkers" were still on the road. One of these units covered New Jersey, Delaware, Pennsylvania, and Maryland; a second, New York, Connecticut, and Massachusetts.[12] Kinemacolor was another example. Since theaters did not have the projection equipment necessary to handle the system of alternating red and green filters, road-show units toured with equipment, a trained projectionist, and often a lecturer. The advance man who arranged special publicity was a key part of all these shows.

The new generation of traveling exhibitors handled the vast majority of early feature-length films, both nonfiction and fiction. This trend blossomed after Pliny P. Craft road-showed films of Buffalo Bill's Wild West Show and *Dante's Inferno* early in 1911.[13] By the fall of 1913, as theater managers relying on "one nighters" were panicking due to the scarcity of touring plays and musicals, traveling showmen easily filled the gap with early dramatic features like *Traffic in Souls*.[14] This film, which claimed to depict the white-slave trade as documented by respected reformers, played for two weeks at the Grand Opera House in Wilkes-Barre.[15] Other companies soon covered the entire United States. Many films were handled on a states rights basis so that an exhibitor bought the rights to exhibit in one or more territories and then covered them with one or more exhibition companies.[16]

The exhibition companies that mounted these services operated on a much larger, qualitatively different scale than the itinerant showmen of the pre-nickelodeon era. Prior to 1908 most roadmen were small-time entrepreneurs, members of what Harry Braverman calls "the old middle class."[17] This new generation, requiring much larger sums of capital, tended to exclude small-time businessmen. Most company managers were employees working for comparatively large corporations. Multi-unit structures unusual before 1908 became the norm in these later years. Howe's operations had expanded and changed in ways consonant with these new conditions. He offered a specialty rarely seen in the nickelodeons, news and travel films. He produced many of his own pictures, and his multi-company structure permitted efficient operations. Moreover, his high-quality exhibition could not be duplicated in regular motion picture houses. Yet changes within the motion picture industry and American cultural life gradually challenged Howe's elite position.

CHANGING ATTITUDES TOWARD MOTION PICTURES

During the 1910s Americans rethought and reworked their earlier attitudes and ideas about the relationship between society and cinema. Adolph Zukor, who brought famous plays and famous players to the screen, contributed significantly to this process. By 1915 the motion picture industry had become an entrenched part of America's cultural and socioeconomic life. In February of that year, D. W. Griffith released *The Birth of a Nation*. Despite the film's racist subject and treatment, many agreed with James Hamilton's observation that "the art of moving pictures is here, leaping forward as nothing artistic ever leaped before. Ignoring it does not stand particularly in its way—it merely makes whoever is so blind slip behind his contemporaries and lose a lot of real enjoyment."[18] Nor were Hamilton's claims simply the casual assertions of a journalist looking to surprise his readers. During the same year, poet Vachel Lindsay published *The Art of the Moving Picture*, and Harvard philosopher Hugo Munsterberg wrote *The Photoplay: A Psychological Study*. Munsterberg contended that cinema was a major art form "as different from that of the theater as the painter's art is different from that of the sculptor's."[19]

Elite institutions and some religious groups acknowledged mainstream cinema's new status. The Brooklyn Institute sponsored an unusual week-long run of J. Stuart Blackton's *The Battle Cry of Peace*. It was so successful that the screenings were extended for an additional week. The Reverend H. E. Robbins, pastor of St. James Church, opened a regular moving picture house in Hartford, Connecticut (1910 population: 98,915), in late 1914 or early 1915. He wanted to run "a high class motion picture house and to demonstrate, if possible, the teaching and reaching power of motion pictures."[20] Recognizing cinema's unparalleled ability to mold the thoughts of children and immigrant Americans, Robbins was anxious for the church to participate in that process. The minister contended that "for every child who goes to Sunday school five go to the movie."[21] His enterprise also attracted middle-aged men who had never previously entered a movie theater. These proper, morally upright spectators were exactly the type who had been Howe's past patrons, while religious leaders had frequently endorsed Howe's exhibitions. Robbins's experiment, accorded wide publicity in the Hearst papers, was subsequently duplicated by two dozen clergymen and social workers across the country. Increasingly they were considering mainstream, popular cinema, not as a cancer to be removed or contained, but as a cultural force to be cultivated and shaped in a positive fashion.[22]

During the early 1910s, Howe gained in local and national prestige along with motion pictures. A day in 1915 was dedicated to him at San Diego's Panama California Exposition. A few months later he was elected president of the Wilkes-Barre Chamber of Commerce. Yet these honors involved hidden ironies, for although Howe appeared to be a prophet of the cinema's new respectability, film had won its new standing through its recognition as art, not as educational entertainment. Moreover, the very success of what might appropriately be called "the Hollywood cinema" finally began to affect Howe's business adversely. His coalition of diverse cultural groups was increasingly fragmented and appropriated by the mainstream cinema. The audience for his distinctive programming shrank steadily after 1911, lured away from several directions.

THE RISE OF THE AMERICAN NEWSREEL

Howe, Hadley, and other traveling exhibitors relied on news films, many of which were acquired from Urban and other European producers. As

Charles Bosworth explained to a *Kansas City Star* reporter, "The motion travel business has developed into a sort of 'wait-a-while' newspaper."[23] But this "wait-a-while" component turned out to be the form's weak point. In August 1911, Pathé Frères began to release its newsreel, *Pathe Weekly*, in the United States. Every week showmen could integrate a new set of nonfiction subjects into their motion picture or vaudeville programs. The wait had become much shorter.

Pathe Weekly became immediately popular and was shown on the Keith and Orpheum vaudeville circuits. Theaters discovered that it attracted a more desirable, well-to-do clientele than typical nickelodeon fare. Howe's Travel Festival and *Pathe Weekly* used strikingly similar subject matter. For instance, in September 1911, the newsreel presented

> Queen Wilhelmina of Holland as seen riding through the streets of Brussels while visiting Belgium. The funeral of Queen Mary Pia, which took place in Rome recently, is very clearly portrayed. From London comes the pictures of Beaumont, "King of the Air," at the conclusion of his great all England flight. Vienna presents the most picturesque scenes in its "flora fete," which is very pretty. The whole world is represented in a picture of Jager-Schmidt boarding the "Olympic" in New York on the last stage of his "round the world in forty days" trip.
>
> . . . America is represented by a series of views showing National Guard officers in camp at Fort Myers, Virginia, a typical camping scene. The Aviation meet at Chicago presents some thrilling aeroplane ascents. Politics are not forgotten, as a picture of Congressman Rucker, of Missouri, brings to mind his near-fight in the House of Representatives in Washington a few weeks ago. Paris fashions for ladies are always an acceptable conclusion to Pathe's illustrated views.[24]

Every film mentioned in this description had one or more counterparts in earlier Howe programs.

Pathe Weekly had adapted nonfiction material to the exigencies of the release system. Like the daily newspaper, the newsreel was released simultaneously throughout the country on a given date at regular, frequent intervals.[25] The company relied not only on its worldwide network of studios and offices but a host of stringers to gather films. By 1913 Pathé had seven or eight full-time cameramen scattered across the United States, dwarfing Howe, who depended on a solitary camera crew.

Pathe Weekly was quickly followed by other newsreels, including *The Vitagraph Monthly of Current Events*, first distributed in mid-August 1911, and *The Animated Weekly*, released by the Motion Picture Sales Company early in 1912.[26] In some cities producers started newsreels featuring regional events. *Cincinnati in Motion* appeared in late 1913, with scenes of sporting contests, railroad wrecks, parades, and important personages. Like other localized efforts, this one failed in less than a year.[27] The number of national newsreels continued to increase, however, for the format provided a fast, efficient way to present actuality material within the emerging Hollywood system. Preempting much of the traveling exhibitors' repertoire, the newsreel eliminated many of the distinctive qualities of Howe's shows.

FEATURE LENGTH "DOCUMENTARIES"

Howe's magazine format stood between the newsreel and elaborate feature-length documentary. Two films of this latter type were the *Durbar in Kinemacolor* and *Rainey's African Hunt*. These feature-length programs functioned within the tradition epitomized by Burton Holmes's travelogues but differed in several important respects. Although they relied on live narration to accompany the projected films, they were not identified with a particular lecturer. Whereas Holmes used slides and films, these programs used only motion pictures. As a result, they could be toured by multiple exhibition units.

Kinemacolor had established itself in the United States by offering spectacle and pageantry with its special color system. In 1912, the company offered its most successful program, *Durbar in Kinemacolor*. The Durbar, held on December 12, 1911, in Delhi, India, celebrated King George's accession as emperor of India. Unlike the Durbar of 1903, in which King Edward was represented by a duke, King George and Queen Mary took part in the ceremonies. The ritual of coronation was transferred to an exotic locale.

Not only was the Durbar ideally suited for Kinemacolor but Charles Urban and his chief photographer Joseph DeFrenes received full cooperation while filming the spectacle. Although Urban claimed to be a friend of King George,[28] personal generosity would not have been the principal reason for such assistance. The event had considerable ideological value. The Durbar "emphasizes the might of England throughout the world," remarked the *New York Times*. "It forces anew upon the minds of the discontented millions of the British Isles the fact that they belong, after all, to the supreme nation, and are subjects of an amiable King, upon whose possessions the setting of the sun seems, in this period of the twentieth century, to be as remote as ever."[29] The Durbar was appropriate in theme and subject matter for Howe's programs, yet his companies did not show it. Special releases by American producers and distributors, including Gaumont, Edison, and Powers, provided moviegoers with glimpses of the Durbar in black and white.[30] They were soon followed by *Durbar in Kinemacolor*, which opened in New York City on February 19, 1912. Presented with an explanatory lecture by Lawrence Grant, the film became a

"Lenten fad," played for several months in different New York theaters, and eventually achieved nationwide success.[31]

Paul J. Rainey's African hunt pictures opened commercially in New York City on April 15, two months after the *Durbar in Kinemacolor* premiere. The subject recalled President Roosevelt's African safari in 1909–1910 and the films of that famous expedition. Rainey, like Burton Holmes, was a member of the social elite, a Cleveland millionaire whose family had made its fortune in the coal trade. Earlier he had taken motion pictures of the Arctic and unveiled them at private soirées for friends.[32] As Holmes did, Rainey both produced and appeared in his programs. Except for private screenings, however, he did not narrate. At the New York debut of his African films, cameraman J. C. Hemment provided a whimsically earnest commentary that portrayed Rainey as a dynamic can-do American: "[Rainey] had one hundred American dogs, which were first trained in hunting big game in the canebrakes of Mississippi and Louisiana. Their courage so impressed Mr. Rainey that he felt sure that the dog, and not the lion, was the king of the beasts. To prove this he set out from America for Africa and the achievements of these dogs is told in a series of marvelous motion pictures."[33] The dogs were shown treeing and killing a cheetah and attacking a lion, events that often brought applause from American audiences.[34] At the same time, publicity emphasized the educational value of these films, citing an endorsement by Professor Osborn, president of the American Museum of Natural History and Dean of the Faculty of Pure Science at Columbia.[35]

By 1912, full-length feature films were proving popular. Although soon established as a predominantly dramatic form, features initially included many nonfiction subjects like *Durbar in Kinemacolor* and *Rainey's African Hunt*. The star system was also emerging; both films had star equivalents—King George and Paul Rainey. In these respects, Howe suffered. His name merely guaranteed a certain kind of exhibition and did not provide a star alternative. Similarly, Kinemacolor lacked star power when there was no king to sell the show. Howe and Urban's mutual concern for creating a lifelike illusion of the world often dominated efforts to create coherent narratives and foreground unified characters. *Rainey's African Hunt* was episodic, lacked a strong narrative line, and finally, never developed Rainey as a screen personality in the way that Robert Flaherty would do, in a different way, with *Nanook of the North*. Rainey's presence was felt more in the extensive newspaper coverage that surrounded the release of the film than as an on-screen personality. Full-page stories in the Sunday magazine section of big-city newspapers were common. The *Cincinnati Commercial Tribune* published "In the Jungle With Paul Rainey," which combined pictures of the millionaire with an extensive interview in which Rainey described his exploits as a big-game hunter.[36]

During 1911 and 1912, the audience for nonfiction subjects grew substantially, drawing patrons primarily from the middle and upper-middle
classes. In New York, the opening night for *Durbar in Kinemacolor* was "a
full dress affair and resembled a night at the opera." Spontaneous applause
occurred through the exhibition. At the conclusion, patrons were
whisked away in "automobiles by the score."[37] Hugo Munsterberg went to
see *Rainey's African Hunt* long before he condescended to enter a regular
picture house. The film escaped the high-minded sneers normally directed
at the movies. As one critic remarked, "That the Lyceum is temporarily a
motion picture theater is no reflection on the Lyceum while the Rainey
pictures are the attraction."[38] Most significantly, *Durbar in Kinemacolor*
and *Rainey's African Hunt* appealed to different elements of the middle
classes: not only people interested in refined or educational entertainment
but those who found amusement in the exotic, in spectacle and in the
depiction of violence.

Both programs opened in prominent Philadelphia theaters on May 6:

DURBAR REVIEWED IN FULL COLOR

*Gorgeous Indian Pageant Reproduced by
Kinemacolor Process at the Forrest*

The gorgeous spectacle of the Durbar, as presented in Kinemacolor last
night at the Forrest proved a source of inspiration such as is seldom, if ever,
provided by motion pictures. The results obtained by this new process are
remarkable, representing as great an advance over the black and white films
as these in their turn do over the old "stereopticon lecture." The colors of
nature are reproduced with an accuracy which is astonishing; the hues are
comparable to those obtained by the finest methods of three-color printing.

Much of the success of the pictures is doubtless due to the subject. The
Durbar, which took place under the open sky, in the strong tropical sunlight
of India, offered a unique opportunity for the photographer and the vivid
pageantry of the celebration, together with its gorgeousness and infinite variety, produced a continuous series of effects that were kaleidoscopic in their
richness and novelty. The pictures taken by the Urban Kinemacolor photographers were made by special command of the King, and every opportunity
was permitted to make them as complete and perfect as possible. The result
will not disappoint anyone's expectation. The idea thus conveyed of the
splendid spectacle comes appreciably near that which might have been had
by actual presence at the ceremony; and surely no one could have had so
many points of view as those revealed by the pictures.

Although the medium is not faultless, the sweep and realism of the views
is such that one can forget mechanical process and share much of the spirit
of triumphal holiday that was so manifest at the actual Durbar. Particularly
is this true with the films which show the processions—the review of troops,
and the massing of the British Army in India around the amphitheater on
the plain of Delhi. The magnificence of the native princes and their retinues

> is beyond description; a mere cataloging of the gold, silk, velvet and cloth-of-gold fails to give any adequate impression of the splendor. There is infinite picturesqueness in the smallest details of the great celebration, such as the washing and painting of the royal elephants, or the harbor views of Calcutta.
>
> It is only fair to add that the films shown this season represent far better work than that seen last year in the king's funeral pictures. The entertainment would, however, be improved by showing the scenes in some definite order, frequently more slowly; and by a better descriptive lecturer who would eliminate some of the bombast heard last night.[39]

Rainey's African Hunt remained six weeks while *Durbar in Kinemacolor* more than doubled that run. Kinemacolor proved extremely popular in Boston, where the Durbar program opened at the Tremont Temple in May and played twenty weeks.[40]

While still exhibiting *Durbar in Kinemacolor*, the Kinemacolor Company embarked on an ambitious attempt to compete within the mainstream industry. During the summer of 1912, the corporation commenced full-scale production of dramatic films. By fall there were six active production units, two of which were based in Los Angeles. From its elegant headquarters, Kinemacolor marketed a film service that quickly boasted over four hundred customers.[41] Although Kinemacolor continued to tour programs, it did not vigorously pursue traveling exhibition. During 1913 it presented films of the Panama Canal and the Balkan Wars in many metropolitan theaters, and in 1915 the company briefly exhibited *With the Fighting Forces of Europe* in selected cities.[42] Pursuing diverse commercial strategies, the company became overextended and dropped out of sight.[43]

Rainey's African hunt pictures, like Kinemacolor programs, appeared in major cities during the next several years but received shorter and shorter runs. The original series returned to some theaters in 1913. Then a new edition of *Rainey's African Hunt* played the following summer in Cincinnati, Cleveland, Pittsburgh, Kansas City, Washington, and elsewhere. Initially, distribution arrangements relied solely on the methods of traveling exhibitors. Later Rainey's Jungle Film Company sold states rights to regional distributors.[44] This allowed for more thorough exploitation, and while many of the subdistributors continued to road-show the film, they also rented it to theaters. States rights methods were also used for such documentary programs as *Captain Scott's South Pole Expedition.*[45] In some cases they were booked into regular motion picture theaters. The nonfiction film had ceased to be the nearly exclusive province of the traveling exhibitor.

Other feature-length, nonfiction subjects succeeded among the "better classes" over the next several years. Most were shot in isolated or inaccessible portions of the world—underwater, in Antarctica, or in unmapped portions of Africa. An entire expedition was devoted to each undertaking.

In May 1912, *Roping Big Game in the Frozen North*, a two-hour film of the Carnegie Alaska-Siberian Expedition taken by Captain F. E. Kleinschmidt, was hastily booked into a New York theater where Kleinschmidt lectured in a nervous and often inaudible voice.[46] These "intimate views of Eskimo life" also appeared in Philadelphia for three weeks. "What the Rainey pictures have done to render the life of the fauna of equatorial Africa real to spectators in more civilized regions of the globe, the Kleinschmidt views have accomplished with portions of the north frigid zone, particularly Siberia and Alaska," remarked one reviewer.[47] The photographic quality of the film was poor, the exhibition badly handled. In Philadelphia, the piano player was inexperienced and uninspired. Although the lecturer had been on the Carnegie expedition, he delivered his spiel hesitantly.[48] The films soon appeared in Pittsburgh, St. Louis, and Chicago, but their impact was undermined by these technical failings.

Thirty Leagues under the Sea was taken by George and Ernest Williamson, whose father developed the submarine technology that made the pictures possible. Based in Norfolk, Virginia, they shot their documentary in the Bahamas and promoted it as the first underwater film. The subject played for a week at the Brooklyn Academy of Music under Institute auspices late in 1914 and in Philadelphia for two weeks the following May. Applauded for showing the educational possibilities of moving pictures, the film presented "the wonders of animal and vegetable life at the bottom of the sea."[49] Audience interest was maintained by a scene showing "a thrilling battle to the death between J. Ernest Williamson and a man eating shark." The results were "amusing as well as scientific."[50]

Through Central Africa, a six-reel account of James Barnes's year-long African expedition, followed the path of explorer Henry Morton Stanley. Barnes's cinematographer was Cherry Kearton, who had earlier photographed Roosevelt's African expedition.[51] Barnes provided the lecture at Philadelphia's Garrick, where it opened in May 1915. To increase its drawing power, Nixon and Zimmerman supplemented it with a Chaplin comedy. Barnes later lectured with the films at the Brooklyn Institute as well.

Sir Douglas Mawson's Marvelous Views of the Frozen South offered motion pictures and still photographs of "the strange animals and birds and inexpressibly picturesque backgrounds of the Antarctic continent south of Australia and Tasmania."[52] This subject was also shown in Philadelphia during the summer of 1915, in direct competition with the Williamson's film. The lecturer emphasized the bravery of the explorers, but the critic was more impressed by the cameraman's daring and cunning. In filming the wildlife, he produced "a collection of close-ups so far unrivaled in this sort of research." Here an extra reel of comedy was not needed. "Unlike most educational subjects, the films have the advantage of frequent comic relief. This quality is provided by the penguins, with their curious, almost artificial markings, and their waddling gait, which has been aptly likened (or vice versa) to the walk of Charlie Chaplin."[53] Like those programs on the underwater world of the Carribean or on Africa, these views of Antarctica were only shown for two weeks. Already exotic locales were becoming familiar to movie audiences, and the attraction of documentary, feature-length programs was fading.

Not surprisingly, traditional travel lecturers relied on motion pictures with increasing frequency. From October 1910 to March 1911, the Brooklyn Institute sponsored weekly illustrated travel lectures given by Dwight Elmendorf, Burton Holmes, Emanuel Newman, and R. G. Knowles. All relied on films as well as slides.[54] For the 1913–1914 season, all the special lecture courses at the Brooklyn Institute incorporated motion pictures, with Holmes, Elmendorf, Newman, and John C. Bowker taking their own films. Two years later, lecturers at the Brooklyn Institute had expanded their reliance on motion pictures still further. A "Young Members Course" offered musical concerts and illustrated lectures, many accompanied with "Educational Motion Pictures." Among the topics were the lectures "My Wild Animal Guests" and "Interpretations of Child Life."[55] By 1913, New York motion picture theater owners were complaining that free movie lectures, sponsored by the Board of Education, were popular enough to force some commercial houses to shut down.[56] The rise of specialized motion picture theaters clearly did not harm the traveling lecturer using moving pictures. Rather, the lecturer's use of films was one more example of the increasing presence of motion pictures in American life.

The growing band of lecturers using motion pictures even included Theodore Roosevelt, who in December 1914 presented *The Exploration of a Great River* at the Museum of Natural History in Manhattan and at the Brooklyn Institute. The slides and films were taken by his son Kermit and the ornithologist George Cherrie. The illustrated talk focused on the Colonel's difficult journey down an "unknown river" in South America. This advocate of "the strenuous life" entertained his audiences with descriptions of hunting expeditions and his participation in a snake fight. On the screen Roosevelt handled a black snake which outfought its poisonous opponent. As the victor swallowed the vanquished, Roosevelt held it up to give the camera a better view. "My snake was a perfectly philosophical snake," he told his audience, "and went right on eating the other while the pictures were being taken."[57] When projection difficulties developed, Roosevelt entertained his impatient crowd with ad-libbed stories of four-foot catfish eating monkeys as they drank from the river.[58]

Although Burton Holmes was still the nation's foremost travel lecturer, his shows lacked the technical excellence of Howe's exhibitions. "I certainly expected better photography and newer prints than those shown," remarked one reviewer. "One film had interest more for its historic value than its intrinsic worth, being made ten years ago during the Russo-Japanese war at Port Arthur. It was badly worn and rainy, and its seems to me that Mr. Holmes should by all means have a new print of it." The critic was even more irritated by the out-of-date projection technology. "The machine was, I think, an old Edison, with an aperture with square corners, and not by any stretch of the fancy could it be called flickerless," he complained. "I am very much surprised indeed to find that a lecturer of the reputation of Burton Holmes could be content with the projecting standards of four or five years ago."[59]

Holmes's programs relied on the traveler being beside the screen delivering the lecture.[60] His reputation was such, however, that he could exploit new industry conditions. In 1914, even as his personal appearances continued, he took advantage of the demand for nonfiction subjects by offering *Burton Holmes' Travelettes*.

> The original travelogues of two hours' duration, and which were given by Mr. Holmes at admission prices of $1.00 and $1.50, will be condensed to approximately fifty minutes and prices will range from twenty-five to fifty cents. The short, popular form of these travel lectures will be known as travelettes, and will be given first in Chicago, Cleveland, Milwaukee and St. Louis, and the service will be extended elsewhere as rapidly as possible. Mr. Holmes believes the time is ripe for placing before the masses the results of his twenty-two years of travel in every quarter of the globe, and realizes this can be done to greater advantage through the moving picture theaters than by any other method.[61]

These programs did not rely on Holmes's customary exhibition practices. Although accompanied by a lecture in many (if not all) instances, the films were rented by the theaters.[62] Whether the theater hired a local lecturer or one was supplied by Holmes's organization is unclear. What is important was that the lecturer had become relatively anonymous. Holmes had adopted commercial practices more compatible with the dominant industry. The travelettes proved popular and were actively distributed for a number of years, during which they appeared in prominent venues.

For the first Cleveland run, Holmes's travelettes were the principal attractions on programs that included unnamed comedies and dramas. The opening selection, *New Manila,* was a condensed version of a lecture Holmes had given during his regular 1913–1914 season. It showed Emilio Aguinaldo, the Philippine leader who had once fought the American army but now lived quietly as a U.S. subject. Holmes's program argued that "Manila had been regenerated from a plague and pestilence spot to one of health, peace and prosperity."[63]

By 1915 an array of expensively produced feature-length subjects were available to theaters and prestigious noncommercial institutions. Just as Howe was unable to match the newsreels, his production capabilities could not equal those of ambitious, well-funded expeditions sent to exotic locales. Inevitably, his role as purveyor of nonfiction subjects declined. This decline, however, not only resulted from challenges within the nonfiction field, but from fundamental changes within dominant film practice. The appearance of the feature-length dramatic film and the rising recognition of cinema as an art adversely affected not only Howe but all nonfiction filmmakers and exhibitors.

Cinema as Art

During the 1910s, the cinema gained significant acceptance as an art form. As early as 1906 industry spokesmen had argued for cinema as an art in response to the accusation that moving pictures were evil and corrupting influences.[64] As theatrical personnel entered the expanding industry, some observers started to take the new form seriously. In June 1908, the New York Dramatic Mirror established a regular weekly motion picture section. "There is just as much art in moving picture acting [as in the theater] and more scope for individuality," declared actress Gene Gauntier in 1910. "Who knows what will be the status of the motion picture actor in ten years? It is on the flood, while the theatrical situation, to put it mildly, is uncertain."[65] Her assertions were soon echoed outside the industry.

In 1911 the first full-length fiction films brought new recognition to cinema's claims as an art. Dante's Inferno, a five-reel film (approximately 1½ hours) produced by the Milano Company in Italy, was declared the "non plus ultra of the moving picture art."[66] The Dramatic Mirror concurred:

> The film in its entirety impresses one of being a vast and wonderful achievement, and one that shows to what heights the motion picture can attain in treating a great subject. The picture will, no doubt, impress many people with the value of a motion picture not only as a work of art, but as a moral and regenerative force. It is significant, however, in this case that in order to fully appreciate these pictures one must see them either from the artistic or philosophical viewpoint.[67]

Dante's Inferno combined art and morality, in part through the skillful accompaniment of a lecturer. "Rarely has an exhibition of this character aroused such general interest as has the graphic depiction of Dante's story," reported the Baltimore Sun. "So effective are some of the scenes that more than one of the audience have been overcome with emotion.

Several of the scenes are harrowing in detail and leave an impression on the spectator not readily forgotten."[68]

Claims that cinema was a serious art form were boosted still further as theatrical stars moved into the motion picture field. Sarah Bernhardt appeared in several films during 1912. These early "art films" continued to have an instructive dimension that was linked to an assumed faithful recording of reality. *Camille* was offered as a record of Sarah Bernhardt's art. When the three-reel *Queen Elizabeth* was released by Adoph Zukor's Famous Players Film Company in summer 1912, promotional ballyhoo declared that Bernhardt would some day die but her art would live. "Historical accuracy, swift and clear action, a sustained splendor of settings and the supreme art of Sarah Bernhardt combine to make this play stand out as a rare and credible achievement," according to motion picture lecturer and critic Stephen Bush.[69] Zukor and his associates, including Daniel Frohman and Edwin S. Porter, used this opportunity to bring top American actors to the screen.

Art films offered an elevated subject matter that had much in common with Howe's conception of what cinema should be. Howe's Travel Festival, *Rainey's African Hunt, Dante's Inferno,* and *Queen Elizabeth* all claimed to instruct and inform as well as entertain. They presented a form of refined culture that satisfied even the more skeptical members of the elite classes. Whether or not these films were really art was not a crucial issue in the end as long as they were instructive. But this convergence of art and refined subject matter did not endure for very long. As critic Frank Woods pointedly asserted, "Art is universal; it is possible in everything. The commonest and least pretentious picture productions can be done in artistic ways. The most lurid melodrama, appealing to the least cultivated tastes can yet be produced with an approach to artistic ideals. It is not necessary that a motion picture to be a work of art must be over the heads of the crowd."[70]

Increasingly mainstream critics differed with Howe over their conception of film and film art. When Howe was concerned with his art, he was really concerned with his skill—his ability to give high-quality, well-executed exhibitions. The greater Howe's art, the more his audiences felt transported to another time and place. To this notion of the art of cinema was counterposed a conception of cinema as art. As these critics conceived film art, it transformed and elevated its subject matter just as a statue or painting of a nude had transformed something potentially pornographic into something sublime. Woods was pointing toward a broad-based mass entertainment form that appealed to different classes both as art and as amusement.

While the "cinema as art" argument did not originate with the feature film, it achieved new credibility because of it. Claims that cinema could elevate its subject matter to the realm of art were increasingly pertinent to features such as the Italian spectacle *Quo Vadis,* the big box-office hit of 1913. As *Quo Vadis* began its fourteen-week Philadelphia run in mid-May, the *North American* remarked,

> "The remarkable film-pageant . . . triumphs with startling brilliancy over difficulties, which would be insuperable in a theatrical production. Surprising feats are possible to moving pictures, but when Neronian Rome is vividly reconstructed, as in the present instance, when the burning of the world capital is revealed and with absolutely [sic] conviction; when arena combats, involving gladiators, Christians and wild beasts are exhibited with a realism that is at times overpoignant, then it must be confessed that a climax of cinematography has been reached.[71]

Howe believed that the spectator should "realize history by visiting the ancient shrines of art, the homes of sepulchres of heroes and the arenas of their heroic deeds."[72] In showing a film of Rome, he presented the artifacts of a distant past. In contrast, the makers of *Quo Vadis* staged its actions in those same ruins but sought to recreate past events for the spectator. In terms of prestige and acceptability to cultural elites, film as art was an alternative to film as instruction.

Feature films with artistic reputations became increasingly plentiful in late 1913 as the Famous Players Film Company released three features (usually four or more reels) per month. By 1914 Jessie Lasky and Cecil B. DeMille had moved into production. Notable foreign imports included *Anthony and Cleopatra* and *Cabiria.* By 1915 feature-length films had become the standard industry product. *The Birth of a Nation* was only the best known. In Pittsburgh during one summer week in June, people could see D. W. Griffith's *The Avenging Conscience,* a reworking of Edgar Allan Poe's *The Tell-Tale Heart;* Selig's dramatization of Rex Beach's best seller, *The Spoilers;* Lois Weber's religious parable, *The Hypocrites;* Mary Pickford in *The Dawn of Tomorrow,* or a variety of less memorable multireel "photoplays."[73]

The challenge of fiction features to nonfiction programs was theoretical as well as commercial. Howe and Kinemacolor sought to reproduce the perfect illusion of reality with sound effects and tinted images. Travel programs, as publicists never tired of remarking, served as substitutes for real voyages which were difficult, expensive, and time-consuming to undertake. Hugo Munsterberg, however, argued that the goal of art was diametrically opposed to this proposition. The philosopher declared that "every demand which is made by the purpose of true art removes us from reality and is contrary to the superficial claim that art ought to rest on skillful imitation. The true victory of art lies in the overcoming of real appearance."[74] Munsterberg opposed the use of sound and color and celebrated the ways in which silence and black and white removed cinema further from reality. Finally, he concluded that "the greatest mission which the photoplay may have in our community is that of esthetic cultivation."[75] Although Munsterberg's views were not fully shared by critics or industry spokesmen, they indicate that Howe, Kinemacolor, and the intrepid cameramen accompanying various expeditions were losing their mandate as purveyors of morally desirable culture for the better classes.

COMPETITION IN THE SUMMER SEASON

Howe, nonfiction features, and various high-class dramatic films vied for patrons even more ferociously than the number of subjects suggests. In metropolitan centers, commercial expediency restricted their exhibitions primarily to the summer months, when legitimate theaters became available. During the later part of the 1911 summer season, Howe found himself competing not only with Kinemacolor's *The Coronation of King George V* but with *Dante's Inferno*, which was exhibited "as a regular traveling attraction in the large cities of the country."[76] The Monopol Film Company, which acquired the American rights to this Italian spectacle, arranged with the Shuberts to show it in their theaters. It had its American premiere, with W. Stephen Bush as lecturer, at their Baltimore house while Howe was at Ford's.[77] *Dante's Inferno* proved so popular that its run was extended until it was supplanted by *Durbar in Kinemacolor*. It also played one of the Shuberts' St. Louis theaters during early September while Howe exhibited at another. A local critic declared, "Nothing hitherto attempted in the matter of motion pictures has proved more daring or caused more comment than the staged scenes from Dante's Inferno."[78] In city after city, *Dante's Inferno* received the same extensive publicity as Kinemacolor and Howe's programs.[79]

By 1912, the competition had intensified still further. In Philadelphia, Howe's Travel Festival was starting its second week when *Durbar in Kinemacolor* and *Rainey's African Hunt* opened on May 6. Although large audiences enjoyed Howe's "wonderful" new program, his Travel Festival left at the end of the week and did not return until *Durbar in Kinemacolor* had finished playing in late August.[80] *Rainey's African Hunt* had also departed, but memories of it lingered. After watching Howe's program, one reviewer noted, "The most thrilling feature of the bill presents the spectacle of a horse and rider attacked by a lion. In sensation[al] interest this film vies with those of the Rainey pictures."[81] During their Philadelphia summer runs, Kinemacolor totaled thirteen weeks, Rainey's pictures six, Howe's five, the Carnegie Alaska-Siberia films three, *Camille* three, and *Dante's Inferno* two.[82]

Competition contributed to the reduced lengths of many Howe engagements. In Kansas City his run fell from five weeks to two, in Baltimore from six to four, and in Chicago from seven to five. Instead of presenting programs throughout the summer, Howe's companies gave several week-long programs at the beginning and/or end of each regular theatrical season. Howe's employees once again enjoyed a respite. In Pittsburgh, Howe played for three weeks in May and June and then returned for another two weeks in August. Similar split seasons occurred in Philadelphia and St. Louis.

During the summer of 1913, dramatic features demonstrated even greater popularity; the Italian superproduction *Quo Vadis* proved a smash hit. Its Pittsburgh debut prevented Howe's Travel Festival from returning for the second half of its split summer season. In Cleveland, where Keith played *Quo Vadis* and another theater offered Famous Players' *The Prisoner of Zenda* starring James Hackett, Howe did not have a summer playdate.

By 1915, as the multi-reel feature film consolidated its supremacy, ex-hibitors of documentary subjects struggled to find play dates in many cities. By this point Howe's companies were only showing films for two weeks of the year in Philadelphia, Pittsburgh, Baltimore, and Cincinnati. In Philadelphia several other nonfiction features equalled Howe's stay. None, however, approached the lengthy runs that Howe's Travel Festival and other nonfiction subjects had enjoyed earlier in the decade. In Washington, D.C. and Cleveland, the showman played for a single week—a very different situation from his extended runs of 1909 and 1911. Yet, despite intensified competition and changes in audience tastes, Howe's battered exhibition circuit remained afloat. His companies still delivered popular programming in smaller cities and towns during the regular theatrical season. Such an achievement, when compared to the fate of Rainey's African pictures or Kinemacolor, suggests that Howe responded to changing circumstances in the industry with considerable perspicacity.

HOWE'S TRAVEL FESTIVAL

Howe had adapted to earlier changes in exhibition practices when his contemporaries often failed. In 1912, the exhibitor seemed ready to adjust to new circumstances—pressures from newsreels, kinemacolor, documen-taries, and early dramatic features—once again. That fall, he announced plans to open a chain of moving picture houses. The *Wilkes-Barre Times-Leader* reported,

> The leases for the different houses have all been prepared and Mr. Howe is leaving to-night to conclude several of them; upon his return the detailed plan will be given out.
>
> The theaters are all located in cities of between eighty and two hundred

10-2. Letterhead (ca. 1912).

thousand population and at the present time are playing what is known as legitimate offerings.

The moving picture business within the past few years has taken wonderful forward strides with the result that the local promoter realizing the big future in store has decided to open up the first big chain of moving picture houses in the country.

Mr. Howe intends to give plenty of pictures with a high class vaudeville performance at popular prices and it is safe to say that the new venture will be a big financial success. . . .

After the chain of twelve theaters are in operation which is expected will be about October 15 or November 1 at the latest it is the intention of the local man to branch out still more and it would not be a surprise if by early spring he had a chain of one hundred theaters from coast to coast playing Howe pictures daily.[83]

This radical break from his customary exhibition practices might have enabled the showman to retain a significant role in the moving picture field. Yet, for reasons that remain unclear, Howe did not follow through on these plans. The financial risk may have been too great. In any case, he missed an opportunity to escape his increasingly constricted circumstances and assured his receding role in the motion picture field.

The rapid decline in Howe's fortunes, however, was not immediately apparent. His programs remained popular in many cities during the 1912–1915 period. When a Howe company opened in Cincinnati during August 1912, "attendance, both in the afternoon and evening, packed the theater solidly and the pictures displayed were of such excellence as to keep the spectators thoroughly entertained from the first to the final reel."[84] Two years later in Pittsburgh, long lines at the box office demonstrated "the extraordinary public appreciation for Lyman H. Howe's travel wonders."[85]

Howe's previously established exhibition practices continued to enhance his programs. One reviewer maintained,

> Those who regard the exhibitor merely as a reproducer of the usual films
> have something to learn and are the poorer for not learning it sooner. For it
> is not alone in the absorbing interest of the subjects and their photographic
> quality that Howe stands pre-eminent, but equally so in the methods of pre-
> sentation. Each scene is accompanied by thrilling effects, which make every-
> thing so realistic that the spectator momentarily feels they are actually trav-
> eling. Just as there are classics in literature, classics in scripture, classics in
> painting, classics in architecture, so, too our modern era has now brought us
> classics in films, and these are exhibited by Howe.[86]

Not all commentators agreed with this assessment. At least a few found
Howe's use of live sound to be somewhat unsatisfactory. While gently
praising some effects, one reviewer observed that "Malay, Turk and Russian all seem to speak the same tongue."[87] Another felt "the near realistic
noises that accompanied the pictures had their wonted distracting and
irritating power."[88] Nonetheless, the results "fairly put to shame" the synchronized, recorded-sound motion pictures of the Edison Kinetophone.[89]

Patrons continued to flock to Howe's diverse selection of subjects.
Travel scenes had become the program's key ingredient. "Travel is attractive because of a legitimate longing for that broad education which only
personal study of other races, civilizations and religions can bestow,"
claimed Howe. "To realize history by visiting the ancient shrines of art,
the homes of sepulchres of heroism and the arenas of their heroic deeds;
to meet people who live differently and look differently than ourselves;
these are more interesting to Americans than any other people in the
world."[90] Thus patrons saw films of France, Italy, Holland, Turkey,
Greece, Egypt, India, and tropical Africa.

American subjects, taken exclusively by Howe's cameramen, frequently
celebrated the country's natural beauty—at Yellowstone National Park,
the Grand Canyon in Arizona, and Niagara Gorge. Since similar films had
been taken by other producers, it was necessary to film these subjects from
new, striking vantage points. One critic commented, "Representation by
motion pictures of the falls and geysers of Yellowstone National Park are
by no means unfamiliar, but here again Mr. Howe has tried to give those
objects a different visual angle. In interesting and picturesque succession
were shown the various gigantic waterfalls and numerous geysers, all more
or less in active operation, throwing up boiling water to distances of from
fifteen to eighty feet."[91] The demand for originality pressured Howe's production crew—still presumably Crowhurst and Bosworth—to take risks
that, according to publicity reports at least, nearly resulted in serious in-

jury. One item claimed that Howe's cameraman narrowly avoided plunging to the bottom of the Grand Canyon:

A RISK THAT A PHOTOGRAPHER TOOK.—Lyman H. Howe's photographer had many moments of peril recently while cinematographing the Grand Canyon in Arizona. While splendid views may be photographed there from many different locations, nevertheless it is usually the points that are considered accessible that offer the most commanding views. And it was the overpowering desire to photograph a scene from a position in midair that brought Howe's photographer within an inch of death. To be exact, it was within a quarter of an inch. A quarter of inch rope was all that held him suspended over a chasm one mile deep. Moreover the rope was caught in the pulley and was gradually sawing through.

He had scrambled on his hands and knees to a pinnacle which had become detached like a solitary sentinel, from the main cliff. One of the guides had lowered him over the cliff and left him dangling in midair until the moment when the swinging movement to and fro over the chasm died down enough to enable the daring photographer to take a steady picture. While he was thus suspended, the rope became twisted and "jammed" in the pulley so that he could not be drawn up again. Meanwhile the rope was momentarily weakening and creaking from the excessive strain.

In this precarious position, seconds seemed like years to the cameraman who had boldly defied earth in his ambition to photograph from such a startling viewpoint. Providentially the rope was finally untangled by the photographer himself, who revolved on its end and then the guide by heroic efforts succeeded in pulling up the now half-conscious camera man to terra firma after an experience so thrilling that he insists he will confine his activities in future to the safer way of photographing from a firm foothold.[92]

Another story described a hair-raising brush with death during filming of *Building New York's Biggest Skyscraper*: "The photographer wanted to show Broadway with the hurrying crowds, that looked like flies in the distance, and one of the ironworkers who was being hoisted from the street. The picture taking mechanism was recording the scene when one of the steel cables caught in the tripod, holding the chain in midair for several minutes until he could frantically cry to his fellows on the ground to reverse the engine."[93] In general, reports of near disaster were common, and many were undoubtedly the creation of the press agent's pen. They effectively emphasized, however, the fact that the camera provided the spectator with views taken from unusual and hard-to-reach vantage points.

Films taken from unnerving viewpoints remained a signature of Howe's shows. Unusual modes of transportation often provided a moving platform and resulted in films, like *A Thrilling Ride with Lincoln Beachy*, that gave the spectator a sensation of being thrust through space:

The sensation of flying in a hydroplane while the air machine races with swift motor boats at Monte Carlo [is one] of the twenty features promised at the Nixon this week. . . . It is a new sport, the test of speed of motors in machines that rush through the air and others that plunge through the water. The moving picture camera was placed in the hydroplane and the tiny films record the views of the racer about three hundred feet high. At several points during the contests the drivers in the rival machines are so close to each other that they exchange cries of defiance.[94]

"Hunting by Aeroplane" is unusual. Two hunters and an aviator skim over fields in a biplane, the result of much shooting being a rabbit and a grouse. The machine did not stop to gather all the trophies of the chase. A peculiar sensation is had as the aeroplane glides and dips over forests and fields.[95]

Perhaps the strangest journey of all is the trip in a dirigible balloon from Gotha to Dusseldorf, Germany. It affords an opportunity to experience the thrills of gliding through the air, yet without the constant danger to life and limb to which aviators are subjected.[96]

The experience of moving through space was intensified by the camera-man's use of lenses with short focal lengths that increased the sensation of depth. According to two veteran projectionists, Howe "then brought his audience right into the scene by making his projected picture nearly large enough to fill the average stage opening."[97] He was celebrating the technologies: first, the transportation that made these sensations possible, and

10-3. Poster (1912).

second, the motion pictures that presented these sensations in the safety of the theater.

Howe also produced A *Rousing New Ride on a Runaway Train*, modeled after the 1908 hit, in the summer of 1914. According to Donald Malkames, who later reshot portions of this film, it was taken from the front end of a train on the switchback railroad in Mauch Chunk, where Howe had once shown his miniature coal breaker.[98] Howe manipulated the footage so that the train's trip down the mountainside seemed out of control. The sharp turns of the switchback railway further heightened this sensation. Here technology created the illusion of danger and left shaken spectators relieved to find themselves in the safety of their seats. Claiming to use film as a window on reality, Howe prepared the prospective viewers in a way that intensified their experience of the film. In the case of A *Runaway Train* it concealed its true genre, the trick film.

Educational purposes often justified the manipulation of the camera, as with the science films purchased from Charles Urban. Time-lapse photography captured the growth of plants and flowers.[99] One 1914 novelty presented "an interesting set of pictures on the precipitation of various metals from solution by the process of electrolysis."[100] Views of aquatic and reptile life relied on extreme magnification. Other studies examined birds and animal life in the wild. Another film offered "the science of palmistry, which showed types of hand and signification of characteristic lines."[101]

Camera manipulations were most readily accepted in the realm of animated cartoons. Becoming an important and popular part of Howe's programs, these were made by Paul Felton and Howe's production staff in Wilkes-Barre. An unusual newspaper article, preserved in Felton's scrapbook, offers a detailed account of the early animator's work:

Funny Folks of the Films

The Downfall of Liberty

The new world that Mr. Felton has created is a kind of travesty on the real world that most motion pictures show. For instance, following a film showing the construction of the Woolworth Building in New York City, you are invited to enter Mr. Felton's "Looking Glass Land." You see the Goddess of Liberty in New York harbor. Across from it, without any perspective at all, is a skyscraper, looking as if it were made of white toothpicks.

Suddenly a little white papier mache kind of a man pops out of the top of the building. After him he hauls a rope and with an easy twist of the wrist flings it over the head of the dignified goddess. Then he nimbly dances over to her. Another manikin follows, walks over the tiny thread from the tall building and lights his pipe on the torch the goddess holds aloft. A tugboat passes by and a policeman appears on top of the skyscraper. Whereupon manikin No. 1 suddenly flits into the black throat of the boat's smokestack. Another boat passes, and the second figure goes in like fashion. When the

FROLICING FILM FUN
FAST AND FURIOUS
CLEVER-COMIC-CARTOONS
AND AMUSING ANTICS
BY LYMAN H. HOWE'S STAFF of
CAMERA MEN AND ARTISTS

10-4. Cartoons made Felton's lantern slides move. They also brought back the comic relief of chalk acts and rapid clay modeling that had amused Howe's audiences in the early 1900s (ca. 1913).

corpulent policeman balances himself on the tightrope it sags in the middle, and both structures are pulled together and with a splash fall into the bay.

A plentitude of silver drops are splashed high into the air. They form into the words, "All Over." You are getting ready to go when this quaint trickster drops the "all" and adds a few letter to what is left, "Overture" is what you see.

A Hippo with the Toothache

Here is a funny little monkey dentist, sitting in his jungle dental parlor waiting for patrons in pain. Along comes a hippopotamus with an aching tooth. You can see by the expression on the big beast's countenance that a hippo with the toothache is about as bad off as a giraffe with a severe attack of tonsillitis. A comical parrot, perched above the dentist's chair, watches the proceedings with the amusing expressions of awe that only Mr. Felton's birds have.

The monkey's efforts to pull that tooth, his final boring a hole in it with a bit and auger—the audience audibly wincing meanwhile—and blasting it out by a charge of gun powder with attendant annihilation of dentist, patient, bird and that whole section of the jungle is about as funny a picture as anybody saw.

Simple, but Laborious

It is a very simple trick, though a great deal of slow labor is back of it all.

"In our laboratories at Wilkes-Barre," Mr. Felton said yesterday afternoon, "we have a large blackboard. On this we train one of the motion picture cameras. Every movement that you see in one of these trick films represents a different sketch. The whole scene is planned first. Then the first picture is sketched on the blackboard and photographed. The next movement of the figures is sketched and photographed, and so on until we have gone through the whole story. You can see it takes a great deal of time and labor. A regular film can be taken at the rate of sixteen pictures a second. But it takes one minute to make even one picture for the trick film."

Mr. Felton has done most of the thinking, designing and drawing for the trick films being shown by the Lyman Howe companies.[102]

The methods described in this article, drawing on a blackboard and using cutouts, had been used by J. Stuart Blackton when making *Humorous Phases of Funny Faces* (1906). In the intervening years both Emile Cohl and Winsor McCay had developed more sophisticated techniques. These may have gone unmentioned, since animation techniques were generally considered trade secrets.

Howe's programs incorporated two disparate mimetic modes—animation and actuality—that were at the margins of proto-Hollywood film practice. By finding imaginative ways to tie the two modes together, Howe, Walkinshaw and Felton created a distinctive, enjoyable style. Felton's animations often played off the nonfiction subjects and offered a "Looking Glass Land" or travesty of the world Howe sought to represent as faithfully as possible. For instance, *A Hippo with a Toothache* almost certainly followed *Thrilling Escape from Lions*, although its conclusion, the use of dynamite to extract the tooth and incidentally blow up the jungle animals, also evoked *Dynamiting a Mountain* on the same program.[103] The nonfiction film of constructing skyscrapers typically celebrated American daring and technological superiority. In the looking-glass world of the cartoon, where anything is possible, the skyscraper collapses. The animation, however, neither undercut the celebratory nature of the nonfiction subject nor encouraged multiple or critical readings. It relegated chaos and disaster to another, unreal realm.

Throughout the early 1910s, cartoons provided Howe's programs with a distinctive look. While they received frequent, favorable comment, their titles were rarely specified in program notes and reviews. *Motor Trip Through France* was probably followed by a "very remarkable picture of the 'freak' variety" showing an auto race in Toyland. A critic declared, "The 'made up' pictures shown by Mr. Howe are positively uncanny, and seem actually beyond human power. The auto race in toy machines driven by dolls was most remarkable."[104] Reviewers often could not classify these films at first, calling them freak pictures, trick photographs, comic pictures, funny pictures, and so on. Yet by 1915, dominant film practice was incorporating animated films into its repertoire, with reviewers increasingly referring to them as "animated cartoons."[105] Here again a key element in the Howe repertoire ceased to provide a distinctive attraction.

THE ISSUE OF MILITARY PREPAREDNESS

Howe's most important group of films dealt with American military power and its effective exercise overseas. *Our Navy* showed the naval review, attended by Secretary of the Navy George von L. Meyer and President Howard Taft, in New York Harbor on November 1 and 2, 1911. Meyer gave Howe permission to film the naval parade, "believing that the country at large should become more familiar with this important phase of our national life." Advance notices for Howe's spring 1912 program called it "the greatest naval review in American history."[106] The effect that Howe hoped to achieve was suggested by the *Baltimore Sun*:

> They furnish a lesson of the efficiency of men, guns and machinery of our mighty war vessels that is of incalculable value. The combined power of the ships represented gives the beholder a fresh, vivid and entirely new conception of the country's resources and power. The ships, in their holiday dress, presented a scene that is profoundly impressive, and this further is intensified at the thrilling climax when the stately procession moves at full speed out to sea in a driving gale and at the same time salutes directly in front of Mr. Howe's camera.[107]

Howe also incited patriotic sentiments in *Burial of the* Maine. In early March 1912, the U.S. battleship *Maine* was raised from the bottom of Havana harbor where it had lain for fourteen years. After the bodies of sailors were removed and the ship was covered with flowers, the *Maine* was towed out to sea and sunk in an elaborate, solemn ceremony.[108] Although films of the event were taken by many different producers, including the Kinemacolor Company, Howe publicity typically claimed exclusivity, unique government facilities, and the fact that copies would be "kept for posterity in the archives of the library of congress and at the rooms of principal societies throughout the country."[109] However questionable such claims might have been, it was "the most popular [film] shown this season by Mr. Howe."[110]

> The general public is familiar with the details of the removal of the wreck of the ill-fated Maine from the harbor of Havana, but the Howe motion pictures give so much of the actuality of truth to the operations that the spectators feel as though they were direct participants in the obsequies, an event carried out with the most sincere patriotism by the government. After the

taking of the caskets of the dead aboard the warship North Carolina you see the scarred and battered wreck towed slowly to sea, the convoy of vessels on either side, and then the impressive ceremonies of the last rites as she sinks from sight beneath the waves. The pictures are clear and distinct and so full of the atmosphere of the real that they leave an indelible impression on every patriotic mind.[111]

The film reminded Americans of the dominant role that their government had assumed in the Caribbean and presented the *Maine* as a justification and symbol for such intervention.

Another popular film, taken by Howe's cameramen and shown during the summer of 1912, documented "daily life" at Culver Military Academy in Culver, Indiana. When shown in Baltimore, a critic reported, "All the boys are inspired by 'Horsemanship, Artillery Maneuvers and Drills at the Culver Military Academy,' and one little tot amused yesterday's matinee audience by calling to his mother, a few seats away, 'Mama, let me go there, will you?' "[112] Fewer films focused on patriotic subjects and the American military during 1913, when "the trick pictures that are only shown by the Howe exhibition come in for the most enthusiasm."[113] Some of Howe's companies presented "the latest invention and labor-saving devices as employed in the manufacture of armor plate at the Bethlehem steel works."[114]

Films of the Panama Canal headed Howe's spring 1914 and fall 1915 tours. The canal provided Howe with a subject that united many of the ideological and political threads of his work. It testified to the national benefits derived from Theodore Roosevelt's "big stick" policy, and to America's technological accomplishments. Its opening strengthened American defense, by effectively uniting the Atlantic and Pacific fleets, and benefited American commerce. The sheer scale of the project synecdochically demonstrated America's ascendancy on the world scene.

Howe's camera crew was sent to Panama, where it filmed the last stages of the canal's construction late in 1913. Although later publicity sometimes claimed they had shot the construction over a four year period, the Howe employees—still Bosworth and presumably Crowhurst—filmed under difficult conditions during a concentrated three-month period.[115] "Two of the photographers contracted malaria while they were 'on the job' and on more than one occasion they had stirring experiences when blasting operations had to be photographed from behind armored screens. The 'stirring' came from flying boulders."[116] The final film conveyed the ambitious scope of the canal project: "What is shown here, while naturally skipping from place to place, furnishes a splendid idea of the work that was done. In the list of scenes given were the 100 horsepower dredge excavating three tons of dirt or rock with one dip; the Gatun Lock, 1000 feet long and 110 feet wide; a busy 400 ton crane; air drills boring for

10-5. Poster (1914).

blasting, washing away earth by water power; preparing dynamite, the explosion caused by it, and scores of other happenings educational, picturesque and amusing."[117] One newspaper captured the spirit of Howe's undertaking when it claimed, "The only reason nobody knows who built the
pyramids is that Lyman H. Howe was born a few centuries too late. You
may be sure that if Lyman had been alive and out of the cradle he would
have swamped Egypt with cameras, obtained the exclusive motion-picture
rights from the Ptolemy family and showed us what pre-historic contracting was like."[118] Howe sought to convince Americans that they were becoming the world's foremost power. Instead of the British-built Aswan
Dam in Egypt, Howe showed the Panama Canal. Instead of British naval
power, Howe heroized the American navy. Instead of British colonies and
pageantry, American colonies and natural beauty were featured.

Soon after the Lyman H. Howe Film Company was incorporated in
June 1914, Howe and Walkinshaw, the two principal owners, had a new
cameraman, Joseph DeFrenes. DeFrenes had been one of Charles Urban's
leading photographers until his Austrian citizenship and the advent of
World War I created problems. Based in England, DeFrenes and his wife
had to either leave the country or be incarcerated. The couple came to
the United States, where DeFrenes was soon hired by Howe at fifty dollars
a week.[119] DeFrenes was set to work on the production of *U.S. Navy of
1915*, a difficult and ambitious project that took several months to film.[120]

The making and showing of such films occurred within the context of
a debate over national preparedness. Josephus Daniels, Secretary of the

Navy under Woodrow Wilson, was eager to increase the size of the American fleet. This meant convincing Congress and their isolationist constituents of the Navy's value and efficiency. As Charles Bosworth told a reporter, "Joseph Daniels believed in publicity. He is a newspaper man and thinks the best way to get a better navy from the American people is to tell them as much as possible of the navy as it is."[121] Maximizing his impact on this debate, Howe showed *U.S. Navy of 1915* in Washington during February rather than wait for the summer season. The run included a well-publicized performance "to which members of Congress, members of the diplomatic corps, government officials and others are to be special guests."[122] The showman hoped to affect government opinion, particularly in Congress.

The Washington screenings were designed to create the kind of publicity coup that *The Birth of a Nation* had just achieved. When Thomas Dixon, Jr., screened the dramatic film for Woodrow Wilson, an old college friend, the President reputedly said that it was "History written by

10-6. Poster (1915).

lightning." This endorsement helped the epic at the box office and undermined groups opposed to its ideological viewpoint.[123] Although Howe's
program did not receive such adulation, government officials did provide
favorable public comments. Daniels wrote a laudatory letter that was frequently quoted in ads and promotional material:

February 23, 1915

My dear Mr. Howe:

One of the most delightful hours I have spent in all my life was the hour I
spent yesterday morning witnessing your pictures of the United States Navy
of 1915. In common with the large audience present, I was greatly pleased
with the splendid representation which you make of the Navy.

The pictures have movement and action and life. They illustrate nearly
every phase of naval activity. Some of the scenes were thrilling; all were
effective. I congratulate you upon the consummation of your work. Those
who are so fortunate as to see the Navy at work and at play, as you have
portrayed it, will have a high appreciation of its strength and power. I wish
every American citizen could see your pictures. Their pride in their Navy and
their country would be increased.

Cordially yours,
(signed) Joseph Daniels[124]

The *U.S. Navy of 1915* filled three reels, providing almost an hour of
screen time. Although a copy does not survive, its contents are described
in reviews:

Howe's film aims to impart the pulse-beat of the complex life that throbs
through our dreadnoughts from reveille to "taps." It shows the bluejackets
washing themselves and scrubbing their clothes as if this were their favorite
pastime. It shows them cleaning the decks with the water running ankle
deep, scrubbing boats, polishing bright work, etc. It takes spectators to the
ship's "galley" where the cook reigns supreme. It depicts a general inspection,
the big gun drills, boat drills under oars, signal drills, infantry and field artillery exercises, clearing ship for action and manifold duties that go to make
"variety the spice of life" for man-o'-warsmen.

In doing this it depicts how naval discipline and efficiency is attained and
maintained. Besides it also shows "jack at play"—boating and swimming,
diving, deck games, etc. Even coaling the ship is no bugbear when it comes
to beating another club's record.

An unusual vivacious scene will show the race-boat crew manning their
12-oared cutter for a 10-mile pull through the fleet and a brush with a rival
ship, also the sturdy bluejackets pulling away at a 50-pound pulley weight in
order to qualify for the crew.[125]

The group of motion pictures . . . gives an excellent idea of the character,
size and efficiency of this country's battleships and coast defenses.

The United States ships Wyoming, Arkansas and Oklahoma were shown:

also the collier Orion and the torpedo boat Patterson, together with the torpedo flotilla and war ships in action.

Statistics giving the number and class of ships and men in the service were shown and life on board ship was visualized so well as to give an impressive lesson from life as to what service in the United States Navy really means.

One picture showed the cadets at the Naval School of Culver, Ind. Portraits of many officers high in rank in the navy elicited applause and that of President Wilson received an ovation.[126]

Howe's filming of the American fleet focused on the quotidian experiences of the sailors, supplemented by a diversity of additional materials including recycled Howe scenes of the Culver Military Academy and footage of Wilson and the naval officers acquired from outside sources. The picture also relied on extensive intertitles to provide identification and statistical information.

Howe did not make an explicit case for a larger navy. As in the past, he strove to represent reality in the belief that it would speak for itself. If the images were there, people would agree not only on the problem but on the solution. One reviewer, however, suggested that Howe's tendency to show the Navy in a heroic mode did not necessarily have the effect that Daniels and Howe desired:

> Notwithstanding what reams of magazine articles he may have read on the "pitiable inadequacy" of the United States navy, the layman who viewed Lyman H. Howe's pictures on "Our Navy in 1915" last night probably left the Garrick Theater entirely satisfied that the national honor can be properly maintained and that his New Jersey seashore bungalow is immune from bombardment.
>
> And there was reason in his assurance, for he had seen a vast array of the materials of warfare. He had seen imposing battleships and fleet cruisers, inside and outside. He had watched the stealthy submarine, the fatal torpedo, the disappearing coast rifles, the gaping mortars, and behind these instruments, the smoothly running organization of sworn defenders of his land.
> . . .
> Mr. Howe may present a one-sided picture but it is certainly calculated to inspire whole-hearted confidence in the United States navy.[127]

Images that Howe and Daniels thought would inspire Americans to support a larger fleet often had the opposite effect. Certainly, his argument was not as explicit or effective as J. Stuart Blackton's *Battle Cry for Peace.* In Blackton's film one thought was consistently brought out: "unless prepared against war, which alone is security, this country can easily be attacked and destroyed."[128] Howe's effort at propaganda failed to depart from the paradigm of his cinema of reassurance and so did not achieve the goals he desired.

The Philippines Yesterday and Today appeared on the same program with

Chapter Ten

U.S. Navy of 1915 and focused on America's colony acquired after an earlier application of American naval power at Manila Bay. According to one reviewer, it "shows native life in the Philippines, mostly among the savages. The concluding pictures of the series show the progress that is being made in redeeming and educating the people. It may readily be seen that it will take many years to fit all of the natives for the responsibilities of self-government."[129] Howe's 1915 spring tour thus revealed ways in which preparedness and large military budgets for defensive purposes—the protection of a citizen's New Jersey bungalow—went hand in hand with the projection of American military power overseas.

Underlying Howe's interest in military preparedness was a strong faith in the Anglo-American alliance. The Lyman H. Howe Company, owned equally by the American Howe and the Canadian Walkinshaw, in fact reflected this alliance. As part of the British Empire, Canada was at war with Germany. Aiding Canada's military efforts, Walkinshaw organized a benefit for the Red Cross Society and the Ladies of the Nineteenth Regiment at the Armoury in St. Catherines, Ontario, on June 28, 1915. The special program featured films of the British Empire with *In India* and *Salmon Fishing, British Columbia*; of England's allies with *Through the Gorges of Southern France* and *Venice—The City of the Sea*; and scenes of their armed forces with *Military and Naval Maneuvers in England and France*. Views of the still-neutral United States were absent from the program.[130] The exhibition was "nothing short of a revelation" and raised $614.54 for the cause.[131]

While Howe's companies exhibited films of the navy and America's colonial possessions, DeFrenes photographed the completed Panama Canal in active operation. According to Charles Bosworth, who may have accompanied DeFrenes on the trip, "the picture gives one the experience of passing through the Canal and also of being at Points along the Canal when ships are passing; they also reveal the occupation of the Canal seen in 1915 by the United States army, incidents of U.S. army life in the Jungle, scenes at Colon and Panama City, with studies of individual types of Panama natives as they are at the present day."[132] To complement this film, DeFrenes and Bosworth filmed the Panama-Pacific Exposition at San Francisco and the Panama-California Exposition in San Diego, both of which marked the opening of the canal.

The San Diego Exposition designated July 7 as Lyman H. Howe Day, an honor it extended to former President Roosevelt and William Jennings Bryan.[133] Missing the formal ceremonies, Howe was represented by Bosworth, who gave the exposition historian a copy of the Panama Canal and San Diego Exposition films. In his speech Bosworth also emphasized Howe's interest in the spirit that prompted the Panama-California Exposition.[134] To take films of the San Diego Exposition, Bosworth and De-

Frenes used two automobiles. The first towed the second "so as not to have the vibration of an automobile whose motor was in operation." The results, Bosworth assured the local press, "will be shown all over the East and will do the Fair much good from an advertising standpoint."[135] After the San Diego filming, Howe's crew moved north to San Francisco and filmed the Panama-Pacific Exposition, including ceremonies surrounding the installation of the Liberty Bell at the fair. Once anonymously appearing in films of the 1900 Paris Exposition, Howe now was part of the spectacle.

Two Expositions by Moving Pictures

Always better than the one that's gone before. That seems to be Lyman H. Howe's ambition in moving pictures—and he manages to achieve it. Last evening's exhibition was certainly the most entertaining and the most instructive he has yet given. One saw about all of the Panama-California Exhibition at San Diego and the Panama-Pacific Exposition at San Francisco without undergoing the fatigue of the journey, a trip through the Panama Canal as though one were on the spot together with a number of other most interesting scenes; and marvelous effects in color and clearness were obtained by the camera.

The trip through the canal was by permission of the Secretary of War and every assistance was given the photographer. All of the interesting points were shown—the great ships passing through the immense locks, the difficulties encountered by slides in the famous Culebra cut, the whole thing from ocean to ocean.

The San Diego exposition is quaint with many reminders of the olden times. A comprehensive view of the buildings and grounds is taken from the California Tower. It seems hardly possible that this is part of the United States. To one who has only read about the San Francisco exposition the marvels can be only fairly comprehended. As a preliminary there is a bird's eye view of the whole affair, then in detail the entrancing scenes and the wonderful effects achieved by the landscape artist, sculptor and architect. A ramble through the courts is like a dream in fairyland. An incident is the arrival of the Liberty Bell, attended with a remarkable demonstration. Even the night illuminations are clearly shown. An enjoyable part of these pictures is the triumph in photography, without a blur or quiver. The whole impression is as though one had spent days in the very midst of the exposition.

Scenes in the parks of Paris, a railway journey in Norway and Sweden, scenes in Holland and Belgium, reveal magnificent color effects and give an intimate view of the geographical characteristics and the home life of the natives. The steel industry in France is shown in ponderous working order, and there are views of the United States submarine fleet off Pensacola, together with a number of humorous pictures, including the ingenious outline effects that always "bring tears of laughter."

It is almost needless to say that the house was crowded. The Howe exhi-

10-7a. Howe's film of the
California expositions is
introduced by an animated
sequence (1915).
b. Howe's cameras were in San
Diego for Lyman H. Howe
Day (1915).
c. The San Francisco exposition by night (1915).

bitions always bring out record breaking audiences. They are in a class by
themselves and they are the best in the moving picture line.[136]

The year 1915 brought recognition and honor to Howe as it did to the
motion picture industry as a whole. He was lauded at the San Diego Exposition and elected president of the Wilkes-Barre Chamber of Commerce
(see Appendix A). His films of the U.S. Navy were seen by high government officials and became part of the growing discourse on military preparedness. Though becoming a man of stature, as a showman, Howe was
increasingly out of step with his times. By 1915, the newly established
Hollywood industry had achieved power, status, and influence. Subject
matter not treated by the mainstream film practice in 1909 had been incorporated into the emerging Hollywood system. Many finally recognized
cinema as an art, making the respectability of Howe's programs strategically unnecessary. Moreover, his programming strategies were losing their
inventiveness, their elasticity, and their ability to surprise. Howe's finest
public moment was the moment that signaled his decline.

10-8. Letterhead (1915).

11 ✳

Later Years: 1916-1933

✳ ✳ ✳

> Lyman H. Howe's Travel Festival . . . is the same perennially delight-
> ful hodge podge of news, travel, science, nonsense and adventure and
> it carried a large audience, mostly composed of youngsters, to a land
> of enchantment for two hours.
>
> "Howe's Pictures at Ford's," *Baltimore Sun*, August 20, 1918

TRAVELING EXHIBITION remained a significant form of motion picture
distribution until the end of the "silent era," i.e., of films without synchronized recorded sound. As the Hollywood industry was consolidated
between 1914 and 1917 and applied the regular release system to most
feature-length dramatic films, it fostered several increasingly distinct practices. Road-showing continued as part of Hollywood's marketing repertoire for "specials." For a blockbuster feature film, units would tour with
effects truck, orchestra, and advance representative. Nine such companies presented Griffith's *Intolerance* in the United States during 1916.[1]
The process, however, was fraught with risk. *Variety* later claimed that
between the road showing of *The Birth of a Nation* (1915) and late 1925,
only about one in four ventures was a box-office success.[2] Touring proved
increasingly perilous for Howe as well.

HOWE AND THE SPONSORED DOCUMENTARY

Howe's business suffered as Hollywood increasingly duplicated his repertoire of subject matter within its own distribution system. To shore up his
company's profitability, Howe reduced the scale and ambition of his activities. Several developments forced this move. First, Howe's ability to purchase foreign travel films was severely hampered by the war. Second, his
summer runs in metropolitan theaters had become shorter and fewer in
number. They ended in Shubert houses after 1914, as the Shuberts became more actively involved in motion picture production and exhibition.[3] The acquisition of additional programs for those few venues where
Howe's engagements exceeded two weeks was no longer profitable. From
1915 onward his summer runs did not depart significantly from those of

the regular theatrical year. These two-week stands were booked for August or early September and presented the old program from the previous spring and the new program for the upcoming fall.

The always cost-conscious Howe further reduced his expenses by shifting to making and showing sponsored industrial films. In the spring of 1915, Howe presented *The Making of a National Cash Register* which was either shot by his cameramen or acquired directly from the National Cash Register Company, presumably for a fee. National Cash Register had been using moving pictures to promote its products since 1903, when the American Mutoscope and Biograph Company made a series of short films to show off the company's activities and its principal officers. Such promotional schemes continued. In January 1913, for example, *A Free Trip to the Home of the National Cash Register Company* was shown at Wilkes-Barre's Grand Opera House to several large audiences. The film was in kinemacolor and accompanied by a lecture. It demonstrated:

> how the city of Dayton, Ohio, had been made beautiful, how the employees of the plant, which engages over 7,000 people, have been benefited morally, physically and financially, how the plant and products themselves have been developed beyond all expectations, simply because the president and other officers of the company recognize that to spend six cents a day in surrounding each of the men and women with beautiful environments, and conditions which tend to health and happiness, brought back returns in dollars.[4]

A few years later National Cash Register used the film *Troubles of a Storekeeper and How to Regulate Them* to sell its latest cash registers.[5] National

11-1. Letterhead (ca. 1917).

Cash Register not only pioneered the use of industrial psychology but recognized that cinema could be used to advance a favorable company image.

Howe lent his reputation as an exhibitor to National Cash Register's
promotional efforts. Spectators were naturally more receptive to the company's message if they paid to see the subject and believed it was part of
the independent exhibitor's regular program. Certainly Howe suggested
the subject was selected by him for its unusual interest. As one promotional item declared:

> The romance of industry as expressed in the making of a National cash
> register constitutes another feature of the program. Howe selected this par-
> ticular plant not alone because it is typical of American skill, enterprise and
> organization but because it is recognized the world over as the model manu-
> facturing plant—a monumental realization of an idea and an ideal. The va-
> riety of the scenes may be imagined when it is remembered that ninety trades
> and professions are engaged here in manufacturing machines from 8,800 dif-
> ferent kinds of raw material coming from all quarters of the globe.[6]

Consistent with earlier Howe presentations of industrial processes, the
film did not betray its shift toward a more full-blown form of industrial
propaganda.

Howe continued this profitable strategy with *The Making of a Willys-
Overland Automobile,* shown in his spring 1916 tour.[7] He produced this
sponsored documentary, for which he was paid by the manufacturer.
DeFrenes and Bosworth each received expenses plus a fifty-dollar salary
every week while they spent almost three months at the Willys-Overland
plant in Toledo, Ohio. The company also provided the personnel and
technical equipment necessary to light the factory. Bosworth explained,

> To move our picture-taking apparatus through the miles of factory area
> required the services of five electricians and the use of ten specially con-
> structed trucks, operated by twenty men. The wire for supplying the electric
> current was a single item requiring more than a month of preparation. The
> move of a "switch" illuminated any corner to a brightness that permitted
> every form of photography. When everything was in place we had before us
> by far the greatest moving picture studio in the world.[8]

The Making of a Willys-Overland Automobile was designed to bring the
auto company's message across in moving picture form.[9] Lyman Howe, a
current president of Wilkes-Barre's Chamber of Commerce and a former
president of its Automobile Club, knew how to articulate that viewpoint.
He also offered an arrangement that no other producer could match.
Howe could exhibit the films he made to his regular patrons, people whom
Robert Grau called the "automobile clientele."[10] Showing "the development of the great industry of automobile manufacturing from the stamping

of the first bolt to the finished machine running on its own power," the industrial film impressed prospective automobile purchasers.[11]

The making and exhibition of industrial films was profitable but belied the claim Howe had made in 1909—that he would not accept money from clients to show his audiences pictures.[12] The showman thus traded on a reputation for integrity that he had developed in earlier years. The move paralleled Howe's activities as a civic leader.[13] He had become an apologist for American industry as well a proponent of American military preparedness.

Howe's cameramen also took sponsored films of a more traditional kind. At least since the making of *The Black Diamond Express*, transportation companies had subsidized producers making films that promoted their business. *Hawaii: The Paradise of the Pacific* was aided by the Great Northern Steamship Company. Shown in the fall of 1916, it displayed the island's exotic beauties.[14] A Howe program described the scenes:

> A ride is taken with the engineer of the Hilo Railway, affording splendid vistas of the seas through luxuriant tropical vegetation. Immense sugar cane flumes are passed en route. Cutting sugar cane is also shown, as well as notable scenic points, such as Waisha Falls, "the Boiling Pots," Rainbow Falls, etc. Pastimes and pursuits of the natives are also depicted, including the rather unique but exciting business of catching sharks in the high seas. In another portion they are seen surf-riding—for the Hawaiians have mastered the art of riding on the crest of rolling waves with a skill and dexterity that has never been equalled nor even imitated successfully by any other race. The concluding portion of the series is of a most spectacular nature. For a veritable inferno—the active volcano of Kilauea—is found in the midst of this tropical Eden and spectators are taken to the innermost recesses of this "everlasting house of Fire."[15]

The Great Northern Railroad assisted DeFrenes as he photographed Glacier National Park in the summer of 1915.[16] The film was exhibited during the spring of 1916 along with *The Making of a Willys-Overland Automobile*. Like the later Hawaii film, it showed natural scenery and the activities of the local natives, the Blackfoot Indians on their reservation.

Howe's 1916 programs revealed the increasingly predictable nature of his selections. Films of national parks had been shown to the better class of audience for more than twenty years.[17] Howe had resurrected scenes of mountain climbing in the Alps (spring 1916) every few years since 1901. *Norway: Land of the Midnight Sun* (fall 1916) recalled *From Christiania to North Cape*, which Howe presented in the spring of 1905. *Life at the United States Military Academy at West Point* (fall 1916) had many antecedents, including *War Games*, shown in 1910. Scenes of France (spring 1916) and Italy (fall 1916), animal studies, and cartoons had appeared on Howe's programs for many years in various forms. In the past, Howe and Walk-

11-2. Hawaii: The Paradise of the Pacific (1916).

inshaw had enriched their offerings with new genres like the cartoon or innovations within established genres like *Ride on a Runaway Train* or *A Thrilling Ride With Lincoln Beachy*. Now they found themselves in a cul de sac.

Howe's organization ended the 1916 year in upheaval. The production staff—Charles Bosworth, Joseph DeFrenes, and Paul Felton—decided to leave and start their own company. Howe's low salaries were as usual a factor.[18] By mid-January, the trio had formed B.D.F. Industrial Motion Picture Company, specializing in industrial motion pictures for advertising purposes. They continued much as before, but without Howe. Bosworth served as salesman and producer, DeFrenes did the camerawork, and Felton was animator. Through animation and industrial cinematography, they would aid the promotional goals of their corporate clients. The new partners went on to make films for Eastman Kodak (*A Trip Through Filmland*) and the Goodrich Rubber Company (*The Striking Tires*). After a few years, difficulties were encountered; Bosworth suffered from delusions, claiming that he had closed major contracts which later proved fictitious. He eventually entered a sanatorium. The company continued as DeFrenes and Felton until the cameraman bought out the animator in the late 1920s.[19]

Of the old group, Robert Gillaum, Linn Hallet, Russell Blake, and Bob Jones were among the few who remained with Howe and Walkinshaw. Harry Manhart had died. Ralph Barber had left in 1915. The departure of booking manager W. C. Pflueger at about the same time increased the organization's difficulties in finding and maintaining first-class venues for their road units.[20] Gillaum assumed Pflueger's role. More often, the partners ended up replacing veterans with eager young men who would work for modest salaries. They relied on a twenty-two-year-old from Wilkes-Barre, Archie Griffith, to head the animation. DeFrenes's position was filled by eighteen-year-old Fred Jayne, who had acquired his cinematographic experience working for Howe. In June 1917 the Howe organization opened a New York office "to inspect all artistic and scientific yet humanizing films of [fact] that appear in this market and to buy all that are of exceptional merit."[21] They were becoming less committed to production and more interested in acquiring outside films as the exhibition circuit continued to shrink.

The defections that disrupted Howe's production had counterparts in exhibition. Before the 1917 summer season, Howe lost his venues in Philadelphia and Pittsburgh. Nixon and Zimmerman may have been disturbed by Howe's melange of sponsored industrials and clichéd subjects as well as his declining box-office appeal. Howe continued to show his Travel Festival in Cincinnati at the Lyric and in Baltimore at Ford's Opera House. Both theaters were independently owned and managed, making them more sympathetic to the activities of an entrepreneur such as Howe. The first program for the 1917 summer season, shown in smaller cities during the previous spring, featured views of Yosemite National Park and films of Sir Douglas Mawson's Expedition to Antarctica. This last selection was a shortened version of *Views of the Frozen South,* shown two years earlier at Nixon and Zimmerman theaters.[22] The documentary had apparently not been shown in Baltimore, and Howe's version pleased the local press.[23]

The program readied for the fall 1917 season was produced after the United States declared war on Germany. It featured *Scenes at Annapolis Naval Academy* and *Somewhere in the Atlantic.* Although publicity claimed that *Somewhere in the Atlantic* was filmed after the commencement of hostilities, descriptions suggest that he basically reworked footage gathered for *U. S. Navy* in 1915. "Seeing Uncle Sam's sailor boys at work and at play, at the serious business of taking the enemy's measure and preparing a warm reception for him, makes one feel very much like jumping into the picture himself and lending a hand," declared one reviewer.[24] The political context more than the images had changed. These scenes were complemented by animated cartoons that poked humiliating fun at the Germans and intensified American hatred for the "Hun." One showed "the battle in the air between a Zeppelin and a British airplane over London, which ends in the total destruction of the big Teuton craft."[25] In another, "the Kaiser meets his waterloo . . . when a captured submarine makes an air voyage to Germany and blows up the Krupp gun works."[26]

Howe's circuit continued to shrink in 1918. In Baltimore, Ford's reduced the showman's season to a single week. The program was "the same
perennially delightful hodge podge of news, travel, science, nonsense and
adventure" but the large audience consisted primarily of children.[27] In a
time of war, Americans sheltered their children by sending them to
Howe's cinema of reassurance, but for themselves they found it less and
less compelling. Cincinnati was one of the few large cities where patrons
continued to greet Howe's Travel Festival with enthusiasm. Both programs opened to a capacity audience at the Lyric and received extensive,
warm reviews in the press. The *Cincinnati Commercial Tribune* remarked,

> Mr. Howe has the happy faculty of leavening his educational subjects with
> just enough comedy to remove the faintest suspicion of appearing pedagogi-
> cal. His cartoons, while not the feature of his program, are nevertheless an
> interesting part of each subject and are to be commended for their originality.
> A striking part of all his pictures are the bright, snappy subtitles.
>
> But it is in leading the public thru foreign countries and picking out the
> most interesting points where Howe and his camera men excel.[28]

Despite these positive remarks, the onset of the war put Howe at a further
disadvantage.

NONFICTION FILMS IN WARTIME

Although wartime increased the popularity of military subjects, Howe was
unable to benefit from this boom. The U.S. government prohibited motion picture producers from filming American armed forces. The ad hoc
government cooperation that Howe and others had received in the past
was impractical in wartime. Processing, assisting, supervising and censoring hordes of freelance cameramen seeking sensational war scenes would
have been chaotic and inefficient. Instead, photographing America's war
effort was centralized within the U.S. government. Pictures were shot by
the U.S. Signal Corps, censored by the military, and then passed through
the Committee on Public Information headed by George Creel. The Creel
Committee released a variety of official U.S. government war films including the *Official War Review* (a newsreel) and special documentaries.[29]

Several official war pictures received broad theatrical release. By March
of 1918, moviegoers were seeing *America at War*. Like future Creel Committee productions, it relied on extensive intertitles rather than a lecturer
for explanatory information. These may have slowed the flow of images
but they permitted the rapid distribution of a uniform program. When it
played at Baltimore's Academy of Music, an American who had fought
with the Canadian Expeditionary Force gave a brief speech before the
film, graphically describing alleged German atrocities. The film itself was

much tamer, only "showing the means by which the men of the draft army are clothed, housed and fed. Each step in the training of an enlisted man is illustrated by views of setting-up exercises, drill-bayonet practice, machine gun and rifle practice and the life and routine at the great cantonments are shown in detail."[30]

Subsequent Creel films showed U.S. troops in the war zone. With *Pershing's Crusaders,* "The real thrill . . . is in the scenes of France, which were taken by the United States Signal Corps and United States Navy photographers. They show the 'Yanks' 'over there,' from the arrival of General Pershing, with his first men, till within a few weeks ago."[31] This was soon followed by *America's Answer,* which presented "the visualized story of America's first year in the War."[32] Critics were enthusiastic about the Creel Committee's war-filled documentary. One declared, "it is inconceivable that a better selection [of pictures] might have been made. Thruout the picture there were frequent outbursts of applause from the audience, which packed the house from orchestra pit to gallery. . . . 'America's Answer' is a notable successor to 'Pershing Crusaders,' and should be seen by every person in Cincinnati."[33]

The activities of the Creel Committee preempted one of Howe's last remaining strengths. Moreover, the committee sold footage to the film studios, which packaged it for commercial exhibition. Carl Laemmle, for example, acquired Creel footage to make *Crashing Through to Berlin,* a historical panorama of the war that ended with "aviation pictures that never fail to thrill."[34] It was released through regular distribution channels. Howe, of course, was not seeking to offer an independent, alternate view of the war. The position he had obliquely advocated had become national policy. Nor did he present his own personal account of the war, as would numerous traveling lecturers. Instead, his programs were limited to the training of military personnel and the demonstration of technology. Howe's subjects paled compared to *America's Answer,* which competed with the second week of his run in Cincinnati.

Howe's new military films often fetishized the technology of modern warfare even as they provided his viewers with the vicarious experience of being in its machines, the tank and airplane. *Thrilling Tests of Gigantic War Caterpillars in Uncle Sam's Army* revealed "the huge caterpillars, under the skillful manipulation of daring 'Sammies,' accomplishing the seemingly impossible in negotiating roads, fields and trenches torn up by shell fire and covered with mud, fallen trees and other obstructions."[35] *Up in the Air with the Marines,* perhaps taken by Fred Jayne, who had joined the Aerial Photographic Service early in January 1918, depicted dangerous military air maneuvers from the pilot's perspective. "It remained for a Howe camera man to risk his neck in getting pictures of the hazardous tail spin and nose dive—conceded to be the most dangerous of all birdmen activities. That it was some 'risk' can best be appreciated by those who see the pictures."[36] Placing the camera on the latest technological innovation in military transportation maintained the viewer-as-passenger convention. The films were topical and patriotic, but Howe had only limited access to this kind of material. Within his variety format Howe continued to offer many other kinds of subjects: scenes of Coney Island, Alaska, and a canoe trip through South America.

Although his cartoons ridiculed the "Huns," Howe's programs did not contain the kind of virulent propaganda that raised emotions to a fever pitch. In the comparatively rational debate over military preparedness, the exhibitor had played a modest role. With the onset of hostilities, fiction films provided a more effective means to inflame wartime hatred of the enemy. *To Hell with the Kaiser* "was received with cheering, for it pictured the death of the Kaiser and the Crown Prince, all as the result of the quick wittedness and heroic work of an American girl."[37] *My Four Years in Germany* reenacted the experiences of former U.S. Ambassador to Germany, James Watson Gerard. As the *Baltimore Sun* told its readers, "If you want the loose ends of your hatred of German militarism gathered together and concentrated in a steady resolve for war until the beast is brought cowering and whining to earth—as beasts do when they find their masters—and if you want to enjoy thoroughly the process of concentration of hate go . . . see the pictorial version of Ambassador Gerard's book."[38] Beside these efforts, Howe's cartoons were almost playful.

Although travel programs were plentiful during the war years, they were increasingly distributed and exhibited according to dominant industry practices. Holmes had extended his series of travelettes, signing a contract with Paramount in 1916.[39] The films that President Roosevelt had shown with his lecture on South America were made into a documentary. The resulting *Colonel Theodore Roosevelt's Expeditions into the Wilds* was shown at the Strand Theater in New York and elsewhere. Roosevelt, the star attraction, could be seen "as only wild animals and jungle companions are permitted to see him in the flesh."[40] S. L. "Roxy" Rothafel, the leading theater manager and exhibitor of his day, showed Martin E. Johnson's *Among the Cannibal Isles of the South Pacific* at his Rivoli Theater in July 1918. The *New York Times* commented, "One goes into another world— not an altogether pleasant, but surely an interesting and instructive world—when he sits and watches the people whom Mr. Johnson has brought to New York." The *Times* critic praised Rothafel who "has once more got away from monotonous movie routine and given [patrons] a chance to see something that raises the motion picture beyond the reach of those who would keep it trash."[41]

Despite the broad application of mass communication practices to the nonfiction film, illustrated motion picture lectures remained popular although perhaps not quite as plentiful. By 1918 the Brooklyn Institute had reduced its number of full-course travel lecturers from four to two. Dwight Elmendorf retired while Frederick Monsen became inactive; only Emmanuel Newman and Burton Holmes remained. For the 1916–1917 season, Holmes gave a course of lectures on the European powers: *Imperial Britain, La Belle France* and *The German Fatherland.* The last was noteworthy for its sympathetic portrayal of Germany on the eve of America's entrance into the war.[42] Even at this late date, Holmes tried to avoid taking sides. For many lecturers, this was not the case. Several toured the United States with official British and French war films. Frederick Palmer, an American correspondent, presented the British view of the war and praised the leading French generals in unabashed propaganda.[43] Once America joined the battle, British officers like Captain Radclyffe Dugmore also toured and lectured with the appropriate war films.[44]

The year after America's entry into the war, Holmes and Newman visited countries and territories in the Pacific.[45] Other exhibitors followed suit; Dr. Leonard Sugden, for example, gave lectures on *The Lure of Alaska* using motion pictures he had taken using the Prizma Color process.[46] This shift in focus was undoubtedly due to government policy that kept freelance cameramen out of the war zone. For the 1918–1919 season, however, Holmes and Newman successfully reached war-ravaged Europe and returned with courses on the allied countries during the conflict. Holmes's course included *Yanks in Paris, Yanks in Italy,* and *Yanks at the Front.* Newman offered *Wartime France, Paris 1918, Wartime England,* and others.

The Demise of Howe's Road Companies

The end of the war did not help Howe, either. Like all in the film industry, he was adversely affected by the influenza epidemic that killed half a million Americans in the fall of 1918. Ralph Barber incorrectly suggested that this forced Howe to disband his touring companies, bringing his road show business to a quick end.[47] While the epidemic frequently either cancelled playdates or reduced his box-office receipts, Howe continued to send out at least two companies through the fall of 1919.

Howe's organization had lost its vitality and lacked new programming ideas. The 1919 spring program even included *New and Surprising Achievements of Caterpillar Tractors,* returning to a subject treated the previous year. Other films were just as familiar: views of Yellowstone National Park and Japan, *Who's Who in the U. S. Army, Flying Over Washington,* and *Thrilling Capture of Huge Seal Elephants.*[48] In the fall of 1919, Howe presented his fiftieth semiannual tour and celebrated what he claimed was his twenty-fifth anniversary in the motion picture field:

LYMAN HOWE'S ANNIVERSARY BILL

It is just twenty-five years since the Lyman H. Howe people entered the
moving picture field and in celebrating their silver anniversary they have put
together the best collection of motion photographs that has ever been given
in one evening's entertainment. Industry, sports, landscape, beauty spots,
adventure, animal and comedy subjects make up the program, and they are
so diversified and wonderfully projected, with lifelike sounds and accessories,
that, as always, the Howe show stands in a class by itself and is the only
survivor of the hundreds of like concerns that have attempted to enter the
field made and controlled by this company.

The industrial shown was the Bethlehem Steel Works, with its wonderful
system of handling immense masses of iron resulting in big guns, building
material and manufactured steel. Beauty spots were shown in the Magnolia
gardens near Charleston, S.C.; landscape and scenic views were provided by
a trip over the Andes in Peru, showing the wonders of construction and the
lives and customs of the people in that country. Tarpon fishing in Florida
furnished the scenes that made every follower of the rod and reel thrill with
excitement. Scenes in a girls' camp in Maine, with its water sports, were most
enthusiastically received, and excitement was furnished by the reckless dis-
regard of mountain climbers in the Canadian Rockies. There were clay mod-
elings of famous composers, with appropriate musical accompaniment and
intimate views into the home life of all the famous moving picture stars.

The comedy was furnished by those eccentric creations of the Howe artists
who have made this field their own and which have won for them the reputation of being the most original and laugh provoking of any innovation in
moving pictures.[49]

His companies still provided sound effects and voices from behind the
screen. Subject matter and its arrangement as well as Howe's commercial
methods had narrowed and then frozen into a form that was frequently
referred to as "a national institution." But this national institution had
become a relic of a bygone era. The fiftieth tour was Howe's last.

Howe closed his Travel Festival for many reasons. Methods of theatrical
exhibition had been transformed over the previous twenty-five years.
Howe had built his business by showing films in regular theaters that also
presented plays, musicals, and other theatrical entertainment. At the turn
of the century, most venues were either owned by local entrepreneurs or
associated with small circuits. By the late 1910s many of these theaters
had either become part of large circuits no longer available to Howe or
been converted to regular motion picture houses.[50] Even in his hometown, Howe sometimes found it difficult to locate a desirable venue.[51]
Near the end, Howe's companies were frequently playing in state armories
and other makeshift spaces.

Adolph Zukor spearheaded the move toward large-scale corporations.
As head of Paramount, he created a vertically integrated, national cor-

poration with extensive production, distribution, and exhibition capabilities in strategically placed spots. Paramount was only the most visible symbol of this consolidation. When Howe's Travel Festival closed, Scranton-based M. E. Cummeford had fifty-seven theaters in northeast Pennsylvania and effectively controlled motion picture exhibition in Wilkes-Barre and surrounding areas.[52] Theaters had become increasingly luxurious during the teens and were capable of presenting a technically excellent show. In comparison, even Howe's projectionists could not overcome all the limitations of the old opera houses and makeshift halls. The quality of his exhibitions was now judged against the standards of elegant, specially designed motion picture theaters built or renovated in the mid and late teens.

The disappearance of the old opera houses paralleled the loss of Howe's original role. Mass culture was triumphant, and Howe's role as a mediator between urban commercial entertainment and local communities uneasy with its values was no longer needed. Although Howe had adapted by offering genres excluded from mass entertainment, by 1919 the new mass culture had incorporated these subjects into its repertoire with the concept of the balanced program.[53] Movie houses often showed a newsreel, a cartoon or travelogue, and a comedy before the main feature. What was once absent from the regular theater found a subservient role there.

Most importantly, World War I exposed the inadequacy and dishonesty of Howe's cinema of reassurance. The pomp, spectacle, and technological wizardry of his many military subjects obscured their awful destructive power. The semiannual proclamations that all was right with the world, that beneficent elites were firmly and properly in control, no longer washed in the midst of revolutions and civil wars in Eastern Europe and Asia. As Robert Sklar has put it, genteel culture—which achieved unprecedented hegemony during World War I—was "smashed like an old and brittle eggshell" in its aftermath.[54] Its power to convince was lost. The middle classes saw their social and economic status, once the basis for their self-confidence, deteriorate. Even they could no longer believe in Howe's ideological message.

NEW DIRECTIONS FOR THE HOWE COMPANY

As his road companies approached their demise, Howe had essentially withdrawn from all business activities. He struggled with a protracted illness and entered a Christian Science sanatorium in June 1922. He died on Jan. 30, 1923, at age sixty-six.[55] As the road shows closed, Walkinshaw looked for new ways to keep the Howe business alive. The organization had always developed its own negatives and prints.[56] In 1919, he expanded these facilities and opened a commercial film laboratory with eight employees. A year later forty Wilkes-Barre residents were working in the lab. By 1924, there were almost one hundred. Under Walkinshaw's careful supervision, the Howe company became one of the motion picture industry's leading film labs, with William Fox, Eastman Kodak, and various independent producers among its customers. According to Irvin Marvel, who worked in the plant, the lab's success was dependent on Walkinshaw's active supervision.[57] When Walkinshaw became ill and then died in 1926 at age fifty-three, the laboratory declined and eventually closed.[58]

Lyman H. Howe Company, Incorporated, was taken over by a new generation. Howe had left his shares in the company to his son, Harold, who became known as Lyman Howe, Junior. Walkinshaw had no children: his shares in the company were divided among his wife and several trusted employees including Robert Gillaum, Linn Hallet, and Bob Jones.[59] The easy accord between Howe and Walkinshaw did not carry over with the next generation. Harold Howe wanted to become the company president, but the other shareholders refused. Robert Gillaum, a faithful employee since 1905, assumed that role.

Although the balanced program had undermined Howe's road shows, one of its leading proponents, the Educational Films Corporation of America, run by Earl W. Hammons, eventually became a Howe ally. Hammons was given credit for "having lifted the educational and scenic film from the place of 'filler' or 'time killer' on the programme of small theaters to a position where they are featured on the electric light signs of the newest motion picture houses in the country."[60] Using the distribution practices of the mainstream industry, Educational Films placed its "high-class motion pictures" in conventional theaters across the country. By 1918 Educational Films was distributing "scenic numbers" like *Mexico Today* to the Rivoli and other prominent theaters.[61] The company consolidated its position in the fall of 1919 and assumed the most powerful position in the short subject field.[62]

Educational Films used Howe's lab[63] and probably helped the company rent its films to select theaters. In June 1917 "Roxy" Rothafel showed *A Flying Trip through the Hawaiian Islands* and *Our Navy To-day* at his Rialto Theater in New York City. These were films that Howe was then showing on his exhibition circuits, which did not include New York, as *Hawaii: The Paradise of the Pacific* and *Somewhere in the Atlantic*.[64] In 1920, a few months after Howe's road companies finally closed, the Rialto again showed a Howe subject, *Sculptured Impressions of Musical Personages*, with Paramount's feature film *Paris Green*, starring Charles Ray.[65] These appearances indicate that Howe's company was hesitantly moving toward the industry's standard form of distribution even before its road companies disbanded.

Once the road companies closed, the Howe organization distributed an occasional film through Educational. Early in 1921 Hammons's company released *Lyman Howe's Famous Ride on a Runaway Train*. Donald Malkames, who later worked for the Howe organization, believes that the film had been used by Howe's road companies and was simply brushed off for release through Educational.[66] If so, it must have been *A Rousing New Ride on a Runaway Train*, shown by Howe in 1914. In any case, the film proved a successful venture. The experience of being on the front of a train hurtling down a mountain once again thrilled and delighted audiences. Rothafel showed it at his Capitol Theater in April 1921 and brought it back for an unusual return engagement in May. Rothafel declared, "In my opinion 'The Ride on a Runaway Train' is the best short subject I have ever seen. It is the only short subject which we ever brought back for a second presentation and on both occasions, it created a sensation."[67] Less than a

11-3. Educational advertised Howe's *Ride on a Runaway Train* with a letter from Roxy.

year later, it was shown before the King and Queen of England.[68] Other
one-reel films, such as *Scenic Distortions*, shown at the Capitol Theater in
January 1922, followed.[69]

   Robert Gillaum soon came up with the idea of reworking material from
Howe's semiannual tours into a regular monthly release known as *Lyman
H. Howe's Hodge-Podge*. Even during semiannual tours, Howe personnel
had often found ways to reincorporate old footage into new programs. This
practice became the basis of the series that began with *King Winter*, released on October 22, 1922, through Educational Films. One 1924 subject, *Snapshots of the Universe*, was described in a trade journal:

> Like all of the issues of Hodge-Podge released by Educational this one is a
> combination of interesting and instructive views and ingenious and amusing
> cartoon work. The serious part of the reel shows contrast between wash day
> in Siberia where the natives wash clothes in icy water and wash day with the
> sailors aboard a warship. There are also contrasting views of hair cutting in
> Borneo and Mexico, fire fighting in Alaska and drill maneuvers by students
> of Culver Military Academy. The latter are snappy and well done. The car-
> toon work is especially novel and clever, and this reel is one of the best of
> the series.[70]

Building on a name that was widely recognized, *Lyman H. Howe's Hodge-
Podge* found its way into many theaters across the country. It showed at
the Central Market Theater in Philadelphia, Loew's Aldine Theater in

11-4. A title card for *Lyman H. Howe's Hodge-Podge* (1927).

Pittsburgh, Loew's State Theater in St. Louis, the Wisconsin Theater in Milwaukee, and other theaters in cities where Howe had once played.[71]

Since most of the film used in *Howe's Hodge-Podge* was already owned by the company, the series was inexpensive to make and proved remunerative. Altogether there were 110 releases.[72] *Howe's Hodge-Podge* even survived the transition to sound, adopting the use of the omniscient narrator and reintroducing some overly familiar sound effects. A script of *Traffic*, submitted for copyright purposes in 1932, indicates that the conventions of spectator as passenger and traveler continued to be reworked along with the material until both were tired clichés:

> Ladies and Gentlemen: Tune in on the latest news flashes about how people go places and do things in Zanzibar . . . and Timbuctoo . . . and other places you may have heard of. Just observe the traffic regulations and keep your mind on the road. There's the green light . . . and we're off. . . .
>
> Naples, Italy: (Within the shadow of Vesuvius). . . . Most famous of Volcanoes . . . lies the city where the feet of tourists follow the paths beaten by the illustrious statesmen, philosophers, and poets of the great Roman Empire. . . .
>
> Budapest, Hungary: Here we have the twin cities of central Europe. Built on both sides of the stream which Strauss called the Beautiful Blue Danube. At this point it unromantically takes on the muddy yellow tint of split-pea soup.[73]

In 1933, as the full impact of the Depression was felt, the Howe company needed an infusion of capital if the business was to continue. The Walkinshaw shareholders were eager to risk their funds, but Lyman Howe, Junior declined. Thus the company that bore Lyman H. Howe's name finally closed its doors.

THE "sound era" brought the practice of road-showing special features with an orchestra and effects trucks to an abrupt end. From a strictly commercial standpoint, the practice of road-showing continued and even flourished, for the costs of paying and transporting personnel was all but eliminated.[74] Yet this practice had been so altered that it bore little resemblance to traveling exhibition. The closing of Howe's road shows had earlier signaled the end of a certain kind of traveling showman. Although D. W. Robertson continued to supply church groups with entertainments, his business shifted away from motion picture exhibitions just as Howe was disbanding his road shows. His American Entertainment Bureau remained in business throughout the 1920s and 1930s.[75]

The tradition of the traveling exhibitor, however, continued in many forms either on the fringe or completely outside the Hollywood system. The Huntleys went back on the road in 1922, using trucks for transportation and showing films in a tent. Amusement films continued to be exhibited in this way by showmen who rarely, if ever, used regular theatrical outlets. Mark Swartz has studied traveling exhibition in North Carolina, then one of the most rural and underdeveloped parts of the country, where numerous showmen made a living into the 1930s and 1940s.[76] Such practices remained viable in some portions of the country until television dealt a final blow.

At the Brooklyn Institute during the 1919–1920 season Burton Holmes gave a complete course on Europe in the aftermath of the war while Newman, nearing the end of his career, appeared only for a day. Other speakers, including Robert Flaherty, who lectured on *The Eskimo*, and Ernest Thompson Seton, who talked on *The Yellowstone National Park*, also provided the Institute with film programs.[77] The Brooklyn Institute's sponsorship of touring lecturers who appealed to its refined membership changed very little over the next fifteen years. In 1933, the year the Howe company folded, Holmes was still giving his annual lecture series. His efforts were supplemented by Branson De Cou, whose eight talks with moving pictures covered such topics as *Old Mexico* and *Soviet Russia*.[78] Single lectures also continued as Air-Commodore P.F.M. Fellows gave an illustrated talk, using films and lantern slides, on *The Mount Everest Flight*. *Four Hundred Fathoms Down* was presented by William Bebe, Director of Tropical Research at the New York Zoological Society. The technology had improved, and the speaker had an impressive institutional affiliation,

11-5. Moredock's Traveling Movie Palace (1926–1927).

but the subject differed little from Williamson's *Thirty Leagues under the Sea* presented almost twenty years before. In the interim, however, the Institute had also developed a sizable motion picture program that offered Hollywood films twice a week. [79]

As the U.S. film industry expanded its scope, elaborated on its methods, and improved its facilities, itinerant exhibitors survived by finding (or more often creating) increasingly limited opportunities at the periphery of the commercial industry. The Howe enterprise had less and less room in which to operate after 1915. Howe's cinema of reassurance appeared bankrupt in the wake of the Great War's devastation. This, along with the onset of extensive vertical integration, and the development of the balanced program, which integrated all genres within a hierarchy dominated by the feature, ensured the post-World War I demise of his exhibition units. Howe's associates then adapted by opening a film lab, taking advantage of lower business costs compared to New York-based operations. They also traded on Howe's still substantial reputation and aesthetic identity to create a series of shorts that could be run in theaters before the main feature. The company experienced a new burst of activities, until Walkinshaw's death, the coming of sound, the Depression, and Hollywood's shift to double features brought these operations to a final close.

12   ✳ ✳ ✳ ✳ ✳ ✳ ✳ ✳ ✳ ✳ ✳ ✳ ✳ ✳ ✳ ✳ ✳ ✳ ✳

Conclusion

✳ ✳ ✳

THE TRAVELING motion-picture lecturer continues to this day. Burton Holmes entertained his audiences with motion pictures into the 1950s. By that time, Jay Leyda recalls, the Holmes travelogue had become cliched and hokey.[1] The National Audubon Society provided its local organizations with speakers and films into the late 1970s. Given in nontheatrical settings, the showings served as social gathering for friends, with tea and cake afterwards.[2] The wide diffusion of the 16 mm format, which reduced costs and made projection in nontheatrical settings much easier, after World War II revitalized the practice of traveling exhibition. Within the last ten or fifteen years sports enthusiasts have lectured extensively on surfing, skiing, and other activities, using films that might be described as polished home movies. Independent filmmakers now tour the college and museum circuit to discuss their work; the more avant-garde sometimes talk or perform while the films are being projected. The practices of the traveling exhibitor have not been entirely eliminated, even though the increasing size and complexity of the moving-image industry has kept such practices more and more at the periphery. The audiences that Howe once addressed might now be found watching public television.

In the annals of American entertainment, traveling exhibition has had a long and important history. Even before there were good roads, hardy exhibitors traveled along the eastern seaboard providing phantasmagoria performances and other screen events.[3] The development of a railway network produced a boon for those eager to move quickly and easily from one location to another. Until entertainment had become a complete technological product that could be cheaply shipped, itinerant showmen were a crucial component of the American cultural landscape. Howe had moved into this world well after the railroads on which he had earlier worked began to criss-cross the country. He achieved prominence at a time when all sorts of traveling exhibitions flourished, and he remained successful even after they went into decline.

The study of Lyman H. Howe and his fellow showmen reveals elements of turn-of-the-century American culture that have been previously neglected or misunderstood. Traveling motion picture exhibitors, who were much more pervasive than generally recognized, reached large sections of the U.S. population that would have otherwise been deprived of the motion picture experience, people living outside major cities as well as urbanites who rejected commercial amusement. Unlike other types of showmen who were inextricably bound to the amusement world, traveling exhibitors regularly shaped their programs and operations in ways that appealed across a spectrum of church-oriented conservatives, cultural elitists, and the more familiar amusement goers.

This study has shown that traveling exhibition fluctuated in response to rapidly changing circumstances in the world of prerecorded entertainment. Historians have often noted that Edison saw motion pictures as a technological extension of the phonograph. Here we have seen how Howe applied the same logic to exhibition. By the 1896–1897 theatrical season, traveling showmen were touring small-town opera houses or playing in nontheatrical settings such as church halls and YMCAs. Yet, despite the promise of cinema's first, novelty year, financial returns proved disappointing to many. The popularity of Spanish-American War films in 1898 provided a brief window of opportunity for some, but determination, showmanship, and a clearly targeted audience were the chief ingredients for success, or at least commercial longevity. In the early 1900s, the loss of audience and commercial difficulties bedeviled these peripetetic exhibitors as much as their urban counterparts. By late 1903, several factors, including improved projection and the rising popularity of story films, provided the groundwork for revival and the increasing use of commercial venues. By 1905, traveling picture shows and vaudeville were directly competing for patrons in cities as large as New York (1900 population: 3,437,202) and as small as New Britain, Connecticut (1900 population: 28,202). By then traveling exhibitors had helped to inculcate audiences throughout the United States with the film-going habit. But, as showmen soon found out, patrons readily transfered their allegiance to the new quotidian storefront picture houses.

Although it has sometimes been assumed that traveling exhibition disappeared with the arrival of mass entertainment practices in 1907–1908, such was not the case. As Howe quickly realized after a brief period of uncertainty, the practice survived in specialized areas that the new exhibition mode had not yet absorbed. Howe, Burton Holmes, and a few others continued to prosper as purveyors of travel films and news subjects. Companies offering technological innovations like Kinemacolor or the Edison Kinetophone depended on traveling exhibition units for much of their income during the 1908–1915 period. As Terry Ramsaye remarks in relation to Howe, they never really became part of the "screen institution."[4] Feature films also were exhibited using road-show methods, first as an alternative to the nickelodeon system of distribution and exhibition and then as one of several commercial strategies available to the dominant Hollywood system. The subject matter and formats that the Hollywood cinema excluded in its earliest stages it gradually incorporated until Howe and others were driven from the field. Thus, to understand fully the practices of the classical Hollywood cinema, we must not only look at feature films but at the majors' efforts to totalize their control over all forms of filmmaking through the introduction of the newsreel, the balanced program, and eventually the capital investment that sound on film required.[5] Yet complete domination and elimination of potential rivals remained an elusive goal. Resistance to hegemonic control, if eliminated in one area, only seemed to thrive in some other.

BY LOOKING at apparently marginal figures such as Howe, historians are forced to reexamine the framework in which they conceive the cinema as well as more general cultural practices. Film history as codified in an array of one-volume surveys and auteurist studies of directors offers too narrow a structure to explore such a dynamic yet diverse phenomenon as motion pictures. In recent years, avant-garde filmmaking, radical social and cultural history, feminist and psychoanalytically oriented film theory, and historical examinations of third world cinema and early film practices are some of the avenues that are leading to the reconceptualization of cinema practices.

Most previous writing on pre-nickelodeon motion picture exhibition has focused on vaudeville theaters.[6] Now vaudeville's contributions can be better situated in relation to other formats. Even in urban environments, vaudeville was never the only mode of motion picture exhibition. Although sometimes competing directly for patrons, vaudeville exhibition and traveling shows interacted symbiotically, sustaining and nurturing the small film industry of the pre-nickelodeon era. Vaudeville, often functioning as a kind of first-run theater, had much more importance to the industry than the number of machines it employed. Its urban exhibition services developed production capabilities that provided itinerant showmen with popular films of national events—subjects often crucial for their survival. Correspondingly, by buying their projectors and films, traveling picture men provided many producers with crucial markets for their goods. Without such financial support, some companies might not have survived.

This study does not seek to elevate the traveling exhibitor to the position of dominance some have ascribed to vaudeville during the first ten years of cinema. No single form of exhibition can adequately characterize this period. Specialized motion picture theaters were more popular along the Pacific coast in the 1890s and early 1900s than either vaudeville or traveling exhibition. Although five-cent vaudeville began to flourish in the Far West during the first years of the new century, all but supplanting the old storefront picture shows, few traveling showmen were prepared to surmount the prohibitive distances between towns. In the deep South, outside of New Orleans, vaudeville was never well established and traveling showmen, typically attached to carnivals, provided the principal opportunities to see films. Between 1904 and at least 1906, exhibitors operated more projectors at Coney Island during the summer months than in all other New York City venues during each of the previous winters. All of these modes of exhibition need study. An examination of film showings in penny arcades, summer parks, and small storefront theaters will allow us to appreciate the diversity of motion picture exhibition and the shifting importance and success of these different forums.

By looking at early film exhibition in general, traveling motion picture showmen in particular, and Howe and his enterprises in specific, we have explored some of the tensions between individual and larger practices. In some areas, Howe was fairly typical: there were many phonograph exhibitors who moved into cinema. In other respects he was atypical or extraordinary: he was one of the very few whose programs appealed across cultural divisions. Sometimes he was in the vanguard, as with "pictures that talk." Other times, rivals took better advantage of new opportunities, as did Archie Shepard when he expanded his operations in 1903–1904. In dialectical fashion the general illuminates the particular and vice versa.

The largely quantitative analysis of traveling exhibition, which provided the basis for our preliminary mapping, points to a second level of exploration. In their modes of production and representation, early motion picture programs were much more sophisticated than historians have recognized. Traveling exhibitors customarily selected and structured short films into complex programs sustained by live sound accompaniment that included music, sound effects, and voices. Howe proved a master of the creative possibilities allowed by these generalized practices. During the 1890s and early 1900s, he displayed flair both for organizing his film subjects along variety lines and for creating sustained narratives. It was in the creative tension between these two poles that Howe realized his programs. Later he applied such knowledge to his company's own filmmaking endeavors. Howe sometimes acted as an author in a deeper sense, by expanding the very parameters of motion picture practices. He perhaps made his greatest contribution with the creative interplay of image and sound— with narration, synchronous voices, music, and effects. Perhaps he did not "invent," but in some real sense he certainly "authored" the use of actors behind the screen, at least as it became a fad in 1907–1909.

Howe's practices, as well as those of other traveling exhibitors, provide new insight into the historical relations between image and sound. From the outset, many showmen accompanied their films with sound effects and crudely synchronized recordings. This phenomenon was so widespread that it cannot be dismissed as an interesting but deviant experiment. Rather, the relation between image and sound remained an issue throughout the "silent" era, a "problem" that was never "solved" until the successful introduction of synchronized recorded sound in the late 1920s. Because Howe had become sensitized to audio presentation during the early 1890s, he subsequently explored its many possibilities in conjunction with motion pictures, playing recordings with films in the 1890s and then shifting to live accompaniment from behind the screen. It may be asking too much to call the "silent cinema" by some other name, but it is not too much to remember that early cinema screenings were anything but silent.

Howe's early experiences enrich our understanding of the pre-cinema as well. Elsewhere, we have argued that the whole concept of "pre-cinema" is fraught with difficulties.[7] Traditionally, histories of pre-cinema have focused on certain discoveries and inventions that formed the technological basis for cinema. Within the last twenty years, this emphasis and its assumptions of technological determinism have been effectively questioned. As a result, almost any nineteenth-century activity that strikes the historian's fancy—in law, culture, technology, and social and economic life—has become part of the cinema's pre-history.

One way to redefine the pre-cinema is to place cinema within a history of screen practice—the history of projected images and their sound accompaniment. Within such a framework there remains an extensive but now definable pre-cinema including magic lantern practices and illustrated lectures. However, it remains essential to see how other cultural activities influence the screen's production and representational methods. Robert C. Allen, for example, has traced the early development of vaudeville and shown how its format readily incorporated a twenty-minute presentation of motion pictures. Howe's experience as a traveling phonograph exhibitor and the ways in which his concerts adopted and adapted to motion pictures have added significance since Edison and his team of inventors initially thought of motion pictures as an extension of the phonograph. Not surprisingly, Howe was one of many showmen to articulate a similar conceptual framework.

Howe and his fellow practitioners, particularly those who catered to such institutions as the Brooklyn Institute of Arts and Sciences, also demonstrate the ways in which the "documentary tradition" was a more sustained and coherent practice than standard histories of the documentary have acknowledged. These usually begin with the topical films of the 1890s and early 1900s (particularly those of the Lumières) and then jump forward to the beginnings of the newsreel and the documentary films of Robert Flaherty.[8] Although Flaherty's prominent role need not be disregarded, he is part of a long and prestigious lineage, including such figures as John Stoddard, Burton Holmes, Dwight Elmendorf, and Jacob Riis. (Truly, "illustrated lecture" was the nineteenth-century term for documentary.) Within this tradition, Howe had a modest role. Although he received many of his nonfiction films from European sources, he also took his own news and travel films. Before Pathé introduced the first newsreel in 1911, Howe offered "wait-a-while" news films with a semiannual release schedule. In many instances, he devoted extensive portions of his programs to events or issues of special interest. Although he helped to keep the nonfiction film alive during the late 1900s and early 1910s, his magazine formats limited its scope and ambition. In contrast, many of his contemporaries devoted entire evenings to single subjects, as Burton Holmes did with the Russo-Japanese War. Our awareness of the strong, continuous tradition of nonfiction film can be greatly enriched by looking at the traveling exhibitor.

Finally, Howe foregrounds the position of ideology in cinema. Throughout much of his career, he played to diverse cultural groups. His predominantly middle-class patrons were divided by strongly held beliefs about pleasure, the role of the church in daily life, and definitions of art and enlightened cultural activity. Despite the longevity of Howe's operations and the frequent upheavals experienced in the world of traveling exhibition, his work displays strong continuities. From his days with the phonograph and even the miniature coal mine, he appealed to audiences through an ideology of reassurance. He avoided the very issues that created anxiety, issues readily apparent in films that Howe chose not to show. In 1896, for example, the Edison Manufacturing Company made numerous films savoring the possibilities that metropolitan life held for amusement, licentiousness, and excitement. Through careful selection and organization, Howe recast their implicit suggestions of freer sexuality and reduced morality. The controversial—and much about city life was controversial to rural audiences—was eliminated. It is hardly surprising that Howe never showed *The Ex-Convict*, *The Kleptomaniac*, or similar social dramas that took a critical stance toward the social inequities of a rapidly industrializing America. Howe expunged much that was new and dynamic in both celebrations and criticisms of the city. But he did not seek refuge in the restrained refinement of the illustrated lectures addressed to cultural elites. Instead he avoided what was divisive and eschewed a critical stance by claiming to recreate the phenomenal world with sound and often color. He renounced overt interpretation and in the process made the world seem manageable, knowable, and even comforting. Like John Philip Sousa, he knit diverse groups together into a unified audience using patriotism, enthusiasm, and a sense of national destiny.

Howe provided the thrill found in popular amusements without their customary incorporation of desire. He focused on the quotidian, the ordinary, the everyday, and found ways to make it fresh and appealing. There was pleasure and sensual texture in the images themselves rather than in what they represented. His viewer-as-passenger subjects—a ride on "a runaway train," a dirigible, a speed boat or airplane—provided a key method of achieving this goal. They offered the sensation of dynamism without engaging the deeper, more unsettling psychological issues of modernity. As the operational aesthetic shifted from Barnum to Howe it became a way of avoiding rather than fostering social meaning or insight. By depicting industrial processes—building locomotives, making steel, or publishing a newspaper—Howe could laud technological achievements while circumventing discomforting questions about their social impact.[9]

For Howe the technologies of transportation and heavy industry had counterparts in the communication systems he embraced. Through his advocacy and presentation of a "model" cinema, the veteran exhibitor demonstrated the kinds of roles that he believed enlightened management should take. On multiple levels, his approach resembled the ideology of corporate liberalism, a faith in social engineering, efficiency, and enlightened reform flowing from the top down.[10] If Howe's long-running Travel Festival had a recurring hero, it was Theodore Roosevelt, who accepted large corporations as the logical culmination of the country's industrial development even as he insisted that they act responsibly. Howe even advocated this corporate ideal directly when showing films of the National Cash Register Corporation. Likewise, citizen Howe exercised his own zeal for reform through civic organizations such as the Wilkes-Barre Chamber of Commerce. Benevolent if stern paternalism, epitomized by Howe's 1903 letters to Edwin Hadley, can be found in a variety of forms throughout his work. In the most literal sense, Howe's Travel Festival offered a world view, one not only of obedient colonial subjects basking in the assumed benefits of Western civilization but of ordinary Americans finding everyday pleasures in the world as it was, and as it was becoming through the transformation of an unproblematic technology. This appeal was crushed by World War I, and although it had a parodic revival in the 1920s with *Lyman H. Howe's Hodge-Podge*, its unproblematic message was ended, seemingly forever, by the Great Depression. Of course, one day the politics of reassurance would be revived by another motion picture entrepreneur with political aspirations, Ronald Reagan, but that is another story.

Appendix A
Howe: A Civic Leader

* * *

HOWE'S ROLE as a Wilkes-Barre civic leader is reminiscent of Phineas T. Barnum's role in his hometown of Bridgeport.[1] As Barnum's showmanship became more respectable and his financial holdings more extensive, he grew in the esteem of his fellow townspeople. Likewise, the growing recognition of cinema's importance and worth coincided with Howe's changing role within his Pennsylvania community. In the early 1900s, as shown in Chapters 5 and 6, Howe carefully cultivated his hometown audience. This practice continued between 1904 and 1908 as he filmed noteworthy local events and showed them to Wilkes-Barreans at his semiannual shows. Howe devoted considerable energy to the Wilkes-Barre's Centennial Jubilee, photographing the military and firemen's parades on May 10, 1906 and the civic and industrial parades on the following day. These films were the headline attraction for Howe's next appearance, September 6 through 8. The *Wilkes-Barre Record* reported, "This year's program contains a number of films of special interest to this city and vicinity, consisting of an excellent series showing the most important centennial scenes. The military, firemen's and the civic and industrial parades are given with all the detail that marked the original. The effect is heightened by the playing of the bands, the clatter of the horses' hoofs, the shouting of the multitude, and so forth, the whole stirring up the audience to marked enthusiasm."[2] Howe gave a print of the centennial films to the local historical society.[3]

The showman used his production capabilities not simply to attract local audiences but to enhance his standing in the Wilkes-Barre community. He repeatedly suggested that his local views were shown across the country and served as advertisements for the city. (The centennial films, however, were only shown in Nanticoke and other northeastern Pennsylvanian towns.) The fact that he presented Wilkes-Barre to the outside world gave him a significant role within the community. In the process, moreover, he presented himself as a model Wilkes-Barre citizen: industrious, up-to-date, temperate, religious, well-traveled, worldly yet moral.

Howe's commercial success added to his prominence. Many local citizens found jobs with the Howe enterprise while other employees settled in the city. His twentieth wedding anniversary in 1908 became an occasion for the office staff and road employees to express their fealty with "a set of engrossed resolutions or congratulations." In addition, two hundred

A-1a,b. Howe's film of the Wilkes-Barre Centennial celebration (1906).

neighbors paid their respects, presenting a "magnificent array of gifts . . . a splendid assortment of cut glass, hand painted china, linens, pictures, etc." The local paper offered an elaborate description of the event, noting everything from the presence of Oppenheim's seven-piece orchestra to Mrs. Howe's gown, "a Paris creation of the directoire style imported especially for her by Mr. Howe."[4]

Howe's prosperity enabled him to acquire the outward symbols of material wealth. In late 1907, the showman purchased one hundred acres of land in Schenectady, New York, where he intended to build an amusement park. Instead, it became the home of a minor-league baseball team partially owned by Howe.[5] Unlike Wilkes-Barre, Schenectady allowed Sunday baseball, a key element in a team's profitability. In 1910 he consummated Wilkes-Barre's "Biggest Real Estate Deal of the Year," purchasing a strip of land along River Street for approximately $200,000. To reduce the dangers of flooding he raised the land and in 1911 built a palatial home on one lot and sold others to wealthy local citizens.[6] With this deal, the newspapers began to call Howe "the motion picture magnate" and the "Moving Picture King."[7]

Somewhat earlier, around 1905, Howe acquired an automobile and became a leading member of the Wilkes-Barre Automobile Club. Owning a car in those earlier years placed him among the economic elite of the city and provided him with a means to socialize with the city's leading citizens. The annual hill climb, which Howe filmed in May 1907, was the club's main venture for several years. But in 1911, as the club lost some of its early vigor, Lyman Howe was elected its president. In his inaugural address to the membership, Howe offered his philosophy of action, "We

A-2. Lyman H. Howe's house (1911).

must wake up and come to life. We must get moving. Idleness means dis-integration. . . . There is work for us to do, and there is nothing that will bring people into closer harmony and make them happier in their social relations than the accomplishment of something."[8] Howe successfully ap-plied the promotional rhetoric he had learned as a showman to the local organization. At the end of March, the club sponsored a four-day Wilkes-Barre automobile show at the Armory. Visiting motor men declared that "outside of the national shows the Wilkes-Barre Show is as fine as any of them." The club split the receipts with the participating car dealers and used the event to conduct a vigorous membership campaign.[9]

Howe established himself as a "doer" and soon headed the Industrial Exposition Committee formed by the Wilkes-Barre Chamber of Com-merce. His job was to ascertain the desirability of a local exposition. Late in 1912 Howe announced the committee's strong support for such an ac-tivity. Again his chairman's report reflected the fervor that led to Howe's success in the motion picture field:

> [An exposition] would be the means of kindling new interest and enthusi-asm throughout our whole valley; it would enthuse and fuze together the members of this organization into such a live working body as it never en-joyed before.
>
> This Chamber of Commerce has the brains and ability to do what other cities have done and it only needs some worthy object that is big enough to enlist the efforts of its members to bring about this unity of action. There is nothing that will grip and develop this organization like some big, interesting work to do.
>
> It is the unanimous opinion of this committee that the exploiting of this exposition be handled and conducted by the Chamber of Commerce, instead of employing at large expense a professional promoter for that purpose. To do it ourselves will give it more of a local color and relieve it of that cold, com-mercial atmosphere that would result from outside influence and it will unite the working forces of the Chamber of Commerce and bring its members closer together in a concentrated effort to awaken a new interest in the wel-fare of our city.[10]

Howe then ran the Greater Wilkes-Barre Industrial Exposition, which lasted for eight days in May 1913, accumulated over 25,000 paying visitors and earned almost $6,000 over expenses. Many felt that the exposition "in a financial way, in an artistic way, in a hustle and bustle way was more than was anticipated." The *Wilkes-Barre Record* editorialized, "Mr. Howe and his co-workers labored industriously. They gave unstintingly of their time and energy—and they accomplished results. The whole city reaps the benefit. The exposition is valuable for the city not only in the direct benefit that will come to the many exhibitors but because it has stirred up the community and created the contagion of progress. It has sent a good Spring tonic coursing through the veins of the old town."[11]

Howe was given a loving cup for his work on the exposition and was viewed as one of the town's leading citizens. When the Wilkes-Barre Citizens' Committee of one hundred was formed in August 1913, Howe was elected its president. Who after all could better head a group that wished to support and promote "selected candidates for city councilmen who would measure up to certain requirements of character and ability and commit themselves to a thorough, conscientious enforcement of the laws"?[12] In June 1914 he was elected president of the first City Art Jury, attached to the city council. The jury approved all plans for bridges, buildings, gates, lampposts, and other structures erected on city property. Howe and the committee eventually found themselves opposing Civil War veterans who wanted a shaft monument in Public Square Park.[13]

Howe became a city benefactor, donating land for tennis courts on Riverside Drive near his home in June 1914. A few months later, after a disastrous cyclone swept the city, he held a benefit at the Grand Opera House under the auspices of the general relief committee. Matinee and evening shows featured a special program of "film masterpieces which Mr. Howe has exhibited in this city at various times and which so many have asked to see again."[14] All the expenses associated with the screenings were assumed by Howe and others. The result yielded a large sum that was soon distributed by an appreciative Federation of Churches.[15]

On a modest scale, Howe followed the example of Theodore Roosevelt. In circumstances that he believed were in the general interest of the populace, Howe took action. In June 1915 he was elected head of the Susquehanna River Improvement Association of the Wyoming Valley, organized to facilitate the prevention of floods and the proper disposal of sewage.[16] Floods were then as now a major destructive threat in the Wyoming Valley. Leading citizens, anxious to reduce "the danger that hangs over us," ensured that the activist Howe became chairman. Convinced "it would be better to spend money for prevention than to spend it to recover and repair," Howe set up a committee to look into the removal of the Nanticoke Dam, advocated by the United States government.[17] His plan quickly won the support of the *Wilkes-Barre Record*.

In October 1915, Howe was elected president of the Wilkes-Barre Chamber of Commerce. The local papers praised the selection. "The election of Lyman Howe as the president of the Chamber of Commerce is fitting recognition of the ability of one of Wilkes-Barre's most prominent businessmen," editorialized the *Record*. "Mr. Howe is one of the large number of men who have reached positions of high influence in the business world through their exertions and such men are particularly well qualified to understand what a community needs."[18] Soon after Howe assumed his position, he was called upon to mediate a trolley car strike in which the owners threatened to break a deadlock by employing strikebreakers.[19] Although initially optimistic, Howe found that his theories of reassurance, his exhortations, and his homilies had little impact on the situation. The strike lasted more than fourteen months, casting a shadow over his term of office.[20] In a similar move, he headed a committee of one hundred businessmen from the anthracite coal region. The group planned to visit New York City, where coal operators and miners were negotiating a new contract.[21] They wished to urge both sides to avoid a strike that would disrupt the economy of northeastern Pennsylvania and devastate their businesses. Before such a meeting could occur, the negotiators agreed to continue working under the old contract until a new accord was reached. The principal pressure to resolve their differences, however, came from the radical Industrial Workers of the World, which was organizing the mine fields and threatening both the established union and the owners.[22] In both instances, Howe's prestige did not translate into real power, a situation not unlike his position in the film industry.

After Howe stepped down from his position as president of Wilkes-Barre's Chamber of Commerce in October 1916, his role as a civic leader declined, paralleling the waning prosperity of his road shows. He remained a public figure, becoming a board member of the Miners Bank and other local institutions. He also served as chairman of the local War Savings Stamps campaign in 1918 and organized several successful drives. With the slogan "Put Wilkes-Barre on Top," Howe had enthusiastic school children canvas for funds.

Howe's increasing involvement with the Christian Science movement, which he helped to establish in Wilkes-Barre, made him the subject of local controversy. In October 1918, when local authorities shut the theaters and churches because of influenza, Howe protested the closings as ungodly. In a letter to the *Wilkes-Barre Record*, he demanded, "Where are we drifting to as a people when we are ordered to close our places of worship in order to keep from contagion?"[23] Howe's plea was subsequently debated and ridiculed in the Wilkes-Barre newspapers.[24] Feeling out of touch with the public mood, declining business fortunes, and the onset of serious illness all caused Howe to withdraw from a prominent role in local affairs as the decade came to a close.

Appendix B
Exhibition Patterns among Traveling Motion Picture Showmen, 1896-1904

* * *

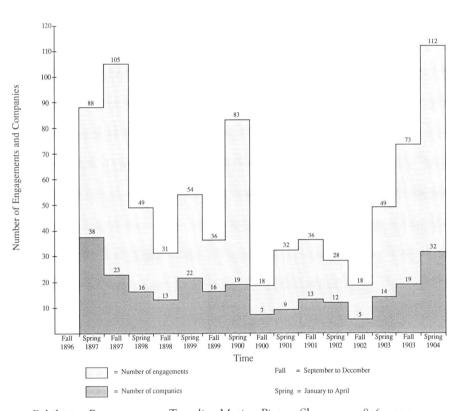

Exhibition Patterns among Traveling Motion-Picture Showmen, 1896–1904

SOURCE: *New York Dramatic Mirror* "Correspondence" and "Misc. Route" sections. For each time period, three issues two weeks apart were surveyed.

The graph is designed to illustrate relative levels of activity and is not a comprehensive analysis of exhibition in this period.

Exhibition Patterns among Traveling Motion-Picture Showmen, 1896–1904

	Total Engagements	Engagements Showing Fight Films	Engagements Showing Non-fight Films	Howe Engagements	Number of Companies
Fall 1896	0	0	0	0	0
Spring 1897	88	0	88	2	38
Fall 1897[a]	105	90	15	1	23
Spring 1898[a]	49	16	33	1	16
Fall 1898[a]	31	4	27	13	13
Spring 1899	54	0	54	16	22
Fall 1899[b]	36	7	29	12	16
Spring 1900[c]	83	56	27	13	19
Fall 1900	18	0	18	12	7
Spring 1901	32	0	32	9	9
Fall 1901	36	0	36	10	13
Spring 1902	28	0	28	9	12
Fall 1902	18	0	18	10	5
Spring 1903[d]	49	11	38	22	14
Fall 1903[e]	73	11	62	18	19
Spring 1904	112	0	112	15	32

SOURCE: New York Dramatic Mirror "Correspondence" and "Misc. Route" sections. For each time period, three issues two weeks apart were surveyed. The number of engagements was calculated and the number of companies estimated.

[a] Veriscope: Corbett-Fitzsimmons fight.
[b] Fitzsimmons-Jeffries fight.
[c] Biograph: Jeffries-Sharkey fight.
[d] Jeffries-Fitzsimmons fight.
[e] Selig Polyscope: Root-Gardner fight.

Appendix C
Selected Film Exhibitions in
Wilkes-Barre, 1896-1919

* * *

29 June–4 July 1896: Edison's Vitascope, Grand Opera House (1,200 seats)

4 December 1896: Lyman H. Howe, Animotiscope, YMCA (1,000 seats), auspices of First Baptist Church

11–23 January 1897: Waite's Comedy Company, Animatograph, Grand Opera House

21–23 January 1897: Edison's Vitascope and Troubadour Company, Music Hall (1,500 seats)

February 1897: Cinematoscope, Ferguson and Federick's Store

25 February 1897: Lyman H. Howe, Animotiscope, Germania Hall, benefit of St. Conrad's Society

29 May 1897: Edison's kinetoscope on exhibition at 86 South Main Street

10–11 September 1897: Veriscope Company, *Corbett-Fitzsimmons Fight*, Grand Opera House

22 October 1897: Lyman H. Howe, Animotiscope, YMCA, auspices of John Knox Commandery, Knights of Malta

2 November 1897: Alexander Black, *Miss Jerry* (Picture Play), YMCA

26 January 1898: Lyman H. Howe, Animotiscope, YMCA, auspices of Ladies Aid Society of Christ Lutheran Church

15–16 April 1898: Cinematograph with *The Passion Play of Oberammergau*, Nesbitt Theater (1,200 seats)

1 June 1898: Lyman H. Howe, Animotiscope (wargraph-stereopticon), YMCA, auspices of Mr. Lord's Bible class of Derr Memorial Church

16 September 1898: Lyman H. Howe Moving Picture Company (Wargraph), Nesbitt Theater

17–19 November 1898: Spooner Repertory Company, Magniscope showing films between fourth and fifth acts of plays, Grand Opera House

24 January 1899: Lyman H. Howe's Wargraph, Nesbitt Theater

25 October 1899: Lyman H. Howe's High-Class Exhibition of Moving Pictures, Nesbitt Theater

9 December 1899: Biograph, *Jeffries-Sharkey Fight*, Fitzhugh Hall

30 January 1900: Lyman H. Howe's High-Class Exhibition of Moving Pictures, with Channing Darling, Nesbitt Theater

19–20 March 1900: *Jeffries-Sharkey Fight Pictures*, Nesbitt Theater

19–25 March 1900: Klimt-Hearn Company, films shown between acts of plays, Grand Opera House

19 October 1900: Lyman H. Howe's High-Class Exhibition of Moving Pictures, with monologist Ackland Lord Boyle, Nesbitt Theater

19 January 1901: Lyman H. Howe's High-Class Moving Pictures, also presenting
Ackland Lord Boyle, Nesbitt Theater

22 November 1901: Howe's Moving Pictures, also presenting Jay Paige, sculptor,
the Armory, auspices of Knights of Malta.

28 November 1901: *The Passion Play*, St. Cecilia's Church

4–5 April 1902: Lyman H. Howe's Presentation of the Most Marvelous Moving
Pictures in the World, with J. Paige, sculptor, Nesbitt Theater

7–8 November 1902: Howe's Moving Pictures, sixteenth semiannual tour, Nesbitt Theater

27–28 March 1903: Howe's Moving Pictures, seventeenth semiannual tour, Nesbitt Theater

7 October 1903: Hadley's Moving Pictures, the Armory, auspices of Uniformed
Rank, John Knox Commandery No. 12, A and I, O. Knights of Malta

20–21 November 1903: Lyman Howe Moving Pictures, eighteenth semiannual
tour, Nesbitt Theater

23 November 1903: Lyman H. Howe Moving Pictures, Broadway Armory, auspices of Presbyterian Church Choir

17 March 1904: Hadley's Moving Pictures, Broad Street Theater, auspices of the
Ladies Auxiliary of the YMCA

9 April 1904: Lyman H. Howe Moving Pictures, nineteenth semiannual tour,
Nesbitt Theater

29–30 November 1904: Lyman H. Howe Moving Pictures, twentieth semiannual
tour, Nesbitt Theater

3 April 1905: Lyman Howe Moving Pictures, twenty-first semiannual tour, Nesbitt Theater

3–4, 7 November 1905: Lyman H. Howe's Lifeorama, twenty-second semiannual
tour, Nesbitt Theater

22 March 1906: Edwin J. Hadley's Moving Pictures, Nesbitt Theater

30 March 1906: Moving Pictures at 3 Public Square, Pictures Changed Twice a
Week, Admission 5 Cents

5 April 1906: *A Trip Through Yellowstone*, lecture with moving pictures by E. C.
Culver, at YMCA Hall, auspices of YWCA Travel Club

21–23 April 1906: Lyman H. Howe's Lifeorama, twenty-third semiannual tour,
Nesbitt Theater

6–8 September 1906: Lyman Howe, America's Greatest Traveler, Lifeorama,
twenty-fourth semiannual tour, Nesbitt Theater

24 November 1906: *Gans-Nelson Fight*, Nesbitt Theater

9 January 1907: *O'Brien-Burns Fight*, Nesbitt Theater

11 March 1907: Edwin J. Hadley's Famous Moving Pictures, the Armory

30 March 1907: Dreamland Theater (nickelodeon) opens at 33 South Main Street

16 April 1907: Lyman H. Howe, twenty-fifth semiannual tour, Nesbitt Theater

27 May 1907: Lyman H. Howe, films from twenty-fourth semiannual tour, Nesbitt
Theater

June 1907: Star Theater (nickelodeon) opens at 66 East Market Street

Summer 1907: Bijou Dream (nickelodeon) opens at 51 Public Square

26 August 1907: Unique (nickelodeon) opens at 70 Public Square

21–22 October 1907: Shepard's Moving Pictures, Nesbitt Theater

7–8 November 1907: Lyman H. Howe, Nesbitt Theater

16 November 1907: Liberty Moving Picture Co., Nesbitt Theater

28 February, 2–4 March 1908: Cullison-Mitchell Company, Talking Pictures, the Cameraphone, Nesbitt Theater

24–25 April 1908: Lyman H. Howe, Nesbitt Theater

11–?? May 1908: Archie Shepard's Advanced Moving Pictures, Grand Opera House

27–28 November 1908: Lyman H. Howe, Nesbitt Theater

1 December 1908: Fred Niblo, Second Talk of the Humorous Tourist, *Cairo To Khartoum* (colored slides and motion pictures), Nesbitt Theater

8 December 1908: Fred Niblo, Travel Talk, *From Vesuvius to the Alps*, Nesbitt Theater

10 April 1909: *Burns-Johnson Fight*, Nesbitt Theater

30 April–1 May 1909: Lyman H. Howe, Nesbitt Theater

19–20 November 1909: Lyman H. Howe's New York Hippodrome Travel Festival, Grand Opera House

22–23 April 1910: Lyman H. Howe's Travel Festival, Grand Opera House

18–19 November 1910: Lyman H. Howe, Grand Opera House

27 February 1911: Pictorial Reproduction of Passion Play of 1910

30 March–1 April 1911: Lyman H. Howe, Grand Opera House

28 September 1911: Kinemacolor, *Coronation of King George V*, Grand Opera House

23–25 November 1911: Lyman H. Howe, Grand Opera House

14–16 March 1912: Lyman H. Howe's Travel Festival, Grand Opera House

March 1912: *Dante's Inferno*, Savoy Theater

18–19 October 1912: Lyman H. Howe's Travel Festival, Grand Opera House

14–16 January 1913: *A Free Trip to the Home of the National Cash Register Company*, Grand Opera House

14–15 February 1913: Lyman H. Howe's Travel Festival, Grand Opera House

3–4 October 1913: Lyman H. Howe's Travel Festival, Grand Opera House

1–5 and 8–10 December 1913: *Traffic in Souls*, Grand Opera House

29–31 January 1914: Lyman H. Howe's Travel Festival, Grand Opera House

26 April 1914: Howe's Travel Festival, for the benefit of cyclone sufferers, Grand Opera House

6–7 November 1914: *Rainey's African Hunt Pictures*, Grand Opera House

4–5 December 1914: Lyman H. Howe's Travel Festival, Grand Opera House

3–6 February 1915: Lyman H. Howe, Grand Opera House

1–6 November 1915: German War Pictures, Grand Opera House

26–27 November 1915: Lyman H. Howe's Travel Festival, Grand Opera House

13–18 December 1915: *The Birth of a Nation*, Grand Opera House

10–11 March 1916: Lyman H. Howe's Travel Festival, Grand Opera House

1–2 January 1917: Howe's Travel Festival, the Armory

17–19 May 1917: Lyman H. Howe's Travel Festival, Majestic Theater

31 December 1917–2 January 1918: Lyman H. Howe's Latest Travel Festival, the Armory, auspices of the Craftsmen's Club of Wilkes-Barre

12–13 April 1918: Lyman H. Howe's Travel Festival, Grand Opera House

3–4 January 1919: Lyman H. Howe's Travel Festival, Grand Opera House

21–22 February 1919: Lyman H. Howe's New Travel Festival, fourty-ninth semi-
    annual tour, Grand Opera House

12–13 December 1919: Lyman H. Howe's Travel Festival, fiftieth semiannual
    tour, Grand Opera House

Appendix D
Selected Film Exhibitions in Philadelphia, 1908-1916

* * *

Dates: Exhibitor and/or Program, Theater	Length of Run in Weeks
7–27 September 1908: Lyman H. Howe, Garrick Theater (1,516 seats)	3
28 June–18 September 1909: Lyman H. Howe, Garrick Theater	12
9 May–11 June 1910: Lyman H. Howe, Garrick Theater	5
1–13 Aug 1910: Kinemacolor, Garrick Theater	2
29 May–28 August 1911: International Amusement Company, *World Travel Pictures*, Garrick Theater	13
31 July–19 August 1911: Lyman H. Howe, Lyric Theater (1,614 seats)	3
22 August–2 September 1911: Lyman H. Howe, Adelphi Theater (1,341 seats)	2
4–11 September 1911: Kinemacolor, *Coronation of King George V*, Adelphi Theater	1
30 April–11 May 1912: Lyman H. Howe, Garrick Theater	2
6 May–14 June 1912: *Rainey's African Hunt*, Walnut Street Theater (1,539 seats)	6
6 May–15 June 1912: Kinemacolor, *Durbar in Kinemacolor*, Forrest Theater	6
13 May–8 June 1912: *Dante's Inferno*, Chestnut Street Opera House (1,512 seats)	4
20 May–8 June 1912: *Roping Big Game in Alaska-Siberia*, Garrick Theater	3
10–29 June 1912: *Camille* and *Mme. Sans Gene*, Garrick Theater	3
10–15 June 1912: *Dante's Inferno*, Hart's Theater	1
1 July–17 August 1912: *Durbar in Kinemacolor*, Garrick Theater	6
12–19 August 1912: *Johnson-Flynn Fight*, Gayety Theater	1
2–16 September 1912: Lyman H. Howe, Garrick Theater	2
28 April–10 May 1913: Kinemacolor, *Panama Canal* and *Balkan Wars*, Chestnut Street Opera House	2
12 May–14 August 1913: *Quo Vadis*, Garrick Theater	14
16 August–13 September 1913: Lyman H. Howe, Garrick Theater	4
11–16 May 1914: *How Wild Animals Live*, with lecture by John W. Ruskin, Forrest Theater	1
18 May–6 June 1914: *Neptune's Daughter*, Forrest Theater	3
1–13 June 1914: Lyman H. Howe, Garrick Theater	2
24 August–5 September 1914: *The War of Wars*, Forrest Theater	2
24 August–5 September 1914: Lyman H. Howe, Garrick Theater	2
7–26 September 1914: *Cabiria*, Chestnut Street Opera House	3

10–29 May 1915: Submarine Pictures (30 *Leagues under the Sea*),
   Garrick Theater   3
17–29 May 1915: *Sir Douglas Mawson's Marvelous Views of the Frozen
   South*, Forrest Theater   2
31 May–12 June 1915: *The James Barnes Expedition Through Central
   Africa*, Garrick Theater   2
31 May–12 June 1915: Kinemacolor, *With the Fighting Forces of Europe*,
   Forrest Theater   2
23 August–4 September 1915: Lyman H. Howe, Garrick Theater   2
7–13 May 1916: *The Spoilers* (Deluxe Edition), Forrest Theater   1
8–20 May 1916: *Deutschwehr War Films*, Chestnut Street Opera House   2
15–20 May 1916: *Defense or Tribute?*, Casino   1
3–8 July 1916: *How Britain Prepared*, Garrick Theater   1
19 June–15 July 1916: *The Ne'er Do Well*, Forrest Theater   4
28 August–9 September 1916: Lyman H. Howe, Garrick Theater   2

Appendix E
Howe Exhibitions in Selected Cities

* * *

Dates: Theater	Length of Run in Weeks

Baltimore

14–20 May 1906: Ford's Grand Opera House (2,250 seats) — 1
20–25 May 1907: Ford's (21,477 paid admissions) — 1
4–31 August 1907: Ford's — 4
18–30 May 1908: Ford's — 2
3 August–6 September 1908: Ford's — 5
2 August–5 September 1909: Ford's — 5
25 July–3 September 1910: Ford's — 6
24 July–2 September 1911: Ford's — 6
5–31 August 1912: Ford's — 4
4–30 August 1913: Ford's — 4
10 August–5 September 1914: Ford's — 4
23 August–4 September 1915: Ford's — 2
21 August–2 September 1916: Ford's — 2
20 August–1 September 1917: Ford's — 2
19–24 August 1918: Ford's — 1
25–30 August 1919: Ford's — 1

Chicago

4 June–22 July 1911: Garrick (1,257 seats) — 7
26 May–30 June 1912: Palace (1,346 seats) — 5

Cincinnati

18–19 January 1907: Music Hall — 2 days
23, 25–29 December 1907: Lyric (2,000 seats) and Auditorium — 6 days
1–14 June 1908: Lyric — 2
30 August–13 September 1908: Lyric — 2
4–10 April 1909: Lyric (Easter week) — 1
1 August–5 September 1909: Lyric — 5
20–27 March 1910: Lyric (Easter week) — 8 days

Dates: Theater	Length of Run in Weeks

14 August–10 September 1910: Lyric — 4
6 August–9 September 1911: Lyric — 5
11 August–14 September 1912: Lyric — 5
17 August–13 September 1913: Lyric — 4
30 August–26 September 1914: Lyric — 4
5–18 September 1915: Lyric — 2
3–16 September 1916: Lyric — 2
26 August–8 September 1917: Lyric — 2
25 August–7 September 1918: Lyric — 2
24 August–6 September 1919: Lyric — 2

Kansas City

16 May–19 June 1909: Shubert (1,603 seats) — 5
12 June–25 July 1910: Shubert — 6
7 May–10 June 1911: Shubert — 5
28 April–11 May 1912: Shubert — 2
4–24 May 1913: Grand (1,500 seats) — 3
16–28 August 1914: Grand — 2

Pittsburgh

22–23 January 1908: Nixon (2,295 seats) and Carnegie Hall — 2 days
29 June–8 August 1908: Nixon — 6
17 June–14 August 1909: Nixon — 8
13 June–16 July 1910: Nixon — 5
29 May–1 July 1911: Nixon — 5
26 May–June 15, 1912: Nixon — 3
19 August–1 September 1912: Nixon — 2
19–31 May 1913: Nixon — 2
17 May–5 June 1914: Nixon — 3
15–28 August 1915: Nixon — 2
21 August–2 September 1916: Nixon — 2

Reading, Pennsylvania

9–21 November 1896: Waite Comedy Company and Animatograph between acts of plays (first showing of moving pictures in Reading)

17–18 January 1899: Academy of Music (1,475 seats, receipts of $771.45)
20–22 April 1899: Academy of Music (receipts of $761.40)
6–7 February 1900: Academy of Music (receipts of $702.05)
22–23 October 1900: Academy of Music (receipts of $782.55)
17–18 December 1901: Academy of Music (receipts of $714.10)
11–12 April 1902: Academy of Music (receipts of $1,131.95)
21–22 November 1902: Academy of Music (receipts of $1,436.90)
15 April 1903: Academy of Music (receipts of $713.00)
9–10 December 1903: Academy of Music (receipts of $881.95)
13–14 April 1904: Academy of Music (receipts of $973.45)
9–10 December 1904: Academy of Music (receipts of $1,277.75)
17–19 April 1905: Academy of Music
8–9 November 1905: Academy of Music (receipts of $1433.15)

October 1906: Theatorium motion picture theater opens, admission five cents

Howe exhibitions continued in subsequent years.

Troy, New York

2–7 November 1896: Vaudeville and Edison's Vitascope at Gaiety Theater (first showing of moving pictures in Troy)

2 March 1899: YMCA Hall (1,100 seats, auspices of Ladies Aid Society of 5th Avenue Church)

2 May 1899: listed in Howe date book but screening not reported in newspapers

10 October 1899: Troy Savings Bank Music Hall (1,255 or 1,285 seats [*Variety*, 15 October 1980, p. 325]; built in the 1870s; excellent acoustics; benefit of 13th St. Union Chapel)

21 November 1899: canceled

22 January 1900: YMCA Hall (auspices of Fairview Home)

10 October 1900: Rand Opera House (1,450 seats, auspices of the First Congregational Church)

24 October 1901: YMCA Hall (auspices of the Troy Tent, Knights of the Maccabees; receipts of $88.74)

12 March 1902: YMCA Hall (auspices of the First Congregational Church)

21–22 October 1902: Music Hall (auspices of Cluett, Peabody, and Company Beneficial Association; receipts of $559.25 for October 22)

23 October 1902: Powers Opera House in Upper Troy (auspices of Sunday Night Club of the Memorial Baptist Church; receipts of $555.75)

3 March 1903: Music Hall (auspices of Cluett, Peabody, and Company Beneficial Association; receipts of $519.50)

29 October 1903: Music Hall (auspices of Cluett, Peabody, and Company Beneficial Association; receipts of $467.50)

15 March 1904: Music Hall (auspices of Cluett, Peabody, and Company Beneficial Association)

3 November 1904: Music Hall (auspices of St. Peter's Lyceum; receipts of $753.25)

17 March 1905: Music Hall

25 October 1905: Music Hall

23 March 1906: Music Hall

14 November 1906: State Armory (auspices of Citizens Corps)

A penny arcade at 311 River Street was placed under the new management of the Troy Arcade Company in November 1906. On 20 December, it reopened as the Nickolet, apparently the first moving picture house in Troy. It was followed by the Empire at Third and Congress Streets on 9 March 1907 and the Novelty at 324 River Street, which seated five hundred people and opened on 21 March.

8 April 1907: Music Hall (full house)

Howe exhibitions continued in subsequent years.

Washington D.C.

15, 22, 29 August, 12 September 1909: Columbia Theater (1,450 seats)
4 Sunday concerts
31 July–11 September 1910: Columbia Theater   7 Sunday concerts
9–16 April 1911: Columbia Theater
8 days
30 July–27 August 1911: Columbia Theater   4 Sunday concerts
11 August–1 September 1912: Columbia Theater   4 Sunday concerts
10–31 August 1913: Columbia Theater
4 Sunday concerts
23 August–12 September 1914: Columbia Theater   3 weeks
22–28 February 1915: Columbia Theater   7 days

Appendix F
Howe Filmography

∗ ∗ ∗

Photographer is listed if known.

Ca. December 1900: Wilkes-Barre street scenes. "Among the views to be shown at the coming exhibition will be several street scenes from our own town which were taken several weeks ago. These views were taken on Public Square and North and South Main streets and East and West Market Streets and should prove unusually interesting."[1]
  Photographers: James White of the Edison Manufacturing Company or J. Stuart Blackton and Albert Smith of American Vitagraph.

March 9, 1904: Flood in Wilkes-Barre. "Lyman Howe employed the Auto Machine Repair Co.'s large auto yesterday and went up and down the street taking moving pictures of the flood."[2] "Two local scenes dealing with the late high water were shown. One was a view of South River street showing horses and carriages driving through the water up to the axles of the vehicles. The other was taken at Academy street, looking towards Carey avenue. This showed the men and boys in their wading boots with a number of boats and canoes taking the people from their houses to places of safety."[3]
  Photographer: Lyman H. Howe.

September 7, 1904: *The Wilkes-Barre, Pa. Crack Fire Department Responding to a General Alarm.*[4]
  Photographer: Lyman H. Howe.

Summer 1905: Carnegie Steel Works. "Showing the complete operation of smelting the ore and producing the finished article."[5]
  Photographer: Lyman H. Howe.

August 10, 1905: President Roosevelt's visit to Wilkes-Barre. "The series dealing with President Roosevelt's visit to Wilkes-Barre is a triumph of the moving picture art. It includes the President approaching the platform on the river common from his carriage through the mass of humanity; the President delivering his speech; shaking hands with Cardinal Gibbons after the speech; visit to the Wyoming monument; acceptance of bouquets from three children at the monument. There are some views of the President so clear that the observer seems face to face with the most eminent man in the world. Even those who took part in the great celebration will be deeply interested in having this scene again brought before them, without straining to see and without the excitement of the crowds."[6]
  Photographer: Lyman H. Howe.

September 21–23, 1905: Allentown Fair. "Scenes of the Allentown Fair, where many familiar faces were recognized, especially those of 'Uncle' Jere Roth,

Secretary Schall and others. Scenes along the midway were the exact reproduction of the sights seen during the week of September 21 to 23.

"Don Patch was also seen breaking the world's record and having the
'Good Luck Horseshoe' placed around his neck by the president of the
Lehigh County Agricultural Society, Hon. Jeremiah Roth."[7]

Photographer: Lyman H. Howe.

May 10–12, 1906: Wilkes-Barre Centennial Jubilee. "To a program of national
and international interest, Mr. Howe has added a series of moving pictures
that reproduce virtually every notable scene of the Wilkes-Barre centennial jubilee. The military parade in all its splendor may again be seen
marching past with martial tread. The many bands, the various regiments,
their staffs, the local and visiting firemen and equipments; even the Dark-
town Fire Brigade, down to the last man and Moxie bottle will once more
parade in all the festive spirit of the historic jubilee.

"To secure these remarkable pictures, Mr. Howe spared no pains or expense. He imported for the occasion special lenses and cameras from Paris
that would insure the most perfect photography. Forewarned by the many
cloudy days, he forarmed himself with lenses and cameras that alone could
record the scenes so superbly under conditions that would have been impossible otherwise. Through courtesies extended by the city officials, he
was enabled to photograph the pageants from the most commanding positions. Every spectator will see the scenes again from a new and better
point of vantage than was possible in the crowded streets."[8]

Photographer: Lyman H. Howe.

September 19–22, 1906: "The Midway of the Great Allentown Fair as seen from
an Automobile and photographed by Mr. Lyman H. Howe last September
will be included in the program."[9]

Photographer: Lyman H. Howe.

May 30, 1907: The Wilkes-Barre hill climbing contest.[10]

Photographer: Lyman H. Howe.

July 1908: "The most stirring scenes and incidents of the last annual encampment
of our state troops on the famous Gettysburg battlefield. The pictures can
of course be seen only at Mr. Howe's exhibition, and at no other as they
were taken by Mr. Howe personally for his own exclusive exhibition purposes. They are of absorbing local interest because of the prominence of
our own 9th Regiment in the scenes depicted. Before the battle maneuvers, the 3rd brigade is shown on review and then the parade of the massed
bands. Following this, Gov. Stuart, General Wiley, Gen. Stewart and
Gen. Dougherty are shown in conference and viewing the maneuvers.
The 9th Regiment is shown in action, and the return march gave Mr.
Howe splendid opportunities for some close facial portraits of the members
of the various local companies. The latter are also shown engaged in camp
pastimes. Prof. Alexander's great popularity is attested by the enthusiastic
appreciation shown by the boys following a cornet solo."[11]

Photographer: Lyman H. Howe.

Late June 1909: Cleveland. (??) "The operators of the Lyman H. Howe 'Travel
     Festival' at Keith's Hippodrome have taken the first of a series of views of
     Cleveland which will be used by Mr. Howe as part of his program abroad
     next fall. Seated in a slowly moving automobile the operators rode up
     Euclid av. through the crowded shopping district and residential section
     to E. 105th st., catching all that was typical and most interesting."[12]
September 1909: *Wild Animals' Impression of Music*. Animals in the Washington
     Zoo. "WILD ANIMALS AND MUSIC—For the purpose of ascertaining the ef-
     fect of music upon the various animals, one of Lyman H. Howe's photog-
     raphers took a phonograph and a moving picture apparatus to the Zoo one
     day last September and tried an experiment, the result of which will be
     made apparent at the Columbia Theater tonight.
     "The superintendent of the Zoo, alive to the importance of the effort,
     and in hearty sympathy with it, gave the photographer every facility to
     make the novel experiment.
     "A division of all the animals was first made, so that the music could be
     played and the impression photographed in animated scenes for a repre-
     sentative of each animal family. Care was used to make the test at the
     'leisure time of the day' in the life of each animal. More than a week was
     given to the task and the 'records' used on the phonograph were changed
     to completely determine the effect on each animal.
     "It was found that a band record or a song with a loud voice frightened
     some of the species. In such instances the more quiet melodies and voices
     were used.
     "Contrary to expectations, the snakes and monkeys paid little heed.
     The lion, tiger, leopard and other 'wild cat' types were evidently attracted
     for a time by the noise only. The deer enjoyed the music in a fashion, but
     kept several hundred feet away. Badgers straight away began to fight at the
     first sound. The buffalo gave the phonograph his ear for a minute, then
     laid down and slept. The bear was the only animal that kept close to the
     machine and clearly displayed affection."[13]
Fall 1909: "A series of pictures of the military life in West Point, Annapolis, Fort
     Myer and other military posts for which Mr. Howe was granted a special
     permit from the government through the good offices of congressman
     Henry W. Palmer and attorney Andrew Hourigan."[14]
February 9–12, 1911: Duluth: ski jumping on February 12 and local views at about
     the same time. "Five men are now in Duluth making final preparations for
     the making of the first moving pictures in this part of the United States.
     "They are H. A. Crowhurst and C. R. Bosworth, photographers; and
     D. J. Tasker, Fred C. Morgan and John Carleton, imitators: all of Lyman
     H. Howe's Travel Festival organization with headquarters at Wilkesbarre,
     Pa.
     "Beginning with the first day of sunshine this week these men, who are
     trained in reproducing real life scenes, will search Duluth and the sur-
     rounding country for typical subjects that interest people everywhere. Lo-
     cal organizations anxious to present the best side of Duluth to the world

have assisted in the plans and hearty cooperation is assured Mr. Howe's representatives wherever they go.

"The skee tournament will be the big feature of the series of pictures to be made."[15]

Photographers: Charles Bosworth and H. A. Crowhurst.

March 18–19, 1911: Dedication of Roosevelt Dam near Phoenix, Arizona.[16]

Photographers: Charles Bosworth and H. A. Crowhurst.

April 1911: *Shoshone Falls, Idaho.*[17]

Photographers: Charles Bosworth and H. A. Crowhurst.

April 1911: *Black Canyon in Northern Colorado.* "The ride through the canyon follows the winding of the river, and as the train rounds each curve new scenic vistas and wild rock formations are shown."[18]

Photographers: Charles Bosworth and H. A. Crowhurst.

May 1911: *Cleveland.* " 'Press' Series CLEVELAND As the World will See it! Garfield Monument, Public Square, giant chutes loading lake steamer, jack knife bridge in operation, Rocky River bridge, Superior viaduct at midday, auto ride on Euclid Ave from Public Square, University Circle and many other interesting points."[19]

Photographers: Charles Bosworth and H. A. Crowhurst.

May 30 and June 4, 1911: *A Thrilling Ride on an Aeroplane with Lincoln Beachy over Wilkes-Barre.* "Beachy made the next flight with a moving picture camera, owned by Lyman Howe, fastened to the front of his machine and so arranged that Beachy could operate it. . . . Beachy made a wide circle over the centre of the valley training his camera on the new court house, the Susquehanna River and parts of the city and West Side. He alighted on the field skimming over it with undulations so gentle that it was most fascinating to watch him."[20]

"Excellent flights were made by Beachy yesterday. He operated a moving picture camera on several of his trips and created a sensation among the spectators by taking some daring low dips so as to include the crowd on the field in the pictures."[21]

Photographer: Lincoln Beachy, assisted by H. A. Crowhurst.

Summer 1911: Washington, D.C. "A tour will be made to Washington, D.C. where the Army and Navy Building, the State Department, Patent Office, Postoffice, Carnegie Library, Library of Congress and finally the National Capitol will be visited and the audiences will be introduced to some of the popular statesmen."[22]

September 26–29 1911: Cornell College and Ithaca, New York: Local Views.[23]

Photographers: Charles Bosworth and H. A. Crowhurst.

Sept 30, 1911: Disaster at Austin, Pennsylvania. "Within a brief time after the first reports of the terrible calamity which wrought such disaster at and around Austin, Pa., on Sept. 30, had been flashed to the outer world, Lyman H. Howe started several of his most expert motion picture photographers for the scene of devastation. They arrived at Austin hours ahead of any other camera men and were photographing the sad spectacle almost before any newspaper men were on the scene to write about it."[24]

Photographers: Charles Bosworth and H. A. Crowhurst.

November 1–2, 1911: *Our Navy*.[25]

March 16, 1912: *Burial of the "Maine."*[26]

Spring–Summer 1912: *Culver (Ind.), Military Academy*. "Horsemanship, Artillery Maneuvers and Drills at Culver Military Academy."[27]

July 27, 1912: *Automobile Races at Driving Park, Wilkes-Barre*. "In order to show just what happened not only at one curve but at each of the four on the track, Mr. Howe stationed a camera man at each turn, and therefore Mr. Howe's reproduction shows exactly how each car swung around each curve on every lap around the track."[28]

Summer 1912: *A Ride through the Niagara Gorge*. "The film is taken from the rear of a moving train."[29]

Summer–Fall 1912: *Building N.Y.'s Biggest Skyscraper*.[30]

Fall 1912: *The Downfall of Liberty*. Animator: Paul Felton.

Spring 1913: *Recent Ohio Valley Floods*.[31]

Spring–Summer 1913: *Manufacture of Armor Plate*. "The latest inventions and labor-saving devices as employed in the manufacture of armor plate at the Bethlehem steel works."[32]

Summer 1913: *Grand Canyon of Arizona*. "Lyman H. Howe's photographer had many moments of peril recently while cinematographing the Grand Canyon in Arizona."[33]

Summer 1913: "A novel lot of incidents connected with the Hopi and Navajo Indians as shown in their native haunts. Not the least novel feature of this exhibit is where the aborigines are seen employed in making baskets, blankets and other articles after the method followed by their race for centuries."[34]

Summer 1913(?): *Yellowstone Park*. "Representation by motion pictures of the falls and geysers of Yellowstone Park are by no means unfamiliar, but here again Mr. Howe has tried to give those objects a different visual angle. In interesting and picturesque succession were shown the various gigantic waterfalls and numerous geysers, all more or less in active operation, throwing up boiling water to distances of from fifteen to eighty feet."[35]

Fall–Winter 1913: *Panama Canal*. "It is remarkable in every sense—but especially so for its matchless photography. Two of the photographers contracted malaria while they were 'on the job' and on more than one occasion they had stirring experiences when blasting operations had to be photographed from behind armored screens. The 'stirring' came from flying boulders."[36] Photographers: Charles Bosworth and H. A. Crowhurst(?).

Spring–Summer 1914: *A Rousing New Ride on a Runaway Train*.[37]

Summer–Fall 1914: *U.S. Navy of 1915*. "The moving pictures of the Navy you obtained through the cooperation of the Department, have been reviewed by officers of the Navy in Washington, and I desire to congratulate you upon the remarkable success you achieved."[38] "I was permitted to make complete moving picture records of the Atlantic fleet battleships, cruisers and submarines in action."[39] Photographers: Charles Bosworth and Joseph DeFrenes.

Fall–Winter 1914: "The romance of industry as expressed in the making of a National cash register constitutes another feature of the program. Howe selected this particular plant not alone because it is typical of American skill, enterprise and organization but because it is recognized the world over as the model manufacturing plant—a monumental realization of an idea and an ideal."[40]

Photographers: Charles Bosworth and Joseph DeFrenes

March–May 1915: *Through the Panama Canal.* "Mr. Howe presents to the exposition historian, a moving picture print, the first from the moving picture negatives that have been made during the last few months at the Panama Canal. . . . The pictures give one the experience of passing through the Canal and also of being at Points along the Canal when ships are passing. They also reveal the occupation of the canal seen in 1915 by the United States army, incidents of U.S. army life in the Jungle, scenes of Colon and Panama City, with studies of individual types of panama natives as they are at the present day."[41]

Photographer: Joseph DeFrenes.

Summer 1915: *U.S. Submarines.* "Some fine scenes photographed upon the deck of a United States submarine were secured at the recent maneuvers of the Atlantic submarine flotilla off Pensacola, Fla."[42]

Photographer: Joseph DeFrenes

July 7, 1915: The Panama-California Exposition in San Diego. "Tomorrow will be Lyman H. Howe Day at the Exposition. Camera men will take official motion pictures of the Exposition from automobiles between 1 and 3 PM."[43]

Photographer: Charles Bosworth.

July 17, 1915: Panama-Pacific Exposition at San Francisco. Filmed Liberty Bell Parade on this date.[44] Other scenes filmed at approximately the same time. "To one who has only read about the San Francisco exposition, the marvels can be only fairly comprehended. As a preliminary there is a bird's eye view of the whole affair, then in detail the entrancing scenes and wonderful effects achieved by the landscape artist, sculptor and architect. A ramble through the courts is like a dream in fairyland. An incident is the arrival of the Liberty Bell, attended with a remarkable demonstration. Even the night illuminations are clearly shown."[45]

Photographer: Joseph DeFrenes.

Summer 1915: *Over the Trails at Glacier National Park.* "Inquiry of Max Walkinshaw, the general manager of the Howe establishment, established that their photographer spent several months at the place with every facility afforded him that the Great Northern Railway had at its command."[46]

Photographer: Joseph DeFrenes.

Fall 1915–Spring 1916: *Making of a Willys-Overland Automobile* (alternate title: *The Making of an Automobile*). "The development of the great industry of automobile manufacture from the stamping of the first bolt to the finished machine running on its own power was fully shown."[47] Filmed in Toledo, Ohio, over three months.

Photographers: Charles Bosworth and Joseph DeFrenes.

Winter 1915–1916: *Hawaii: The Paradise of the Pacific.* "Some splendid scenes in the harbor of Honolulu, views of the craters of active volcanoes and pictures of the inhabitants make up a good reel. 'Close-ups' of the molten mass inside the fiery crater of the most active volcano in the world are vividly portrayed. These scenes were taken at midday and midnight for contrast effect."[48]

"At Waikiki Beach, 'The Atlantic City' of the islands, natives are shown surf riding."[49]

Photographer: Joseph DeFrenes.

Spring 1916: *Life at the United States Military Academy at West Point.* "The film shows the strenuous training and grind, as well as the glamor, of life at the school."[50]

Summer 1916: *Yosemite National Park.*[51]

Summer 1916: *Through the Cascade Mountains in Washington.*[52]

Summer 1916(?): *The Real Wild West* (alternate title: *Broncho Busting Contest*).[53]

September 24, 1916: *Hill Climbing Contest,* Wilkes-Barre. "Showing the recent [sic] automobile race over Giant's Despair at Wilkes-Barre, Pa., where fearless drivers race their cars at tremendous speed up steep inclines and around many sharp curves."[54]

By Summer 1917: *U.S. Naval Academy.*[55]

Summer 1917: *Somewhere in the Atlantic* (alternate title: *With Uncle Sam's New Navy*). Filmed "at the outset of hostilities." May be reworked footage from *U.S. Navy in 1915.*[56]

Summer 1917: *Charcoal and Chalk.* "An imaginary Zeppelin raid."[57]

Animator: Archie Griffith.

Summer 1917: *The Kaiser Meets His Waterloo.*[58]

Animator: Archie Griffith.

June 1917: Howe opens New York office to purchase film. The following films may have been made by the Lyman Howe Company, but cameramen and animators are unknown.

Summer 1917: *Logging in Maine* (alternate title: *Timber Life in Maine*).[59]

Summer 1917: *Alaska—Its Icebergs and Glaciers.* "Pictures the grotesque totem poles of the Northwest during a fascinating motion picture trip of Alaska."[60]

Summer 1917: *Capturing Mountain Lions* (alternate title: *Mountain Lion Hunt in Montana*). "We see an intrepid mountaineer go into the wilds of the Northwest and capture, with the assistance of trained dogs, a wild mountain lion."[61]

By Spring 1918: *Coney Island by Day and Night.* (alternate title: *Visit to Coney Island*).[62]

By Summer 1918: *Thrilling Tests of War Caterpillars in Uncle Sam's Army.*[63]

By Summer 1918: *Up in the Air with the Marines.*[64]

Photographer: Fred Jayne

By Winter 1919: *Ocklawaha River.*[65]

By Summer 1919: Fishing Expedition, Ft. Myers Florida. "Shows the spectacular dives and twists these game fish go through. A feature of this episode is the successful landing of a 185-pound tarpon by a young woman weighing 105 pounds."[66]

By Summer 1919: *Magnolia Gardens*, Charleston, South Carolina. [67]
1919: "*A Day in Dogville.*"
      Animator: Archie Griffith. [68]
1919: "*Jungle Vaudeville.*"
      Animator: Archie Griffith. [69]

Appendix G
Documents

* * *

MOVING WAR PICTURES

Some Very Interesting Views Shown by Lyman Howe———A Couple of Bombardment Scenes

All of the seats in the Nesbitt Theatre were occupied last evening and there was scarcely standing room at the exhibition of moving war pictures, interspersed with others, by Lyman H. Howe. Mr. Howe has given a number of exhibitions in this city but none so successfully as the one of last evening. Never before has he had such a variety of pictures. Some of them are so thrillingly realistic that the audience broke out in the most enthusiastic applause.

Mr. Howe has, at the expenditure of a considerable sum of money, secured a number of war scenes photographed on the spot, and they proved intensely interesting. The great risk taken in getting these photographs makes them very expensive and Mr. Howe is one of only three who are showing them in the country.

One picture shows the bombardment of Cabanas Fortress by the New York. The vessel steams briskly by the fortress, throwing shell after shell against it. The ship rocks and heaves from the concussion and seems instilled with life, the smoke pouring in volumes from her stacks and the shells flying from her sides. Shells may also be seen coming from the fortress but they fall in the water, the aim of the Spaniards being poor. After the bombardment great holes may be seen in the fort, showing the work of destruction.

Another scene shows the bombardment of Matanzas by the New York and the monitor Puritan. Shot after shot are thrown into the city and the awful possibilities of the modern war vessel are seen in the rapidity with which the shells are sent on their way of destruction.

The dynamite cruiser Vesuvius in action is one of the best of the series. The vessel looms up in the picture as a small craft, but it is readily seen that she is one of the most destructive war machines yet invented. From her pneumatic guns may be seen coming the terrible charges of guncotton and their effect in tearing away portions of a hill over a mile away creates a deep impression on the audience. One of the shots takes away the whole side of the hill. The ship scarcely makes a quiver while working this awful damage.

"Defending the flag" is the title of a thrilling scene showing a land battle. Men and officers may be seen shot and falling on all sides. An officer who stands by the side of a cannon grabs the flag and holds it against all, defending himself with pistol and then with sword until all about him are dead and wounded.

Other interesting war pictures were the following. The 71st Regt. of New York parade before leaving for the front, arrival of troops at Tampa, morning wash in

camp, blanket court martial, troops embarking for Cuba, troops landing at Carnegie pier, troops marching to the front, packing ammunition on mules, pack
train en route, wagon train en route with supplies, Spanish soldiers capturing and
shooting insurgents, battleship Maine before leaving New York harbor for Havana. The above are only some of them, however. All were taken from life and
were enthusiastically received by the audience.

Mr. Howe in his miscellaneous group of pictures also showed some new ones.
One of the most interesting was the ride on the front end of a locomotive approaching and going through Chiselhurst tunnel in England at sixty miles an
hour. One sees the scenery flying before him and when the tunnel looms up in
the distance the effect upon the audience is thrilling. It appears as if the tunnel
with its black mouth, were about to dart from the picture and swallow up the
audience. Another fine view was that showing cattle fording a stream in the West.
Every movement is perfectly natural. When the cattle have crossed the stream
they seem as if walking out of the pictures and some in the audience were seized
with an uncomfortable feeling until they realize that there is no danger.

The effect is very realistic. A photograph of the ocean, taken after a storm from
the deck of the steamer Coptic, is another awe-inspiring view. The ocean may be
seen lashed into fury and tossing itself into mountains. Mr. Howe's entire collection is along this line of novelty and excellence. There are quite a number of
moving picture exhibitors, but everywhere that Mr. Howe goes he is conceded to
have the finest and most interesting lot. He exhibits them with less flicker and
blur than any ever seen here, and this is a great advantage. Mr. Howe also gave a
few pleasant selections on his improved phonograph.

SOURCE: *Wilkes-Barre Record*, 17 September 1898, p. 5.

DOCUMENT 2

THOUSANDS SAW PICTURES

*Lyman H. Howe Draws an Immense Audience
to the Armory*

One of the largest crowds the armory has ever held last night saw the Lyman
H. Howe moving pictures and it was also one of the best pleased audiences ever
assembled there. Heretofore, Mr. Howe has given his exhibitions, first in the
Y.M.C.A. auditorium and then in the Nesbitt and as on every occasion the
houses were filled he conceived the idea of giving an entertainment in the armory,
with its vast floor space. The fact that he succeeded in filling this great audience
room also is the biggest kind of a testimonial for him.

Before 8 o'clock the people began arriving and by 8:15 there was a jam in front
of the edifice that filled the vestibule and extended across the street. Hundreds
crowded about the entrance way until the scene reminded one of the Nordica
concert crowd or that which clamored for admission to the McKinley memorial
service.

The street leading to the armory were a lively scene. About thirty ushers, members of the Knights of Malta, did excellent work in seating the crowd, not one of the number losing his presence of mind. When all were seated there was a sea of faces from the door to the stage and the galleries were also filled. Dozens stood in the small space in the rear and then the sale of tickets was stopped and many people went home unable to gain admission. It is estimated that nearly four thousand people saw the exhibition.

Mr. Howe's entertainment was well worth the immense audience. He has the reputation everywhere in the country of giving the best moving picture entertainment on the road and everywhere he goes there are big houses. Mr. Howe spends big sums of money for the latest and best pictures and is thus enabled to get exclusive subjects both from European and American manufacturers. He makes his annual trip to Europe to see what is being produced there.

The series is the best Mr. Howe has ever given in Wilkes-Barre. Perhaps the most interesting just at this time are those of the Pan-American Exposition and the McKinley scenes. In the former the camera was on naphtha launch that made a circuit of the Exposition grounds in the canal and the audience was enabled to see the buildings, etc., just as if it had been on the launch with the camera.

An impressive scene was that showing the martyred President delivering his last speech. The features of the late President are quite distinct and the view had a marked effect upon the audience. The excited crowd in front of the Temple of Music after the shooting was also shown, the surging mass going backward and forward, the commotion plainly visible. The carrying of the casket containing the body to the city hall, the crowd standing in front of the place in the rain waiting for the opportunity to enter, the funeral procession at Washington were all realistically shown. There was also a picture of President Roosevelt's arrival at Canton, Ohio.

There was an excellent series of miscellaneous views. One of them showed a ride on front of an engine through a pretty section of country in Devonshire, England. The sensation produced was just as if the beholder were actually on the engine. Farms, lakes and hills were passed and the engine also crossed a bridge. Another realistic scene showed a storm in mid-ocean, the view being taken from an Atlantic liner. The heaving of the ship with the waves was plainly shown and the dashing of the water over the deck. A surf scene was one of the best of the evening.

The audience was not a little stirred by an automobile scene. In the distance the machine is seen swiftly coming. It comes closer and closer and finally apparently jumps out from the canvas when there is an explosion and the machine disappears. Humorous views kept the audience laughing and there was plenty of them.

During an intermission J. P. Kern, whose stage name is J. Paige, entertained with clay modeling. Clay on a block was molded in representations of the face of Admiral Dewey, of a Chinaman, of an Indian, etc.. There are very few who can do this kind of work and Mr. Kern is certainly an expert. He was heartily encored. Mr. Kern was a few years ago employed as artist on the Record.

SOURCE: *Wilkes-Barre Record*, 23 November 1901, p. 5.

SEE HISTORIC SIEGE

*Burton Holmes Gives Graphic Portrayal
of Port Arthur Scenes
Photos Taken During Action*

"The Russian soldiers before every battle went to service conducted by one of the priests at the front, and, whenever possible, partook of the sacrament. The Japanese, before battle, cleaned their guns, bathed their brown bodies, and whenever possible, changed their linen so that poison would be less likely in the event of being wounded and to be ready for the supreme embrace in case of death. The Japanese always smiles. When we should weep he smiles; when we should sob, he giggles; but when we come to know him, we realize that the smile and the giggle are eloquent of self-control."

These two characteristics of the Japanese soldier were related by Burton Holmes during his travelogue on "Port Arthur, the Siege and Surrender" which drew two immense audiences to the Pabst theater yesterday afternoon and last evening, to give insight into the marvelous scenes portrayed by the pictures taken during the Siege and by brilliant word descriptions with which the lecturer told their story. This travelogue is the crown of all the achievements which have made the name of Burton Holmes famous the world over, and is a contribution of distinct literary and historic value. Superior to any lecture before given in its graphic interest and its realistic presentation of scenes of the remarkable Siege, it holds the intense attention of the audience from the portrayal of the departure of the troops to the orient until the following final tribute to President Roosevelt, accompanying the picture of the peace party at Portsmouth: "This war might have dragged on another year had not one man been brave enough to bury the traditions of diplomacy and with compelling voice, say, 'Let us have peace.' "

Admiral Togo's flagship, moving full speed ahead, the launching of torpedoes and explosion of submarine mines, Russian troops crossing the frozen lake in Siberia, the arrival of Gen. Kuropatkin, reviews of Russian troops by the czar and grand dukes, the seventeen ton guns which the Japanese took from their coastal defences, hauled by teams of 1,000 men across the country and installed on cement foundations three miles from Port Arthur to demolish the fortifications and the warships in the harbor, field guns in operation, the Japanese in their wonderful trench approaches by which they were able to reach the tops of the surrounding hills and which they kept concealed from the Russians by carrying every basket of earth for miles back through the trenches to the rear of their own troops, the blowing up of the Double Dragon fort and the advance of the Japanese troops to take possession, the capitulation, the departure of the Russian troops as prisoners and the triumphal entry of the Japanese with their peculiar marching step, inspiring in its confident swing, were portrayed in realistic moving pictures, while scores of other photographs from the war were shown.

The photographs were chiefly taken by James Ricalton, war photographer, and the motion pictures by Joseph Rosenthal and George Rogers, bioscope war operators. In showing the pictures of the war correspondents, their camps, and their methods of work the lecturer paid special tribute to Richard Barry, a Wisconsin man, and his book on the Siege. The entire travelogue is powerful in its realism, and it is to Burton Holmes that thousands of people will be indebted for their most vivid conception of the siege of Port Arthur.

SOURCE: *Milwaukee Sentinel*, 11 October 1905, p. 4.

DOCUMENT 4

HOWE'S VIVID WAR PICTURES

*Scenes about Port Arthur Are Revived
at Pabst Theater*

Scenes and incidents of the memorable Siege and tragic surrender of Port Arthur were vividly brought before two audiences yesterday afternoon and evening through the medium of Lyman H. Howe's Lifeorama. That most of the same series had been shown here only a few weeks before by Burton Holmes detracted little if any of their interest but on the contrary served to refreshen the memory and print the more indelibly upon the mind the horrors as well as the sublimities of war. The stubborn resistance of the Russian soldier in the face of certain death, the daredevil bravery of the little Japs, who surmounted inconceivable obstacles that led to the attainment of an object and purpose staked out by Japanese statesmanship decades ago, can not but make the heart of every man swell with pride and admiration. Mr. Howe accompanies his pictures with the clanging of sabres, the rattle of musketry, the fanfare of trumpets, the roll of the drum, the booming of cannon, in short with the semblance of strife and struggle that adds to the realism of the photographic reproductions and brings the scene close to home until the spectator fairly lives in the atmosphere and is translated in imagination to the spot where history is being made.

The tension of these appalling war pictures is relieved by several humorous conceits, like "Brown's Half Holiday," showing the misadventures of a man who is made to assist his wife in the semi-annual housecleaning when he desires to spend his holiday with a companionable friend on the tennis court. Highly interesting pictures showing graphically the processes of steelmaking as in vogue in the Carnegie mills add to the instructiveness of the entertainment. The process is followed from the time the ore is brought to the furnace until the finished sheet of steel or steel rail is ready to be sent to the market. One of the prettiest as it is one of the most enthusiastically received picture, is that showing the boys at the Reedham, England, Orphanage, at drill. The precision and the neatness of evolution of these boys as reproduced is marvelous indeed, and calls forth spontaneous applause. Mr. Howe put on for the first time on any stage "The Boy Tramps" yesterday afternoon, the success of which is already assured.

Combining vistas of the beautiful scenery of France with exciting episodes that almost make the heart stand still in awe and fear of imminent danger, the Gordon Bennett International Automobile Race of 1905 pictures are a feature of the program at once interesting and fascinating. Other pictures that won the approval of the audience were those in connection with the President's visit to Wilkesbarre, Penn., last August, when he spoke to 100,000 miners on the River common.

Another capacity house greeted the entertainment last night. The performance will be repeated tonight and tomorrow, matinee and night.

SOURCE: *Milwaukee Sentinel*, 1 December 1905, p. 4.

DOCUMENT 5

Lyman Howe is doing a great public service in dignifying the motion picture. It is no small undertaking to challenge a verdict from the public at such a vast and beautiful place of entertainment as the New York Hippodrome, and on Sunday evening when I went there, I had my doubts as to the possibilities of his success. Is a modern audience educated up to such a pitch of intelligence that it is ready to accept the motion picture as the staple of an entire evening's entertainment? Last Sunday's great crowd gave an emphatic reply to the question, and Lyman H. Howe emerges triumphantly from the ordeal. He has conquered the public by sheer force of excellence, and a firm faith in the drawing powers of high class motion photography.

I have seen the motion picture displayed in every imaginable kind of theater, and in many large cities, but never in a hall of such size and beauty as the Hippodrome, where every possible visitor can see the stage and a large size picture is possible. The programme was diversified; the photographs splendidly good, and the title slides delicately refined and telling. A master hand was at the projector, for the pictures were very skillfully shown. Then the tinting was effective and artistic. The audience, in fact, saw moving picture photography displayed to its best advantage.

And with what rapt attention these beautiful views were followed by the vast house! The travel note is a safe one to strike in cosmopolitan New York where all sorts and conditions of men from all parts of the world are gathered together. Lyman Howe, shrewd man, knows this and plays his cards accordingly. Rome, India, Nice, the Rockies, London, Sicily, Niagara were some of the places we visited the other night. The mind was ever kept in motion; ever stimulated; ever refreshed; ever excited. I cannot conceive of a more delightful and rational way of passing an evening. It is a positive brain rest. Before the Indian films were shown a gentleman came on stage and read us a short lecture about them. Positively I resented the intrusion of that man; I did not want anybody to talk then; I wanted the pictures to do that, and so did all the people round about me. So Mr. Howe, no more lecturing, please; your pictures are eloquent enough and we are quite content to look at them and listen to your effects.

And such effects! How wonderfully clever and well timed these are, to be sure. It is the very perfection of stage management. In one picture a dog is seen scampering across a field of view. He is made to bark as he runs. The guide who hustles the sightseers through the streets of Rome seems to talk glibly after the manner of his kind and the words are spoken in unison with the actions of the man on the screen. Nothing more humorous could be imagined than the speech of Cicero in the guise of a statue come to life. Its the very quintessence of broad farce and the audience shook with laughter. When we went to Niagara, we shivered at the icy grandeur of Winter, and felt the roll and roar of the great waters in Summer, so subtly skilful were the introduced effects. So too, as the train tore through the Frazer River Canon of the Rockies; as the automobile swept over the rocky gorges of the Savoy; as the merrymakers disported themselves at the Nice Carnival of 1908—there were the accompanying toots and rattle of locomotives, the tumultuous swirl of tumbled waters, the weird ear-splitting sounds of the carnivallers. In a word these accompanying effects were splendidly done and they added much to the attractiveness of the pictures.

The programme, which is to be repeated next Sunday evening, contains a series of Sicilian views, apropos the recent earthquake, and many other items of a humorous character. All New York should see this fine collection of moving pictures. They are educative, they are entertaining, they are humorous, they are inspiring, and above all they are beautiful. I mingled with the great crowd in and about the gorgeous house, young and old, rich and prosperous, and I listened to what they said of the display. They had come to see the pictures "so we thought we'd come and see the pictures" was a common remark of Madame New York, who meant filling an evening to the best advantage—they saw them; and they were contented. I take off my hat to you, friend Howe; you have a great public at your back, and you are doing so well with your exhibition and its quality is so fine that, especially in these critical times of the moving picture when the hand of the enemy is against it, you deserve every praise and encouragement in your work.

Source: *Moving Picture World*, 1 February 1909, p. 169.

Notes

* * *

Chapter One

1. Since almost every exhibitor from this period was male, we will apply male nouns and pronouns in general references.

2. Terry Ramsaye, *A Million and One Nights* (New York: Simon and Schuster, 1926), pp. 75, 312–14; Robert Grau, *The Stage in the Twentieth Century* (New York: Broadway Publishing Co., 1912), pp. 121–22.

3. Harry M. Geduld, *The Birth of the Talkies: From Edison to Jolson* (Bloomington: Indiana University Press, 1975), p. 3.

4. General knowledge of early film history has progressed significantly in the last twelve years. The work of Noël Burch, Tom Gunning, André Gaudreault, John Fell, Eileen Bowser, Paul Spehr, Robert C. Allen, Janet Staiger, and others has enabled current historians to begin a major reassessment. Nonetheless, significant gaps remain in our understanding. Useful bibliographies can be found in John Fell, ed., *Film before Griffith* (Berkeley: University of California Press, 1983); and Charles Musser, *The Emergence of Cinema: The American Screen to 1907* (New York: Scribner's, 1990).

5. See, for example, Roy Rosenzweig, *Eight Hours for What We Will: Workers and Leisure in an Industrial City, 1870–1920* (Cambridge: Cambridge University Press, 1983); Kathy Peiss, *Cheap Amusements: Leisure in Turn-of-the-Century New York* (Philadelphia: Temple University Press, 1986); Stephen Hardy, *How Boston Played: Sport, Recreation and Community, 1865–1915* (Boston: Northeastern University Press, 1982); and Melvin L. Adelman, *A Sporting Time: New York City and the Rise of Modern Athletics, 1820–1870* (Urbana: University of Illinois Press, 1986).

6. Elizabeth Ewen, "City Lights: Immigrant Women and the Rise of the Movies," *Signs: Journal of Women in Culture and Society* 5, no. 3, supplement (1980).

7. Robert Sklar, "Oh! Althusser!: Historiography and the Rise of Cinema Studies," *Radical History Review* 41 (April 1988), pp. 11–35; see also Miriam Hansen, "Early Silent Film: Whose Public Sphere?" *New German Critique* 29 (Winter 1983), pp. 147–84.

8. Douglas Gomery, "The Economics of U.S. Film Exhibition and Practice," *Ciné Tracts* 12 (Winter 1981), pp. 38–46; Rosenzweig, *Eight Hours*, pp. 191–228.

9. See, for example, Robert C. Allen, *Vaudeville and Film, 1895–1915: A History of Media Interaction* (New York: Arno Press, 1980); Robert C. Allen, "Motion Picture Exhibition in Manhattan: Beyond the Nickelodeon," in Fell, ed., *Film before Griffith*, pp. 162–75; and Russell Merritt, "Nickelodeon Theaters, 1905–1914: Building an Audience for the Movies," in Tino Balio, ed., *The American Film Industry* (Madison: University of Wisconsin Press, 1976), pp. 59–82.

10. Neil Harris, "John Philip Sousa and the Culture of Reassurance," in John Newsom, ed., *Perspectives on John Philip Sousa* (Washington, D.C.: Library of Congress, 1983), pp. 11–40.
11. Calvin Pryluck, "The Itinerant Movie Show and the Development of the Industry," *Journal of the University Film and Video Association* 35 (Fall 1983), pp. 11–22.
12. Two useful looks at such specialized traveling motion picture exhibitors in North America are Edward Lowry, "Edwin J. Hadley: Traveling Film Exhibitor," in Fell, ed., *Film before Griffith*, pp. 131–42; and Germain Lacasse with Serge Duigou, *L'Historiographe* (Montreal: Cinemathèque Quebecoise, 1985).
13. Carlo Ginzburg, *The Cheese and the Worms: The Cosmos of a Sixteenth-Century Miller* (New York: Penguin, 1982), p. xxi.
14. Michel Foucault, "What is an Author?" in *Language, Counter-Memory: Selected Essays and Interviews* (Ithaca: Cornell University Press, 1977), pp. 113–38.
15. Boris Tomashevsky, "Literature and Biography," in Ladislav Matejka and Krystyna Pomorska, eds., *Readings in Russian Poetics: Formalist and Structuralist Views* (Cambridge: MIT Press, 1971), p. 55.
16. David Bordwell, *The Films of Carl-Theodor Dreyer* (Berkeley: University of California Press, 1981), p. 9.
17. Neil Harris, *Humbug: The Art of P. T. Barnum* (Boston: Little, Brown, 1973), pp. 77–78.
18. Tomashevsky, "Literature and Biography," p. 50.
19. Bordwell, *Films of Carl-Theodor Dreyer*, p. 10.
20. In a recent *New York Times* survey, 85 percent of those responding considered themselves middle class ("Poll Reveals Gains by Democrats Among Vital Middle Class," *New York Times*, 7 August 1988, pp. 1, 24).
21. Harry Braverman, *Labor and Monopoly Capital: The Degradation of Work in the Twentieth Century* (New York: Monthly Review Press, 1974), pp. 403–9.
22. Albert F. McLean, Jr., *American Vaudeville as Ritual* (Lexington: University of Kentucky Press, 1965), pp. 2–3.
23. Thomas Kessner, *The Golden Door: Italian and Immigrant Mobility in New York City, 1880–1915* (New York: Oxford University Press, 1977).
24. John Kasson, *Amusing the Million: Coney Island at the Turn of the Century* (New York: Hill and Wang, 1978), p. 11.
25. Daniel Czitrom, *Media and the American Mind: From Morse to McLuhan* (Chapel Hill: University of North Carolina Press, 1982), p. 43.
26. See Alan Trachtenberg, *The Incorporation of America: Culture and Society in the Gilded Age* (New York: Hill and Wang, 1982).
27. Albert F. McLean, Jr., is one of the few to have acknowledged their quite different agendas (*American Vaudeville as Ritual*, pp. 66–90).
28. Henry F. May, *Protestant Churches and Industrial America* (New York: Harper and Brothers, 1949).
29. Although this does not exhaust the number of cultural clusters, these are key for cinema of this period. Political radicals, for example, may have generated

their own cultural institutions but they did not support identifiable traveling showmen. By the mid-1910s, however, they were constructing a distinct film culture (Steve Ross, "Cinema and Class Conflict," in Robert Sklar and Charles Musser, eds., *Resisting Images: Essays on Film and History* [Philadelphia: Temple University Press, 1990]).

30. Woodrow Wilson, *Mere Literature and Other Essays* (Boston: Houghton, Mifflin, 1896), p. 212, cited in Robert Sklar, *The Plastic Age* (New York: George Braziller, 1970), pp. 2–3.

CHAPTER TWO

1. Phineas T. Barnum, *Struggles and Triumphs of P. T. Barnum* (1882; reprint, London: Macgibbon and Kee, 1967), pp. 11–46; Harris, *Humbug*, pp. 20–23.
2. Broadside, ca. 1840s, Ohio Historical Society.
3. Harris, *Humbug*, p. 57.
4. *New York Clipper*, 4 April 1914, p. 3.
5. As McLean points out, this format catered to city dwellers' varied schedules (*American Vaudeville as Ritual*, p. 203). Both principles, however, had been anticipated in Barnum's Museum.
6. *New York Times*, 29 March 1884, p. 4.
7. Donald C. King, "S. Z. Poli: From Wax to Riches," *Marquee* 2, no. 2 (1979), pp. 11–18. Although generally well researched, its chronology of Poli's early life needs more work. King has Poli working for the Eden Musee several years before it opened.
8. Wilkes-Barre was the county seat for Luzerne County, which included Scranton and what is now Lackawanna County until the 1870s. Wilkes-Barre became a city in 1871. The major source for information about nineteenth-century Wilkes-Barre is Oscar Jewell Harvey and Ernest Gray Smith, *A History of Wilkes-Barre and Wyoming Valley*, 6 vols. (Wilkes-Barre: Smith Bennett Corp., 1909–1930). The principal source for Howe's early life and family background is Rev. Horace Edwin Hayden, the Hon. Alfred Hand, and John W. Jordan, *Genealogical and Family History of the Wyoming and Lackawanna Valleys, Pennsylvania*, vol. 2 (New York: Lewis Publishing Co., 1906), pp. 579–82.
9. *Luzerne Union*, 22 October 1873.
10. The Wilkes-Barre city directories from 1872 onward provide much of this information.
11. Philip S. Foner, *The Great Labor Unrest of 1877* (New York: Monad Press, 1977).
12. Harvey and Smith, *A History*, 4: 2117.
13. Lyman H. Howe and Robert M. Colborn, "A Marvel of Mechanism," HCS.
14. Ibid.
15. Ibid.
16. Lyman H. Howe, "Third Season at Glen Onoko," HCS.
17. See Chapter 8.
18. Howe, "Third Season at Glen Onoko," HCS.
19. Howe & Colborn, "A Marvel of Mechanism," HCS.

20. Francis G. Couvares, *The Remaking of Pittsburgh: Class and Culture in an Industrializing City, 1877–1919* (Albany: State University of New York Press, 1984), pp. 31–50; E. P. Thompson, "Patrician Society, Plebeian Culture," *Journal of Social History* 7 (1974), pp. 382–405.
21. "The Story of Lyman Howe," *Pittsburgh Post,* 18 May 1913, p. 3b.
22. *Baltimore Sun,* 9 January 1884, p. 1.
23. Samples of these survive in HCS.
24. Advertisements appearing in *Baltimore Sun,* January 1884.
25. *Baltimore American and Commercial Advertiser,* 13 January 1884, HCS.
26. Theo L. Mumford, *The Switzerland of America* (Mauch Chunk, Pa.: 188?).
27. *New York Times,* 1 January 1884, p. 3, and 29 March 1884, p. 7.
28. Ralph Barber, manuscript, n.d., PW-BH.
29. Harvey and Smith, *A History,* 3: 2142.
30. *Wilkes-Barre News,* ca. 1912, HS. The chronology in this newspaper article is badly out of order. For instance, the *News* indicates that Howe sold these transmitters before he had his miniature coal breaker, although neither Wilkes-Barre nor Scranton had a phone system at that time. We have followed the chronology offered in Hayden, Hand, and Jordan, *History,* pp. 579–582.

CHAPTER THREE

1. The telephone, for example, was presented at the Clinton Avenue Reformed Church in Newark, New Jersey, on May 16 and 17, 1878. According to one report, "The apparatus, though perfectly plain and simple in construction, transmitted messages and vocal and instrumental music in a way that demonstrated the importance of Mr. Edison's invention, and the great results it is destined to accomplish in the future" (*Newark Daily Advertiser,* 17 May 1878; *Thomas A. Edison Papers: A Selective Microfilm Edition* reel 25: frame 195). In the 1870s the telephone was closely associated with Edison's name. Such telephone exhibitions obviously provided a model for the phonograph concerts that followed.
2. Czitrom, *Media and the American Mind.*
3. *New York World,* 17 May 1878, p. 1; *Edison Papers,* reel 25: frame 225.
4. "Church Entertainments," brochure, 22 July 1879; *Edison Papers,* reel 25: frame 294.
5. "Successful Phonograph Exhibitors," *The Phonogram* (February 1893), p. 322.
6. Robert Conot, *A Streak of Luck: The Life and Legend of Thomas Alva Edison* (New York: Seaview Books, 1979), pp. 265–69.
7. *Rome Sentinel,* 29 January 1889, NJWOE.
8. Edison's quadroplex enabled telegraph companies to send four messages simultaneously over a single wire, thus saving millions of dollars.
9. "How to Give Concert Exhibitions of the Phonograph," *The Phonogram* (February 1893), p. 324.
10. *The Phonogram,* February 1893, pp. 322–23.
11. See clippings relevant to the phonograph for 1889–1891 at NJWOE.
12. Howe's scrapbook brings together a collection of scattered, hard-to-locate reviews, many of which come from newspapers no longer extant.

13. *Proceedings of Second Annual Convention of Local Phonograph Companies of the United States, 16–18 June 1891* (New York: Linotype Reporting and Printing Co., 1891), p. 128.

14. "Bottled Music," *Bethlehem Daily Times*, 23 April 1890, p. 1.

15. *Allentown Daily City Item*, 2 and 4 April 1890, HPS.

16. *Scranton Republican*, 12 March 1890, pp. 2, 5.

17. *Scranton Truth*, 11 March 1890, HPS.

18. *Scranton Daily Times*, 15 March 1890, HPS.

19. "Exhibition of the Phonograph," *Scranton Republican*, 11 March 1890, p. 5.

20. *Scranton Republican*, 20 March 1890, HPS.

21. *Scranton Republican*, 21 March 1890, HPS.

22. *Scranton Free Press*, 23 March 1890, HPS.

23. *Allentown Daily City Item*, 2 April 1890, HPS. A Boston phonograph exhibitor who operated in similar fashion reported that his patrons were "of all classes—rich and poor, young and old, male and especially *female*" (*The Phonogram*, July 1892, p. 163).

24. *Allentown Daily City Item*, 8 April 1890, HPS.

25. *Allentown Critic*, 10 April 1890, p. 4.

26. *Allentown Daily City Item*, 11 April 1890, HPS.

27. "The Wonderful Phonograph," *Bethlehem Daily Times*, 22 April 1890, p. 4.

28. "Listen to the Talking Machine," *Bethlehem Daily Times*, 29 April 1890, p. 1.

29. Ibid.

30. Lyman H. Howe, broadside, December 1890, and *Carbondale Evening Leader*, 17 December 1890, HPS.

31. Lyman H. Howe, contract form, early 1890s, PW-bH.

32. *The Miltonian*, 9 January 1891, HPS.

33. *Danville Daily Record*, ca. 14 January 1891, HPS.

34. *Scranton Republican*, 22 January 1891, *Scranton Truth*, 10 December 1891, and *Allentown City Item*, 27 November 1891, HPS.

35. John Ward was recording and playing cylinders in Pottsville during December 1890 (*Pottsville Journal*, 20 December 1890, NJWOE).

36. *Gettysburg Compiler*, 10 March 1891, and *York Daily*, 25 April 1891, HPS.

37. *Scranton Republican*, 14 March 1890, p. 3.

38. *Scranton Truth*, 10 December 1891, HPS.

39. Harris, "John Philip Sousa," pp. 11–40.

40. *The Phonogram* (February 1893), pp. 324–26. This is only an excerpt of an interesting article.

41. *Miner's Journal*, 14 January 1893, HPS.

42. *The Age*, 24 February 1891, *Danville Gem*, 17 January 1891, HPS.

43. *Canastota Journal*, 15 March 1893, HPS.

44. *Lancaster Daily Examiner*, 13 February 1891, HPS.

45. Barbara Kirshenblatt-Gimblett graciously shared her thoughts with me on the importance of the quotidian. See "Objects of Ethnography," in Ivan Karp and Steven Lavine, eds., *Exhibiting Culture: Poetics and Politics of*

Museum Display (Washington, D.C.: Smithsonian Institution Press, forthcoming).

46. *York Daily*, 25 April 1891, HPS.

47. *Cortland Standard*, 29 March 1893, HPS.

48. *Daily Advertiser*, 14 March 1894, HPS.

49. *Proceedings of Second Annual Convention*, p. 63.

50. *Lebanon Daily Report*, 6 February 1891, HPS.

51. McLean, *American Vaudeville as Ritual*, pp. 138–64.

52. *Lebanon Daily News*, 6 February 1891, HPS.

53. *Hazleton Plain Speaker*, 17 December 1892; see also *The Miltonian*, 9 and 23 January 1891, HPS.

54. *Scranton Republican*, 22 January 1891, and *Lancaster Daily Examiner*, 13 February 1891, HPS.

55. *Allentown Daily City Item*, 27 November 1891; see also *York Daily*, 25 April 1891, and *Bethlehem Daily Times*, 28 March 1891, HPS.

56. *Penny Evening News*, 23 November 1894, HPS. This metaphor was probably quite common. Several years later, a promotional item claimed, "The Graphophone is to the ear what the photographic camera is to the eye, and more for the Graphophone catches instantly every tint and shade of sound" (*Danbury Evening News*, 1 June 1898, p. 4).

57. *Proceedings of Second Annual Convention*, p. 102.

58. Ibid.

59. *Chambersburg Valley Spirit*, 10 March 1891, HPS.

60. *Kingston Morning Times*, 21 February 1891, HPS.

61. *York Daily*, 25 April 1891, HPS. A concert given two years later in Bellefonte, Pennsylvania, for the benefit of the YMCA, was also witnessed by about five hundred people (*Bellefonte Republican*, 4 May 1893, HPS).

62. *Marathon Independent*, 29 March 1893; *Nunda News*, 15 April 1893; *Susquehanna Transcript*, 5 October 1893, HPS.

63. "The Exhibition Parlors of the Ohio Phonograph Company," *The Phonogram* (November–December 1891), pp. 248–49.

64. *Proceedings of Second Annual Convention*, pp. 52–53.

65. *Proceedings of Second Annual Convention*, p. 62.

66. "Lyman H. Howe's Phonograph Concerts," circular, 8 February 1894.

67. *Scranton Truth*, 10 December 1891, and *Deposit Journal*, 15 March 1893, HPS.

68. *Kingston Morning Times*, 21 November 1891; see also *Marathon Independent*, 29 March 1893, and *Spencer Herald*, 7 April 1893, HPS.

69. *Bellefonte Daily Gazette*, 3 May 1893, HPS.

70. *Lansing Journal*, 18 January 1895, NJWOE.

71. Their more modest churches and social institutions generally had to wait until the mid- or late 1890s, when the price of the phonograph had fallen, before they could sponsor concerts by semiprofessional or amateur exhibitors.

72. *Pottsville Evening Chronicle*, 14 January 1893, HPS.

73. *Shamokin Daily Herald*, 11 January 1893, HPS.

74. *Miner's Journal*, 14 January 1893, HPS.

75. *Hazleton Sentinel,* 17 December 1892, HPS; see also *Bellefonte Daily Gazette,* 3 May 1893, HPS.

76. *Miner's Journal,* 11 January 1893, HPS, for example, lists Howe's forthcoming exhibitions.

77. Hayden, Hand, and Jordon, *History,* 2: 581.

78. *Assembly Daily,* 5 July 1893, HPS.

79. *Philadelphia Press,* 5 July 1894, HPS.

80. Thomas A. Edison, caveat 110, 8 October 1888, filed 17 October 1888, transcribed in Gordon Hendricks, *The Edison Motion Picture Myth* (Berkeley: University of California Press, 1961), p. 158.

81. "The Kinetograph," *The Phonogram* (October 1892), pp. 217–18.

82. Tate to Howe, 8 June 1893, Edison letter books, NJWOE.

83. Quoted in Conot, *A Streak of Luck,* p. 312.

84. Conot, *A Streak of Luck,* p. 315.

85. Broadside, 23 April 1894, NJWOE.

86. *Norwalk Daily Reflector,* 9 March 1895, HPS.

87. *Wyoming County Times,* 15 March 1894, HPS.

88. *Rome Daily Sentinel,* 18 December 1893, HPS.

89. *Camden Advance-Journal,* 21 December 1893, HPS.

90. *Troy Daily Times,* 18 April 1894; *Jamestown Evening Journal,* 21 November 1894; *Evening Times,* 16 February 1895; *The Courant,* 3 April 1895; and *Saginaw Courier-Herald,* 4 May 1895, HPS.

91. *The Journal,* 11 January 1896, HPS.

92. Oliver Reed and Walter L. Welch, *From Tin Foil to Stereo,* 2d ed. (Indianapolis: H. W. Swan, 1976), p. 60; and Conot, *A Streak of Luck,* p. 316.

CHAPTER FOUR

1. Robert Fischer to Norman Raff and Frank Gammon, 3 April 1896; A. Holland to Norman Raff, 1 August 1896; MH-BA.

2. The Washington-based inventors originally called their projector a "phantoscope." After they separated on bad terms in late 1895, Armat approached Raff and Gammon and asked them to market the machine. They agreed, signing a formal contract in January 1896. Raff and Gammon had been marketing Edison's peephole kinetoscope in the United States and Canada when they became the commercial agents for this machine.

3. Raff and Gammon to Lyman H. Howe, 17 February 1896, MH-BA. Unfortunately, Howe's letters to Raff and Gammon do not survive.

4. Raff and Gammon to Howe, 25 February 1896, MH-BA.

5. Raff and Gammon to Howe, 4 March 1896, MH-BA.

6. A. F. Rieser to Edison Kinetoscope Company, 29 February 1896, Raff and Gammon Collection, MH-BA.

7. Ibid. Rieser went on to acquire the vitascope rights for Ohio and induced his friend, Peter W. Kiefaber, to acquire rights to New Jersey, Massachusetts, Illinois, and Maryland.

8. Raff and Gammon to Howe, 9 March 1896, MH-BA.

9. A. F. Rieser to Raff and Gammon, 28 May 1896, MH-BA. The myth of Howe's primacy was already established by the 1920s (clipping, Wilkes-Barre news-

paper, 2 May 1924, FS). It was never challenged, since the *Wilkes-Barre Record*, on which later histories of the city have been based, neglected to cover the earlier vitascope exhibition in any detail ("Late Lyman H. Howe First to Show Motion Pictures in City," *Wilkes-Barre Record*, 31 May 1955; "Valley Once a Movie-Making Center," *Wilkes-Barre Times-Leader Evening News*, 12 November 1966, p. 10). In this respect, Howe was fairly typical, for many local newspapers have valorized the reputation of their "old-time" exhibitor in this way. Another Wilkes-Barre resident, George J. Llewellyn, purchased vitascope rights for Michigan from Raff and Gammon. Both Jones and Llewellyn had probably been approached by Howe when he was trying to raise money for purchasing the Pennsylvania rights. Appropriate volumes of Julius Cahn, *Cahn's Official Theatrical Guide* (New York) are the source for seating capacities unless otherwise noted.

10. *Scranton Times*, 23 June 1896, p. 1, and 24 June 1896, p. 1; *Wilkes-Barre Record*, 29 June 1896, p. 12.
11. "Wizard Edison's Vitascope," *Wilkes-Barre Times*, 1 July 1896, p. 8.
12. *Wilkes-Barre Record*, 3 July 1896, p. 5.
13. Holland Brothers to Raff and Gammon, 23 September 1896, MH-BA.
14. Holland Brothers to Raff, 28 December 1896, MH-BA.
15. *New York Clipper*, 26 September 1896, p. 480; 31 October 1896, p. 554; and 14 November 1896, p. 595.
16. *Wilkes-Barre News*, ca. 1912, HS.
17. News item, quoted in *Wilkes-Barre Times-Leader Evening News* 12 November 1966, p. 10.
18. Raff and Gammon, *The Vitascope* (New York: 1896).
19. Kinetoscope Company to Lyman H. Howe, 17 February 1896, 3: 215, MH-BA.
20. Terry Ramsaye credits Howe as the first (*A Million and One Nights*, p. 313), but the Lathams (and probably Biograph) used take-up reels before him.
21. *Wilkes-Barre News*, 2 July 1903, cited in Edwin J. Hadley, program, 7 October 1903, Hadley Collection, TXU-H.
22. *Wilkes-Barre Record*, 28 November 1896, HPS.
23. "The Animatiscope," *Wilkes-Barre Leader*, 3 December 1896, p. 2.
24. *Wilkes-Barre Leader*, 3 December 1896, p. 2.
25. *Bloomsburg Daily*, 29 December 1896, HPS.
26. Erik Barnouw, *Documentary: A History of the Non-Fiction Film* (New York: Oxford University Press, 1974), pp. 5–20.
27. "The Animotoscope," *Wilkes-Barre Record*, 5 December 1896, p. 12.
28. *Wilkes-Barre Record*, 5 December 1896, p. 12.
29. *The Union*, 12 December 1896, HPS.
30. *Evening Gazette*, 12 December 1896, HPS.
31. *Daily Record*, 30 December 1896, HPS.
32. "The Animotiscope," *Owego Gazette*, 18 March 1897.
33. Lacasse, *L'Historiographe*.
34. The separation of these two commercial methods is reflected in Raff and Gammon's sale of Philadelphia and Pittsburgh exhibition rights apart from

the rest of Pennsylvania and their retention of New York City rights while selling those for New York state.

35. Charles Musser, "Another Look at the Chaser Period," *Studies in Visual Communication* 10, no. 4 (Fall 1984): 24–44.

36. For example, *Lancaster Intelligencer*, 9 December 1896, p. 6.

37. *New York Dramatic Mirror* (henceforth NYDM), 9 January 1897, p. 7.

38. *Reading Eagle*, 9 January 1898, pp. 2, 3; *Brooklyn Eagle*, 10 February 1901, p. 8.

39. *Reading Eagle*, 28 March 1897, pp. 1, 2; NYDM, 20 and 27 February 1897.

40. "Amusements," *Williamsport Sun*, 10 December 1896, p. 4.

41. "Gave a Performance," *South Bethlehem Daily Globe*, 26 February 1897, p. 1.

42. Himmelein's Ideals, for example, did not show moving pictures the following year (*Reading Eagle*, 23 December 1897, p. 2).

43. "The Projectoscope Will Do," *Harrisburg Daily Telegraph*, 30 November 1896, p. 1.

44. *Harrisburg Patriot*, 13 January 1897, p. 5.

45. "An Attractive Exhibition," *Hanover Evening Herald*, 19 January 1897, p. 1.

46. "New Advertisements," *Hanover Evening Herald*, 11 May 1897, p. 2; The American Cineograph Company, promotional brochure, ca. April 1897, NjWOE.

47. NYDM, 5 December 1896, p. 8.

48. NYDM, 12 December 1896, 23 January 1897, p. 8, and 10 April 1897, p. 7.

49. "High Class Vaudeville," *Phoenix Gazette*, 20 May 1897; "Look Out for the Big Show," *Tuscon Citizen*, 27 May 1897, courtesy of George C. Hall. See Hall, "The First Moving Picture in Arizona, or Was It," *Film History* 3, no. 1 (1989), pp. 1–10.

50. Charles McCoy Clark, "The First Motion Picture in Arizona," Arizona Pioneers Historical Society, courtesy of George C. Hall.

51. NYDM, 3 April 1897, p. 7.

52. *Geneva Advertiser*, 6 April 1897, p. 3.

53. Sutton's Opera House, Hillsdale, Michigan, broadside, 8–10 April 1897.

54. *Geneva Advertiser*, 6 April 1897, p. 3.

55. *Hanover Evening Herald*, 11 May 1897, p. 2.

56. NYDM, 5 December 1896, p. 8.

57. *Wilkes-Barre Record*, 5 December 1896, p. 12.

58. "At the Frothingham," *Scranton Times*, 23 June 1896, p. 4.

59. "Wizard Edison's Vitascope," *Wilkes-Barre Times*, 1 July 1896, p. 8.

60. *Port Jervis Evening Journal*, 12 December 1896, HPS.

61. *Danville Sun*, 30 December 1896, HPS.

62. *Wilkes-Barre Record*, 29 October 1897, p. 7.

63. *Daily Record*, 22 December 1896, HPS.

64. *Danville Sun*, 30 December 1896, HPS.

65. *Wilkes-Barre Record*, 19 May 1896, p. 5.

66. *Wilkes-Barre Record*, 8 January 1897, p. 5.

67. *Wilkes-Barre Record*, 9 January 1897, p. 5.

68. *Rome Daily Sentinel*, 3 May 1897, HPS.

69. *Albany Evening Journal*, 10 February 1897, HPS.
70. *Wayne Independent*, 5 March 1897, HPS.
71. *Geneva Advertiser*, 9 March 1897, p. 2; 6 April 1897, p. 3.
72. Hadley to Howe, 17 September 1899, TXU-H.
73. *Wilkes-Barre Times-Leader*, ca. fall 1912, WS.
74. *Bloomsburg Daily*, 29 December 1896, HPS.
75. *Port Jervis Evening Gazette*, 12 December 1896, HPS. See also *Daily Record*, (Mahonoy City, Pennsylvania), 22 December 1896, HPS.
76. *Cohoes Republican*, 27 February 1897, p. 1.
77. *Cohoes Republican*, 11, 12, and 13 March 1897. In Williamsport, where Howe showed films at the local YMCA in January, although he was preceded by Hopkins' Trans-Oceanics with their kinematographe, the hall was jammed with a large and appreciative audience. An additional screening was immediately scheduled, filling an otherwise vacant playdate (*Williamsport Grit*, 17 January 1897, HPS).
78. *Middletown Daily Times*, 11 December 1896, HPS.
79. *Port Jervis Evening Gazette*, 12 December 1896, HPS.
80. *Middletown Daily Times*, 3 February 1897, HPS.
81. *Albany Evening Journal*, 10 February 1897, HPS.
82. *Danbury Evening News*, 16 June 1897, HPS.
83. *Danbury Evening News*, 20 November 1897, HAS.

CHAPTER FIVE

1. "The introduction of this scientific achievement in the art of accurate reproduction of living scenes has attracted the attention and patronage of many people who never before attended the continuous and popular price form of amusement," observed one reporter in 1896 (*Chicago Tribune*, 19 July 1896, p. 31).
2. This survey was based on the "Correspondence" section and listings of road companies in NYDM. For the fall and spring of each year, three issues, two weeks apart, were examined. The different playdates were tallied and the number of different companies estimated. This survey has limited though still valuable utility. Although it considers only a minuscule sample of exhibitions, it suggests the relative level of specialized film exhibitions in commercial venues outside the major cities.
3. "The Brutal Show," *Wilkes-Barre Record*, 16 February 1897, p. 4.
4. "No Prize Fight Pictures," *South Bethlehem Daily Globe*, 23 March 1897, p. 2; *New York World*, 20 March 1897, p. 8.
5. "The Veriscope Shows the Fight," *New York Tribune*, 23 May 1897, p. 8.
6. See, for example, "Does its Work Well," *Boston Herald*, 1 June 1897, p. 7.
7. *Wilkes-Barre Record*, 11 September 1897, p. 5.
8. *The Argus*, 22 April 1894; *Albany Evening Journal*, 10 February 1897, HPS.
9. *Rome Daily Sentinel*, 18 December 1893 and 3 May 1897, HPS.
10. "Church and Amusements," *Hartford Courant*, 21 May 1896, p. 3.
11. *Scranton Tribune*, 14 April 1897, HPS.
12. *Danbury Evening News*, 12 February 1898, HAS.
13. *Ellenville Journal*, 18 June 1897, HPS.

14. The Epworth League was founded in 1889 and had more than eight thousand chapters by 1893. In Reading, for example, the social committee of the Memorial Church Epworth League provided one entertainment a month, which "brought our young people of Memorial Church closer together than they have ever been before" (*Reading Eagle*, 13 May 1901, p. 4).

15. *Wilkes-Barre Record*, 19 January 1897, p. 4.

16. *Wilkes-Barre Record*, 29 October 1897, p. 7.

17. *The Phonoscope* (March 1898), p. 7.

18. See Musser, *The Emergence of Cinema*, for a consideration of theatrical and screen passion plays in 1880, and see, e.g., "The Passion Play Denounced," *New York Times*, 16 November 1880, p. 2, and "Mr. Abbey's Decision," *New York Times*, 28 November 1880, p. 7.

19. *Moving Picture World*, 22 February 1908, p. 132.

20. "Moving War Pictures," *Wilkes-Barre Record*, 17 September 1898, p. 5.

21. *Reading Eagle*, 18 January 1899, p. 2.

22. *Wilkes-Barre Record*, 20 September 1898, p. 8.

23. *Amsterdam Morning Sentinel*, 3 March 1898, p. 4; *Amsterdam Daily Democrat*, 21 November 1898, p. 4.

24. See Appendix E for more detailed information of his Troy exhibitions.

25. New Haven city directories (New Haven: Price and Lee), 1895–1909.

26. *Hartford Courant*, 22 March 1898, p. 3.

27. *Hartford Courant*, 21 March 1898, p. 5, and 19 March 1904, p. 7; *Meriden Daily Journal*, 20 January 1904, p. 9.

28. Brooklyn directories 1884–1892; letterhead, New York and Brooklyn Entertainment Bureau, May 1892, box 16E, Bella Landour Collection, NNHi.

29. Edison Projectoscope Company, advertising brochure, 1900, TXU-H.

30. Clipping, 22 February 1896, COS, p. 11.

31. Program, COS, pp. 6–7.

32. See, for example, program for Opera House, Milan, Ohio, 11–12 October 1898, COS, p. 13.

33. Edwin Hadley to Howe, 17 September 1899, TXU-H.

34. "The Animotiscope," program for Odd Fellows' Hall, Gorham, New York, 7 April 1899, TXU-H. Many of the endorsements in this program cite church announcement sheets, which suggest that the screenings were not reviewed in local newspapers.

35. Hadley to Howe, 17 September 1899, TXU-H.

36. The Hadley Kinetoscope Concert Company, leaflet for exhibition at Lyons, Indiana, Methodist Episcopal Church; Hadley's Animated Picture Machine, letterhead, ca. 1899; Hadley to Howe, 24 August 1899, TXU-H.

37. Lowery, "Edwin J. Hadley," p. 132.

38. "Life, Color and Motion," *Brooklyn Daily Eagle*, 28 November 1896, p. 9.

39. "A Cycle Tour in Europe," *Brooklyn Eagle*, 27 April 1896, p. 7.

40. Brooklyn Institute of Arts and Sciences, *Ticket No.* 19, 1896–1897 season; *Brooklyn Eagle*, 9 March 1897, p. 7. Northrop often gave the same lecture outside New York without the benefit of moving pictures.

41. "Prof. Northrop's Lecture," *Brooklyn Eagle*, 16 January 1898, p. 13.

42. "The Hardships of Klondike," *Brooklyn Eagle*, 12 February 1898, p. 3.

43. Brooklyn Institute of Arts and Sciences, tickets, 1897–1898, NN.

44. *Cincinnati Enquirer*, ca. 1894–1895, BHS.

45. "The First Lenten Lecture," *New York Tribune*, 25 February 1898, p. 7.

46. "A Successor to Stoddard," *Brooklyn Eagle*, 13 March 1898, p. 32.

47. E. Burton Holmes, *The Burton Holmes Lectures*, 1897–1898, p. 3, BHS.

48. "Cycling Through Corsica," *New York Tribune*, 1 March 1898, p. 7; see also *New York World*, 25 February 1898, p. 9.

49. E. Burton Holmes, *Lectures for Sixth Year*, 1898–1899, BHS.

50. Elmendorf had earlier given stereopticon lectures on such subjects as the Rocky Mountains of Colorado ("Mr. Elmendorf's Lecture," *Brooklyn Eagle*, 8 February 1898, p. 12). This earlier lecture was not sponsored by the Institute, however.

51. "The Santiago Campaign," *Brooklyn Eagle*, 4 April 1899, p. 3. Many of the war films were undoubtedly taken by William Paley for the Edison Manufacturing Company in the spring and summer of 1898; James White, manager of Edison's Kinetograph Department, took many of the Mexican films during the winter of 1897–1898.

52. Maguire and Baucus, Ltd., *Lumiere Films, Edison Films, International Films*, fall 1897, NjWOE.

53. *Evening Herald*, 28 October 1897, HAS.

54. *Evening Herald*, 28 October 1897, HAS.

55. *Wilkes-Barre Record*, 1 June 1898, HAS.

56. *Carbondale Evening Leader*, 28 October 1897, HAS.

57. *Wilkes-Barre Record*, 27 January 1898, HAS.

58. Cecil Hepworth, *Came the Dawn* (London: Phoenix House, 1951), p. 33.

59. *Amsterdam Daily Democrat*, 5 March 1898, HAS.

60. *Amsterdam Morning Sentinel*, 3 March 1898; HAS.

61. *Wilkes-Barre News-Dealer*, 27 January 1898; *Danbury Evening News*, 20 November 1897, HAS.

62. *Danbury Evening News*, 20 November 1897; *Evening Herald* (North Adams, Massachusetts), 9 November 1897; *Morning Sentinel* (Amsterdam, New York), 3 March 1898, HAS.

63. *Hartford Courant*, 22 April 1899, p. 5.

64. Many war films were taken in Florida and Cuba by the Edison Company's motion picture photographer William Paley. Others, primarily reenactments of naval battles filmed in miniature, were made by Edward Amet of Waukegan, Illinois, and by Blackton and Smith of New York City. Sigmund Lubin also photographed ship launchings, parades, and battle reenactments.

65. *Wilkes-Barre Times*, 2 June 1898, HAS.

66. For example, Vitagraph used slides by the *New York Herald*. On Eberhard Schneider's use of slides see: *Reading Eagle*, 6 September 1898, p. 2.

67. *Scranton Truth*, 20 January 1899, p. 3.

68. Howe may have used a few sound-effect instruments for his pictures as early as 1897 (*Danbury Evening News*, 20 November 1897, HPS).

69. *Wilkes-Barre Times*, 2 June 1898, HAS.

70. "Realistic Noises," *St. Louis Republic*, 21 June 1896, p. 16.
71. "Howe's Realistic Pictures," *Wilkes-Barre Record*, 25 January 1899, p. 10.
72. "Lyman Howe Co. President Dead," Wilkes-Barre newspaper, ca. 1926, FS.
73. Wilkes-Barre newspaper, ca. 1915–1916, WS.
74. Howe and Walkinshaw, contract, 1 September 1898, WS.
75. Bloomsburg newspapers from this period unfortunately have not been preserved, so it is impossible to offer details of this program.
76. *Reading Eagle*, 16 April 1899, p. 3; Lyman Howe Motion Picture Company, promotional literature, ca. 1905, PW-BH.
77. *Reading Eagle*, 18 January 1899, p. 2.

CHAPTER SIX

1. Roadmen who showed films between acts of a play or in conjunction with some other touring theatrical amusement like burlesque usually retained the one-reel, twenty-minute format.
2. Musser, "Another Look," pp. 24–52. The Biograph Company with its 70 mm film had established a permanent relationship with the Keith organization by late 1896.
3. Hadley to Howe, 17 September 1899, TXU-H.
4. Hadley to Howe, 19 October 1899, TXU-H.
5. "Howe's Realistic Pictures," *Wilkes-Barre Record*, 25 January 1899, p. 10.
6. Howe and Walkinshaw, contract, 1 September 1899, WS. Howe's demand for a hundred-dollar guarantee is further evidence of Walkinshaw's increased responsibilities.
7. NYDM, 12 August 1899, p. 23.
8. Hadley to Howe, 24 August 1899, TXU-H.
9. NYDM, 11 March 1899.
10. "The Moving Pictures," *Wilkes-Barre Record*, 26 October 1899, p. 5.
11. Lyman H. Howe Moving Picture Company, leaflet for Corning, New York, ca. February 1900, PW-BH.
12. "Moving Pictures and Fairview," *Troy Daily Times*, 23 January 1900, p. 5.
13. Hadley to Howe, 6 February 1903, TXU-H.
14. "Howe and His Pictures," *Wilkes-Barre Times*, 26 October 1899, p. 3.
15. In the United States, Edison sued Maguire and Baucus for patent infringement. Rather than contest the suit, the partners acknowledged Edison's patents and gradually curtailed their American operations.
16. *Wilkes-Barre Times*, 26 October 1899, p. 3.
17. Ibid., p. 3.
18. *Wilkes-Barre Record*, 26 October 1899, p. 5.
19. *Wilkes-Barre Times*, 26 October 1899, p. 3.
20. *Wilkes-Barre Record*, 26 October 1899, p. 5.
21. "The Moving Pictures," *Scranton Truth*, 25 October 1899, p. 3.
22. *Wilkes-Barre Record*, 26 October 1899, p. 5.
23. For a discussion of the Charity Bazaar Fire, see Jacques Delandes and Jacques Richard, *Histoire Comparée du Cinéma* (Tournai, Belgium: Casterman, 1968), vol. 2, *Du Cinematographe au cinéma*, pp. 23–25.
24. *The Phonoscope* (August–September 1897), p. 11.

25. *Owego Times*, 9 November 1899.
26. *Troy Daily Times*, 23 January 1900, p. 5.
27. Walkinshaw datebook, pw-bh.
28. Leaflet, Corning, N.Y., 1900; broadside, Bloomsburg Opera House, 8 September 1898, gs.
29. Howe, draft of promotional letter, ca. 1900, pw-bh.
30. Jas C. Weber, caption on back of photo, ca. 1900. Maude Adams was a popular actress of the period.
31. Hadley to Howe, 17 September 1899, txu-h.
32. "Mr. Howe's Exhibition," *Wilkes-Barre Record*, 14 November 1899, p. 6.
33. "The Howe Moving Pictures," *Wheeling Register*, 24 March 1900, p. 5.
34. Lyman H. Howe Moving Picture Company, program, 1900–1901 season, gs. The five thousand-foot film of an English circus was not mentioned in Wilkes-Barre and other reviews. Requiring more than an hour to show, it may have never been used. This program dates from early 1901, shortly after the death of Queen Victoria.
35. "The Moving Pictures," *Wilkes-Barre Record*, 20 October 1900, p. 5.
36. *Wilkes-Barre Record*, 20 October 1900, p. 5.
37. Hadley to Howe, 6 February 1903, txu-h.
38. *Wilkes-Barre Record*, 20 October 1900, p. 5.
39. "A High Class Exhibition," *Wilkes-Barre Times*, 21 January 1901, p. 8.
40. *Hartford Times*, 12 April 1897, p. 1; *Hartford Courant*, 20 April 1897, p. 3. For local views taken in Rochester, New York, by the Biograph Company see George C. Pratt, " 'No Magic, No Mystery, No Sleight of Hand': The First Ten Years of Motion Pictures in Rochester," in Marshall Deutelbaum, ed., *"Image" on the Art and Evolution of the Film* (New York: Dover, 1979), pp. 39–46; for Providence, Rhode Island, see Robert C. Allen, "Contra the Chaser Period," in Fell, ed., *Film Before Griffith*, pp. 105–15.
41. "Vaudeville Correspondence," nydm, 7 April 1900, p. 11.
42. "Howe's Moving Pictures," *Wilkes-Barre Times*, 14 January 1901, p. 8.
43. "Death of Prominent Mason—Alexander B. King," *Troy Times*, 12 April 1911, ws.
44. *Variety*, 15 October 1980, p. 325, gives the Music Hall's capacity as 1,285 seats. Although it was consistently referred to as Troy's largest theater, the Rand Opera House had more seats—1,450.
45. *Troy Daily Times*, 22 October 1902, p. 4.
46. J. Stuart Blackton, testimony, 20 November 1913, Equity No. 889, September Sessions 1912, U.S. v. Motion Picture Patents Company, U.S. District Court, District of Eastern Pennsylvania, printed record, p. 1879.
47. Rachel Low and Roger Manvell, *The History of the British Film, 1896–1906* (London: George Allen and Unwin, 1948).
48. *Oneonta Star*, cited in *Glens Falls Times*, 5 November 1901, p. 7.
49. *Danbury News*, 19 October 1901, cited in *Glens Falls Times*, 8 November 1901, p. 7.
50. Lyman Howe Motion Picture Company, program, 22 November 1901, gs.
51. Searchlight Theater, program, 1901, dlc.

52. See *Before the Nickelodeon*, chapter 6, for the Edison Manufacturing Company's "preferred" arrangement of these films.

53. It is often impossible to make such judgements for other traveling exhibitors due to insufficient information.

54. *Oneonta Star*, cited in *Glens Falls Times*, 5 November 1901, p. 7.

55. *Wilkes-Barre Record*, 23 November 1901, p. 5.

56. NYDM, 26 October, 2 and 16 November 1901.

57. Lyman H. Howe Moving Picture Company, advertising brochure, ca. 1905, PW-BH. The John Knox Commandry, which sponsored the show and supplied the hall, received forty-five percent of this sum (exhibition report, WS).

58. "Howe's Famous Pictures," *Wilkes-Barre Times*, 23 November 1901, p. 3.

59. *Reading Eagle*, 3 November 1901, p. 3, 15 December 1901, p. 3; Howe Moving Picture Company, promotional material, ca. 1905.

60. "Amusements," *Reading Eagle*, 21 November 1902, p. 2; Lyman H. Howe Moving Picture Company, press sheet, 1901 season, PW-BH.

61. "Amusements,"*Reading Eagle*, 11 April 1902, p. 2.

62. Arbitrary numerations of seasons were made by Hadley in his 1897–1899 advertisements, but not by Dibble. See Lowry, "Edwin J. Hadley," p. 131.

63. Harris, "John Philip Sousa," pp. 32–33.

64. Howe and Walkinshaw, contract, 10 June 1901, WS.

65. *Chatham Courier*, 30 October 1901, WS.

66. "Allentown," NYDM, 5 April 1902, p. 23; "An Enjoyable Entertainment," *Allentown Morning Call*, 15 April 1902, p. 1.

67. "At the Empire," *Glens Falls Times*, 10 September 1902, p. 5.

68. "Howe and His Pictures," *Wilkes-Barre Times*, 8 November 1902, p. 6.

69. "World in Moving Pictures," *Wilkes-Barre Record*, 8 November 1901, p. 5.

70. *Hartford Courant*, 6 April 1900, p. 7.

71. *Utica Observer*, 22 October 1901, p. 5, and 19 October 1901, p. 7.

72. "Moving Pictures," *Hartford Courant*, 1 April 1902, p. 7.

73. Ibid.; *Hartford Courant*, 31 March 1900, p. 7.

74. NYDM, 23 March 1901, p. 5.

75. "Successful Moving Pictures," *Elmira Daily Advertiser*, 8 March 1902, p. 7.

76. "Edison's Projectoscope Co. Coming again," *East Hampton Star*, 18 August 1899, courtesy of Easthampton Historical Society; Edison Projectoscope Company, advertising brochure, 1900, TXU-H.

77. *New York Clipper*, 11 August 1900, p. 527; *Billboard*, 14 December 1901, p. 12.

78. "New England Figures Theater Values by Millions," *Moving Picture World*, 15 July 1916, p. 407.

79. *New York Clipper*, 24 April 1897, p. 125.

80. "The Three Bonheurs," *Billboard*, 15 December 1900, p. 19.

81. "The Bonheur Bros. Show," *Billboard*, 16 November 1901, p. 8.

82. "Notes From the Bonheur Bros. Show," *Billboard*, 23 November 1901, p. 10.

83. *Billboard*, 26 October 1901, p. 13.

84. Lacasse, *L'Historiographe*, p. 33.

85. *Hartford Courant*, 22 April 1899, p. 5, 5 April 1900, p. 7.

86. Burton Holmes, program, 1899–1900 season, BHS.
87. "Japan, Land of Flowers," *Brooklyn Eagle*, 6 January 1900, p. 11.
88. Burton Holmes, program, 1899–1900 season, BHS.
89. "Holmes Lecture on Hawaii," *Brooklyn Eagle*, 28 December 1899, p. 13.
90. "Manila and the Philippines," *Brooklyn Eagle*, 30 December 1899, p. 14.

CHAPTER SEVEN

1. *Film Index*, 21 November 1908, p. 3.
2. Obituary, Fred Willson, *Wilkes-Barre Record*, 11 December 1922, p. 7; *Daily Review* (Towanda, Pennsylvania), 11 December 1922, WS.
3. Hadley to Howe, 6 January 1903, TXU-H.
4. Hadley to Howe, 18 January 1903, TXU-H.
5. Draft of letter, Howe to Hadley, ca. January-February 1903, TXU-H.
6. Hadley to Manhart, 14 May 1903, TXU-H.
7. NYDM, 21 February 1903.
8. The second unit performed at the Opera House (932 seats) in Warren, Ohio (1900 population: 8,529), on Friday, February 27, and at the Grand Opera House (1,200 seats) in Salem, Ohio (1900 population: 7,582), on February 28 (NYDM, 14 March 1903); at the New Croswell Opera House (1,158 seats) in Adrian, Michigan (1900 population: 9,654), under auspices of the local Elks lodge on March 12, and at the New Bradley Opera House (900 seats) in Tecumseh, Michigan, on March 13 (NYDM, 28 April 1903); and in LaPorte, Indiana (1900 population: 7,113), on March 24, and Valparaiso, Indiana (1900 population: 6,280), on March 27–28 (NYDM, 11 April 1903).
9. Lyman H. Howe Moving Picture Company, program for Cortland Opera House, Cortland, New York, 27 May 1903, GS.
10. "Mr. Howe's New Pictures," *Wilkes-Barre Record*, 28 March 1903, p. 7.
11. Lyman Howe Moving Picture Company, program, 27 May 1903, GS. King Edward did not attend the coronation but was represented by Viceroy and Lady Curzon and the Duke and Duchess of Connaught.
12. "Will C. Smith," *Moving Picture World*, ca. 1918, WS.
13. NYDM, 30 April 1910, p. 22.
14. Howe and Walkinshaw, contract, 29 January 1903, WS. Edwin S. Porter, the Edison Company's chief filmmaker, was then being paid one-third to half this amount.
15. For a more detailed discussion of this phenomenon see Musser, "Another Look," pp. 24–52.
16. Lyman H. Howe Moving Picture Company, program for Armory in Jamestown, New York, 8 January 1904, GS.
17. *Wilkes-Barre Record*, 21 November 1903, p. 5. A few scenes of this film survive in the collection of Edison negatives at the Museum of Modern Art.
18. A dupe of this subject was listed in Edison's catalog as 135 feet. Howe's program notes suggest that he might have shown only the final portion of this subject, making its running time even shorter. Certainly an abbreviated version would have been less expensive to tint.
19. In Reading, his first company grossed $881.95 for four performances, an amount that represented little more than half the previous year's receipts.

Although attendance was hampered by rain, figures for Troy tell a similar story. Howe, who once again appeared under the auspices of the Cluett, Peabody, and Company Beneficial Association, grossed $467.50, a decrease of approximately ten percent from the previous spring. These box-office figures are too scattered to support firm conclusions.

20. This selection again "pleased large business" in Chambersburg, Pennsylvania (NYDM, 3 October 1903, p. 8). In Tiffin, Ohio (1900 population: 10,989), nearly every seat on the first floor of Noble's Opera House (1,000 seats) was taken at fifty cents and the gallery was also well filled at twenty-five cents per person. "The pictures were shown in a manner that does away with many of the objectionable features, especially the wavering effects so tiresome to the eyes. For the greater part the scenes were all new to Tiffin and nearly all were applauded" (*Tiffin Daily Advertiser*, 1 October 1903, p. 4). In Elyria, Ohio, where Howe's pictures were seen by a small audience on the previous tour, they were greeted by large houses over a two-day stay and declared "a fine exhibition" (NYDM, 14 March 1903, p. 8). Despite the first company's difficulties, Howe's overall profitability increased as his second company began to establish itself in the Midwest on its return dates.

21. Edwin J. Hadley, program for Wilkes-Barre Armory, 7 October 1903, TXU-H.

22. J. A. Carroll to Lyman H. Howe, 4 December 1903, TXU-H.

23. *Beaver Falls Daily Tribune*, ca. 3 December, 1903, clipping, Hadley file, TXU-H.

24. *New Britain Record*, 14 October 1903, p. 14; *Reading Eagle*, 10 April 1904, p. 4.

25. *Troy Times*, 19 September 1903; 26 October 1903, p. 5.

26. Hadley to Howe, 24 September 1903, TXU-H.

27. See Chapter 6.

28. Edwin J. Hadley, program for Casino, Bath, New York, 18 April 1904, TXU-H.

29. *Wilkes-Barre News*, 9 October 1903, cited in Edwin J. Hadley, program for Casino, 18 April 1904, TXU-H.

30. "The Moving Pictures," *Wilkes-Barre Record*, 8 October 1903, p. 5.

31. *Reading Eagle*, 10 April 1904, p. 4, and 8 May 1904, p. 2.

32. *Amsterdam Recorder*, 26 September 1903, and *The Mirror* (Warren, Pennsylvania), 19 November 1903, cited in Edwin J. Hadley, program for Casino, 18 April 1904, TXU-H.

33. Lyman H. Howe Moving Picture Company, program for Armory, Jamestown, New York, 8 January 1904, GS.

34. *Elmira Daily Advertiser*, 10 February 1902, p. 6; *Reading Eagle*, 10 April 1903, p. 3.

35. Archie L. Shepard, program, fall 1903, TXU-H. The antiquated spelling for Batie's first name had more refined, upscale associations.

36. *Norwich Bulletin*, 1 January 1904, p. 1.

37. Archie Shepard, program for Manchester Opera House, 28 February 1904, TXU-H; *Lewiston Evening Journal*, 5 March 1904, p. 16.

38. *Lewiston Evening Journal*, 7 March 1904, p. 8.

39. *Lewiston Evening Journal*, 6 January 1904, 8 and 22 March 1904.

40. *Glens Falls Times*, 17 October 1903.

41. Morgan and Hoyt Moving Picture Company, program for Opera House, Great Barrington, Massachusetts, 8 May 1903, TXU-H.

42. *Zanesville Daily Courier*, 28 April 1903, p. 5, and 24 September 1904, p. 5.

43. *Geneva Advertizer-Gazette*, 23 February 1904.

44. *Zanesville Daily Courier*, 21 October 1904, p. 5.

45. Pryluck, "The Itinerant Movie Show," p. 20; Ronald Johnson, receipt, 25 May 1904, WIWHI.

46. Huntley Entertainers, route book, April 1906–January 1907, WIWHI; newspaper evidence suggests that they had visited these or similar towns in prior years. Myrtle Huntley to Brandon, 3 June 1905, mentions towns on their route like Cambria (1900 population: 561), Markesan (1900 population: 706), Portage (1900 population: 5,459), and Fox Lake (1900 population: 890).

47. *New York Clipper*, 30 July 1904, p. 532.

48. *Waushara County Argus*, 30 May 1906, p. 1.

49. Myrtle Huntley to Brandon, 3 June 1905, WIWHI.

50. Dodge-Bowman Amusement Company, program for Empire Theater, 29 January 1905, TXU-H.

51. Lacasse, *L'Historiographe*, p. 35; NYDM, 19 March and 4 April 1904; *Film Index*, 8 September 1906, p. 3.

52. *Hartford Courant*, 15 September 1903, and 19 March 1904 through 25 April 1904; *Meriden Daily Journal*, 20 January 1904, p. 9. Searches through various newspapers for the 1905–1906 and 1906–1907 seasons have produced no indication that Dibble was active during these years. A broadside for Dibble's 9th season 1906–1907 survives in the Bella Landour Collection, NNHI. New Haven directories continued to list Dibble as a show manager until his move to Branford, Connecticut, in 1911.

53. *Norwalk Hour*, 15 October 1904, p. 6.

54. Brooklyn Institute of Arts and Sciences, tickets, 1903–1904, NN.

55. Lyman Howe Moving Picture Company, program, Nesbitt Theater, Wilkes-Barre, 9 April 1904, GS.

56. *Glens Falls Times*, 28 January 1904, p. 6.

57. *Wilkes-Barre Leader*, 12 April 1904, p. 8.

58. *Reading Eagle*, 10 April 1904, p. 4.

59. *Reading Eagle*, 14 April 1904, p. 2. Attendance at the matinee was 679; at the evening performance, 1,457.

60. "Better Than Ever Before," *Wilkes-Barre Record*, 21 November 1903, p. 5. Since most cameras were deemed to infringe on Edison's camera patents, camera technology developed more rapidly in Europe than the United States.

61. *Wilkes-Barre Record*, 10 March 1904, p. 8.

62. Lyman Howe Moving Picture Company, program, Nesbitt Theater, Wilkes-Barre, 9 April 1904, GS.

63. "The Moving Pictures," *Wilkes-Barre Record*, 11 April 1904, p. 3.

64. *Wilkes-Barre Record*, 10 March 1904, p. 8.
65. *Reading Eagle*, 14 April 1904, p. 2.
66. See Appendix A for a more general look at Howe's civic role in Wilkes-Barre.
67. *Wilkes-Barre Record*, 8 September 1904, HS.
68. Although the picture was of marginal technical quality, Howe's hometown audience responded to it with enthusiasm. The *Wilkes-Barre Times* reported, "The light was not as good as it might be and the picture seemed a trifle hazy. One critic remarked that the horses went too fast for a good picture, but nevertheless each company could be distinguished and the picture was so enthusiastically applauded that the view had to be reproduced as an encore" ("Howe's Moving Pictures," 30 November 1904, p. 5). The film was regularly shown by the first company but not the other two (Lyman Howe Moving Picture Company, program for Casino, Pittsfield, Massachusetts, 24 October 1904, GS).
69. Another traveling exhibitor taking local views in the northeast was William Steiner's Imperial Moving Picture Company.
70. *Views and Film Index*, 21 November 1908, p. 3.
71. *The Norwalk Hour*, 7 October 1904, p. 7.
72. *New Britain Record*, 23 November 1904, p. 3.
73. *New Britain Record*, 25 November 1904, p. 3.
74. *New Britain Record*, 3 December 1904, p. 4.
75. *Views and Film Index*, 21 November 1908, p. 3; *New Britain Record*, 24 February 1905.
76. *The Era*, 12 December 1903, cited in Low and Manvell, *History*, pp. 60–61.
77. Hadley to Howe, 6 February 1903, TXU-H.
78. Hadley to Howe, 20 February 1903 and 14 May 1903; and Hadley to Harry Manhart, 14 May 1903, TXU-H.
79. *Wilkes-Barre Record*, 8 September 1904, HS. The ordeal may have influenced Howe in his conversion from Presbyterianism to Christian Science in 1912.
80. *New York Clipper*, 7 May 1904, p. 244.
81. *Wilkes-Barre Record*, 8 September 1904. The *Wilkes-Barre Record* of 30 November 1904 suggests that Howe had four companies all doing "big business." Evidence to substantiate this larger figure, however, is lacking. For example, a photograph of Howe personnel taken for the 1904–1905 season included just enough personnel to run three companies.
82. *Grit*, ca. November 1904, WS.
83. It is also possible that Pflueger, who was a pianist, assumed Walkinshaw's old position with the first company and that Walkinshaw remained based in Wilkes-Barre.
84. *Cleveland Press*, 20 May 1905, p. 11; "Ed Mayo of the Lyman Howe Moving Picture Company," Pittston, Pa. newspaper, ca. 1 September 1905, WS.
85. Russell Blake was from Hartford, Connecticut, Will C. Smith from Washington, D.C. The nature of the film industry prior to 1906 was such that projection experience could only be gained in large cities or traveling on the road. This mitigated against finding experienced operators from eastern Pennsylvania.

86. Lyman H. Howe Moving Picture Company, program for Casino, Pittsfield, Massachusetts, 24 October 1904, GS; Lyman H. Howe Moving Picture Company, program for Sumter, South Carolina, 20 October 1904, GS.
87. *Billboard*, 8 October 1904, p. 7, and 5 November 1904.
88. See *New Britain Record*, 4 January 1905, p. 4, and 18 February 1905, p. 2; *Northern Budget* (Troy, New York), 19 March 1905, p. 6; see program for Sherman, Dodge-Bowman, and Shepard at TXU-H or look at almost any advertisement or publicity blurb for a traveling exhibitor during this period.
89. *Northern Budget*, 23 and 30 October 1904. Howe exhibited November 3. The Sunday concert at Griswold's Opera House on October 30 featured films of the Russo-Japanese War.
90. Lyman Howe Moving Picture Company, program for Grays' Armory, Cleveland, 19 May 1905, GS.
91. Ibid.; *Reading Eagle*, 18 April 1905, p. 2.
92. "Found Husband in Moving Pictures," *Wheeling Register*, 26 February 1905, p. 13. Such stories were too common to be believed, but their O. Henryesque like notion of coincidence remains delightful.
93. "A Great Pageant for Americans," *Wilkes-Barre Leader*, 1 April 1905, p. 4.
94. These assertions, moreover, became more strident not only in the face of competition but in the face of production companies' claims to authorship. As creative responsibilities became increasingly centralized in production companies, the role of the exhibitor became less important in this regard.

CHAPTER EIGHT

1. *Billboard*, 18 November 1905.
2. *New York Herald*, 3 December 1905, p. 14c. Admission was twenty-five cents for matinees, twenty-five and fifty cents for the evening shows.
3. *Billboard*, 27 January 1906, and 24 February 1906, p. 27.
4. "The Projectoscope," *Views and Film Index*, 23 June 1906, p. 5.
5. *Philadelphia Record*, 5 January 1906, p. 12; *Troy Times*, 4 February 1906, p. 6.
6. *New York Clipper*, 30 September 1905, p. 800.
7. "Miscellaneous," *New York Clipper*, 21 October 1905, p. 887. Many known exhibitors were never mentioned in amusement journals. Dibble, for example, remained active during this period, although extensive searches have not revealed his name.
8. *Billboard*, 30 September 1905, p. 5.
9. *Billboard*, 4 February 1905, p. 27. Manager Frank Moore of the Moore Moving Picture Show supplied the *New York Clipper* with a list of Maine and Vermont towns that he visited during September 1905. Most were so small that they could not be located with even the most detailed maps (*New York Clipper*, 9 September 1905, p. 728).
10. *Film Index*, 19 May 1906, p. 8.
11. Lloyd Davey to Carol Nelson, La Canada Flintridge, California, July 1982. Precisely when the Howe-Walkinshaw partnership commenced as well as the form it took is unclear. Walkinshaw's scrapbook, however, does not contain contractual information from the post-1905 period, suggesting that their re-

lationship changed at this time. Yet Walkinshaw was mentioned as a "helper" in the 1908 Wilkes-Barre directory and as "manager" in the 1909 edition.

12. For the next two years, Smith projected moving pictures that illustrated songs sung by Diamond. After receiving an inheritance in 1907, he acquired the stock and goodwill of Nicholas Power's New York Film Exchange. In 1912, Smith entered the employ of the Nicholas Power's Company, makers of a popular projector. In late 1917, he became general manager of the company. See *Moving Picture World*, 28 September 1908, p. 468, and clipping, ca. 1918, ws.

13. "Mr. Howe's Big Strike," *Wilkes-Barre Record*, 9 August 1905, p. 18.

14. "President the Honored Guest of Wyoming Valley," *Wilkes-Barre Record*, 11 August 1905, p. 1.

15. "World Famous Scenes," *Wilkes-Barre Record*, 4 November 1905, p. 10.

16. Howe donated the film to the Roosevelt Memorial Association; it is now catalogued under the title *Theodore Roosevelt as Father Curran's Guest at Wilkes-Barre, Pa., August 10, 1905*. The scene of Roosevelt speaking from the platform may have been cannibalized for stock footage. An intimate, extended take of Roosevelt and Father Curran standing on some steps was probably taken when Roosevelt returned to Wilkes-Barre in 1912.

17. *Wheeling Register*, 7 October 1905, p. 3.

18. "Last Night's Performance," *Allentown Morning Call*, 11 November 1905, p. 1.

19. Named after the publisher of the *New York Tribune*.

20. As Robert A. Brackett, head of the western company, proudly announced, "The Lyman H. Howe Moving Picture Co. (western) . . . is booked solid until June 10, 1906. Owing to the fact that we have [a] new and improved mechanism which practically eliminates the 'flicker,' and that Mr. Howe brought over from Europe some pictures which will be exclusive, and are masterpieces of animated photography, we expect this to be a banner year" (*Billboard*, 16 September 1905, p. 3). The company opened on August 30, 1905.

21. *Wheeling Register*, 7 October 1905, p. 3. Howe's show was in Wheeling on 6 and 7 October 1905.

22. *Northern Budget*, 22 October 1905, p. 6.

23. Lyman H. Howe Motion Picture Company, advertising brochure, ca. 1906, pw-bH. In Wilkes-Barre "the theatre was crowded from end to end and the demand for seats was almost unprecedented." The Port Arthur series was the main attraction, but Howe's films of Roosevelt also aroused excitement: "The series dealing with President Roosevelt's visit to Wilkes-Barre is a triumph of the moving picture art. . . . There are some views of the President so clear that the observer seems face to face with the most eminent man in the world. Even those who took part in the great celebration will be deeply interested in having the scenes again brought before them, without a straining to see and without the excitement of the crowds" (*Wilkes-Barre Record*, 4 November 1905, p. 10). Howe scheduled an additional playdate. For the three days he grossed $2,437.75, over one thousand dollars more than the Wilkes-Barre

gross for his Pan-American–McKinley program (*Wilkes-Barre Leader*, 4 November 1905, p. 6). In Allentown, Howe's views of the local fair helped to generate a $1,550.60 box office in two days. The figure for Reading came to $1,433.15, a new Howe record for that city.

24. *Boston Globe*, 2 April 1905, p. 3b and 1 October 1905, p. 3b.
25. *Boston Herald*, 6 October 1905, p. 10.
26. *Detroit Journal*, 27 October 1905, cited in Lyman Howe Moving Picture Company (western) program, 7 March 1906.
27. *Chicago Evening Herald*, 14 October 1905, BHS, no. 2.
28. *Milwaukee Sentinel*, 11 October 1905, p. 4.
29. *Milwaukee Sentinel*, 1 December 1905, p. 4.
30. Harrison, "John Philip Sousa," p. 23.
31. "Exciting and Entertaining," *Wilkes-Barre Record*, 21 April 1906; *Boston Herald*, 28 January 1906, p. 2b.
32. "Howe's Moving Pictures," *Boston Herald*, 6 February 1906, p. 8.
33. "Howe at the Armory," *Detroit Free Press*, 25 March 1906, p. 11a.
34. Lyman H. Howe Moving Picture Company, program for Huntington Theater, Huntington, West Virginia, 7 March 1906, GS.
35. *Baltimore Sun*, 13 May 1906, p. 8. Although Howe claimed that the earthquake films were taken by his own photographer, it seems more likely that Howe acquired them from the Vitagraph Company of America.
36. "Theatres Last Night," *Baltimore Sun*, 15 May 1906, p. 11.
37. *Wilkes-Barre Record*, 30 March 1906, p. 5.
38. *Boston Herald*, 30 and 31 August, and 2, 9, 16, 23, and 30 September 1906.
39. *Reading Eagle*, 27 October 1906, p. 2.
40. By the end of 1906, one trade journal had listed over three hundred picture houses in thirty-five states (*Billboard*, 15 December 1906, pp. 32–33).
41. *Lewiston Evening Journal*, 6 March and 6 April 1907; *Moving Picture World*, 9 March 1907, p. 9.
42. *Moving Picture World*, 9 March 1907, p. 9.
43. "Binghampton," *Billboard*, 5 January 1907, p. 34.
44. American Film Exchange, letterhead, COS.
45. "The Inception of the 'Black Top,' " *Moving Picture World*, 15 July 1916, pp. 368–69, and "Chicago Reports Many Variations in Picture Shows," *Moving Picture World*, p. 413.
46. *Milwaukee Sentinel*, 29 November 1906, p. 5. This last film was taken by Joseph DeFrenes, who would eventually become a Howe employee. An Austrian who managed the Kodak lab in Naples, Italy, DeFrenes sold a copy of the Vesuvius film to Burton Holmes, who provided him with an introduction to Charles Urban. Urban distributed the news film and sold prints to Howe. DeFrenes also became one of Urban's principal cameramen, and many of his films were to end up in Howe's programs (Richard DeFrenes to Carol Nelson, Schwenksville, Pennsylvania, May 1982).
47. *Baltimore Sun*, 13 May 1906, p. 1; *Milwaukee Sentinel*, 29 November 1906, p. 5.

48. As Rosenzweig has pointed out in his study of leisure in Worcester (1910 population: 145,986), some working-class groups, for example evangelical Swedes, avoided commercial popular amusement (*Eight Hours*, pp. 202–4). Since Worcester was on Howe's circuit from the turn of the century onward, his exhibitions may well have offered an alternate, acceptable form of moving pictures.

49. "Lifeorama Delights," *Boston Herald*, 12 October 1906, p. 14.

50. "Lyman H. Howe, the Lecturer Who Praises Animated Camera," *Cincinnati Commercial Tribune*, 18 January 1907, p. 5.

51. Howe could not control the weather, however, and his Cincinnati debut was marred by a destructive flood that swept through the city (*Cincinnati Commercial Tribune*, 19 January 1907, p. 1).

52. *Pittsburgh Post*, 19 January 1908, p. 6.

53. *Wheeling Register*, 14 September 1907, p. 4.

54. *Pittsburgh Dispatch*, 19 January 1908, p. 4d; *Boston Herald*, 12 October 1907, p. 3.

55. "Talking Pictures at the Nixon," *Pittsburgh Post*, 23 January 1908, p. 4; *Pittsburgh Post*, 28 June 1908, p. 2f.

56. *Pittsburgh Post*, 23 January 1908, p. 4; and *Pittsburgh Dispatch*, 23 January 1908, p. 7.

57. A similar problem emerged later in the year in Boston where *A Stag Hunt in France* was announced as part of the bill. The Society for the Prevention of Cruelty to Animals protested its exhibition and the controversial film was replaced by *Scenes in Japan* (*Boston Transcript*, 5 October 1907, p. 5, pw-bh). Such protests were becoming a problem in other amusement forms such as vaudeville (Albert McLean, Jr., *American Vaudeville as Ritual*, pp. 138–64).

58. "21,477 Paid Admissions," *Wilkes-Barre Record*, 27 May 1907, p. 7 offers a substantially higher figure for the same week-long run.

59. The third company, for example, had its last play date at Marion, Ohio, on June 18th (*Billboard*, 15 June 1907, p. 13).

60. The 1,500-seat Lowell Opera House, the Savoy Theater (Fall River), the Franklin Theater (Worcester), the 1,582-seat New Bedford Theater, the 1,300-seat Salem Theater, the 1,450-seat Strong Theater (Burlington), the 2,210-seat Smith's Theater (Bridgeport), the 1,300-seat Empire Theater (Lewiston), and the 1,400-seat Grand Opera House (Wilmington). *New York Clipper*, 8 June 1907; *Lewiston Evening Journal*, 29 May 1907. Shepard was undoubtedly showing films in many theaters not listed in the *New York Clipper*.

61. *Variety*, 20 March 1909, p. 11, gives capacity and location.

62. *Baltimore Sun*, 4 August 1907, p. 1.

63. "Pictures at Ford's," *Baltimore Sun*, 6 August 1907, p. 9.

64. Ibid.

65. " 'Lifeorama' at Ford's," *Baltimore Sun*, 20 August 1907, p. 7.

66. "Last Week of Pictures," *Baltimore Sun*, 27 August 1907, p. 7.

67. Ibid.

68. "Lifeorama at Ford's," *Baltimore Sun*, 13 August 1907, p. 6.
69. *Baltimore Sun*, 20 August 1907, p. 7.
70. Ibid.
71. *Billboard*, 7 September 1907, p. 14. Emphasis added. Howe was thus seen usurping the role that Stoddard assigned to Holmes.
72. *Billboard*, 17 August 1907, p. 14.
73. Wilson, *Mere Literature*, p. 212.
74. *Billboard*, 14 September 1907, p. 11.
75. *Baltimore Sun*, 1 September 1907, p. 1.
76. *Baltimore Sun*, 1, 8, 15, and 22 September 1907, p. 1.
77. *Bay City Tribune*, 29 October 1907, p. 4, PW-BH.
78. "Howe's Moving Pictures," *Cincinnati Commercial Tribune*, 23 December 1907, p. 7.
79. *Moving Picture World*, 5 October 1907, p. 486.
80. Brackett exhibited at the Crawford Theater in Wichita, Kansas (1910 population: 52,450), in March 1907 (*Billboard*, 9 March 1907, p. 10), but his show was not encountered in searches for later years.
81. Clippings, WS.
82. *Moving Picture World*, 9 May 1908, p. 411.
83. Pryluck, "The Itinerant Movie Show," p. 20.
84. *Moving Picture World*, 9 May 1908, p. 411; Lowry, "Edwin J. Hadley," p. 141.
85. Brooklyn Institute of Arts and Sciences, Ticket No. 15, 5 January 1907.
86. Brooklyn Institute of Arts and Sciences, Ticket No. 31, 27 April 1907.
87. Brooklyn Institute of Arts and Sciences, Tickets, 1907–1908, NN.
88. "The Elmendorf Lectures," *Moving Picture World*, 5 October 1907, p. 485.
89. Brooklyn Institute of Arts and Sciences, Ticket No. 15, 5 January 1907.
90. *Philadelphia North American*, 8 September 1908, p. 6.
91. *Philadelphia Record*, 8 September 1908, PW-BH.
92. *Buffalo Express*, 8 June 1909, p. 7.
93. Lloyd Davey to Carol Nelson, July 1982.
94. *Wilkes-Barre Record*, 15 May 1908, p. 3.
95. "The Nixon Theater," *Pittsburgh Post*, 28 June 1908, p. 2f. Theater managers often placed large cakes of ice in the basement and blew the cool air upstairs with fans.
96. *Pittsburgh Post*, 5 July 1908, p. 2f, and 19 July 1908, p. 2f.
97. "In the Theaters and Parks Last Evening," *Pittsburgh Post*, 14 July 1908, p. 4.
98. "Nixon Theater," *Pittsburgh Post*, 26 July 1908, p. 2f.
99. *Cleveland Plain Dealer*, 16 August 1908, p. 8; 17 August 1908, p. 1; 18 August 1908, p. 12; 20 August 1908, pp. 1, 8; 28 August 1908, p. 4.
100. "How Talking Pictures Are Made," *Moving Picture World*, 22 August 1908, pp. 136–37.
101. *Moving Picture World*, 22 August 1908, p. 136; 28 November 1908, p. 419.
102. The transformation of representational methods during this period is examined in Charles Musser, "The Nickelodeon Era Begins: Establishing a

Framework for Hollywood's Mode of Representation," *Framework*, no. 22–23 (August 1983): 4–10. The increased popularity of the exhibitor's intervention during this period—a key point in the article—is disputed by Barry Salt in "What We Can Learn From the First Twenty Years of Cinema," *Iris* 2, no. 1 (1984): 87. Our references here to the wave of talking pictures in pertinent cities should refute Salt's dismissal.

103. *Baltimore Sun*, 17, 24, and 31 May 1908.

104. "Pictures at the Columbia," *Cincinnati Commercial Tribune*, 31 May 1908, p. 21.

105. *Cincinnati Commercial Tribune*, 10 June 1908, p. 7.

106. *Pittsburgh Post*, 30 June 1908, p. 4.

107. *Pittsburgh Post*, 21 July 1908, p. 4.

108. "Views of Many Lands," *Baltimore Sun*, 11 August 1908, p. 5.

109. *Cleveland Plain Dealer*, 17 August 1908, p. 4.

110. *Topeka Daily Capital*, 14 April 1907, p. 16; Jim McDonald to Carol Nelson, Boonton, New Jersey, January 1982. Jim McDonald was one of the students hired by Howe.

111. Edward Plottle to Carol Nelson, Scranton, Pennsylvania, February 1982.

112. "In the Theaters and Parks Last Evening," *Pittsburgh Post*, 21 July 1908, p. 4.

113. *Cincinnati Commercial Tribune*, 22 August 1909, p. 18.

114. The world of urban working children in the early twentieth century is examined in David Nasaw, *Children of the City at Work and at Play* (Garden City, New York: Anchor/Doubleday, 1985).

115. *Chicago Tribune*, 1 June 1908, cited in *New York Clipper*, 13 June 1908, p. 440.

116. Henry Lee traveled with his "Cyclo-Homo" for much of the 1908–1909 season, though on a greatly reduced scale. On his way to England, Lee presented a twenty-minute travelogue at the Colonial Theater in New York City in November 1908. At least one reviewer, however, was not tremendously impressed (*Variety*, 5 December 1908, p. 14). The following year, Lee returned to his traditional act as an impersonator.

117. *New York Clipper*, 16 May 1908, p. 350.

CHAPTER NINE

1. "Amusement Houses," *Wilkes-Barre Record*, 28 November 1907, p. 11, reprinted in *Moving Picture World*, 7 December 1907, pp. 648–49.

2. *Wilkes-Barre Record*, 29 November 1907, p. 8.

3. See, for example, "To Station Police at Theater Doors," *Cleveland Plain Dealer*, 16 August 1908, p. 8; "Managers Get Grace," *Cleveland Plain Dealer*, 18 August 1908, p. 12.

4. *Film Index*, 22 September 1906, p. 1.

5. Rosenzweig, *Eight Hours*, p. 192.

6. "Badger Movie Pioneers See Future," *Minneapolis Sunday Tribune*, 21 August 1960, p. 1b.

7. *Moving Picture World*, 7 December 1907, p. 645.

8. *Moving Picture World*, 21 September 1907, p. 454.

9. *Brooklyn Eagle*, 17 March 1908, p. 10.
10. Lyman H. Howe Moving Picture Company, flyer, 18 March 1908, FS.
11. "Amusements Opposed," *Baltimore Sun*, 19 May 1908, p. 9.
12. *Moving Picture World*, 8 June 1907, p. 217, 6 July 1907, pp. 277–78; *Variety*, 16 May 1908, p. 11, 23 May 1908, p. 12.
13. "Down with 'Blue Law Tyranny' Cry Labor Men 250,000 Strong," *Moving Picture World*, 14 December 1907, p. 688.
14. "Supreme Court Decides Sunday Show Legal," *Variety*, 7 December 1907, p. 2.
15. *New York Clipper*, 2 January 1909, p. 1158.
16. "Wage War on Shows," *New York Tribune*, 24 December 1908, p. 4.
17. *New York Clipper*, 2 January 1909, p. 1175.
18. Ramsaye, *A Million and One Nights*, p. 479.
19. *Pittsburgh Press*, 4 August 1908, p. 5. See also *Pittsburgh Post*, 14 July 1908, p. 4.
20. *Cincinnati Commercial Tribune*, 31 August 1908, p. 7.
21. Clipping, ca. February 1909, FS.
22. The preceding Sunday, for example, a benefit performance, endorsed by the King of Italy, had been given for Sicilian earthquake victims (*New York Herald*, 24 January 1909, p. 11c).
23. *New York Herald*, 1 February 1909, p. 10.
24. NYDM, 6 February 1909, p. 18.
25. W. C. Pflueger to Lee Shubert, 25 January 1909, general correspondence, NNS.
26. Shubert and Anderson, endorsement printed in Hippodrome program, 7 February 1909, PW-bH.
27. Lyman H. Howe Moving Picture Company, program for the New York Hippodrome, 7 February 1909, PW-bH.
28. Lloyd Davey to Carol Nelson, La Canada Flintridge, California, July 1982.
29. *New York Herald*, February 8, 1909, p. 1.
30. Clipping, ca. February 1909, FS.
31. Ramsaye, *A Million and One Nights*, p. 480.
32. W. C. Pflueger to J. J. Shubert, 2 March 1909, Pflueger to Shubert, 1 January 1912, NNS; NYDM, 7 June 1911, p. 28.
33. *Moving Picture World* (20 November 1909, p. 717) lists several Gaumont films on a Howe program. Howe apparently acquired Urban films released in 1910 in England with no difficulty. Furthermore, although licensed houses were not supposed to show unlicensed subjects, managers sometimes hired Howe to present programs in these very theaters.
34. Shubert to Howe, 2 March 1909, NNS.
35. Pflueger to J. J. Shubert, 5 March 1909, NNS.
36. *Cincinnati Commercial Tribune*, 22 August 1909, p. 18, where Bayley's name is misspelled "Baily"; NYDM, 16 April 1910, p. 34.
37. *Cleveland Press*, 13 July 1909, p. 2.
38. *Toronto World*, 6 May 1909, p. 2.
39. Pflueger to J. J. Shubert, 5 March 1909, NNS.

40. *Washington Star*, 11 September 1910, p. 6b.

41. *New York Herald*, 31 January 1909, p. 11c.

42. *Cincinnati Commercial Tribune*, 11 August 1909, p. 7, 16 August 1909, p. 7; see Cincinnati exhibition listed in Appendix E.

43. Searches through the *Boston Globe* for 1910 and 1911 indicate that Howe did not have a summer season either year.

44. "About Plays and Players," *Cleveland Plain Dealer*, 21 June 1909, p. 4.

45. *Cleveland Plain Dealer*, 22 June 1909, p. 8.

46. "About Plays and Players," *Cleveland Plain Dealer*, 25 June 1909, p. 4.

47. *Cleveland Plain Dealer*, 27 June 1909, p. 2e.

48. Clipping, ca. July 1909, FS.

49. " 'Drop the Sunday School Picnic,' Says Minister, 'Theater's Better,' " *Cleveland Plain Dealer*, 1 July 1909, p. 1.

50. *Cleveland Press*, 25 June 1909, p. 11.

51. "About Plays and Players," *Cleveland Plain Dealer*, 7 July 1909, p. 6.

52. "About Plays and Players," *Cleveland Plain Dealer*, 16 July 1909, p. 4. This trip was never mentioned in Wilkes-Barre reviews nor in Walkinshaw's extensive scrapbooks.

53. *Cleveland Plain Dealer*, 12 July 1909, p. 4.

54. *Cleveland Plain Dealer*, 8 July 1908, p. 6.

55. *Cleveland Plain Dealer*, 30 June 1909, p. 4.

56. A modest search through *The Bioscope*, England's trade journal, produced no information on activities there by Howe. Perhaps more significantly, nothing in surviving scrapbooks substantiates the claim.

57. Pflueger to Shubert, 5 March 1909, NNS.

58. *Boston Herald*, 18 August 1909, p. 1.

59. "Howe's Travel Festival at Grand," *Wilkes-Barre Record*, 23 April 1910. Some of the scenes, however, were probably selected from earlier programs or purchased from other producers.

60. *Baltimore Sun*, 24 July 1910, p. 9. Such assistance was not unique ("Victory," *Moving Picture World*, 20 September 1913, p. 1267).

61. *Cincinnati Commercial Tribune*, 22 August 1910, p. 3.

62. "Wild Animals and Music," *Washington Star*, 31 July 1910, p. 5b.

63. "Perilous Work of the Moving Picture Man," *Toronto World*, 14 May 1911, p. 6. Many of these films had been used in Howe's earlier shows. It thus appears that Crowhurst had been an employee of Charles Urban.

64. "Show Duluth to the World," *Duluth News Tribune*, 9 February 1911, p. 16.

65. "News of Sporting World," *Duluth News Tribune*, 13 February 1911, p. 8.

66. *Duluth News Tribune*, 9 February 1911, p. 16.

67. *Cleveland Plain Dealer*, 21 May 1911, p. 11e; "Cornell Footballmen Frolic for the Films," *Ithaca Daily News*, 29 September 1911, p. 8.

68. *Duluth News Tribune*, 9 February 1911, p. 16; "Ithaca and Cornell in Motion Pictures" and "Business Men to Cooperate with Howe," *Ithaca Daily News*, 26 September 1911, p. 5.

69. "Cameraman's Catch Seen at the Lyceum," *Ithaca Daily News*, 7 October 1911, p. 5.

70. See Chapter 7.

71. "Roosevelt Opens Gates of Great Dam," *New York Times*, 19 March 1911, p. 16.

72. "American Scenery at Ford's," *Baltimore Sun*, 15 August 1911, p. 13.

73. "Columbia," *Washington Star*, 11 April 1911, p. 3. It is also possible that the impersonators did not have the President's exact words and did not dare make them up in such a situation. The sound specialists who visited Duluth almost certainly did not travel to Arizona.

74. *Baltimore Sun*, 15 August 1911, p. 13.

75. *Kansas City Star*, 14 May 1911, p. 14a.

76. "A Big 'Ad' for our City," *Wilkes-Barre Board of Trade Journal*, July 1911, pp. 8–9.

77. Hale's Tours, started in May 1905, literalized the viewer-as-passenger conceit by placing the audience in a mock railway car from which they watched film of passing scenery out a front "window" which was, in reality, the movie screen. These films were primarily taken from the front end of a train. The popularity of Hale's "tours" faded within a few years, but Howe continued to provide his audiences with the sensation of moving through space and time by introducing either breathtaking scenery or some novel form of transport.

78. *Wilkes-Barre Board of Trade Journal*, July 1911, p. 9.

79. *Chicago Evening Examiner*, 8 July 1911, ws.

80. "Moving Picture Men Everywhere," *Montreal Star*, 1 July 1911, p. 26.

81. *Baltimore Sun*, 6 August 1911, p. 1; *New York Times*, 6 August 1911, p. 1; *New York American*, 6 August 1911, p. 1.

82. Clipping, *San Diego Union*, 25 August 1963, San Diego Historical Society.

83. *Montreal Star*, 1 July 1911, p. 26.

84. *Baltimore Sun*, 2 July 1911, p. 1.

85. Clipping, ws; see also *Washington Star*, 30 July 1911, p. 3b.

86. "The arrangement of the scenes could not be improved upon, and to spice up the otherwise monotonous array of soldiery and carriages, pictures such as the 'Naval Review at Spithead,' 'The U.S.S. Delaware, America's Naval Representative,' and 'Fancy Drills of the School Children' are shown" (*Moving Picture World*, ca. July 1911, ws). Ralph Barber recalled that Howe only acquired exclusive American rights to these films, suggesting that he was not directly responsible for their production. Many contemporary articles, however, indicated that Walkinshaw produced the pictures and developed the negative on the boat back from Europe. Although Barber's often hazy memory may be correct in this instance—making this claim yet another instance of legend-building—we find these articles more convincing. See *Montreal Star*, 1 July 1911, p. 26; clipping, ws; and Ralph Barber, manuscript, pw-bh.

87. "Austin Disaster Pictures by Howe," *Moving Picture World*, 21 October 1911, p. 214. See also *Wilkes-Barre Times-Leader*, 3 October 1911, p. 1.

88. *Allentown Morning Call*, 16 October 1911, p. 8.

89. See Donald Crafton, *Before Mickey: The Animated Film, 1898–1928* (Cambridge: MIT Press, 1982). *Winsor McCay's Drawings* was released by Howe's business friends, J. Stuart Blackton and Albert Smith of American Vitagraph. Emile Cohl, whose work was distributed by Gaumont, was another possible example.

90. *Middletown Daily Times-Press*, 12 October 1911, p. 2, PW-BH.

91. *Chamber of Commerce Journal*, Wilkes-Barre, July 1912, pp. 6–7.

92. NYDM, 30 April 1910, p. 22.

93. Ralph Barber, manuscript, PW-BH.

94. Max Walkinshaw Hallet to Charles Musser, West Hartford, Connecticut, 21 June 1985.

95. NYDM, 24 May 1911, p. 27.

96. "Boy Scouts Cheer Coronation Views at the Princess," *Montreal Star*, 11 July 1911, p. 2; "Color Pictures at Princess are Wonderful," *Montreal Star*, 18 July 1911, p. 2; and clippings, WS.

97. Walkinshaw to Shubert, 15 June 1911; Shubert to Pflueger, 19 June 1911.

98. Clipping, WS; Pflueger to Shubert, 24 July 1911, NNS.

99. *Cincinnati Commercial Tribune*, 14 August 1911, p. 2, 7 August 1911, p. 3.

100. *Philadelphia North American*, 28 May 1911, p. 5c.

101. "Moving Pictures the Garrick Summer Bill," *Philadelphia North American*, 30 May 1911, p. 7.

102. *Baltimore Sun*, 2 July 1911, p. 1.

103. Not to be confused with the mimic Henry Lee, Van C. Lee had written an article, "The Value of the Lecture," *Moving Picture World*, 8 February 1908, p. 9.

104. *Cleveland Plain Dealer*, 14, 21, and 28 May 1911.

105. *Pittsburgh Post*, 17 July 1910, p. 2d.

106. "Kinemacolor Pictures in Nixon," *Pittsburgh Post*, 19 July 1910, p. 2.

107. "Nature's Colors in Films at the Garrick," *Philadelphia North American*, 2 August 1910, p. 2.

108. *Wilkes-Barre Record*, 25 March 1911, p. 23; *Toronto World*, 22 May 1911, p. 9.

109. NYDM, 3 May 1911, p. 34.

110. "Color Pictures at Princess Are Very Wonderful," *Montreal Daily Star*, 18 July 1911, p. 2.

111. *St. Louis Globe-Democrat*, 17 September 1911, p. 5c; "More Amusements Herald Season's Full Swing," *Baltimore Sun*, 27 August 1911, p. 3c; "Kinemacolor Films Shown at Adelphi," *Philadelphia North American*, 5 September 1911, p. 8.

112. NYDM, 1 November 1911, p. 27.

113. *Ithaca Daily News*, 19 September 1911, p. 6.

114. *Cincinnati Commercial Tribune*, 25 March 1910, p. 3.

115. *Pittsburgh Post*, 14 June 1910, p. 5.

116. For instance, *St. Louis Post-Dispatch*, 6 March 1910, p. 6c, cited in Gorham Kindem, "Hollywood's Movie Star System: A Historical Overview," in

Gorham Kindem, ed., *The American Movie Industry* (Carbondale, Illinois: Southern Illinois University Press, 1982), p. 81.

117. *Moving Picture World*, 4 January 1908, p. 9.

118. Clipping, *St. Louis Times*, August 1910, ws.

119. Clipping, *St. Louis Star*, August 1910, ws.

120. *St. Louis Times*, ca. September 1911, ws. The nature of the readership and the fact that respondents had to be reasonably well educated and articulate before they were likely to respond were other factors that helped to determine the kinds of responses received.

121. Clipping, ws.

122. *Cincinnati Post*, ws.

CHAPTER TEN

1. "Moving Picture Barnstormers," *Theatre Magazine* (August 1911), pp. 47–49. Roberta Pearson graciously brought this article to our attention.

2. Ibid.

3. See Chapter 2.

4. NYDM, 21 June 1911, p. 27, 28 June 1911, p. 27, 11 October 1911, p. 34.

5. Lowry reports that the latest Hadley material dates from late 1912 ("Edwin J. Hadley," p. 141.

6. "Church Pictures a Go," *Variety*, 28 November 1913, p. 12; New York City directory, 1915–1916.

7. Clipping, 22 March 1913, WiWHi.

8. Clipping, *La Crosse Tribune*, ca. 1915, WiWHi.

9. "Twenty-Two Humanovo Companies," NYDM, 18 July 1908, p. 7. Because they usually contracted their services at a specific price, Humanovo and its equivalents generally functioned as specialty exhibition services rather than conventional road shows.

10. NYDM, 5 June 1909, p. 18.

11. *Wilkes-Barre Record*, 29 February 1908, p. 7.

12. *Variety*, 15 August 1913, p. 15, 28 November 1913, p. 12, 27 March 1914, p. 17; receipts, Edison Kinetophone Company week of 21 July 1913, NjWOE.

13. Eileen Bowser, *The Transformation of Cinema* (New York: Macmillan/Scribner's, 1990).

14. "Panic Among One Nighters," *Variety*, 12 September 1913, p. 10; *Variety*, 5 December 1913, p. 17.

15. *Wilkes-Barre Record*, 29 November 1913.

16. NYDM, 23 August 1911, p. 20; "Kleine's Price Too High," *Variety*, 30 January 1914, p. 24.

17. Braverman, *Labor and Monopoly Capital*, pp. 403–9. Even men like Howe, Shepard and Robertson had started in this way.

18. *Everybody's Magazine* (June 1915), p. 680.

19. Hugo Munsterberg, *The Film: A Psychological Study* (1916; New York: Dover, 1970), p. 17.

20. "Why Churches Should Run Moving Picture Shows," *Cleveland Plain Dealer*, 13 June 1915, magazine section.

21. Ibid. This attitude might be compared to that of the Cleveland minister who took his Sunday school to see Howe's show in 1909 (see Chapter 8).

22. Ibid.

23. *Kansas City Star*, 12 June 1910, p. 13.

24. "The Weekly Newsreel," *Moving Picture World*, 21 July 1917, p. 419, cited in Raymond Fielding, *The American Newsreel, 1911–1967* (Norman: University of Oklahoma Press, 1972), pp. 74–75. Fielding's excellent book is the principal source for this section.

25. Thus they conform to the definition of mass communication offered by Melvin DeFleur and Everrette Dennis, *Understanding Mass Media* (Boston: Houghton Mifflin Company, 1981), p. 11.

26. *Moving Picture World*, 12 August 1911, p. 393; NYDM, 27 March 1912, p. 34 and *Moving Picture World*, 6 April 1912, p. 42.

27. *Cincinnati Commercial Tribune*, 5 October 1913, p. 2c, 16 November 1913, p. 2c. The last advertisement for *Cincinnati in Motion* located in our survey appeared on 1 March 1914, p. 2c.

28. *New York Herald*, 10 March 1912, ws.

29. *New York Times*, 13 December 1911, p. 10.

30. *Moving Picture World*, 20 January 1912, pp. 196, 198; Fielding, *The American Newsreel*, p. 56.

31. *New York Sun*, 3 March 1912, p. 8b.

32. "Millionaires at Kinemacolor Show," clipping, ca. October 1909, ws.

33. "Mr. Rainey's African Jungle Pictures to be Shown Here," *New York Herald*, 14 April 1912, p. 11c; see also NYDM, 24 April 1912, p. 27.

34. "Films Depict Wild Animals in Varied Moods," *New York Herald*, 16 April 1912, p. 15; *Philadelphia North American*, 7 May 1912, p. 8.

35. *New York Herald*, 14 April 1912, p. 11c. The expeditions were often accompanied by a handful of naturalists from these institutions.

36. *Cincinnati Commercial Tribune*, 9 June 1912, p. 15b.

37. *Moving Picture World*, 2 March 1912, p. 774.

38. *New York Herald*, 16 April 1912, p. 15.

39. *Philadelphia North American*, 7 May 1912, p. 8.

40. *Boston Herald*, 1 September 1912 to 20 October 1912. Films of King George's coronation were then brought back for two weeks and followed by a series entitled *Travel by Kinemacolor* that featured programs such as *Scenes of Yellowstone Park*.

41. *Moving Picture World*, 12 October 1912, p. 231, 16 November 1912, p. 653.

42. *Philadelphia North American*, 4 May 1913, p. 5a, and 30 May 1915, p. 6c; *Washington Star*, 11 May 1915.

43. Although an overview of Kinemacolor in America has yet to be written, Gorham Kindem looks at its later problems in "The Demise of Kinemacolor," in Kindem, ed., *The American Movie Industry*, pp. 136–45.

44. *Moving Picture World*, 20 April 1912, p. 214, 11 May 1912, p. 495; *Variety*, 14 November 1913, p. 26.

45. *Moving Picture World*, 6 April 1912, p. 81.

46. *New York Times*, 21 May 1912, p. 24.

47. "Pictures of Arctic Animals at Garrick," *Philadelphia North American*, 21 May 1912, p. 2.

48. *Moving Picture World*, 25 May 1912, p. 740; and *Pittsburgh Post*, 2 June 1912, p. 3d.

49. *Philadelphia North American*, 11 May 1915, p. 6.

50. *Brooklyn Eagle*, 27 December 1914, p. 7.

51. *Philadelphia North American*, 1 June 1915, p. 6. A brief summary of Kearton's career appears in Kevin Brownlow, *The War, The West, and the Wilderness* (New York: Knopf, 1979). The history also offers useful production information on other documentaries and filmmakers discussed in this section.

52. "Pictures at Forrest Paint the Antarctic," *Philadelphia North American*, 18 May 1915, p. 13.

53. Ibid.

54. *The Bulletin of the Brooklyn Institute of Arts and Sciences*, 30 September 1911, pp. 83–85.

55. *The Bulletin of the Brooklyn Institute of Arts and Sciences*, 1915–1916, p. 40.

56. "Free Movies Hurt," *Variety*, 28 November 1913, p. 13.

57. *Brooklyn Eagle*, 18 December 1914, p. 11.

58. Ibid., p. 11.

59. *Moving Picture World*, 11 November 1911, p. 461.

60. In 1908–1909, Holmes had made an interesting attempt to start a second unit with Wright Kramer as his alter ego. The experiment, however, did not succeed (*The Bulletin of the Brooklyn Institute of Arts and Sciences*, 1908–1909, p. 302).

61. "Burton Holmes Travelettes," *Moving Picture World*, 13 June 1914, p. 1552.

62. For instance, a Homes travelogue at a Keith vaudeville house was shown with a talk by Walter Murray ("Magician of Muscle, at Keith's, is Weird," *Philadelphia North American*, 8 June 1915, p. 6).

63. "How Burton Holmes Shot Aguinaldo," *Cleveland Plain Dealer*, 28 June 1914, p. 3e.

64. "Do Moving Pictures Breed Immorality," *Views and Film Index*, 22 September 1906, p. 1.

65. "The Kalem Girl," *Film Index*, 7 May 1910, p. 3.

66. *Moving Picture World*, 22 July 1911, p. 101.

67. "Dante's Inferno," NYDM, 2 August 1911, p. 26.

68. "Inferno Pictures Extended," *Baltimore Sun*, 20 August 1911, p. 3c.

69. "Queen Elizabeth," *Moving Picture World*, 3 August 1912, p. 428.

70. NYDM, 21 August 1912, p. 24.

71. " 'Quo Vadis'? in Movies Success at Garrick," *Philadelphia North American*, 13 May 1913, p. 6.

72. *Cincinnati Commercial Tribune*, 17 August 1912, p. 3.

73. *Pittsburgh Post*, 6 June 1915, pp. 2b–3b.

74. Munsterberg, *The Film*, p. 71.

75. Ibid., pp. 89, 98–99.

76. NYDM, 26 July 1911, p. 21.

77. *Baltimore Sun*, 13 August 1911, p. 1.

78. *St. Louis Globe-Democrat*, 3 September 1911, p. 7c.
79. Monopol sold states rights for the film in Virginia, Tennessee, Georgia, and other Southeastern states to Jack Wells, who planned to tour the territory with two road companies (NYDM, 23 August 1911, p. 20).
80. *Philadelphia North American*, 7 May 1912.
81. *Philadelphia North American*, 10 September 1912, p. 8.
82. These figures do not include a twenty-minute version of *Durbar in Kinemacolor* that was on the vaudeville bill at a local Nixon and Zimmerman theater during Howe's August return.
83. *Wilkes-Barre Times-Leader*, ca. September 1912, ws.
84. "Lyman Howe Travelogues Begin Season at Lyric," *Cincinnati Commercial Tribune*, 12 August 1912, p. 3.
85. "World Sights Crowd Nixon," *Pittsburgh Post*, 19 May 1914, p. 9.
86. "Lyman Howe at the Lyric," *Cincinnati Commercial Tribune*, 24 August 1913, p. 2b.
87. *Philadelphia North American*, 7 May 1912, p. 8.
88. "The Nixon," *Pittsburgh Post*, 20 May 1913, p. 8.
89. "Lyman Howe Pictures Delight Lyric Patrons," *Cincinnati Commercial Tribune*, 25 August 1913, p. 5.
90. *Pittsburgh Post*, 18 May 1913, p. 3b.
91. "Howe Travel Scenes Again at the Garrick," *Philadelphia North American*, 2 June 1914, p. 8.
92. *Washington Star*, 31 August 1913, p. 3b.
93. *Cincinnati Commercial Tribune*, 10 August 1913, p. 3c.
94. *Pittsburgh Dispatch*, 18 August 1912, p. 5e.
95. "Ford's," *Baltimore Sun*, 27 August 1912, p. 8.
96. *Washington Star*, 25 August 1912, p. 2b.
97. L. M. Townsend and W. W. Hennessy, "Some Novel Projected Motion Picture Presentations," *Transcript of SMPE*, XII (April 1928), 34: 345, courtesy of Richard Koszarski.
98. Donald Malkames to Carol Nelson, Yonkers, New York, February 1982. Malkames worked on the *Lyman Howe Hodge Podge* series; see Chapter 10.
99. *Baltimore Sun*, 16 August 1914, p. 4b.
100. "Howe at Garrick with Pictures of Europe," *Philadelphia North American*, 25 August 1914, p. 9.
101. "Lyman H. Howe Films Open at the Garrick," *Philadelphia North American*, 19 August 1913, p. 9.
102. *Kansas City Star*, 23 May 1913, p. 1b.
103. *Kansas City Star*, 18 May 1913, p. 7c, 23 May 1913, p. 1b.
104. *Philadelphia North American*, 7 May 1912, p. 8.
105. For example, *Pittsburgh Post*, 15 August 1915, p. 4c.
106. *Wilkes-Barre Record*, 11 March 1912, and Wilkes-Barre Grand Opera House, program, 14–16 March 1912.
107. *Baltimore Sun*, 25 August 1912, p. 5c.
108. "The Maine Sinks to Ocean Grave," *New York Times*, 17 March 1912, pp. 1–2.

109. "Lyman Howe at the Lyric," *Cincinnati Commercial Tribune*, 11 August 1912, p. 2c.
110. " 'Maine's Burial'—Ford's," *Baltimore Sun*, 20 August 1912, p. 8.
111. "Lyman Howe Travelogues Begin Season at Lyric," *Cincinnati Commercial Tribune*, 12 August 1912, p. 3.
112. "New Views at Ford's," *Baltimore Sun*, 13 August 1912, p. 8.
113. "Howe's Travel Pictures at Grand," *Wilkes-Barre Record*, 4 October 1913.
114. *Washington Star*, 24 August 1913, p. 3b.
115. "Lyman Howe Coming to Lyric," *Cincinnati Commercial Tribune*, 23 August 1914, p. 3b.
116. "Howe's Panama Canal Pictures," *Wilkes-Barre Record*, 28 January 1914, p. 9.
117. *Philadelphia North American*, 2 June 1914, p. 8.
118. *Binghamton Republican-Herald*, clipping, pw-bH.
119. Richard DeFrenes to Carol Nelson, Schwenksville, Pennsylvania, May 1982. Unfortunately newspaper reports rarely mention the names of the cameramen, and our information remains incomplete. When Crowhurst left and DeFrenes arrived remains speculative.
120. A photograph of DeFrenes appears in *Detroit Free Press*, 1 June 1915, p. 9.
121. "Boosts U.S. Navy," *Cleveland Plain Dealer*, early June 1915, ws.
122. *Washington Star*, 21 February 1915, p. 3b.
123. Thomas Cripps, "The Reaction of the Negro to the Motion Picture *Birth of a Nation*," in Fred Silva, ed., *Focus on The Birth of a Nation* (Englewood, California: Prentice-Hall, 1971), p. 115.
124. pw-bH.
125. "Nixon-Howe's New Naval Scenes," *Pittsburgh Post*, 15 August 1915, p. 4c.
126. "Howe Films Show U. S. Navy," *Baltimore Sun*, 24 August 1915, p. 7.
127. "U.S. Navy in Action Is Depicted at Garrick," *Philadelphia North American*, 24 August 1915, p. 6.
128. *Brooklyn Eagle*, 21 December 1915, p. 8b.
129. "The Navy on Canvas," *Wilkes-Barre Record*, 5 February 1915, p. 14.
130. Lyman H. Howe Travel Festival, program, 28 June 1915, ws.
131. "Nothing Short of a Revelation to St. Catherines People Was the Lyman H. Howe Travel Festival in the Armories," *St. Catherines Standard*, 29 June 1915, ws.
132. *Wilkes-Barre Times-Leader*, 8 July 1915.
133. Sam Hamil to Carol Nelson, San Diego, July 1981.
134. *Wilkes-Barre Times-Leader*, 8 July 1915. The donated copies, shown publicly in early 1933, were not to be located when Carol Nelson made a visit to the San Diego County Historical Society (*San Diego Union*, 28 December 1932; John Gonzales to Carol Nelson, 16 July 1982).
135. *San Diego Union*, 8 July 1915, p. 2.
136. *Wilkes-Barre Record*, 27 November, 1915, p. 11.

CHAPTER ELEVEN

1. These companies traveled with one rumble-round, one gong, one sword machine, four horse machines, one fire-gun effect, one cannon-ball crash and

plate, one train effect, one chime, one train whistle, one drum, and one tom-tom for orchestra (University Publications of America, *D. W. Griffith Papers,* reel 36, frame 134).

2. "Road Show Picture—To Date," *Variety,* 29 December 1926, p. 14. Russell Merritt kindly brought this article to my attention.

3. *Variety,* 26 December 1913, p. 3. The last Shubert correspondence with the Howe organization in the Shubert Archive is from the summer of 1914.

4. "Lecture and Pictures," *Wilkes-Barre Record,* 17 January 1913, p. 5.

5. *Philadelphia North American,* 16 March 1916, p. 2.

6. *Wilkes-Barre Record,* 30 January 1915, p. 21.

7. " 'Traveling With Howe' at Grand," *Wilkes-Barre Record,* 11 March 1916, p. 12.

8. Clipping, ws.

9. Paul Felton, in a speech to the Wilkes-Barre Advertising Club (clipping, fs).

10. Grau, *The Stage,* pp. 121–22.

11. *Wilkes-Barre Record,* 11 March 1916, p. 12.

12. *Cleveland Plain Dealer,* 7 July 1909, p. 6.

13. See Appendix A.

14. Robert K. Bonine had taken somewhat similar films as a cameraman for the Edison Manufacturing Company in 1906. These too were at least partially subsidized by a steamship company; see Musser, *Before the Nickelodeon,* chapter 10.

15. Lyman H. Howe Moving Picture Company, program, Auditorium Theater, Manchester, N.H., 24–25 November 1916.

16. *Wilkes-Barre Record,* 11 March 1916, p. 12.

17. Daniel Crane Taylor, *John L Stoddard: Traveller, Lecturer, Litterateur* (New York: P. J. Kennedy and Sons, 1935), pp. 145–48; "Yellowstone Wonders," *Brooklyn Eagle,* 15 December 1896, p. 7; Brooklyn Institute of Arts and Sciences, tickets, 1903–1904; "A Trip Through Wonderland," *Wilkes-Barre Record,* 30 March 1906, p. 9.

18. DeFrenes in particular was upset by his pay (Richard DeFrenes to Carol Nelson, May 1982).

19. Clippings, fs and ws.

20. Ralph Barber, manuscript, pw-bh. In various scrapbooks and correspondence, the last reference to Pflueger appears on Howe's 1915 stationery. He was almost certainly gone by 1917–1918.

21. *Moving Picture World,* ca. 23 June 1917, p. 2097.

22. *Philadelphia North American,* 18 May 1915, p. 13; *Pittsburgh Post,* 6 June 1915, p. 2b.

23. "Howe's Popular Pictures at Ford's," *Baltimore Sun,* 19 August 1917, p. 2B and "Travel Festival at Ford's," *Baltimore Sun,* 21 August 1917, p 6.

24. "Lyric," *Cincinnati Commercial Tribune,* 3 September 1917, p. 5.

25. Ibid., p. 5.

26. Newspaper clipping, Worcester, Massachusetts, Fall 1917, ws.

27. "Howe's Pictures at Ford's," *Baltimore Sun,* 20 August 1918, p. 6.

28. "Lyric Opens Season," *Cincinnati Commercial Tribune*, 26 August 1918, p. 5.

29. Kevin Brownlow, *The War*, pp. 112–19.

30. "Academy—Official War Pictures," *Baltimore Sun*, 26 March 1918, p. 8.

31. *Baltimore Sun*, 16 June 1918, p. 6.

32. *Baltimore Sun*, 25 August 1918.

33. "America's Answer," *Cincinnati Commercial Tribune*, 2 September 1918, p. 7.

34. *New York Times*, 12 August 1918, p. 7.

35. "Lyman Howe Travel Fest Opens at Lyric," *Cincinnati Commercial Tribune*, 25 August 1918, p. 5.

36. "Lyric," *Cincinnati Commercial Tribune*, 2 September 1918, p. 7.

37. "Theaters," *Baltimore Sun*, 30 July 1918, p. 5.

38. "My Four Years in Germany," *Baltimore Sun*, 28 May 1918, p. 6.

39. *New York Herald*, 18 January 1916, p. 11.

40. *New York Times*, 10 June 1918, p. 9.

41. *New York Times*, 22 July 1918, p. 9.

42. *Bulletin of the Brooklyn Institute of Arts and Sciences*, 1916–1917.

43. *Brooklyn Eagle*, 10 March 1917, p. 7.

44. *Bulletin of the Brooklyn Institute of Arts and Sciences*, 1917–1918, p. 110.

45. Ibid., pp. 211, 2601.

46. "Academy—'Lure of Alaska,' " *Baltimore Sun*, 14 May 1918, p. 6.

47. Ralph Barber, manuscript, n.d., pw-bH. Barber, however, had left Howe's employ by this time.

48. *Wilkes-Barre Record*, 22 February 1919, p. 1.

49. *Wilkes-Barre Record*, 13 December 1919, p. 32.

50. Julius Cahn and Gus Hill, *Theatrical Guide* 20 (1921) lists many motion picture theaters that had once been old opera houses in Pennsylvania and New York.

51. With the Grand closed after a fire, Howe played at the Armory for his fall 1916 tour. In 1917 he moved to the Majestic, a vaudeville and motion picture theater, only to move back to the Armory at the end of the year. Finally the Grand reopened, and he returned there in the spring.

52. *Moving Picture World*, 19 June 1920, p. 1579.

53. Richard Koszarski, *An Evening's Entertainment: The Age of the Silent Feature Picture, 1915–1928* (New York: Scribner's, 1990), chapters 2 and 7.

54. Sklar, *The Plastic Age*, p. 1.

55. "Lyman Howe Dies in Boston," *Wilkes Barre Record*, 31 January 1923.

56. In *Kinetograph and Lantern Weekly* of 9 November 1916 (ws), Walkinshaw had advertised for "a reliable young man capable of taking complete charge of dark rooms."

57. *Moving Picture World*, 19 June 1920, p. 1579; *Wilkes-Barre Record*, 2 May 1920; Irwin Marvel to Carol Nelson, Wilkes-Barre, September 1981.

58. "Lyman Howe Co. President Dead," Wilkes-Barre newspaper, FS; clippings, WS, FS.

59. Maxwell Walkinshaw Hallet to Charles Musser, West Hartford, Connecticut, 21 June 1985.

60. "Famous Comics to Appear in 'Movies,'" *New York Evening Journal*, 20 March 1918, ws.
61. *New York Times*, 10 June 1918, p. 9.
62. *Exhibitors Herald*, 27 September 1919, ws.
63. Max Walkinshaw Hallet to Charles Musser, 21 June 1985.
64. Program, Rialto Theater, 24 June 1917, ws.
65. Program, Rialto Theater, 18 April 1920, ws.
66. Donald Malkames to Carol Nelson, Yonkers, New York, February 1982.
67. Clipping, Capitol Theater scrapbook, NN.
68. "Howe Film Fit for the King," *Wilkes-Barre Record*, 6 January 1922, HS.
69. Programs, Capitol Theater, 17 April 1921, 15 January 1922, ws.
70. Clipping, n.d., courtesy of Andrew McKay.
71. Clipping, n.d., courtesy of Andrew McKay.
72. *Motion Pictures: 1912–1939* (Washington, D.C.: Copyright Office, Library of Congress, 1951), pp. 501–2.
73. Copyright file for *Traffic*, 18 November 1932, DLC.
74. *Variety*, 29 December 1926, p. 14.
75. New York City business directories, New York City telephone books, 1915–1940.
76. Mark E. Swartz, "Motion Pictures on the Move," *Journal of American Culture* 9 (Winter 1986), pp. 1–7.
77. *Bulletin of the Brooklyn Institute of Arts and Sciences*, 1919–1920.
78. *Bulletin of the Brooklyn Institute of Arts and Sciences*, 1933–1934.
79. On Wednesday afternoons and Saturday evenings. *The Emperor Jones*, with Paul Robeson, was shown five months after its New York premiere. Less noteworthy and successful films arrived within a few months—another demonstration of the Hollywood cinema's successful appeal across cultural and class barriers.

Chapter Twelve

1. Jay Leyda to Charles Musser, New York City, 1978.
2. Robert Sklar to Charles Musser, New York City, November 1985. Sklar was a consultant for the National Audubon Society in the early 1970s, when it was concerned about dropping attendance at these events.
3. Musser, *Emergence of Cinema*, chapter 1.
4. Ramsaye, *A Million and One Nights*, p. 312.
5. In terms of David Bordwell, Janet Staiger, and Kristin Thompson's excellent *The Classical Hollywood Cinema* (New York: Columbia University Press, 1985), a broadening of scope to include nonfiction and nonfeature forms is required if we are to gain a full picture of the classical Hollywood industry. The classical Hollywood cinema, moreover, would need to be resituated in relation to alternative and oppositional practices, rather than simply seeing oppositional and alternative practices as a response to Hollywood.
6. See Ramsaye, *A Million and One Nights*; Allen, *Vaudeville and Film*; and Musser, "Another Look."
7. Charles Musser, "Toward a History of Screen Practice," *Quarterly Review of Film Studies*, 9, no. 1 (Winter 1984), pp. 59–69.

8. Erik Barnouw, *Documentary*; Richard Meran Barsam, *Nonfiction Film: A Critical History* (New York, Dutton, 1973); and Fielding, *The American Newsreel*.

9. Spectators no longer really learned how processes worked, nor did they in all likelihood make use of that knowledge in any meaningful way. As the working classes were confronted more and more with the detailed division of labor, they seem to have lost interest in the operational aesthetic. It survived in simplified form as something to be learned by school children, which may partially explain the reason for Howe's youthful audiences in later years.

10. James Weinstein, *The Corporate Ideal and the Liberal State, 1900–1918* (Boston: Beacon Press, 1968).

APPENDIX A

1. Harris, *Humbug*, pp. 185–204.
2. *Wilkes-Barre Record*, 7 September 1906, p. 8.
3. *Wilkes-Barre Times*, 5 September 1906, p. 10. This donation provided the only surviving print of the film. It was subsequently rescued from nitrate deterioration by Ray Barber, and excerpts appear in the documentary film *Lyman H. Howe's High Class Moving Pictures*.
4. *Wilkes-Barre Record*, 28 September 1908, ws.
5. *Moving Picture World*, 28 September 1907, p. 470; *Wilkes-Barre Times-Leader*, 4 March 1908, p. 11.
6. *Wilkes-Barre Times-Leader*, 22 July 1910, *Wilkes-Barre Record*, 23 July 1910, hs.
7. *Wilkes-Barre Evening News*, 18 March 1911, *Wilkes-Barre Times-Leader*, 22 July 1910, hs.
8. *Wilkes-Barre Times-Leader*, 25 February 1911, p. 3, hs.
9. *Wilkes-Barre Record*, 23 March 1911, hs.
10. *Wilkes-Barre Evening News*, 27 November 1912, p. 6.
11. *Wilkes-Barre Record*, 19 May 1913, cited in *Chamber of Commerce Journal*, July 1913, p. 10.
12. *Wilkes-Barre Record*, August 1913, hs.
13. *Wilkes-Barre Record*, 9 June 1914, *Wilkes-Barre Evening News*, 12 December 1914, hs.
14. *Wilkes-Barre Record*, 27 August 1914, hs.
15. *Wilkes-Barre Record*, 16 September 1914, hs.
16. *Wilkes-Barre Evening News*, 17 June 1915, hs.
17. *Wilkes-Barre Record*, 31 July 1915, hs.
18. *Wilkes-Barre Record*, 12 October 1915, ws.
19. *Wilkes-Barre Evening News*, 29 October 1915, p. 1.
20. *Wilkes-Barre Record*, 16 December 1916, p. 1.
21. *Wilkes-Barre Record*, 22 March 1916, hs.
22. "Continue Mine Agreement," *New York Times*, 24 March 1916, p. 8.
23. *Wilkes-Barre Record*, 9 October 1918, hs.
24. For instance, *Sunday Independent*, 20 October 1918, hs.

APPENDIX F

1. "Howe's Moving Pictures," *Wilkes-Barre Times*, 14 January 1901, p. 8.
2. *Wilkes-Barre Record*, 10 March 1904, p. 8.

3. "The Moving Pictures," *Wilkes-Barre Record*, 11 April 1904, p. 3.
4. "Lyman H. Howe's Convalescence," *Wilkes-Barre Record*, 8 September 1904.
5. "World Famous Scenes," *Wilkes-Barre Record*, 4 November 1905, p. 10.
6. *Wilkes-Barre Record*, 4 November 1905, p. 10.
7. "Last Night's Performance," *Allentown Morning Call*, 11 November 1905, p. 1.
8. "Pictures Will Be Good," *Wilkes-Barre Times*, 4 September 1906, p. 8.
9. Lyman H. Howe Company, program, Allentown, 13–15 December 1906.
10. "The Day's Scenes and Incidents," *Wilkes-Barre Record*, 31 May 1907, p. 8.
11. "Our Soldier Boys," *Wilkes-Barre Times*, 21 November 1908, p. 10.
12. "About Plays and Players," *Cleveland Plain Dealer*, 30 June 1909, p. 4.
13. *Washington Star*, 31 July 1910, p. 5b.
14. "Howe's Travel Festival at Grand," *Wilkes-Barre Record*, 23 April 1910.
15. "Show Duluth to the World," *Duluth News Tribune*, 9 February 1911, p. 16.
16. "Columbia," *Washington Star*, 11 April 1911, p. 3.
17. *Kansas City Star*, 14 May 1911, p. 14a.
18. *Baltimore Sun*, 15 August 1911, p. 13.
19. *Cleveland Plain Dealer*, 21 May 1911, p. 11e.
20. "Daring Flights," *Wilkes-Barre Record*, 31 May 1911, p. 4
21. *Wilkes-Barre Record*, 5 June 1911, p. 8.
22. "New Pictures at Ford's," *Baltimore Sun*, 20 August 1911, p. 3c.
23. "Ithaca and Cornell in Motion Pictures," *Ithaca Daily News*, 26 and 29 September 1911, p. 5.
24. "Amusements," *Wilkes-Barre Record*, 20 November 1911.
25. "Amusements," *Wilkes-Barre Record*, 11 March 1912.
26. "Lyman Howe at the Lyric," *Cincinnati Commercial Tribune*, 11 August 1912, p. 2c.
27. "New Views at Ford's," *Baltimore Sun*, 11 August 1912, p. 8.
28. "Howe's Pictures Have Local Color," *Wilkes-Barre Record*, 19 October 1912.
29. *Baltimore Sun*, 11 August 1912.
30. *Kansas City Star*, 18 May 1913, p. 7c.
31. Ibid.
32. "Howe's Travel Festival," *Washington Star*, 24 August 1913, p. 3b.
33. "A Risk That a Photographer Took," *Washington Star*, 31 August 1913, p. 3b.
34. "Lyman H. Howe Films Open at Garrick," *Philadelphia North-American*, 19 August 1913, p. 9.
35. "Howe Travel Series Again at the Garrrick," *Philadelphia North American*, 2 June 1914, p. 8
36. *Wilkes-Barre Record*, 28 January 1914, p. 9.
37. *Baltimore Sun*, 16 August 1914, p. 4b.
38. Josephus Daniels to Lyman H. Howe, 5 January 1915.
39. Interview, C. R. Bosworth in *Cleveland Plain Dealer*, ws.
40. *Wilkes-Barre Record*, 30 January 1915, p. 21.
41. "Lyman Howe," *Wilkes-Barre Times-Leader*, 8 July 1915, ws.
42. "Through Canal by 'Movies,' " *Baltimore Sun*, 31 August 1915, p. 7.
43. *San Diego Union*, 6 July 1915.
44. *San Francisco Chronicle*, 18 July 1915, p. 1.

45. "Two Expositions by Moving Pictures," *Wilkes-Barre Record*, 27 November 1915, p. 11.
46. " 'Traveling With Howe' at Grand," *Wilkes-Barre Record*, 11 March 1916, p. 12.
47. Ibid., p. 12.
48. "Howe Has West Point Scenes," *Baltimore Sun*, 29 August 1916, p. 4.
49. "Lyman Howe To-day," *Wilkes-Barre Record*, 1 January 1917, p. 6.
50. "Howe Has West Point Scenes," *Baltimore Sun*, 29 August 1916, p. 4.
51. "Lyric," *Cincinnati Commercial Tribune*, 3 September 1917, p. 5.
52. Ibid., p. 5; Lyman H. Howe, program, 31 December 1917 to 2 January 1918, Wilkes-Barre.
53. "2d Week of Travel Festival," *Cincinnati Commercial Tribune*, 2 September 1917, p. 6c.
54. "Howe's Antarctic Film," *Cincinnati Commercial Tribune*, 26 August 1917, p. 5e.
55. *Baltimore Sun*, 26 August 1917, p. 2b.
56. *Cincinnati Commercial Tribune*, 2 September 1917, p. 6c.
57. "Howe's Navy Picture at Ford's Theater," *Baltimore Sun*, 26 August 1917, p. 2b.
58. Worcester, Massachusetts, newspaper, ws.
59. Lyman H. Howe, program, 31 December 1917 to 2 January 1918, Wilkes-Barre.
60. *Wilkes-Barre Record*, 13 April 1918, p. 20.
61. "Howe at Ford's," 18 August 1918, p. 2c; Lyman H. Howe, program, 12–13 April 1918, Wilkes-Barre.
62. Lyman H. Howe, program, 12–13 April 1918.
63. *Baltimore Sun*, 30 July 1918, p. 5.
64. Ibid., p. 5.
65. "Howe's Travel Pictures at Grand," *Wilkes-Barre Record*, 22 February 1919, p. 15.
66. "Lyric," *Cincinnati Commercial Tribune*, 1 September 1919, p. 10.
67. Ibid., p. 10.
68. Clipping, Fall 1919, ws.
69. Clipping, Fall 1919, ws.

Index

✳ ✳ ✳

Page numbers in italics refer to illustrations.